An Introduction to Competition Law

Second Edition

Piet Jan Slot and Martin Farley

·HART·
PUBLISHING
OXFORD AND PORTLAND, OREGON
2017

Hart Publishing
An imprint of Bloomsbury Publishing Plc

Hart Publishing Ltd
Kemp House
Chawley Park
Cumnor Hill
Oxford OX2 9PH
UK

Bloomsbury Publishing Plc
50 Bedford Square
London
WC1B 3DP
UK

www.hartpub.co.uk
www.bloomsbury.com

Published in North America (US and Canada) by
Hart Publishing
c/o International Specialized Book Services
920 NE 58th Avenue, Suite 300
Portland, OR 97213-3786
USA

www.isbs.com

**HART PUBLISHING, the Hart/Stag logo, BLOOMSBURY and the
Diana logo are trademarks of Bloomsbury Publishing Plc**

First published 2017

© Piet Jan Slot and Martin Farley 2017

Piet Jan Slot and Martin Farley have asserted their right under the Copyright, Designs and Patents Act 1988
to be identified as Authors of this work.

While every care has been taken to ensure the accuracy of this work, no responsibility for loss or damage
occasioned to any person acting or refraining from action as a result of any statement in it can be accepted
by the authors, editors or publishers.

All UK Government legislation and other public sector information used in the work is Crown Copyright ©.
All House of Lords and House of Commons information used in the work is Parliamentary Copyright ©.
This information is reused under the terms of the Open Government Licence v3.0
(http://www.nationalarchives.gov.uk/doc/open-government-licence/version/3) except where otherwise stated.

All Eur-lex material used in the work is © European Union, http://eur-lex.europa.eu/, 1998–2017.

British Library Cataloguing-in-Publication Data
A catalogue record for this book is available from the British Library.

ISBN: HB: 978-1-84946-180-1
ePDF: 978-1-84946-916-6
ePub: 978-1-78225-013-5

Library of Congress Cataloging-in-Publication Data

Names: Slot, Pieter J., author. | Farley, Martin, author.

Title: An introduction to competition law / Piet Jan Slot and Martin Farley.

Description: Second edition. | Oxford [UK] ; Portland, Oregon : Hart Publishing, 2017. | Includes
bibliographical references and index.

Identifiers: LCCN 2016045796 (print) | LCCN 2016046243 (ebook) | ISBN 9781849461801
(pbk. : alk. paper) | ISBN 9781782250135 (Epub)

Subjects: LCSH: Competition, Unfair—Great Britain. | Competition, Unfair—European Union countries.

Classification: LCC KD2218 .S56 2017 (print) | LCC KD2218 (ebook) | DDC 343.4107/21—dc23

LC record available at https://lccn.loc.gov/2016045796

Typeset by Compuscript Ltd, Shannon
Printed and bound in Great Britain

To find out more about our authors and books visit www.hartpublishing.co.uk. Here you will find extracts, author
information, details of forthcoming events and the option to sign up for our newsletters.

Foreword

Studying the law in our modern societies is not an easy task. A series of varied factors, ranging from globalisation to risk averseness, have led to an increasingly dense body of complex regulations, especially in the area of economic law. Those teaching, studying and practicing the law tend to react to this phenomenon by an increased degree of specialisation. One may wonder whether this is necessarily a positive development. A proliferation of specialisms may affect the consistency of a legal system and the practitioner's understanding of the 'raison d'être' of his specialism. Or, to put it differently, where many know a lot about a little, one may fail to see the wood for the trees.

European competition law is not exempt from this societal trend. It has become a legal system in its own right, in which practitioners tend to focus on discrete areas, such as state aid control, the control of concentrations, liberalisation or private enforcement. Where all European lawyers used to practise competition law, competition lawyers nowadays no longer practise all competition rules. I remember meeting a young lawyer of a large international law firm who proudly claimed that he was 'specialised in section 6 of the Form CO'.

As they focus on increasingly narrow niches, competition lawyers tend to forget the origins of the competition rules. For the vast majority of Member States, these rules have their roots in the European Treaties. They serve the purpose of creating the internal market and making it work. It is perfectly understandable that economic theories, such as welfare economics, provide the tools for better informed decision making and for facilitating a coordinated application of the competition rules at the international level. Even so, without an understanding of the underlying rationale of EU competition rules, namely the creation of an integrated market across Europe, the application of competition rules, in particular by the European Courts, would lack a clear justification.

I therefore consider that teachers and academics cannot limit themselves to explaining the mechanical application of the competition rules. These rules must be put in their wider societal context: they have an origin, a purpose and a direction. All this is easier said than done, especially where publishers, rightly, limit the number of pages to an acceptable maximum. Students and practitioners simply do not have the time to digest voluminous manuals. These constraints imply that authors must set priorities, identifying the main concepts underlying the competition rules and making complex issues easily accessible. This gift of 'simplification' is not a given to all authors. Making complex things look simple requires both in-depth knowledge of the subject matter and superior writing skills.

Now, Piet Jan Slot and Martin Farley meet these standards. It is therefore without hesitation that I recommend that students and practitioners alike read their introduction to the European competition rules, as contained in Chapter 1 of Title VII of Part One of the Treaty on the Functioning of the European Union and the corresponding provisions of national competition law.

Marc van der Woude
Vice President—General Court of the European Union

Preface

Ten years have passed since the publication of the first edition of this book. Ten years is a long time in EU competition law. The Treaty of Lisbon has brought a major change in the structure of the Treaties. We have now the Treaty on European Union (TEU) and the Treaty on the Functioning of the EU (TFEU) with the inevitable renumbering of the articles. The rules on competition are now contained in Articles 101 and 102 TFEU, which respectively prohibit cartels and abuses of a dominant position; Article 106 TFEU treats the situation of undertakings that have been granted special or exclusive rights or entrusted with the operation of services of general economic interest; while Article 107 TFEU contains the prohibition on State aid and Article 108 TFEU sets out the procedural rules concerning State aid. The secondary legislation has also undergone major revision. The same goes for the Notices and Guidelines. Moreover, important developments have also taken place in the case law of the Union Courts. All of this is reflected in the text of this revised edition.

Through all of these changes, the aim of this book has remained the same: to provide a broad category of readers—students, officials and lawyers in practice who do not deal with competition law issues on a daily basis—with the tools for understanding matters of EU and UK competition law.

An important function of this book is to provide an insight into the combined system of EU and UK law. When we were about to finalise the text UK voters indicated their preference for leaving the EU. However, it is, as of yet, entirely unclear whether this choice, even if it ultimately results in the UK leaving the EU, will sever completely the ties that bind EU and UK competition law. Since being reformed in 1998, the UK competition law regime has closely mirrored EU law, and the existence of section 60 of the Competition Act 1998 has ensured that UK competition law is interpreted consistently with EU law. The two regimes, therefore, are built upon a common basis. As such, even if the two regimes diverge in the event that the UK exits the EU, it is unlikely that this will result in immediate revolutionary changes to UK competition law. Hence the present structure of the book is likely to remain useful for quite some time. Furthermore, the interaction of the two systems may provide readers from other EU Member States or third countries with a useful insight into how national and EU competition regimes interact and co-exist.

Most materials on competition law are now ubiquitously available on the internet. This has led us to make some important adjustments to the case law citations of the Union Courts. We now only refer to case numbers as this allows every reader easy access via the website of the Union judicature (www.curia.eu). We have also included limited references to other literature where that was thought to be particularly useful. The novice in competition law should familiarise her or himself with the website of the Directorate General Competition of the EU Commission (short DG COMP).[1] This

---

[1] http://ec.europa.eu/competition/index_en.html.

website provides a very comprehensive and useful source of legislation, decisions, and other materials. Apart from the official website of DG COMP many other organisations, such as law firms which regularly publish client briefs, provide a vast source of information. The caveat here is that the reader is advised to be aware of the fact that such documentation is not necessarily the official version.

Due to the introductory character of this book, we have made a careful selection of the most important case law of the Union Courts, as well as the decisions of the EU Commission, the Competition and Markets Authority (CMA) and the Competition Appeal Tribunal (CAT). The reader is also reminded that the case law contains extensive references to earlier cases. In this regard, the informed reader will be aware of the fact that the EU has evolved several times through its history from the original European Economic Community (EEC), to the European Community (EC) to the European Union (EU). Similarly, the institutional structure of the UK regime has changed, most notably with the Office of Fair Trading (OFT) and Competition Commission (CC) being combined to form the CMA on 1 April 2014. As a result of these changes we have cited older literature and judgments with reference to EEC/EC or OFT/CC whenever appropriate.

Our warm thanks are due to Angus Johnston, co-author of the first edition, for all of his hard work on the first edition of this book.

Finally, sincere thanks are due to everyone at Hart Publishing for their patience and cooperation during the development and production of this book. We have endeavoured to state the law as it stood at 31 July 2016.

Piet Jan Slot, Emeritus Professor, Leiden University.
Martin Farley, member of the European Commission Legal Service and Fellow of the Centre of European Law, King's College London.[2]

---

[2] The views expressed in this work are those of the authors and may not be regarded as stating an official position of the European Commission.

Contents

Table of Cases

CFI / General Court

Commission Decisions

ECHR

USA

Netherlands

Table of Legislation

EU Treaties

United Kingdom

Statutory Instruments

Competition Commission

Competition and Markets Authority

United States

International Treaties, Conventions etc

China

Czech Republic

Netherlands

Introduction to
Competition Law

1.1 The Economic Background to Competition Law

Competition law is, in many ways, the night-watchman of a market economy. In a market economy, the important decisions about production and consumption (ie supply and demand) are taken through the market. Producers and consumers decide, on the basis of prices, whether or not to produce (supply) and/or whether the answer is to consume (demand). The goal of competition law is to ensure that the market functions optimally: ie to let competition do its good work. According to economists, an optimal operation of the market leads to greater welfare. This happens in three ways.

First, a well-functioning market leads to *productive efficiency*. The 'products' (which can be goods or services) are produced at as low a cost as possible. To achieve a certain quality, no more materials are used in production than is absolutely necessary. Companies are forced to look for better production methods so that the product can be produced at lower costs. If they do not do this, they are punished immediately by competition from their competitors.

Secondly, the proper operation of the market leads to *allocative efficiency*. Allocative efficiency is promoted by putting the available resources of production to work where they contribute most to consumer preferences. Production responds optimally to demand. Market power stands in the way of achieving allocative efficiency. Imagine that there is a monopoly over the production of blue pens, while producers of red pens compete strongly among themselves. Consumers generally prefer the blue pens. However, because the producer of blue pens holds a monopoly and charges a (higher) monopoly price, a number of consumers switch over to red pens. Through this shift in demand, more productive resources must be engaged in the production of red pens to satisfy the increased demand. From the point of view of social welfare (ie consumer preference), this is not optimal. If the price of blue pens were to fall, then the use of those productive resources would shift to the production of blue pens. In this way there is an improvement in allocative efficiency, because production is more in accordance with the preferences of the consumers.

Thirdly, the operation of the market leads to *dynamic efficiency*. Competition drives companies to be innovative and strive to create new products. Without this push, industry would continue to produce old fashioned and less useful models. The achievement of dynamic efficiency was also an important driving force for the UK government when introducing the Competition Act 1998, and the more recent reforms of the Enterprise Act 2002.[1]

In the European Union (the EU), competition law has the further goal of promoting the functioning of the internal market. For this reason, close attention is paid to ensuring that the commercial world does not conclude or maintain agreements that restrict the free movement of imports and exports to and from other EU Member States. This objective has played an important role, particularly in the early days of the development of the internal market. The creation and development of the internal market has in no small part been due to the application of competition law.

This book discusses the meaning of competition law for the healthy functioning of the market. First of all, therefore, we will consider the function(s) of competition law. Thereafter, a number of economic concepts and background matters will be introduced and explained. A full treatment of these matters is beyond the scope of this introductory book. However, the reader who aims at a higher level of understanding of economics and wants to practice competition is well advised to familiarise him- or herself more thoroughly with this discipline.

1.2 The Function(s) of Competition Law

Although the function of competition law has already implicitly been touched upon in the preceding section, it is perhaps useful to dwell upon this question for a moment. Antitrust law in the US (competition law in European terms) was developed in a period where trusts (ie, cartels) threatened from all sides to bring the American economy under their control. A cartoon from the 1890s illustrated this by depicting the most notorious cartels and monopolies as a giant octopus that held Uncle Sam in its all-embracing grip. Antitrust law—which seeks to break the trusts (ie, cartels)— was, therefore, also intended above all as a political message that the government recognised the damaging nature of the trusts and wanted to call a halt to them. It was thus a question of control and the redistribution of power and wealth. In other

---

[1] See C Blair, 'Competition Bill [HL]' (House of Commons Research Paper 98/53, 28 April 1998), R Whish, 'The Competition Act 1998 and the Prior Debate on Reform' in BJ Rodger and A MacCulloch (eds), *The UK Competition Act 1998: A New Era for UK Competition Law* (Oxford, Hart Publishing, 2000) and the UK Government's White Paper, *A World Class Competition Regime* (31 July 2001). NB see the even more recent entry into force of the Enterprise and Regulatory Reform Act 2013, and its creation of the Competition & Markets Authority (CMA), which will be discussed further in the relevant chapters below.

words, antitrust law was a strongly populist instrument. Behind this there was also a more economic–political objective, namely to guarantee the operation of the market mechanism. In a famous decision of the US Supreme Court, *Socony-Vacuum Oil*,[2] it was made clear that a price cartel that had been set up to combat ruinous competition simply could not be allowed to stand. The case concerned a price-fixing cartel that had been set up by small manufacturers in an attempt to stabilise oil prices in the face of the economic crisis of the 1930s. Despite the desperate situation faced by the companies concerned, the Supreme Court remained of the view that American antitrust law did not exist to protect the small competitor. It was about the protection of the *competitive process*. This judgment illustrates strikingly the conflict between the objectives of competition law. The current US antitrust law is increasingly directed at protecting the interests of the consumer and carries with it heavy sanctions. For example, prison sentences can be imposed upon individual offenders and claimants can bring so-called 'treble damages actions' against undertakings that have breached the antitrust rules. These sanctions ensure that American antitrust law carries important political and social baggage.

Competition law in the EU, however, was mainly directed at achieving the objectives of the common market, which later became known as the 'internal market'. The function of the promotion of competition was an active part of these objectives. The same is true of the protection of the consumer.[3] Various EU block exemption Regulations have the goal of promoting research and development: this happens by exempting agreements in this field from the prohibition on cartels. This also takes place through encouraging the development of patents. These developments can be seen as a form of industrial policy in which legislators and enforcement agencies recognise that a certain degree of cooperation between competitors can, in certain circumstances, be beneficial for the market—and consumers—as a whole.[4]

In this connection, it is important to note that competition law does not strive to achieve moral goals, nor does it carry any moral baggage other than the promotion of competition. Whenever, for example, a particular undertaking builds up a large market share through a very efficient production process and very effective commercial policy, that position is not in itself prohibited. On the other hand, such praiseworthy market behaviour does not have the consequence that the company is somehow freed from the stricter competition rules that apply to undertakings that hold a position of dominance on the market. Here, again, the issue is the protection of *competition* and not the protection of successful market behaviour.

---

[2] *United States v Socony-Vacuum Oil Co* 310 US 150 (1940).

[3] Above all, this has come strongly to the fore in the creation of various block exemptions. So, in the block exemption for car dealers (Reg 461/2010 [2010] OJ L129/52) it is ensured that, outside the dealer system, consumers can source cars from other Member States. See, eg, J Goyder, *EU Distribution Law*, 5th edn (Oxford, Hart Publishing, 2011), esp chs 3 and 4, and the Supplementary guidelines on vertical restraints in agreements for the sale and repair of motor vehicles and for the distribution of spare parts for motor vehicles [2010] OJ C138/16, which strongly emphasise the central role of the consumer in this area. On consumer law and policy in the EU more generally, see S Weatherill, *EU Consumer Law and Policy*, 2nd edn (Cheltenham, Edward Elgar, 2013).

[4] See, eg, W Sauter, *Competition Law and Industrial Policy in the EU* (Oxford, Clarendon Press, 1995) and T Käseberg and A van Laer, 'Competition Law and Industrial Policy: Conflict, Adaptation, and Complementarity', in KK Patel and H Schweitzer (eds), *The Historical Foundations of EU Competition Law* (Oxford, Oxford University Press, 2013), ch 5.

1.3 The Market

1.3.1 Economic Theory Distinguishes Between Various Market Forms

Economic theory distinguishes between a number of market forms. First, there is the market with full or 'perfect' competition. In this market, there is an infinite number of producers and, as a result of this, no single producer is in a position to influence the price. Similarly, there is an unlimited number of consumers/buyers, who are just as unable to influence the price. The product is homogeneous, so that no single buyer has a slight preference for one type of the product over another. Buyers and sellers have full information at their disposal concerning prices and the sort of goods that will be offered, so that both will buy and sell at the current price. Also, buyers and sellers neither ask nor offer any deviation from the standard quality of the product. There are also low barriers to entry for the producers. The classic example of a market that approaches this model is that of the market for grain in the United States. This market has a very large number of farmers who grow the grain and many purchasers. Furthermore, the grain is all of the same quality. Although the model of perfect competition is hardly ever encountered in practice, it performs an important exemplary function in competition law. In this model, undertakings produce at the point where their marginal costs[5] are equal to the price. That means that the consumer pays the lowest possible price for the product. This price is an equilibrium price because it places the producer in a position to produce in an economically responsible manner. In this situation of equilibrium, no profit is made, apart from a reasonable allowance for the factors of production involved. Furthermore, there are no other forces to ensure that new producers will enter the market. The results of this model are used to explain its normative effects upon competition law. Thus, in the application of competition law the authorities strive to ensure the largest possible number of sellers of products. It also explains why agreements between producers concerning prices and market sharing are undesirable. Such practices keep the price artificially above the equilibrium level.

This market form, however, is only partly of relevance in the daily practice of competition law. The American economist JM Clark, in his article 'Towards a Concept of Workable Competition', made an important contribution to the further development of the theory of market forms.[6] Clark concluded that perfect competition does not exist in practice. In his view, there are always circumstances which ensure that the market does not function perfectly (so-called 'market imperfections'). Thus, producers and consumers are far from having full information at their disposal. The product is also rarely homogeneous, so that different prices can apply to different qualities. Often

---

[5] The marginal cost of an additional unit of output is the cost of the additional inputs needed to produce that output.

[6] (1940) 30 *American Economic Review* 241.

there are also barriers to entry for producers. These imperfections have important consequences. For Clark, the issue was thus to create the conditions in which the market would be, and would remain, workable. As a result, certain restrictions upon competition could be accepted in order to realise other goals, such as a good product or a good service. This concept of workable competition has also been followed in EU and UK competition law, and is even enshrined in the relevant legislation Article 101(3) TFEU and section 9(1) of the Competition Act 1998 (see Chapter 3.5 below). Thus, the Court of Justice of the European Union (ECJ, or 'the Court') in its *Metro I* judgment[7] held that the issue was one of 'effective' competition—that is, the measure of competition that is necessary to comply with the basic demands of the EU Treaty and to achieve its objectives. On the basis of this starting point, the ECJ accepted a certain restriction of price competition, since this could lead to an increase in competition with regard to factors other than price.

A second market form is that of monopoly. In this market form, there is only one producer that puts the relevant product on to the market. Through this, this producer is in a position to demand a price for the product that is far above the equilibrium price (ie, the marginal costs) as there is no competition to constrain its behaviour. The consumer pays much more for this product than would be possible under perfect competition. The extra income that the consumer spends in this way cannot be used to purchase other products. In such a market, allocative inefficiency occurs. Indirectly, the existence of a monopoly can also lead to productive inefficiency. But then we must accept that—due to the absence of competitive pressures—costs will be higher than where competition is present. Alongside this, the pressure for product innovation can also fade: the absence of such pressure can lead to a reduced level of dynamic efficiency. This model of monopoly also has great normative value for competition law. As we will discuss in Chapter 4, those with dominant positions are subjected to stricter rules than undertakings with a lesser degree of market power. The same considerations also form the basis of merger control, with the creation or strengthening of a dominant position being a specific example of the type of significant impediment to competition that can result in the prohibition of a merger under the EU Merger Regulation: on this, see Chapter 5.

The mirror image of a monopoly is a monopsony. In this situation, there is only one buyer. This position gives the buyer the possibility to dictate the conditions of purchase. From a competition point of view, this situation is just as undesirable as a monopoly. An example of a monopsony was the position of the Spanish State telephone company, prior to the liberalisation of the telecoms market. Telefonica was the only company that bought telecoms equipment on the Spanish market. When two large producers of this equipment decided to merge, a dominant position on the equipment market would have been created and the question was whether this dominant position would distort competition. The European Commission (which had to decide whether or not to approve the merger) took the view that, due to the existence of only one buyer of such equipment, the merger in fact would not do so.[8]

---

[7] Case 26/76 *Metro SB-Großmärkte GmbH & Co KG v Commission*, paras 21–22.
[8] Commission Decision *Alcatel/Telettra* [1991] OJ L122/48.

A third market form is that of oligopoly. In this model there is only a limited number of sellers or producers. This provides them with the possibility of influencing market conditions. This possibility is increased still further if this small group of producers conspires to impose their conditions upon the market. In oligopolistic markets the competition authorities must therefore be particularly vigilant. An understanding of the nature of oligopolistic markets is of especial relevance in the contexts of: the notion of concerted practices (see Chapter 3.2.2.3); the concept of collective dominance (see Chapter 4.2.13); and the merger field, when assessing coordinated effects and the likely structure of the market subsequent to the proposed merger (see Chapter 5.2.5).

In the 1980s the theory of the 'contestable market' was developed. The concept of a contestable market implies that such a market is freely accessible. Producers can enter the market freely, and if they wish to exit the market then they similarly face few (or, at any rate, no great) restrictions and costs in doing so. In contestable markets it is not the number of sellers that is so important. The potential[9] competition ensures that there is (and remains) sufficient competition on the market. Thus, for the application of competition law, the matter turns rather upon the question of whether or not the position of the current sellers can be challenged.

1.3.2 Various Market Forms Are Important in Competition Law

In order to give competition law a concrete form, it is necessary to identify the relevant market: that is, the market on which the relevant competitive behaviour takes place. As a result, the need to define the relevant market arises in multiple contexts in both EU and UK competition law. For example, in EU competition law, market definition is relevant under Article 101(1) TFEU for determining whether an agreement has the appreciable effect of restricting competition and an appreciable effect on trade between Member States; under Article 101(3)(b), when considering whether an agreement would substantially eliminate competition; for determining whether certain block exemptions are applicable, such as the block exemption for vertical agreements; under Article 102 for determining whether an undertaking has a dominant position on the market; and in merger control for determining whether the concentration is likely to result in a significant impediment to effective competition.

As a matter of UK competition law, in addition to when it applies the Chapter I and Chapter II prohibitions of the Competition Act 1998 (which are based on the provisions in Articles 101 and 102), the CMA also needs to define the relevant market when determining the level of a penalty under the Competition Act 1998;[10] and under the Enterprise Act 2002 when carrying out its merger control functions or conducting 'market studies' or 'market investigations'.

In 1997, the European Commission published a 'Notice on the Definition of the Relevant Market for the Purposes of EU Competition Law'.[11] This Notice provides

---

[9] Here we are concerned with the possibility that other companies (not in the same line of business) can begin to supply the product: see further s 1.3.2.3 (below).

[10] Guidance as to the Appropriate Amount of a Penalty, OFT 423, September 2012, para 2.7, adopted by the CMA Board with effect from 1 April 2014.

[11] [1997] OJ C372/5. A Commission Notice has no officially binding force: it is not legislation, but rather acts like pseudo-legislation. This Notice provides a summary of 40 years of practice in this field, so it

a useful overview of the most important concepts and further discusses which criteria can be used to decide upon the relevant market.[12] In its Guidelines on Vertical Restraints,[13] the Commission provided further indications of how to determine the relevant market in the application of the block exemption Regulation on vertical agreements.[14]

1.3.2.1 Product Market

Only producers of identical or similar products or services can come into competition with each other. A grain farmer does not compete with the Boeing-McDonnell Douglas aircraft factory. An undertaking always operates on one or more specific product markets. No single undertaking produces everything. And even a big company can be a small player on a particular market.

How is the product market determined? At the heart of the market definition exercise is the identification of those products that are a good alternative for the product in question. In economic terms, this requires a decision on which substitutes are available for that product either from the point of view of the customer (demand-side) or for other suppliers (supply-side). To do this, it is necessary to analyse the characteristic features and intended use of the relevant product.[15]

A well-known example of a case in which the Court focused on the characteristics of the product when assessing the relevant market is to be found in the *United Brands* judgment of the ECJ.[16] This case concerned the question of whether the relevant product market was simply 'bananas' or a broader market of 'fresh fruit' generally. The Court and the Commission were of the view that, for a number of important categories of consumer (such as babies and the elderly), bananas could not be replaced by

---

nevertheless has an important role in the application of EU competition law and (as will become clear in ch 2), UK competition law. The EU Courts have referred with approval to the Notice: see, eg, Case T-321/05 *AstraZeneca v Commission*, para 86. Further, there are often observations to be found in the sectoral directives that concern the delimitation of the market. See, eg, the Commission Guidelines on Market Analysis and the Assessment of Significant Market Power under the Community Regulatory Framework for Electronic Communications Networks and Services [2002] OJ C165/3 or ch 2 of the Commission Notice on the Application of the Competition Rules to the Postal Sector and on the Assessment of Certain State Measures Relating to Postal Services [1998] OJ C39/2. See, for a specific UK example, the CMA's guidance on 'Regulated industries: Guidance on concurrent application of competition law to regulated industries' (CMA 10).

[12] The OFT, too, in December 2004 published its Guidelines on *Market Definition* (OFT 403), and this has now been adopted by the CMA (as of 12 March 2014): https://www.gov.uk/government/uploads/system/uploads/attachment_data/file/284423/oft403.pdf; and see also the International Competition Network's *Recommended Practices for Merger Analysis* (8 December 2009, http://www.internationalcompetitionnetwork.org/uploads/library/doc316.pdf), Part II (on market definition).

[13] [2010] OJ C 130/1.

[14] Reg 330/2010/EU [2010] OJ L102/1.

[15] See, eg the progress of the *Aberdeen Journals* case and, in particular, the Competition Commission Appeal Tribunal's (CCAT's) first judgment in the case (remitting it to the OFT for more accurate market definition) *Aberdeen Journals (No 1)* [2002] CAT 4. The CCAT criticised the OFT's failure properly to describe the different newspapers involved and the types of advertising that they carried: thus, the CCAT was unable to determine whether or not Aberdeen Journals held a dominant position on the market for the supply of advertising space in journals and newspapers in the Aberdeen area. See generally, OFT, *Market Definition* (OFT 403) for further details of the OFT's approach.

[16] Case 27/76 *United Brands v Commission*.

another fruit that was harder to eat. This was the result of the special characteristics of bananas. Bananas are particularly soft, have no pips or stones, are available all year round and are always in sufficient supply. These factors meant that the demand for bananas reacts only very slightly to a reduction in the prices of other fresh fruit. Due to all of these reasons, the Court concluded that the banana market was a product market that was sufficiently differentiated from those of other fresh fruits.

As indicated by the ECJ, however, characteristics and intended use are not sufficient in themselves. One of the key factors that need to be taken into account is the sensitivity of the consumer to any changes in price levels. If a small increase in the price of the relevant product leads to a great reduction in the demand for that product and to a large increase in demand for another product, it is probable that these products are substitutable for one another and therefore belong to the same market.

The Commission's 'Notice on the Definition of the Relevant Market for the Purposes of Community Competition Law'[17] and the OFT's guidance on *Market Definition* (OFT 403)[18] explain one of the principal techniques for assessing whether or not there is demand-side substitutability for a particular product or range of products. This is known as the 'SSNIP test', which stands for a 'Small but Significant, Non-transitory Increase in Price'. The basic purpose of this test is to establish whether consumers would switch from one product to another if the price of all supplies of the first product were increased by a small amount and kept at that level over time.[19] If customers would switch, then this can establish which products are viewed as substitutes for the first product and thus help to delimit the scope of the relevant product market. A similar approach may assist in determining the appropriate scope of the relevant geographic market (on which see section 1.3.2.2 below). This approach is also known as the 'hypothetical monopolist test', given that its premise is that all supplies of the first product are subjected to a price increase. However, the reader should be careful not to associate this nomenclature with a presumption that dominance of the market by the company (under investigation under Article 102 TFEU or Chapter II of the CA 1998) has been shown: this must be established separately, as explained in Chapter 4.2.2 below.[20] Nevertheless, treating this approach as a hypothetical monopolist test does remind us of one key point: for an alternative product to form part of the same market as the product in question, the consumer's switch to alternative products must be such as to render unprofitable the hypothetical monopolist's price increase.[21]

Certain difficulties can arise in using the SSNIP test in particular circumstances: the major problem is determining the appropriate price level to take as the starting point, to which the hypothetical price increase is then added. This can be problematic in cases where the price on the market has already been significantly inflated due to

---

[17] See n 11, above. On horizontal cooperation agreements, see the separate set of Commission Guidelines: [2011] OJ C11/1.

[18] See also the jointly published UK *Merger Assessment Guidelines* (CC2 (revised), OFT1254; September 2010; adopted by the CMA, 12 March 2014), especially section 5.2: a 5% increase will usually be applied when using SSNIP in merger cases.

[19] This does not include short-lived promotions, such as summer sales, etc.

[20] For an illustration of the utilisation of the SSNIP approach in court, see *Attheraces v British Horseracing Board* [2005] EWHC 3015 (Ch), [135]–[231] (esp [174]ff).

[21] Note 11, above, para 17; see also OFT 403, ss 2, 3 and 4 (but esp s 2 for an outline).

anti-competitive practices,[22] or where the case concerns the emergence of a new product for which there is no obvious comparator to provide a starting pricing point.[23] The difficulty in such cases, as the UK authorities have acknowledged,[24] is finding an appropriate alternative methodology for determining what the relevant price starting point for the SSNIP test should be.[25] For a practical illustration of the SSNIP test and some of its difficulties, see section 1.3.2.2 below, which contains extracts from the Competition Appeal Tribunal's judgment in the *Burgess* case.[26]

The more narrowly the market is defined, the greater the chance that a particular undertaking will hold a dominant position on it. This is clear to see from the problems that arose on the acquisition of Elf Aquitaine by TotalFina.[27] Both companies were active in the field of refining and distributing oil and gas, and also supplied petrol to drivers at the retail level. According to TotalFina, the natural advocate of a broad definition of the relevant market, the relevant market consisted of the retail sale of petrol via service stations. Drivers would always have a free choice of service stations at which to fill their tanks. The Commission, however, came to a different conclusion and defined the relevant market as the market for the sale of petrol along the French motorways. This was because the sale of petrol on motorways satisfied different needs from those fulfilled by the sale of petrol off the motorways. In the words of the Commission:

> Motorists use the motorway to benefit from the speed of the traffic, as well as all the other services that result from the operating structure of a motorway, such as the supply of petrol, the restaurants, opportunities to take breaks, etc. A consequence of this choice is a reduced sensitivity to petrol prices.[28]

An important additional factor in the Commission's assessment lay in the French system of motorway tolls. If a driver leaves a toll road to fill up with petrol, then a further toll must be paid to re-enter the motorway if he or she wishes to continue that journey

---

[22] Often known as the 'cellophane fallacy', after the infamous US case of *United States v El du Pont de Nemour & Co* 351 US 377 (1956) (which concerned cellophane products). The danger is that, with the price already at an artificially high level, switching will occur more rapidly, with the result that the breadth of the relevant market will be drawn more widely than is appropriate if the SSNIP test is applied in an overly mechanical fashion. This is why some take the view that the SSNIP test is most appropriate in merger cases, where the question at issue is the likely future market situation if the merger were to be allowed to proceed. The OFT Guideline on Market Definition specifically notes the problem of the cellophane fallacy and seeks to overcome any potential issues that might arise therefrom by ensuring that 'all the evidence on market definition is weighed in the round' (OFT 403, paras 5.4–5.6). See for example the approaches adopted by the OFT in its investigations in Aberdeen Journals II (OFT Decision 25 September 2002, paras 94–99) and BSkyB (OFT Decision 30 January 2003, paras 88–97).

[23] See, eg, the Competition Appeal Tribunal's judgment in *The Racecourse Association and the British Horseracing Board v OFT* [2005] CAT 29. The CAT was critical of the OFT's methodology in defining the relevant market in its Decision in this case (No CA98/2/2004 *Attheraces* (5 April 2004), see ss 135–150.

[24] See OFT 403, ss 5.4–5.6 and the OFT Economic Discussion Paper No 2, *The Role of Market Definition in Monopoly and Dominance Enquiries* (OFT 342) (produced by NERA for the OFT, July 2001).

[25] The CAT is clearly of the view that there is a need to establish the relevant market conditions that would exist after any distortions caused by abusive conduct have been taken into account: see the second Aberdeen Journals case, *Aberdeen Journals Ltd v OFT (No 2)* [2003] CAT 11, s 276.

[26] See n 37 below, and the subsequent text.

[27] Case T-342/00 *Petrolessence SA v Commission*, Judgment of the Court of First Instance on an application for the annulment of the Commission's Decision 2001/402/EC of 9 February 2000 [2001] OJ L143/1 and the Decision (of 13 September) based upon that Decision).

[28] At para 168.

on that road. This creates a barrier to competition between service stations on the motorway and other service stations, thus showing that the two belonged to different markets. As proof of this, the Commission relied on the price differential that existed between the variously located service stations—a difference that could not be justified by objective factors. In any case, the French toll system was only an additional cause.

On the narrow market for petrol supply on the motorways, the Commission considered that the proposed concentration would result in a significant impediment to effective competition as it would result in the creation of a dominant position for the merged entity. In order to obtain clearance for the concentration, TotalFina committed to divest some of the motorway service stations that would otherwise be controlled by the merged entity. Had the relevant market been defined more broadly, it is possible that TotalFina would not have had to commit to such a divestiture in order to obtain clearance of the concentration.

An example of a service market is the market for charter transport. When KLM wanted to take over Martinair, the merger had to be assessed by the European Commission. The Commission decided that there was a separate air transport market for charter flights.[29] This market had different features from the market for regular scheduled services. The European Commission let it be known that the merger between KLM and Martinair would lead to a dominant position on the charter market that would endanger competition. On the basis of this, KLM and Martinair dropped their plans to merge.

Meanwhile, the OFT's Decision in the *West Midlands flat-roofing case*[30] provides a good UK illustration of the general process of market definition (in this case, for 'repair, maintenance and improvement', or RMI, services for flat roofs):

131. Market definition usually starts with the product that is the subject of the complaint. This is the supply of RMI services for a variety of different types of flat roofs.

132. The OFT considers that a buyer requiring RMI services for flat roofs would generally consider flat roofing specialists to be competitors, irrespective of which type of flat roof the contractor specialised in.

133. Flat roofing falls into three broad categories:

— felt (also known as bituminous felt roof coverings);
— single ply membranes; and
— asphalt.

134. Bituminous flat roof coverings are designed to be fixed on to the surface deckings of flat roofs to protect them from the elements. They are supplied in a wide variety and combinations of materials with effective lives that range from less than 5, to over 20 years. Single ply PVC roofs accomplish the same basic function as felt, but have several advantages such as simple installation, the ability of the covering to move more freely and a low installation cost. Asphalt provides a waterproof but inflexible covering. Mastic asphalt is particularly suitable for roofs that carry pedestrians or cars, such as rooftop car parks.

135. The OFT notes that although different flat roofing materials have different specialist uses, the skills employed, and the services provided by flat roof contractors allow contractors

---

[29] *KLM–Martinair II*, Case No COMP/M.1328 (1 February 1999), withdrawn 25 May 1999.
[30] OFT Decision, No CA98/1/2004, 16 March 2004 (footnotes omitted).

that specialise in fitting different flat roofing materials to compete against one another for flat roof contracting work.

136. In addition to flat roofing specialists, there are also contractors who specialise in RMI services for pitched or metal roofing. However, the supply of RMI services provided by pitched or metal roofing specialists is likely to be qualitatively different to the supply of RMI services by flat roof specialists. This is because of a basic difference in material and technology. Therefore the OFT does not consider that the supply of RMI services for pitched and metal roofs are within the same market.

137. In summary the OFT considers that the relevant product market is the supply of RMI services for flat roofs.

As the above extract demonstrates, when defining the relevant market, the OFT first identified the focal product and then sought to identify possible substitutes for this product—first from a demand-side perspective (ie, that of the customer),[31] and then from a supply-side perspective (ie, that of suppliers of similar products—in this case suppliers of RMI services for flat roofs as well as pitched and metal roofs). The OFT ultimately concluded that the relevant market covered RMI services for all flat roofs because, from the demand-side, customers generally consider all flat roof specialists to be competitors, and that flat roof contractors generally compete regardless of the specific roof material. Contractors for pitched or metal roofs did not fall within the relevant market, however, because the materials and technology used by these contractors are different to those used by flat-roof specialists and, as such, they are not in a position to switch quickly and easily to providing RMI services for flat roofs.

1.3.2.2 Geographic Market

An undertaking is always active in a particular geographic area. Undertakings that are located too far away from each other do not pose competitive threats to each other. Exactly how far these distances have to be for this to be the case is heavily dependent upon the nature of the product and factors connected therewith, such as transport costs. An ice cream cone seller in New York, for example, is not subject to any competition from his colleague in Boston. A café in Birmingham is not in competition with a pizza restaurant in London or Bristol. But a restaurant in Brussels that has been awarded three stars by the Michelin Guide does experience competition from a three-star restaurant in Paris. Why? First, because the wealthy diners who frequent this sort of restaurant can easily travel from Brussels to Paris. Secondly, with a high-speed train this journey can be completed in just one hour and twenty minutes. Thirdly, for the users of the Michelin Guide it is clear that a three-star restaurant is definitely worth this journey.

Thus, it comes down to the identification of the factors that give the product a particular geographical reach. Often, these are transport costs. Yet for high value and light products, such as watches, transport costs are rarely a relevant element. In the

---

[31] See also the CMA's investigation in the *Private healthcare* case, where the CMA took into account the results of its patient survey as a useful source of information about the relevant market (Final Report 2 April 2014).

United Brands bananas case discussed above, the legal import regime played a crucial role in determining the geographic market. The nature of the product also has an important role to play. The French eat more snails than the British. The demand for dining establishments is decided locally, while the demand for three-star restaurants is nationally and even internationally determined. Here, sensitivity to changes in price is also a key issue.

In the case of the *KLM–Martinair* merger, the Commission analysed the issues on the basis that the geographic market was The Netherlands. It was considered that holiday makers from that country would not willingly travel to Copenhagen or Berlin in order to pick up a charter flight from there to their final destination: in this situation, the outer limits tend to be Brussels and Düsseldorf. Departing from these latter airports would only be attractive to the holidaymaker if the price differential for the flights was greater than the cost of travel to these airports.

International geographic markets have formed the basis for most EU competition law analysis. For example, in the *Tetra Pak* case,[32] the geographic market for the packaging system was treated as EU-wide, even in spite of the fact that the parent company was present in each Member State through national subsidiary companies. In its judgment, the Court of First Instance[33] (the CFI; now the General Court, GC) followed the Commission's market definition:

91. The Court notes at the outset that in the scheme of Article [102 TFEU] the geographical market must be defined so as to determine whether the undertaking concerned is in a dominant position in the [EU] or a substantial part of it. The definition of the geographical market, as that of the product market, accordingly calls for an economic assessment. The geographical market can thus be defined as the territory in which all traders operate in the same conditions of competition in so far as concerns specifically the relevant products. The Commission correctly points out that it is not at all necessary for the objective conditions of competition between traders to be perfectly homogeneous. It is sufficient if they are 'the same' or 'sufficiently homogeneous' ...

92. It is accordingly necessary to ascertain whether the various factors pleaded by the applicant give rise in the [EU] to objective conditions of competition of a heterogeneous nature. The Court considers that the establishment of major manufacturers of packaging systems in each Member State by way of national subsidiaries, and similarly the practice of dairies of obtaining supplies at local level, are not sufficient, contrary to the applicant's contention, to establish that the conditions of competition are specific to the territory of each of those States. With regard in particular to Tetra Pak's policy, the context of these proceedings suggests conversely that the circumstances which have just been described are attributable rather to its strategy of partitioning the markets than to the existence of local markets characterized by objectively different conditions of competition ...

94. In this case, the Commission was entitled to define a single geographical market covering the whole [EU] for three main reasons. First, as the Commission emphasizes without contradiction by the applicant, demand was stable and not insignificant—even though it varied in intensity from one Member State to another—for all the relevant products, throughout the territory of the [EU], during the period covered by the Decision. Secondly, according to the same sources, from the technical point of view customers could obtain supplies of machinery

---

[32] Commission Decision 92/163/EEC of 24 July 1991 [1992] OJ L72/1.
[33] Case T-83/91, *TetraPak International*.

or cartons in other Member States, the presence of local distribution units being necessary solely to install, maintain and repair machines. Thirdly, the very low cost of transport for cartons and machines meant that they could be easily and rapidly traded between States; the applicant does not deny this ...

98. It follows from the above that the relevant geographical market comprises in this case the whole of the [EU]. It thus extended to the nine Member States until 31 December 1980, to the ten until 31 December 1985 and to the twelve as from 1 January 1986.

As most barriers to inter-Member State trade are removed, a situation will come to pass in which producers from different Member States can actually compete with each other, and thus the relevant geographic market may well often coincide with the EU market.

It should also be noted that, particularly with the ever-increasing move towards globalisation, there will often be situations where reference is made to a worldwide market, in place of one limited to the EU. Such a situation arose in the *Microsoft* case.[34] There, the relevant market was the worldwide market for 'Intel-compatible' computer operating systems.

At the other end of the scale, it is perfectly plausible for markets to be smaller than national. In UK competition law, the OFT's guidelines on market definition—which have been adopted by the CMA—specifically recognise the possibility of the existence of sub-national, local or regional markets.[35] Returning to the example of the *West Midlands flat-roofing* case (discussed in section 1.3.2.1 above), the OFT's Decision also provides a good illustration of the process of defining the relevant geographic market:

138. When defining the relevant geographic market the OFT uses a similar approach to defining the relevant product market. The complaint relates to a series of agreements centred in specific locations in the West Midlands area. These areas are Coventry, Birmingham, Warwick, Dudley and Hereford.

139. The OFT considers that a customer in the West Midlands area would typically choose from suppliers in the same area.

140. In particular, the OFT notes that many local authorities in the West Midlands operate a common standard for council contracts, organised through the West Midlands Forum. The West Midlands Forum consists of BCC, CCC, Redditch Borough Council, SMBC, Walsall Metropolitan Borough Council and Wolverhampton City Council. Any company that cannot meet the West Midlands Forum Common criteria is not recommended for inclusion on the relevant standing lists. These common standards, and the similarity between Council standing lists and tender invitation lists used by private managing agents, is suggestive of a high degree of substitutability between flat roofing contractors in the West Midlands area.

---

[34] *United States v Microsoft* 253 F 3d 34 (2001) (USCA, DC Cir) and 231 F Supp.2d 144 (2002) (DDC, acknowledging the eventual settlement of the case).

[35] Guidelines on *Market definition* (OFT 403). See also the Competition Commission's decision of 6 June 2013 in the Groupe Eurotunnel S.A. and SeaFrance S.A. merger inquiry where the Competition Commission defined the geographic market as short sea routes between the UK and France; various bus transport decisions adopted by the DGFT and OFT over the years (under the pre-CA 1998 regime, the report on *Thamesway Limited: the Operation of Local Bus Services Commencing in, Terminating in or Passing through Southend-on-Sea* (27 August 1993) (discussed in Myers, *Predatory Behaviour in UK Competition Policy* (OFT Research Paper No 5, November 1994), 33–36) and, under the new dispensation, OFT Decision *Market Sharing by Arriva plc and FirstGroup plc* (No CA98/9/2002, 30 January 2002) (concerning the Leeds area). See also the first *Aberdeen Journals* case, n 15, above, para 97.

141. Evidence from local authority standing lists and other parties indicate that the opportunity for customers to use contractors outside the West Midlands area is limited.

142. First, contractors from outside the region that are not already on the approved contractor lists of West Midlands local authorities may be subject to some measure of delay because of the time needed to check that new contractors satisfy the qualification requirements that these local authorities and private managing agents set. Second, contractors from outside the region would be further away from the contract site in question and therefore find it harder to absorb transport costs compared to more 'local' contractors. This position has often led to regional market definitions for other types of building products. Third, contractors from outside the region may have more difficulty securing local labour resources than firms already established in the region because of the shortage of skilled labour.

143. Accordingly, the OFT finds that the relevant geographic market is the West Midlands.[36]

A further helpful example of UK practice can be found in the important judgment of the Competition Appeal Tribunal (CAT) in the case of *JJ Burgess & Sons v OFT*.[37] The case concerned access to the Harwood Park Crematorium in Hertfordshire and much turned on whether or not the OFT had accurately defined the relevant geographic market for the provision of crematoria services: this definition had a clear effect upon whether or not the Harwood Park Crematorium could be said to be dominant in the supply of such services. The CAT reasoned as follows:

187. In the Decision, the OFT comes to the conclusion that the relevant geographic market includes all crematoria within a 30 kilometre radius of Stevenage and Knebworth.

188. We note first that although the OFT rightly distinguishes between crematoria services, and funeral directing services, there is little mention, in the Decision, of the close links between them. Thus, from the consumer's point of view, what is typically purchased is a package of services which consists both of funeral-related services (coffin, hearse, transport etc) and the services of a crematorium, all of which is arranged by the funeral director, as agent, in accordance with the wishes of the consumer, and for which a single account is rendered. We bear in mind that, although the Decision refers to the market for crematoria services, it is characteristic of that market that the services are supplied to end-customers through funeral directors who are themselves serving customers in predominantly local markets such as eg Stevenage and Knebworth.

189. The fact that Austins/Harwood Park is a vertically integrated enterprise which is active in both aspects of the service provided to consumers, namely both funeral and crematoria services, is in our view a highly relevant feature of the present case.

190. We agree with the OFT that, in determining a geographic market, it is convenient to start by looking at a relatively narrow area, such as the area supplied by the parties, and then to consider whether the evidence suggests that the area should be broadened and to include other alternatives that may, geographically speaking, be substitutable from the consumer's point of view (paragraph 38 of the Decision). Accordingly we start by considering whether the Stevenage/Knebworth area is a relevant geographic market for crematoria services.

195. However, it appears to be common ground that, as with funeral directing services, consumers have a strong preference to use local crematoria services, on grounds of convenience.... it

---

[36] See n 30 above (footnotes omitted).
[37] [2005] CAT 25 (footnotes omitted from the extracts reproduced in the following text).

appears that about 95 per cent of cremations arising in [the Stevenage/Knebworth] area were carried out at Harwood Park. ...

199. It is in our view not difficult to identify why consumers would have a strong preference for using the local or most convenient crematorium. Mourners at a funeral, many of whom are likely to be elderly, would not normally wish to travel long distances if that could be avoided; many elderly mourners may not have transport available to take them longer distances; extra travel is likely to increase the time needed, and also to add to the cost of the funeral in terms of fuel and labour costs; and there may be sentimental reasons for choosing the local crematorium, for example to facilitate subsequent visits to view a memorial tablet, to visit a garden of remembrance, or because a previous family member was cremated there. Those considerations, of a common sense nature, are in our view supported by the evidence before the Tribunal. ...

204. It is true that the evidence does not show that business at Burgess' [*sic*] Knebworth office dried up completely in the relatively short period between March and July 2004 when access to Harwood Park was denied. However, in our view, the totality of the evidence shows that there is a strong preference on the part of consumers in the Stevenage/Knebworth area for a cremation to be carried out at Harwood Park. Even, if for a while, Burgess was able to persuade some customers to accept an alternative, despite their apparently expressed wish, we are satisfied that the demand from the vast majority of customers in that area is to have the cremation at Harwood Park. When one compares, for example, the evidence as to the relevant drive times between Stevenage/Knebworth and Harwood Park and West Herts (the best part of two hours, there and back, for West Herts, compared with about half an hour or less, there and back, for Harwood Park) that does not seem to us to be a surprising conclusion to reach.

The CAT went on to discuss the evidence as to the pricing levels of the Harwood Park Crematorium and the ability of funeral directors and end consumers to switch to other crematoria were Harwood Park to increase its prices by a small but significant amount.[38] The analysis showed that:

221. ... Harwood Park increased its prices by 55% between 1998 and 2003, as compared with price increases of 32% by the other crematoria. Over the same period Harwood Park increased its number of cremations by 17.5%, as compared with –15% to +8% for the other crematoria. ...

224. In any event, even if the OFT's figure of [a] 9.6% [increase in Harwood Park's prices] was correct, in terms of a conventional SSNIP test even a price increase by Firm A of around 10% above the weighted average price increase of competitors, which yields no evidence of switching away from Firm A, would normally be regarded as a strong indication that Firm A is able to exercise market power without significant competitive constraint.

---

[38] Applying the so-called 'SSNIP test' (Small but Significant, Non-transitory Increase in Price), discussed in the Commission's Notice on the definition of the relevant market (n 11, above) and the OFT's Guideline on Market Definition (OFT 403, para 2.10): see the text accompanying n 35, above, for discussion. Note further that the CAT agreed with the appellant's argument that 'the relevant purchase is typically made by a consumer who is in a distressed state, who has to take a decision quickly, and who has little or no previous experience of making such a purchase. Those factors—not mentioned at all by the OFT in the Decision—seem to us to point to a market which may not be particularly sensitive to small but significant changes in price. The circumstances in which the purchase is made suggest to us that, for crematoria services, a conventional SSNIP test is likely to show less sensitivity to price changes than in other consumer markets' ([2005] CAT 25, para 216). Thus, there was even doubt, in the CAT's view, as to the utility of the SSNIP test on the facts of the *Burgess* case.

225. In the present context the above evidence in our view strongly supports the conclusion that Harwood Park is shielded from competition to a material extent and operates in an identifiably separate geographic market.

Finally, on the issue of consumer choice in the geographic market definition, the CAT's judgment was also instructive.

242. We stress, in that latter connection, that we do not accept the OFT's apparent submission that in defining a relevant geographic market it is sufficient that the end-consumer should have 'a choice', however inconvenient the 'choice' may be, and however much that 'choice' may diverge from the consumer's 'preference'. As the Commission's *Notice on the Definition of the Relevant Market* points out at paragraph 46, it is consumer *preferences* which have a strong potential to limit geographic markets. Such preferences in our view are highly relevant to the analysis.

243. Stated in general terms the issue, it seems to us, is whether and in what circumstances a sufficient number of consumers situated in Stevenage/Knebworth may reasonably be expected to switch to an alternative crematorium in a neighbouring geographic location. In our view, the totality of the evidence considered above, viewed in the round, points overwhelmingly to the conclusion that it is difficult to envisage realistic circumstances in which a material number of consumers in the Stevenage/Knebworth area would be willing to switch to a crematorium other than Harwood Park. ...

245. For all those reasons we find that there is a discrete geographic market for crematoria services in at least the Stevenage/Knebworth area.

The CAT then proceeded to substitute this assessment for that of the OFT and ruled on the evidence before it that an abuse of a dominant position had occurred (on which see further Chapter 4.2.4.5 and 6.3.5.3 below).

1.3.2.3 The Development of the Market Over Time

The temporal dimension is sometimes important in the definition of the relevant market. This is the case whenever supply or demand is strongly dependent upon time factors. Supply-side examples include agricultural products or Christmas-related items. The Commission's *ABG* Decision provides an illustration of how exceptional factors can also require careful examination of this issue: the relevant market here was for oil and was limited to the period immediately following the crisis that resulted from OPEC's conduct in the early 1970s.[39] On the demand side, one could think of garden furniture and electricity. During the peak periods in each day—the early morning and the evening—there is a substantial increase in the demand for electricity. Similarly demand for garden furniture is highest in the spring and summer. As a result of this, dominant positions can occur during these periods.

  The economy is constantly developing. This has the consequence that the concept of a 'market' is not static. The relevance of the time factor is, once again, dependent upon the nature of the product and the nature of the demand. Thus, fashion articles have a very short temporal market. The market for Tipp-Ex, a correction fluid

---

[39] [1977] OJ L117/1 (overturned on appeal on other grounds: Case 77/77 *BP v Commission*). For guidance on the UK approach, see OFT, *Market Definition* (OFT 403), paras 5.1–5.3.

that was widely used when texts were still produced using traditional typewriters, has largely disappeared. The same is true of the market for telexes, which first made way for faxes and now for e-mail. And e-mail now has largely done away with the viability of the fax. The developments in the IT sector have greatly increased the importance of the temporal element in market definition. A strong market position can be eroded in a very short period of time. The rapidity of technological developments has greatly increased the importance of the time factor. The emergence of the tablet (or 'pad') is changing the market for computers, which now seems to be divided into three separate markets: desktops, laptops and tablets. A similar development is taking place in the mobile telephone sector, thanks to the emergence of a new generation of mobile phones with apps that until recently were only available on desktops.

Closely connected to the development of the market over time is the concept of 'potential competition'. The question of whether or not potential competition could appear for a particular product is again dependent upon the nature of the product. In the car market, it was always the case that the following year's model put pressure on the sale of the current year's model, even before the former had been launched. The sale of smartphones has seen a comparable phenomenon develop. As we will see in Chapter 5, potential competition is, above all, important in the assessment of mergers. There, a judgment must be made about the development of competition over a longer time frame. Potential competition can also play a role in defining the relevant product and the geographic market.

1.3.3 Market Share

Once the relevant market has been determined, the next step is to decide what the market shares are. The market share of an undertaking is of great importance in the application of competition law, and it plays a variety of roles.[40] First of all, market share is important for determining whether or not the competition rules are applicable. Very small market shares are not affected by the prohibitions of competition law. This is reflected in the *de minimis* concept, discussed in Chapter 3.2.4. Secondly, market share is key in deciding whether or not particular agreements have the effect of restricting competition. Thirdly, whether or not certain agreements fall under a block exemption requires knowledge of the market shares of the participating undertakings. Thus, the block exemption for vertical agreements applies on condition that the market share of the supplier as well as the buyer does not exceed 30 per cent.[41]

Market share is also extremely important in the application of the prohibition on the abuse of dominant positions. It is not possible to hold a dominant position without having a large market share. Market share is also critical in the operation of the merger control system: if, as a result of a merger, large market shares would be created, this could lead to the merger being prohibited.

---

[40] This para contains various concepts that will only be fully explained in the following chapters. Nevertheless, for systematic reasons it is useful here to make clear the importance of an undertaking's market share.

[41] Art 3(1) of Reg 330/2010 [2010] OJ L 102/1; see further Chapter 3.6.3.2, below.

1.3.3.1   Determining the Market Share

Once the product and geographic markets have been identified, it is possible to determine the market share of the individual undertaking by assessing its position in relation to the total dimensions of the market in question. Data concerning the extent of the market as a whole and the market shares are often to be found in annual reports, studies and other sources published by the relevant business association. The undertakings concerned are, furthermore, under a duty to report data concerning their market share when they submit an application to the Commission for merger clearance.[42] In most cases, the market share will be related to the turnover of the undertaking. In some industries other indicators are important: thus, the total production capacity may be relevant, or the size of the transport fleet or the extent of reserves. This last element is a vital issue in the oil industry.[43]

1.3.3.2   The Market Position Is Not Necessarily Simply the Market Share

The position of the undertaking(s) involved is not simply dependent upon market share. The market power of an undertaking is also dependent upon the market power of other undertakings, as well as the existence and extent of barriers to entry into the market. This issue will be discussed further in Chapter 4.2.2 below.

1.3.4   The Price Mechanism Is the Central Element of the Market

Markets can only function if the formation of prices takes place freely. Only free prices give the right signals to producers to manufacture goods and to offer services. For consumers, their consumption needs can only be satisfied optimally by free prices. Each interference with the free formation of prices by business in the form of cartels is thus undesirable. In principle, interference from government in the form of regulation is also undesirable. Such an incursion can only be justified in very special markets or for special goods or services. This issue will be discussed in the next section. If the price mechanism functions well, then the individual behaviour of producers and consumers automatically leads to the proper operation of the market. Through this, striving to serve one's own interests leads to the realisation of social benefits. Adam Smith indicated this phenomenon in his seminal book *The Wealth of Nations*, describing it as 'the invisible hand'.[44]

---

[42] Similar data had to be supplied when submitting applications for an individual exemption in both EC and UK law; however, under Reg 1/2003 and the changes to the UK rules mean that such notifications for individual exemption can no longer be entertained by the authorities. For further discussion of this point, see Chapter 3.5.1, 6.1, 6.3.4 and 6.4.1 (below).

[43] As illustrated only too clearly by the troubles experienced by Royal Dutch Shell and its revision downwards of estimated long-term oil reserves: see, eg *The Times*, 19 April 2004.

[44] Its full title is *An Inquiry into the Nature and Causes of the Wealth of Nations* (New York, The Modern Library, 1956). The book, originally published in 1776, is one of the classic texts of economic theory. 'By

This core function of the price mechanism is an important starting point for competition law. Agreements and practices that could affect the effectiveness of the price mechanism are by definition viewed with great suspicion by competition authorities.

1.4 Competition Law and the Economic Theory of Regulation

Competition law can also be summarised as a form of regulation of the economy. By regulation, we mean the conscious intervention in a country's economy by the government. This leads to the restriction of the freedom to trade of businesses and/or consumers. The government forces the adoption of particular types of behaviour desired by it, with the help of legislation and supported by sanctions. In a free market economy, competition law is the form of regulation that, in principle, interferes least with the market mechanism. Although it might theoretically be possible to make the intervention by competition law in the functioning of the market conform strictly to market principles, in practice this is not the case. The application of competition law makes it inevitable that certain choices will have to be made. This is particularly the case where a competition authority can grant exemptions for agreements that would otherwise fall foul of the prohibition on anti-competitive agreements.[45] As we will discuss in Chapter 3.5.1 below, where a competition authority has a discretionary competence to resolve such questions, such discretion allows for the possibility of steering these matters to some degree. Thus, exemption policy can be applied more flexibly to those agreements that have a beneficial effect upon (for example) the environment. In the past, the European Commission has given weight to considerations of employment, culture, environment, regional policy and industrial policy in its exemption decisions.[46] The very small number of notifications in the UK (until the withdrawal of the notification system in 2004) makes it harder to find examples in this vein,[47] but it should be noted that

---

preferring the support of the domestic to that of foreign industry, he intends only his own gain, and he is in this, as in many other cases, led by an invisible hand to promote an end which was no part of his intention' (ibid, 423).

[45] As will be discussed in Chapter 3.5.1 below, the main forum for the application of Art 101(3) TFEU is the national court, but the Commission still has the competence to declare that the conditions of Art 101(3) TFEU are satisfied. Moreover, the Commission has to address the question whether Art 101(3) applies in cases where defendants raise this defence in infringement cases, see Chapter 3.5.3. The CMA has a similar competence vis-à-vis both Art 101(3) TFEU and the Chapter I prohibition (see s 9 of the Competition Act 1998).

[46] See, eg, R Whish and D Bailey, *Competition Law*, 8th edn (Oxford, 2015) 166 et seq.

[47] eg, the *Ineos/BASF notification* of 5 April 2002 related to the conversion of hazardous chemicals and referred to the considerable environmental pressure on BASF not to incinerate such chemicals; however, the OFT found there to have been no infringement of the Ch I prohibition in any case (Decision CA98/17/02 *Lucite International UK Limited (formerly Ineos Acrylics UK Limited) and BASF plc* (29 November 2002)).

national governments have other policy instruments at their disposal to achieve such aims and are not shy about using them.

Another illustration is the ongoing discussion throughout Europe about fixed book prices. The Dutch book cartel was notified to the Commission immediately upon the entry into force of Regulation 17 in 1962. In spite of this, the Commission has never settled the status of this notified agreement. A great deal of political pressure was exerted upon the European Commission (particularly by the European Parliament) to tolerate fixed book prices. However, to tolerate such fixed prices is at odds with the general competition policy regarding price-fixing agreements. Through the pressure from the European Parliament, as well as from various national governments, a sort of stalemate has emerged; this has led to a situation in which the Commission has never dared to challenge the various national book agreements.[48]

The steering element in competition law comes even more clearly to the fore in the policy applied in the various block exemption Regulations. A block exemption is the result of a lengthy negotiation process between the Commission, the relevant industry and other interest groups, such as consumer organisations. A good example is provided by the block exemption for certain vertical agreements and concerted practices in the motor vehicle sector: Regulation 461/2010 contains a compromise between the interests of the car industry, car dealers and consumers.[49]

In a number of sectors, the government consciously steers commercial and consumer practices. This generally concerns sectors that lack a properly functioning market, such as public utilities.[50] According to welfare economics, regulation is required if there is a situation of market failure. We can distinguish between four forms of market failure.

First, there can be a situation where a single company holds a dominant position. This dominance can be the consequence of a natural monopoly, such as the national high voltage electricity transmission network. The same is true of the national gas transmission pipelines that were formerly owned by British Gas in the UK.

Secondly, external effects can cause a market to fail. Such external effects might include the conduct in the production of a particular undertaking, which cause costs that cannot (or can only with great difficulty) be imposed upon the individual producer. The effects of environmental pollution are a well-known example. The external effects of the production or consumption of particular goods have an impact upon the welfare of third parties. The market failure occurs because an individual does not have to take into account the costs and benefits that are caused by his or her behaviour. These costs and benefits are not discounted by (ie, taken into account in the calculations of) the market mechanism. Environmental goods, such as fresh air and clean water, belong to us all, but if an undertaking uses a particularly large part of that good, such as a soap factory that heavily pollutes the water, then that party does

---

[48] See, eg, Case C-39/96 *KVBBB v Free Recordshop*.

[49] [2010] OJ L129/52-57. The provisions of the old block exemption Reg 1400/2002 remained in force until 31 May 2013. Thereafter, the provisions of the general block exemption Reg 330/210 also apply to the motor vehicle sector. This compromise is well explained in: Christof Swaak, *European Community Law and the Automobile Industry* (Kluwer Law International, 1999) ch. 7.

[50] The following paragraphs are based upon the contribution by EEC van Damme, 'Marktwerking en herregulering' in RAJ van Gestel and P Eijlander (eds), *Markt en wet* (Tjeenk Willink, Deventer, 1996), 19–43.

not pay extra for the costs that have been inflicted upon us all. Extra payments can only be organised if duties (or similar) are imposed via the political decision-making process:[51] a phenomenon often described as the 'internalisation' of such costs, which would otherwise remain outside (ie, external to) the cost base of such undertakings.

Thirdly, there are public goods of which consumption is general. Air transport safety in the form of air traffic control and national defence benefits all citizens. Calculating and requiring individual payment for such goods would be practically impossible. Therefore, these goods are produced in the collective sector.

Fourthly, there is sometimes talk of information asymmetry, as a result of which the consumer cannot judge exactly what use a particular product or service will be. Through this, the situation can arise that certain goods or services are not produced, or at least not in sufficient quantities. Thus, some supervision of the banking and insurance sector is necessary to ensure that reliable products are offered to consumers. Furthermore, such oversight is necessary to counter fraud and money laundering. Without government intervention here, such supervision could not have been introduced.

According to the theory of the 'public interest', regulation is necessary for sectors where there exists a clear market failure. Adherents to this theory are well aware that the costs of regulation can run very high. Furthermore, regulation can lead to rigidity and can cause the body that performs the regulatory function to become too reliant upon the industry that is to be regulated.[52] Regulation must therefore be prevented from working 'back-to-front' in this way if it is to be effective. Further, attention must always be paid to market developments and technological change and innovation.

In the 1980s, a new vision of regulation was developed, alongside the theory of 'public interest'. This new vision gained ground as a result of the liberalisation process that was carried out by various EU Member States in certain sectors. In this vision, the transition from a regulated to a liberalised market requires the accompaniment of a specially designed form of regulation. Thus, in various countries the telecoms, gas and electricity sectors were subjected to a special form of regulation that was intended to make the move to a fully liberalised regime possible: ie, 'regulating for competition'. In the EU, Member States are now obliged (thanks to various Directives) to introduce a regulatory regime in the telecoms, electricity and gas sectors.[53] In the UK, most of these regulatory regimes had already been introduced, although certain changes have had to be made to their institutional structure and organisation over the years. Thus,

---

[51] This was the idea behind, eg, the EU's Emissions Trading System (see Directive 2003/87/EC [2003] OJ L275/32, as amended (see http://ec.europa.eu/clima/policies/ets/documentation_en.htm for details)), which aimed to put a price on carbon dioxide emissions and then require those emitting CO2 to cover the cost thereof in the price that they charged for their output.

[52] This is known in the literature as 'regulatory capture', where the regulator becomes the 'captive' of the industry that it is supposed to be regulating.

[53] In the telecoms sector, this is mainly due to Directive 96/19/EC amending Directive 90/388/EEC with regard to the implementation of full competition in telecommunications markets [1996] OJ L74/13: see, further, I Walden (ed), *Telecommunications Law and Regulation*, 4th edn (Oxford, Oxford University Press, 2012). In the electricity sector, this was begun by Directive 96/92/EC ([1997] OJ L27/20) and is now to be found in Directive 2003/54/EC concerning common rules for the internal market in electricity and repealing Directive 96/92/EC [2003] OJ L176/37; in the gas sector, the founding document was Directive 98/30/EC ([1998] OJ L204/1), and this has been developed by Directive 2003/55/EC concerning common rules for the internal market in natural gas and repealing Directive 98/30/EC [2003] OJ L176/57. On these latter two sectors, see A Johnston and G Block, *EU Energy Law* (Oxford, Oxford University Press, 2012).

the Office of Gas and Electricity Markets (Ofgem) is the regulator for both electricity and natural gas, while the Ofcom covers all UK communications industries, including telecoms (but also television, radio and wireless communications). The task and functions of these (and the other UK) regulators are outside the scope of this book but remain of great significance in practice.

When discussing the economic background of competition law, some coverage of the thinking of the so-called 'Chicago school' must be provided. Mainly in the 1980s, this school of economists exercised an important influence in the US over thinking about the function of competition law. In general, this school advocated a more explicit role for economic learning and scholarship in the creation and application of competition law. The central tenet of the thinking of the Chicago school is the working of the market. Its adherents are convinced, far more strongly than other economists, that regulation should (as far as possible) take place via the market. If market imperfections are noted, then we should strive to get these markets to be subject to competition. The liberalisation process that has developed in the last 20 years in many countries and in the EU has been strongly inspired by the approach of the Chicago school. The same can also be said for the recent changes in EU competition law.[54]

1.5 Various Systems of Competition Law

In competition law, a distinction is usually drawn between an abuse-based system and a prohibition-based system. In a system where control is based upon finding some abuse, agreements that have an effect upon competition are, in principle, allowed. The same holds for the behaviour of undertakings with a dominant position. These matters will only be addressed if a particular agreement or particular practice produces an abuse. This abuse is determined 'after the fact' and is then prohibited. Agreements in such a system are only prohibited once their abusive character has been established. A clear example of an abuse-based system was the Dutch Law on Economic Competition of 1956. Under this system, the Minister of Economic Affairs could prohibit agreements if they ran contrary to the 'general interest' (which was interpreted as meaning 'the hindering of competition').

In a prohibition-based system, the starting point is that agreements that restrict or hinder competition are forbidden. This also holds true for the abuse of a dominant position. The important difference from an abuse-based system is that such agreements and practices are forbidden from the moment that they enter into force or take place. EU competition law and the current UK competition law are both based upon this prohibition system; meanwhile, the former UK system contained elements of this approach (failure to register a registrable agreement rendered the agreement void in respect of any 'relevant restrictions') and elements of a more abuse-based approach

---

[54] In particular, the block exemption Reg for vertical agreements: see Chapter 3.6.3 (below).

(investigation and report by the Monopolies and Mergers Commission, recommending remedies to the Secretary of State for Trade and Industry).[55]

In reality, the difference between the two systems is not as clear as the foregoing paragraphs might suggest. In abuse-based systems, some sorts of agreement that were seen as damaging to competition were often prohibited from the outset by legislation. On the other hand, in the prohibition-based system of the EU, less damaging agreements can be exempted from the prohibition, as will be discussed in Chapter 3.

1.6 The Renumbering of the TFEU by the Lisbon Treaty

The changes to EU law resulting from the entry into force of the Lisbon Treaty have been highlighted in the Foreword. The reader is advised to take due note of these as they have a substantial impact upon the relevant provisions of EU competition law.

---

[55] This pen portrait of the former UK system is necessarily simplified and abbreviated here. For further discussion of the old UK system in all its (often frustrating and inefficient) complexity, see the earlier editions of Whish's work on *Competition Law*, 3rd edn (London, Butterworths, 1993), and for an outline and discussion of the debate surrounding the 1998 reforms, see R Whish, 'The Competition Act 1998 and the Prior Debate on Reform' in BJ Rodger and A MacCulloch (eds), *The UK Competition Act: A New Era for UK Competition Law* (Oxford, Hart Publishing, 2000).

The Basic Structure of Competition Law

2.1 Some Key Concepts in the Application of Competition Law

In this chapter, we will deal first with a number of general concepts that are important for the application of the various subdivisions of competition law. After this, there follows an overview of how the combined system of UK and EU competition law fits together and operates. Finally, the scope of application of competition law will be discussed.

2.1.1 The Concept of an 'Undertaking'

Competition law is directed at 'undertakings' and their dealings. Section I of Chapter I of Title VII TFEU has as its title 'Rules Applying to Undertakings', although nowhere does the TFEU Treaty itself provide a definition or explanation of the concept. In UK competition law, it is clear that the term 'undertaking' will be interpreted in accordance with the position under EU law by virtue of section 60 of the Competition Act 1998 (CA 1998).[1] In this way, the link between the two legal systems is confirmed: the generality of the section 60 requirement allows full account to be taken of the EU material from all relevant sources (including Articles 101, 102 and 106 TFEU and the EU Merger Regulation 139/2004).[2] Undertakings can be natural or legal persons, private companies or state companies, producers, distributors, service providers or professionals: indeed, according to the UK Competition and Markets Authority (the CMA), the term includes any person capable of carrying on commercial or economic

---

[1] *Agreements and Concerted Practices* (OFT 401, December 2004), paras 2.5 and 4.8.
[2] [2004] OJ L24/1.

activities relating to goods or services.[3] In this connection, it is not important what sort of activity the undertaking is carrying out. Equally, it does not matter at which stage of the production process the undertaking operates.

The EU Courts have always taken the position that the legal form of the undertaking is not important in assessing whether or not an entity counts as an 'undertaking'. Neither is the way in which the entity is financed. Furthermore, it does not matter whether or not the entity in question makes a profit. The key point is that the relevant activity can be carried out in competition with other undertakings. This can still be the case where the government has limited the range within which competition can take place.[4]

In competition law, the concept of 'undertaking' is mainly important to indicate the separation between the tasks of government and the activities of undertakings. This separation is sometimes very subtle and can be illustrated by reference to the case law of the ECJ concerning pension funds. Entities that manage pension funds which are based upon solidarity between participants and where the payments are not based upon the contributions of those participants do not fall within the definition of 'undertaking' for the purposes of EC competition law.[5] In the Dutch cases of *Albany*, *Brentjens* and *Drijvende Bokken* the ECJ came to the conclusion that these pension funds *were* undertakings: they worked with a capitalisation system, whereby the amount of contributions was determined by the fund and the extent of benefits depended upon the financial results of the fund's investments. In making those investments, those funds competed with insurance companies and thus pursued an economic activity that rendered them undertakings.[6] Meanwhile, the 'sickness funds' in Germany (providing statutory health insurance, which is compulsory for the great majority of employees in Germany) were not held to be undertakings by the Court.[7]

Government departments or entities and public sector organisations that act on the market count as undertakings insofar as they do not perform specific governmental tasks or functions in so doing.[8] Activities that are carried out in fulfilment of a

---

[3] OFT 401, para 2.5. Note that s 59 CA 1998 makes clear that where the expression 'persons' is used in the CA 1998 it is to be taken to include 'undertakings'. To this effect, see the OFT's decision of 20 November 2006, concerning the exchange of information on future fees by certain independent fee paying schools, in which the Secretary of State for Defence, in his capacity as the person responsible for the governance of the Royal Hospital School was held to be acting as an undertaking.

[4] Cases 240–242, 261, 262, 268 an 269/82 *Stichting SSI v Commission*. See also the conclusion of A-G Jacobs in Cases C-264, 306, 354 and 355/01 *AOK Bundesverband and others*, para 42 of his Opinion. See further paras 45–64 of the ECJ's judgment in the same case. See M Krajewski and M Farley, 'Limited Competition in National Health Systems and the Application of Competition Law: The AOK Bundesverband Case' (2004) 29 *EL Rev* 842, 848 et seq.

[5] Joined Cases C-159 and 160/91 *Poucet and Pistre*.

[6] Case C-67/96 *Albany International BV v Stichting Bedrijfspensioenfonds Textielindustrie*, Joined Cases C-115 to 117/97 *Brentjens' Handelsonderneming BV v Stichting Bedrijfspensioenfonds voor de Handel in Bouwmaterialen* and Case C-219/97 *Maatschappij Drijvende Bokken BV v Stichting Pensioenfonds voor de Vervoer- en Havenbedrijven*: see, eg, *Albany*, paras 77–87.

[7] Joined Cases C-264/01, 306/01, 354/01 and 355/01 *AOK Bundesverband and others*.

[8] The CMA has taken over guidance adopted by the OFT concerning *Public bodies and competition law* (OFT 1389, December 2011), which is relevant to for the purposes of determining when public bodies will constitute undertakings for the purposes of UK competition law.

statutorily or legally imposed task are not the activities of an undertaking for competition law purposes.[9]

A good illustration of these issues involving government, state or 'public' entities and competition law is provided by the UK case of *BetterCare*.[10] The case turned upon the status of the North & West Belfast Health and Social Services Trust for the purposes of competition law. BetterCare provided residential care and nursing home services in Northern Ireland, while the North & West Belfast Health & Social Services Trust bought those services from BetterCare in some areas, while managing its own facilities for residential care in others (where it recouped some of the costs from the residents of its care facilities). BetterCare alleged that the Trust was abusing its dominant position by extracting unfairly low prices and unfair terms in its contracts with BetterCare. This raised the important preliminary question of whether or not the Trust was an 'undertaking' under the CA 1998 and the Competition Commission Appeal Tribunal (CCAT), as the Competition Appeal Tribunal was known then, rejected the Director General of Fair Trading's (DGFT's) view[11] and held instead that the Trust did carry out economic activities such as to render it an undertaking for the purposes of the CA 1998.[12] In the CCAT's judgment, the Trust was a purchaser of services and thus, to that extent, was engaged in an economic activity. Further, the Trust was itself active on the market for residential and nursing care services in Northern Ireland. Also, the Trust did not provide its services gratuitously when it provided such care services. As a result, the case was remitted to the DGFT to reach a decision on the substance of the allegation: the OFT finally decided that no abuse of a dominant position had been perpetrated by the Trust, while not reaching a firm position on whether or not the Trust was an undertaking (taking the view that the matter had yet clearly to be settled by EU competition law).

The approach of the CCAT can be contrasted with the judgment of the CFI (now General Court) in the *FENIN* case,[13] which seems to have been more willing to exclude a public sector body from 'undertaking' status, provided that the purchase of goods or services was made so as to be able to provide a social service. This raises the difficult question of how the CMA should react, in the light of section 60 CA 1998: we discuss this issue more fully in Chapter 7.2.2 below.[14]

---

[9] Case C-343/95 *Cali & Figli v Servizi Ecologici Porto di Genova*. In this judgment, the ECJ held that an undertaking that performed environmental inspections in a harbour did not carry out activities as an undertaking, but rather fulfilled a task imposed upon it by the state.

[10] *BetterCare Group v DGFT* [2002] CAT 7.

[11] DGFT Decision CA/98/11/2002, *North & West Belfast Health & Social Services Trust* (30 April 2002).

[12] *BetterCare Group Ltd v DGFT* [2002] CAT 7, paras 163–277.

[13] Case T-319/99, (noted by V Louri in 'The *FENIN* Judgment: The Notion of Undertaking and Purchasing Activity' (2005) 32 *Legal Issues of Economic Integration* 87); the judgment was confirmed by the ECJ Case C-205/03P, *Federación Española de Empresas de Tecnología Sanitaria (FENIN) v. Commission*. See: M Krajewski and M Farley, *Non-economic activities in upstream and downstream markets and the scope of competition law after FENIN*, ELRev (2007) 111–124.

[14] See the OFT's Policy Note, *The Competition Act 1998 and Public Bodies* (OFT 443, January 2004) for discussion and the OFT's closure of the case (Decision CA98/09/2003, 23 December 2003). See further R Whish and D Bailey, *Competition Law*, 8th edn (London, LexisNexis Butterworths, 2015), 85–103.

Employees' associations, which typically perform trade union functions, are not treated as undertakings. A sickness insurance fund seems likely to be treated as an undertaking if, alongside the fulfilment of a statutory task, it also provides additional insurance or conducts other activities.[15] Thus, sickness insurance funds must be viewed as undertakings in connection with buying health care (including personnel and care resources) and where they offer sickness fund insurance policies. By parity of reasoning, a hospital could in certain circumstances qualify as an undertaking for the purposes of competition law.[16] Equally, as noted above, the German sickness funds have been held not to amount to undertakings.[17]

From this brief discussion of the notion of an undertaking in the context of 'government' or 'public' activities, it should be clear that whether or not an entity should be viewed as an undertaking for the purposes of competition law is a question that must be examined separately in each individual case, taking care to assess each activity involved. The fact that an institution has a statutory task to perform will not necessarily mean that that institution's other activities should not be treated as those of an undertaking.[18]

The concept of an undertaking is also of importance in the assessment of complex business structures and whether or not competition law applies to them. For example, it must be determined which relationships within one concern (parent–subsidiary relations) fall within the scope of the prohibition on restricting or distorting competition. If a parent company forms a single economic entity with its subsidiary, under which the subsidiary has no real autonomy to decide its own conduct on the market, then both together will be viewed as a single undertaking. Agreements and other concerted practices between such a parent company and its subsidiary thus escape the supervision of competition law.[19]

2.1.2 Various Types of Agreement

It is customary in competition law to distinguish between horizontal and vertical agreements. Horizontal agreements are agreements between undertakings that operate

---

[15] See, eg, the Dutch Competition Authority's Decision No 1165, *ANOZ Verzekeringen*, 29 December 1998.

[16] See, eg, the Dutch Competition Authority's Decision No 165, *Sophia Ziekenhuis*, 5 June 1998.

[17] See n 7, above.

[18] See the interesting series of cases in the Netherlands relating to the Centraal Bureau Rijvaardigsbewijzen (CBR) (the Central Bureau for Driving Licences), such as the Dutch Competition Authority's Decision No 119, *Loke and others v CBR*, 21 January 1999 that the CBR was not an undertaking for purposes relating to the fulfilment of its statutory functions—upheld on appeal by the Rotterdam Court (judgment of 12 April 2000) and the Court of Appeal for Commercial Matters (judgment of 3 July 2002: LJN-No AE6021, case No AWB 00/429). Compare this with the judgment of the Den Haag Court (of 17 January 2002) in *Aucon BV v Stichting CBR*, where the CBR's free software package included modules that competed with software offered commercially by Aucon: the court held that the provision of such software by the CBR was the activity of an undertaking and was subject to the competition rules.

[19] Case T-102/92 *Viho Europe BV v Commission*, concerning a challenge to Parker's European distribution system for its pens, which consisted of a wholly owned distribution subsidiary in each Member State. For discussion of whether or not this creates a gap in the system of EC competition law, see paras 31ff of AG Lenz's Opinion on the *Viho Europe* appeal (Case C-73/95 P. In similar vein in UK competition law, see the OFT Decision, *Anaesthetists' groups* (15 April 2003), and *Suretrack Rail Services v Infraco JNP* [2002] Eu LR 659 (Ch D), [16]–[19].

at the same level of the production or distribution process. A price-fixing agreement between all suppliers of flat roofs in the construction sector is a typical example of a horizontal agreement.[20]

Vertical agreements are agreements between undertakings that do not operate at the same level of the production or distribution process. One example would be a selective distribution agreement, such as was dealt with by the European Commission in its *Givenchy* decision.[21] Givenchy is a producer of luxury cosmetic products. In the EU retail sales of Givenchy products take place through a network of smaller dealers. Givenchy concludes individual distribution agreements with these retailers, who have to satisfy certain selection criteria to join the network. Thus, the personnel in the shops must have a good knowledge of perfumes and other cosmetic products, while the location of the shop must be in accordance with the luxury image of the Givenchy name. The shop must be fitted out in accordance with Givenchy's requirements and the environment within the shop in which the Givenchy products are sold must be similarly compliant. In this vein, attention is paid to the quality of the image of shop premises, its signs, the flooring material, the walls, the furniture and the shop counters. The agreement also contains a prohibition on the sale of products of lower quality by the store, which might damage the image of Givenchy. Further, Givenchy requires that these retailers also offer competing products in such a way that the image of Givenchy products comes across clearly to the consumer and their awareness levels thereof are kept high.

Competition law has a general application and is not limited to retail undertakings. Thus, simply because supply contracts are concluded directly with the end-user of the product does not mean that the relevant supply agreements might not run contrary to the competition rules of EU or national law.[22]

2.2 The Combined System of UK and European Competition Law

2.2.1 Introduction

The clear starting point of the UK competition law regime was an intention to introduce a national legal regime that aligned itself as far as possible with the competition

---

[20] See, eg, the OFT's series of Decisions finding collusive tendering practices in the flat-roofing sector in a number of regions of the UK: eg, OFT Decision No CA98/1/2004, *West Midlands flat-roofing* (16 March 2004), discussed in Chapter 3.6.2 below. Further cases followed during 2005: see OFT Decisions CA98/01/2005 *Mastic asphalt roofing contracts in Scotland* (15 March 2005), CA98/02/2005 *Felt and single-ply roofing contracts in North East England* (16 March 2005) and CA98/04/2005 *Felt and single-ply roofing contracts in West and Central Scotland* (8 July 2005).

[21] [1992] OJ L236/11.

[22] See, eg, the Dutch case of *Driessen v Benegas* (Hoge Raad, 15 October 1999) NJB 1999, nr 144C, 5 November 1999, 1062.

rules of the European Union.[23] This was intended to reduce the compliance burden placed upon undertakings by the need to respect the two systems of competition law that applied within the territory of the UK. This approach is underlined by the inclusion of section 60 CA 1998, which provides as follows:[24]

Section 60—Principles to be applied in determining questions.

(1)   The purpose of this section is to ensure that *so far as is possible* (**having regard to any relevant differences** between the provisions concerned), questions arising under this Part in relation to competition within the United Kingdom are dealt with in a manner which is consistent with the treatment of corresponding *questions arising* in [EU] law *in relation to competition* within the [EU].

(2)   At any time when the court determines a question arising under this Part, it must act (so far as is compatible with the provisions of this Part and whether or not it would otherwise be required to do so) with a view to securing that there is *no inconsistency* between—

(a)   the principles applied, and decision reached, by the court in determining that question; and

(b)   the principles laid down by the Treaty and the European Court, and any relevant decision of that Court, as applicable at that time in determining any corresponding question arising in [EU] law.

(3)   The court must, in addition, *have regard* to any relevant decision or statement of the Commission.

(4)   Subsections (2) and (3) also apply to—

(a)   the [CMA];[25] and

(b)   any person acting on behalf of the [CMA], in connection with any matter arising under this Part.

(5)   In subsections (2) and (3), 'court' means any court or tribunal.

(6)   In subsections (2)(b) and (3), 'decision' includes a decision as to—

(a)   the interpretation of any provision of [EU] law;

(b)   the civil liability of an undertaking for harm caused by its infringement of [EU] law.

The major points to be taken from section 60 CA 1998 are as follows:[26]

s 60(1):

(i)   'so far as is possible': this ensures that explicit differences between the UK and EU systems are maintained. In other cases of ambiguity, the policy is to follow the EU approach;

---

[23] See the UK Government's White Paper, *A World Class Competition Regime* (31 July 2001). For discussion, see (inter alia) C Blair, 'Competition Bill [HL]' (House of Commons Research Paper 98/53, 28 April 1998); R Whish, 'The Competition Act 1998 and the Prior Debate on Reform' in BJ Rodger and A MacCulloch (eds), *The UK Competition Act 1998: A New Era for UK Competition Law* (Oxford, Hart Publishing, 2000); and G Borrie, 'Lawyers, Legislators and Lobbyists—the Making of the Competition Act 1998' (1999) *Journal of Business Law* 205. For earlier critique of the assumption that alignment with the EU system would be beneficial see M Furse, 'The Role of EC Law in UK Reform Proposals' (1996) *European Competition Law Review* 134, and for further discussion of the Bill see M Furse, 'The Competition Bill—A Competition Law That Can Compete?' (1998) *Journal of Business Law* 168.

[24] All emphases added.

[25] Word substituted by the Enterprise and Regulatory Reform Act 2013, sch 5, para 39.

[26] For discussion, see K Middleton, 'Harmonization with Community Law—the Euro Clause' and BJ Rodger, 'Interrelationship with Community Competition Law Enforcement', both in BJ Rodger and A MacCulloch (eds), *The Competition Act: A New Era for UK Competition Law* (Oxford, Hart Publishing, 2000), 21–43 and 45–74 respectively.

(ii) 'having regard to any relevant differences': this requires the courts and the CMA to focus upon where clear differences exist (eg the merger control system, on which see Chapter 5; the procedural and enforcement regimes,[27] on which see Chapter 6; agreements specifically excluded from the scope of Chapter 1 by virtue of Schedules 1 to 3 of the Competition Act 1998, on which see Chapter 3.2; and EU competition law's generally strong focus on questions of building the internal market);[28]

(iii) 'questions arising ... in relation to competition': while it is not the intention that section 60 CA 1998 should lead to the development of identical procedural regimes, it seems strongly arguable that the expression 'in relation to competition' allows the inclusion of general principles of EU law where these have been relevant to the development of the EU competition law regime (eg equality, legal certainty, legitimate expectations and proportionality);[29]

(iv) 'corresponding questions': to the extent that there are "relevant differences" between the facts and circumstances considered by the Commission and the facts and circumstances under consideration by the CMA, there will not be "corresponding questions" for the purposes of section 60 CA 1998. The mere fact that one case involves competition in the UK, and the other involves competition within the EU, is not of itself a material difference for the purposes of determining whether "corresponding questions" arise. Rather, it appears that there needs to be a difference in the facts before the CMA and the Commission that would be material to the application of the competition rules.[30]

s 60(2):

'no inconsistency': while a consistent application of the principles of Article 101 TFEU and the Chapter I prohibition, and Article 102 TFEU and the Chapter II prohibition is clearly desirable in view of the goals of alignment of the two systems discussed above, it seems highly unlikely that there was any intention on the part of the legislator to endow the principles deriving from the EU provisions with some kind of direct effect and supremacy over the UK provisions. It is 'with a view to securing that there is no inconsistency', not a guarantee, that the provision was enacted;

s 60(3):

'have regard': on the face of it, this would seem to impose a lesser duty upon the court than the consistency principle under section 60(2), not requiring that Commission 'decisions or statements'[31] be followed and applied strictly. In its decision in *MasterCard*, however, the OFT considered that, while it was not bound to comply with decision or statements of the

---

[27] Which are becoming more aligned in some ways after the EC's modernisation package and the UK's response thereto (discussed in ch 6), while more different in others (eg, the cartel offence under UK law: see Chapter 6.3.5.2 below).

[28] OFT 1025 October 2008, para 4.13, *Newspapers and Magazine Distribution*.

[29] House of Lords Committee, 25 November 1997, columns 960–963. The CAT has made extensive references to principles of EU law in its rulings in, for example, *Pernod-Ricard v OFT* [2004] CAT 10; and *APEX v OFT* [2005] CAT 4.

[30] OFT Decision of 6 September 2005, in *MasterCard*, paras 97–106.

[31] These must be formal expressions carrying the authority of the Commission, covering individual decisions and announcements of policy (such as Annual Reports, Notices, etc): see the OFT's old Guideline *The Major Provisions* (OFT 400), para 6.2 and its more recent statement in the Guideline *Modernisation* (OFT 442), para 4.11.

Commission, it should give serious consideration to them.[32] In practice, however, it seems likely that a detailed and consistent decisional practice of the Commission is likely to carry significant weight in the analysis of competition issues before the UK courts.

Overall, section 60 CA 1998 aims at securing a strong and far-reaching degree of consistency between the application of the UK and EU competition law regimes, but it does not lay down an absolute objective of consistency. Throughout this book, we will be careful to draw the reader's attention to certain areas where explicit differences exist between the two regimes and also to those situations in which practice and interpretation might seem to have diverged or to suggest different approaches to very similar problems. Here, we provide a brief summary of certain elements specific to the UK regime which have been retained, and further aspects which have been introduced, by legislation since the CA 1998. These include, notably, the criminal offence of participating in a cartel and the UK's merger control regime (which aligns itself more closely with the EU regime while retaining important institutional, procedural and certain substantive differences). Both of these aspects were introduced by the Enterprise Act 2002 (EA 2002) and are discussed in some detail later in this book (see Chapter 6.3.5.2 and 5.3 below). Overall, however, in practice, the strong degree to which the new UK competition law regime was modelled upon that of the EU means that it will operate very similarly to EU law.

In general, competition law is aimed at the following types of behaviour by market actors:

(a)   agreements that can restrict or distort competition (cartels, etc);[33]
(b)   the abuse of positions of dominance; and
(c)   mergers (known as concentrations in EU law) between undertakings.

The first two types of behaviour are prohibited under competition law. Cartels are prohibited on the basis of Article 101 TFEU and section 2 of the CA 1998; the latter is often known as the 'Chapter I prohibition' after the chapter of the CA 1998 in which it can be found. Abuse of a dominant position is prohibited by virtue of Article 102 TFEU and section 18 CA 1998 (the latter again often being known as the 'Chapter II prohibition', for the same reason). Mergers between undertakings are not prohibited as such. Where the jurisdictional thresholds are met, however, a merger must be notified in advance to the European Commission under Article 4 of Regulation 139/2004/EC. Under UK law, notification of a relevant merger situation is not compulsory. Nevertheless, many companies involved in mergers do take the opportunity to notify these transactions, so the practical differences may not be as great as it might seem at first sight. This is discussed further in Chapter 5. Once the competition authorities have received such merger notifications, only those mergers that could impede competition to a significant degree will be prohibited.

---

[32]   OFT Decision of 6 September 2005, in *MasterCard*, paras 107–116.
[33]   In Chapter 3.2 below we will make clear that this heading encompasses cartels, other agreements, decisions of associations of undertakings and concerted practices between undertakings: the common thread is that they involve some coordination of behaviour and collusion between two or more undertakings, such collusion being restrictive or distortive of competition.

2.2.2 The Relationship Between UK and EU Competition Law

In the vast majority of cases, UK and EU competition law rules contain the same substantive provisions. This is the consequence of the decision to base the current UK competition law system upon the substantive system of EU competition law. This means that cartels and abuses of dominant positions in the UK are subjected to a single system of substantive norms. The application of this system in the UK is to a great extent entrusted to the CMA[34] and to the ordinary national civil courts. In cases involving a European dimension the European Commission will, in principle, take the lead. However, the precise division of competence between the various institutions and courts involved can be complex. The following paragraphs, therefore, seek to provide an overview of the relevant divisions.

2.2.2.1 Concerning Collusive Practices (Cartels, etc)[35]

(a)   First of all, it must be established whether or not a cartel or other collusive anti-competitive practice falls within the Chapter I prohibition (section 2(1) CA 1998). In this respect, a cartel or other collusive anti-competitive practices will only fall within the Chapter I prohibition if it can be shown that the practice in question will result in an appreciable restriction upon competition in the UK (or a part thereof). We discuss this criterion in more detail in Chapter 3.2.2 and 3.2.4 below.

(b)   For such cartels (etc) that are shown to have an appreciable effect upon competition, the CMA is the competent institution. The CMA can take measures to deal with such practices by requiring the undertakings involved to bring the practices to an end; levy fines on the perpetrating undertakings; or accept legally binding commitments from the undertakings that they will modify their behaviour in the future.[36] Alongside the CMA's role, the national courts have jurisdiction to adjudicate in any disputes involving the Chapter I prohibition, including recognising exemptions from the prohibition under section 9 CA 1998.

(c)   There are also cartels that have a 'European dimension'. This is established if the criterion of an 'effect on trade between Member States' is met. In general, these are large cartels, in the sense that the companies involved (when taken together) have a substantial turnover. Where such cartels are at issue, they often involve

---

[34] Albeit involving the sectoral regulators within their fields of competence (see section 2.3.3 below). For discussion of this relationship and the issues that may be raised by the concurrent application of the competition rules, see R Nazzini, *Concurrent Proceedings in Competition Law: Procedure, Evidence and Remedies* (Oxford, Oxford University Press, 2004).

[35] Note that any concepts used here will be explained more fully in the later chapters of this book; for example, for discussion of 'cartels' and collusion, see Chapter 3.2.3 below.

[36] Sections 4, 5 and 12–16 CA 1998, which provide for a system of notification of agreements for individual exemption, have been repealed. The repeal of these sections followed the introduction of Reg 1/2003, which abandoned a similar notification and individual exemption system that existed under Reg 17/62. Instead, the criteria laid down in s 9 CA 1998 (equivalent to those in Art 101(3) TFEU) will apply automatically to agreements. Undertakings may also rely upon these exemption criteria in proceedings before national courts (a parallel to Art 10 of Reg 1/2003—again, see Chapter 3.5 below).

companies from a number of different EU Member States. It is also possible that purely national cartels may have a European dimension, on the basis that their operation closes off the national market and protects it from competition from other Member States.

(d)   Cartels and anti-competitive collusive practices with a European dimension can be addressed by the Commission, but it is important to note that the CMA will also be competent to deal with such practices *so long as* the Commission has not taken the case on itself.[37] Where the Commission is not acting, the CMA is obliged to apply Articles 101 and 102 (as applicable) in situations where the practice in question has an effect on trade between Member States (Article 3 of Regulation 1/2003) and is empowered so to act on the basis of Article 5 of Regulation 1/2003[38] and sections 31(2)(c) and (d) CA 1998. The UK courts also have jurisdiction to hear cases concerning anticompetitive practices having a European dimension: this jurisdiction is based upon the direct effect of Article 101 TFEU and Article 6 of Regulation 1/2003.[39]

As will be clear from the foregoing summary, it is possible that cartels and other anti-competitive collusive practices with a European dimension may find themselves subject to investigation by both the Commission and the CMA simultaneously. In such a situation, conflicts may arise between these authorities' competences to apply competition law. According to the ECJ, such a conflict must be resolved by reference to the rule that the EU law competence takes priority.[40] This principle has now been enshrined in Article 3(2) of Regulation 1/2003. On the basis of Article 3(1), when applying the Chapter I prohibition to agreements (etc) that affect trade between Member States the CMA and the UK courts (including the CAT) are obliged to apply Article 101 TFEU as well. This must not lead to the UK-level decision or judgment permitting an agreement that breaches Article 101 TFEU. Similarly, agreements that are capable of affecting trade, but which satisfy the criteria laid down by the various EU block exemption regulations cannot be prohibited at UK level (see to that effect Article 3(2) of Regulation 1/2003). The starting point for this priority rule is clear, but its application in practice can sometimes be trickier. The Commission has published 'Guidelines on the Effect on Trade Concept Contained in Articles 81 and 82 of the Treaty'.[41] In this context, Article 11 of Regulation 1/2003 is of great importance. Article 11 provides for close cooperation between the Commission and the national competition authorities (NCAs), including the CMA. Thus, the CMA must keep the

---

[37] This occurs as a result of Art 11(6) of Reg 1/2003 when the Commission adopts a decision to initiate proceedings pursuant to Art 2(1) of Reg 773/2004. This might be done at the same time as the adoption of the SO but does not need to be and ever more frequently is done prior to adopting an SO): on this part of the procedure, see Chapter 6.4.2 below. It should also be noted that according to Art 16(2) of Reg 1/2003, NCAs cannot take decisions regarding the same practice that would run counter to a preceding Commission decision.

[38] Council Reg (EC) No 1/2003 of 16 December 2002 on the implementation of the rules on competition laid down in Arts 81 and 82 of the Treaty [2003] OJ L1/1.

[39] Case 127/73 *Belgische Radio en Televisie (BRT) v SV Sabam (No 1)* 51, para 15.

[40] Case 14/68 *Walt Wilhelm v Bundeskartellamt*, 2–4 (paras 3–9).

[41] [2004] OJ C101/81. The opinion of Advocate General Kokott in Case C-439/11 P, *Ziegler v Commission*, provides a valuable illustration of the problems involved in applying this notice. On this issue, see further Chapter 3.2.5 below.

Commission informed of every case in which the CMA applies Article 101 TFEU. The Commission is empowered to intervene and take over the investigation and decision in individual cases, a decision that is facilitated by this close cooperation between the Commission and the NCAs.[42]

The differences between UK and EU competition law in this area are, in practice, usually of little importance. The substantive norms involved are the same. The national courts will always have jurisdiction in such cases and the CMA is usually competent to deal with such anti-competitive practices.[43] Nevertheless, there are situations in which the division of competences does matter. For example, there are subtle differences between the EU and UK systems concerning exemptions from the prohibition of anti-competitive agreements; these issues are discussed below, in section 3.2.1.[44]

Figure 2.1 provides a schematic overview of the relationship between UK and EU law in the field of collusive anti-competitive practices.

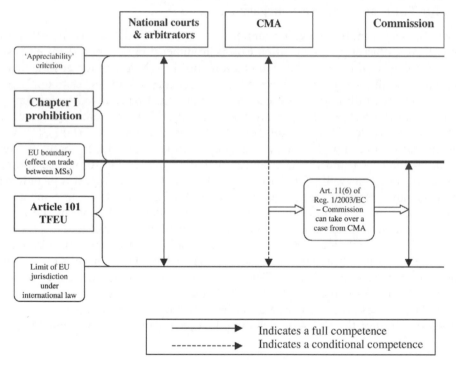

Figure 2.1: Schematic view of the relationship between UK and EU competition law concerning cartels and other collusive anti-competitive practices

---

[42] See further Chapter 6.2.2 below.

[43] The CMA is competent insofar as the Commission has not intervened and taken over the case on the basis of Art 11(6) of Reg 1/2003/EC.

[44] See also the discussion of the EC and UK approaches to the concept of an 'undertaking' (section 2.1.1 (above) and Chapter 7.2.2 (below)) and the operation of block and parallel exemptions in UK competition law (Chapter 3.4.2 below).

2.2.2.2 Concerning Abuse of a Dominant Position

An abuse of a dominant position can be dealt with by the CMA and/or the Commission, depending upon the geographic market on which the abuse takes place. The national courts will have jurisdiction over the application of both sets of rules, by virtue of the direct effect of Article 102 TFEU and the general applicability of the Chapter II prohibition under the CA 1998. There is no *de minimis* threshold that must be passed before either of these provisions can apply.

Here, the criterion of the effect upon trade between Member States plays only a minor role: instead, the demarcation of the competences of the CMA and the Commission is primarily determined through the definition of the relevant geographic market. The Commission is competent if the relevant geographic market coincides with the EU market or a substantial part thereof. Similarly, the Commission is competent where the geographic market is a worldwide one. The CMA is competent to apply the Chapter II prohibition (section 18 CA 1998) where the relevant dominant position is held within the UK and the geographic market is UK-wide or a part of the UK. By virtue of Article 3(1) of Regulation 1/2003, the CMA is also competent (and indeed is obliged) to apply Article 102 TFEU in cases where there is an effect upon trade between Member States. In spite of this, the Commission has the power under Article 11(6) of Regulation 1/2003 to intervene and take over a case from the CMA. It is important to note that, by contrast with the position concerning Article 101 TFEU, Regulation 1/2003 does *not* prohibit Member States from maintaining or introducing stricter rules on the abuse of dominant positions. It seems unlikely that this possibility would be of great significance in the UK system, given the UK system's focus upon aligning itself as closely as possible with the EU competition rules applicable in this field.[45]

The involvement of the CMA in cases concerning fully European or worldwide markets is not likely to be frequent (or, indeed, advisable). It is more likely that CMA involvement under Article 102 TFEU will occur where the geographic market concerns a part of, or at most the entirety of, the UK.

The UK courts and arbitrators retain jurisdiction over disputes concerning the abuse of a dominant position held on an EU or worldwide geographic market. This is based upon the direct effect of Article 102 TFEU and Article 6 of Regulation 1/2003. Of course, the UK courts also have jurisdiction in cases concerning allegations of abuse of a dominant position held in the UK market or a part thereof (see Fig 2.2).

---

[45] See Chapter 4.2.6.2 below for discussion of one possible area of significance here, concerning the UK system's provision of market investigation references pursuant to the Enterprise Act 2002, in respect of unilateral conduct of undertakings: this can lead to far-reaching structural remedies, which might amount to a stricter national approach to such questions, albeit that it is not functionally identical in aims and procedure.

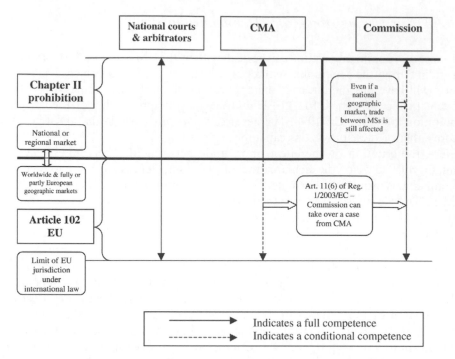

Figure 2.2: Schematic view of the relationship between UK and EU competition law concerning the abuse of dominant positions

The importance of the demarcation of the competences of the CMA and the Commission is even smaller here than where collusive anti-competitive practices are concerned. The starting point of Regulation 1/2003 is that the Commission and the NCAs are to apply EU competition law in close cooperation with each other. Complaints concerning abusive behaviour in the UK market are best dealt with by the CMA. In cases in which the CMA is of the view that the market has a European scope, it can always invite the Commission to take over the case and investigate it at the EU level. The CMA will become involved in cases in which a clear impact upon the UK market is at issue, while the Commission will only spring into action where the case concerns the European market or a substantial part thereof.[46] Finally, the UK courts and arbitrators can rule on disputes where an abuse of a dominant position (which can correspond to the territory of a single Member State) is alleged in the UK or the European market.

2.2.2.3 Concerning Concentrations

While the EU merger control regime[47] obliges prior notification to be made of proposed mergers having a Union dimension (known as 'concentrations'; see Chapter 5 for

---

[46] For discussion of the concept 'substantial part of the common market', see Chapter 4.2.1 below.

[47] The relevant rules from which the scope of the EU merger control is derived are laid down by Reg 139/2004/EC of the Council of 20 January 2004 on the control of concentrations between undertakings [2004] OJ L24/1.

discussion), notification is voluntary under the UK system. In spite of this, a large number of UK mergers are notified to the CMA in any case, raising a need for constant vigilance on the part of the CMA to ensure that it respects the competence of the Commission to scrutinise mergers with a Union dimension.[48] According to the one-stop merger control principle, mergers with a Union dimension should be investigated only by the Commission. This follows from Article 21(3) of Regulation 139/2004 (the EUMR).[49] The following concentrations[50] fall under the EU merger control regime:

(a)   Concentrations between companies:

—   with a combined worldwide turnover of more than €5,000 million;
—   where the total aggregate turnover in the EU of each of at least two of the undertakings concerned exceeds €250 million;
—   unless each of the undertakings concerned achieves more than two-thirds of its total EU-wide turnover in a single Member State.

(b)   Also, concentrations between companies:

—   with a combined worldwide turnover of over €2,500 million;
—   where the total aggregate turnover of all the undertakings concerned is more than €100 million in each of at least three EU Member States and
—   in each of at least three of the Member States used to satisfy the previous condition the aggregate turnover of at least two of the undertakings concerned exceeds €25 million and
—   the aggregate EC-wide turnover of each of at least two of the undertakings concerned is greater than €100 million;
—   unless each of the undertakings concerned achieves more than two-thirds of its EU-wide turnover in a single Member State.

For a merger to fall under the UK's merger control regime, it must qualify as a 'relevant merger situation' for the purposes of section 23 of the EA 2002. A relevant merger situation exists where all three of the following criteria are met:[51]

(a)   first, either:

—   two or more enterprises (broadly speaking, business activities of any kind) must cease to be distinct; or
—   there must be arrangements in progress or in contemplation which, if carried into effect, will lead to enterprises ceasing to be distinct,

(b)   and second, either:

—   the UK turnover associated with the enterprise which is being acquired exceeds £70 million (known as 'the turnover test'); or

---

[48] This concept is discussed in detail in section 5.2.4 below.
[49] See Chapter 5.2.4.1 where we have to explain this further.
[50] This is the EU law term used: for further discussion, see Chapter 5.2.3 below.
[51] See CMA Guidance CMA2, Mergers: Guidance on the CMA's jurisdiction and procedure, January 2014, para 4.3.

— the enterprises which cease to be distinct supply or acquire goods or services of any description and, after the merger, together supply or acquire at least 25% of all those particular goods or services of that kind supplied in the UK or in a substantial part of it. The merger must also result in an increment to the share of supply or acquisition. ('the share of supply test').

(c)   and third, either

— the merger must not yet have taken place; or
— it must have taken place not more than four months before the day the reference is made, unless the merger took place without having been made public and without the CMA being informed of it (in which case the four-month period starts from the earlier of the time the merger was made public or the time the CMA was told about it).[52] The four-month deadline may be extended in certain circumstances.[53]

In the context of mergers that have not yet completed, at Phase 1 the CMA will generally consider that 'arrangements are in progress or in contemplation' for the purposes of section 33 of the EA 2002 if a public announcement has been made by the parties concerned.

While it is clear from the definition of these thresholds that framing a relevant concentration or merger is a complicated process, in practice the application of the combined merger control system operates relatively smoothly.

In summary, the combined merger control system looks like this: mergers where the target has turnover in excess of £70 million but the worldwide turnover of the undertakings concerned (including the UK) is less than €2,500 million will normally fall to be assessed under UK law (see Chapter 5.3 for our more detailed discussion of the operation of the UK system). Concentrations where the undertakings concerned have a worldwide turnover in excess of €2,500 million will normally fall under the scrutiny of the EU merger control regime where the other thresholds are satisfied. Where those other elements of the Union dimension are not satisfied, then the merger will still fall within UK law if the relevant three cumulative criteria under the EA 2002 are met.

Mergers that do not satisfy the thresholds of the UK merger control regime may in certain, very limited, circumstances still be subject to the application of the prohibition on abuses of a dominant position under the Chapter II prohibition.[54] Figure 2.3 provides a schematic overview of the relationship between UK and EU law on merger control.

---

[52] The date of the merger refers to the date when the enterprises cease to be distinct (see s 24(1) EA 2002).

[53] See for example ss 25, 42 and 122 EA 2002.

[54] Given the criterion contained in s 23(2)(b) EA 2002, this will be extremely rare indeed: eg, where a question of joint dominance is raised where the acquired enterprise's turnover is too low and where none of the allegedly jointly dominant undertakings holds more than 25% of the relevant market. See Case 6/72 *Continental Can v Commission*. In theory, the same holds for mergers that do not satisfy the EU thresholds. Such mergers can be subject to scrutiny on the basis of Art 102 TFEU. However, where such mergers are carried out in a Member State, like the UK, which has a system of merger control, such application of Art 102 TFEU is highly unlikely.

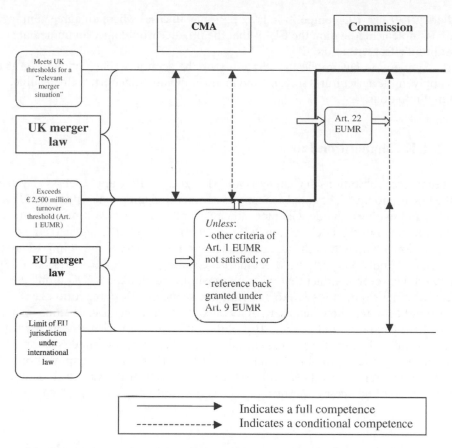

Figure 2.3: **Schematic overview of the relationship between UK and EU competition law concerning mergers**

2.3 The Scope of Application of Competition Law

2.3.1 European Competition Law

First of all, the geographic scope of application of competition law must be established. According to Article 52 TEU, competition law applies in the European territory of the EU Member States. Alongside this, it also applies to the territorial sea and the Exclusive Economic Zone (EEZ), and on board ships and aeroplanes that are registered in a Member State. In the case of the EEZ, competition law applies in all areas and to all activities in the EEZ where the Member States or the EU have legal authority. Further, EU competition law applies in all cases where an agreement or an abuse is implemented within the EU or that the practice would have an immediate and substantial effect within the EU.[55]

EU competition law applies to all sectors of the economy. The competition rules also apply in the agricultural sector[56] and in sea[57] and air transport,[58] albeit subject to certain limitations.[59]

2.3.2 UK Competition Law

In outline, the prohibitions in Chapters I and II of the CA 1998 apply across all sectors of the UK economy.[60] They apply so long as competition and trade within the UK are affected and so long as, under Chapter I, the relevant arrangement 'is, or is intended to be, implemented in the UK' (section 2(3) CA 1998) and, under Chapter II, the dominant position is held within the UK or a substantial part thereof (including where the UK element is only one part of a wider market covering other countries) (section 18(3) CA 1998). However, conduct that takes place wholly outside the UK and only has an 'effect' within it would not seem to be within the scope of UK competition law.[61]

It should be noted, however, that CA 1998 contains a range of exclusions from the scope of the Chapter I and Chapter II prohibitions, while other legislation also introduces certain exclusions from those prohibitions. These operate under section 3 CA 1998 for the Chapter I prohibition and section 19 CA 1998 for the Chapter II prohibition, both by reference to the specific exclusions laid out in the various schedules to CA 1998. In outline, these cover mergers and concentrations (schedule 1), competition

---

[55] Joined Cases 89, 104, 114, 116, 117 and 125–129/85 *Åhlström Osakeyhtiö and others v Commission* (*Woodpulp I*).

[56] Art 2 of Reg 26/62/EEC provides that the prohibition of Art 81(1) EC does not apply to agreements that form part of a national market organisation or are necessary for the achievement of the goals of the Common Agricultural Policy [1962] OJ L30/993 (English Special Edition [1959–62] OJ 129), as amended by Reg 49/62/EEC [1962] OJ L53/1571.

[57] The scope of application of Reg 906/2009 block exemption on liner shipping consortia is limited to transport via liner services to and from EU ports [2009] OJ L256/31. See further R Whish and D Bailey, *Competition Law*, 8th edn (Oxford, 2015), 1022–1031.

[58] The scope of application of Reg 487/2009 on the application of Art 101(3) TFEU to certain categories of agreements and concerted practices in the air transport sector. This Council regulation enables the Commission to enact specific rules. So far the Commission has not used its powers. R Whish and D Bailey, *Competition Law*, 8th edn (Oxford, 2015), 1022–1031.

[59] The reader is referred to specialist works for further details on these matters: see, eg V Rose and D. Bailey (ed), *Bellamy & Child's Common Market Law of Competition*, 7th edn (London, Sweet & Maxwell, 2015), chs 18 (on agriculture) and 15 (on transport). J Faul and A Nickpay *The EU Law of Competition*, 3rd edn (Oxford, Oxford University Press, 2014), ch 11 financial services, ch 12 energy, ch 13 communications, ch. 14 media, ch. 15 transport, ch 16 pharma.

[60] For a topical, controversial example, see OFT Press Release 214/05 (9 November 2005), in which the OFT reported that it had issued a 'statement of objections' (on which Chapter 6.3.5 below) setting out its provisional findings that an agreement between 50 fee-paying independent schools to exchange detailed information about the fees that they intended to charge was in breach of competition law.

[61] See Chapter 8.2 below.

scrutiny under other enactments (schedule 2) and planning obligations and other general exclusions (schedule 3). Table 2.1 attempts to provide an overview of these provisions and the areas in which they operate, while the following section provides a brief discussion of some of the more important areas in which the interaction of the UK competition rules and other legislative provisions is at issue. It should also be noted that, as highlighted by sections 3(2)–(5) and 19(2)–(4) CA 1998, in certain circumstances it is open to the Secretary of State for Trade and Industry to amend schedules 1 and 3 CA 1998 (but not schedule 2) and, indeed, to adopt exclusions for agreements from either or both prohibitions on grounds of compliance with international obligations or 'exceptional and compelling reasons of public policy' (sections 6 and 7 of schedule 3 respectively).

Table 2.1: Exclusions from the chapter I and chapter II prohibitions under UK competition law

Field	Legislation	Ch. I excl	Ch. II excl	Clawback?
Mergers and concentrations[a]	sch 1 CA 1998	Yes	Yes	Possible by CMA, *only* re the ch I prohibition (sch 1, para 4 CA 1998)
Planning obligations[b]	sch 3, para 1 CA 1998	Yes	No	No
Agreements subject to directions under s 21(2) RTPA 1976	sch 3, para 2 CA 1998	Yes	No	After a transitional period ending on 1 May 2007, this exclusion no will longer apply[c]
EEA Regulated Financial Services Markets	sch 3, para 3 CA 1998	Yes	No	No
Services of General Economic Interest[d]	sch 3, para 4 CA 1998	Yes	Yes	No
Compliance with legal requirements	sch 3, para 5 CA 1998	Yes	Yes	No
Certain Orders issued by Secretary of State under specific CA 1998 powers	sch 3 paras 6 (inter-national obligations) and 7 (exceptional and compelling reasons of public policy) CA 1998	Yes	Yes	No (unless specifically included in the Order)
Agricultural products	sch 3, para 9 CA 1998	Yes	No	Yes

(Continued)

Table 2.1: (*Continued*)

Field	Legislation	Ch. I excl	Ch. II excl	Clawback?
Land agreements	s 50(1) CA 1998 *juncto* CA 1998 (Land Agreements Exclusion and Revocation) Order 2004 (SI 2004, No. 1260)[e]	Yes	No	Yes

[a] Covers both mergers qualifying under UK law and concentrations under EU law: see ch 5.

[b] Eg where planning permission is granted subject to an agreement to perform certain services or provide certain facilities: see s 106 Town and Country Planning Act 1990.

[c] Competition Act 1998 and Other Enactments (Amendment) Regulations 2004 (SI 2004, No 1261), Regs 1 and 4 *juncto* sch 1, para 50(a). See *Transitional Arrangements* (OFT 406), for discussion.

[d] See section 7.2 below for details of the operation of this provision.

[e] This order revoked the previous exclusion for vertical agreements, while retaining the exclusion for 'land agreements'. For discussion of the position of vertical agreements, see section 3.6.3 below.

2.3.3 UK Competition Law and Other Legislation

It is important to note how the UK's competition law regime relates to other legislation that touches upon questions relating to markets and the competitive process. Some of these other provisions are highly specialised and involve their own intricate and complicated systems, so we cannot hope to provide a complete picture of their operation and significance here.

The legislation discussed here raises questions that concern the extent to which specific fields and/or sectors of law and/or economic activity are better governed by a regime tailored specifically to the particular issues raised therein. As a basic starting point, it is clear that the general system of UK competition law (covering collusion, abuse of dominant position and merger control) is applicable to *all* areas of economic activity. It is true that the precise application of UK competition law requires careful analysis in the light of the facts of each situation, but the same basic principles apply across all sectors and in all cases.

However, in some sectors the straightforward application of the competition rules is felt not to deal adequately with particular characteristics commonly encountered in such sectors. One way of resolving this problem is to exclude the sector from the application of the normal UK competition rules and instead to lay down a regime tailored to the needs of the sector. For this reason, schedule 2 CA 1998 excludes agreements that are subject to competition scrutiny under other specific pieces of legislation. An example of this can be found in the UK under the Financial Services and Markets Act 2000 (FSMA 2000). Under FSMA 2000, agreements, practices or conduct that were encouraged by any of the former Financial Services Authority's regulating provisions were excluded from the Chapter I and Chapter II prohibitions. This exclusion, however, was repealed by the Financial Services Act 2012 (FSA 2012), which sought to enhance the competition scrutiny of practices adopted by the Financial Conduct Authority (FCA), which replaced the Financial Services Authority, and the Prudential Regulation Authority (PRA).

Following the introduction of the FSA 2012, the CMA may give advice to either the FCA or the PRA that one or more regulating provisions or practices may cause or contribute to the prevention, restriction or distortion of competition in the UK.[62] The relevant regulator is then required to publish, within 90 days, a reasoned statement setting out how it intends to react in light of the CMA's advice.[63] Where, following publication of the regulator's response, the CMA continues to have concerns regarding the provision or practice in question, the Treasury has the power to give directions to the PRA or FCA to remedy the situation. The Treasury is not, however, obliged to give such directions.[64] The CMA has agreed a Memorandum of Understanding with the FCA which sets out how it will cooperate with the FCA on financial services matters.[65]

Another approach to the special nature of problems raised in certain sectors is to introduce detailed specialised sectoral legislation and entrust a sectoral regulator with the task of overseeing activities in that sector,[66] while nevertheless continuing to permit the normal competition rules to apply in that sector as well. The logic behind this idea is that the application of the competition rules in these sectors requires detailed knowledge of the workings and intricacies of the field, so that the combination of the regulatory and competition law functions is likely to be more effective than leaving the latter to the more generalist competition authority. This is the model that has been adopted by the UK when pursuing the liberalisation of the various utilities (electricity, gas, water, rail and telecommunications). A series of regulators was created to perform the oversight function: the Gas and Electricity Markets Authority (supported by the Office of Gas and Electricity Markets (Ofgem)) is responsible for the gas and electricity markets; the Water Services Regulatory Authority (known as Ofwat) for the water industry; the Office of Rail and Road (ORR) for the railways and highways; the Office of Communications (Ofcom) for all manner of activities connected with communications; the Civil Aviation Authority (CAA) for air traffic services; the Financial Conduct Authority (FCA) for the financial services markets; and the Payment Systems Regulator (PSR) for the payment systems industry. Each of these regulatory bodies is also competent,[67] concurrently with the CMA, to apply the provisions of the CA 1998

---

[62] FSMA 2000, s 140B.

[63] FSMA 2000, s 140G.

[64] FSMA 2000, s 140H.

[65] Memorandum of understanding between the Competition and Markets Authority and the Financial Conduct Authority—concurrent competition powers, 21 December 2015.

[66] See C Jones (ed), *EU Energy Law*, 4th edn (Florence, EUI, 2016) 1–1290. For the older general discussion of these phenomena, see (from a wide-ranging and inter-disciplinary literature), eg, C Graham, *Regulating Public Utilities: A Constitutional Approach* (Oxford, Hart Publishing, 2000); D Helm, *Energy, the State, and the Market: British Energy Policy since 1979*, revised edn (Oxford, Oxford University Press, 2004); D Helm and T Jenkinson (eds), *Competition in Regulated Industries* (Oxford, Clarendon Press, 1998); D Newbery, *Privatization, Restructuring, and Regulation of Network Utilities* (Cambridge, MIT Press, MA, 2000); T Prosser, *Law and the Regulators* (Oxford, Clarendon Press, 1997); and T Prosser, *The Limits of Competition Law* (Oxford, Oxford University Press, 2005).

[67] By virtue of s 54 *juncto* sch 10, pts II and III of the CA 1998.

(ie, the Chapter I and Chapter II prohibitions), as well as Articles 101 and 102 TFEU, to activities in relation to their respective sectors. This allows the sector regulators to focus upon broad questions of market rules and the structure of the sector, while enabling intervention in individual cases either on the basis of sectoral regulatory powers or (where appropriate) under UK or EU competition law.

This system raises a number of interesting issues, including the extent to which the sector regulators will seek to secure the objective of a liberalised and competitive market by utilising their wide range of *ex ante* regulatory powers to impose licencing and other conditions upon companies operating in the sector. Alternatively, the sector regulators could choose to rely more strongly upon the *ex post* application of the competition rules, or a combination of both systems could be employed.[68] Following the introduction of the Enterprise Regulatory Reform Act 2013 (ERRA 2013), the relevant regulators are under an obligation to consider whether it would be more appropriate to use their competition powers before taking enforcement action under the relevant sector specific regulatory powers.[69] Furthermore, under the ERRA 2013, the Secretary of State can remove, by order, from a sectoral regulator any of its concurrency functions, if he or she considers that it is appropriate to do so for the purpose of promoting competition for the benefit of consumers.[70]

Another issue concerns the practical procedural operation of these concurrent competences to apply the competition rules: overlaps could occur between the CMA and any of the sector regulators, but it is also possible that one situation or agreement may touch upon the area of expertise of each of two (or more) sector regulators, particularly in these days of multi-utilities with interests across a range of sectors. In an attempt to ensure a coordinated exercise of their concurrent powers, the regulators listed above and the CMA form part of the UK Competition Network ('the UKCN'). The UKCN aims to promote competition for the benefit of consumers and to prevent anti-competitive behaviour by using competition law powers and developing pro-competitive regulatory frameworks. Arrangements are in place in the UKCN to facilitate the coordination of the regulator's concurrent competition law functions.

---

[68] For discussion, see R Whish and D Bailey, *Competition Law*, 8th edn (Oxford, Oxford University Press, 2015) 73. See for older literature T Prosser, 'Competition, Regulators and Public Service' in BJ Rodger and A MacCulloch (eds), *The Competition Act: A New Era for UK Competition Law* (Oxford, Hart Publishing, 2000), 225–41.

[69] Enterprise Regulatory Reform Act 2013, sch 14.

[70] Enterprise Regulatory Reform Act 2013, s 52. This provision applies to OFCOM, OFGEM, OFWAT, the ORR, the CAA and the Northern Ireland Authority for Utility Regulation.

The Prohibition of Anti-competitive Agreements

3.1 Introduction

3.1.1 General

The prohibition on agreements that affect competition has a central place in both UK and EU competition law. This prohibition is to be found in Article 101(1) TFEU and in Chapter I (specifically section 2(1)) CA 1998, and will be discussed in section 3.2 below. A breach of this prohibition leads to the relevant agreement being void, under Article 101(2) TFEU and section 2(4) CA 1998; this will be treated in section 3.3. In both systems it is possible that certain agreements may not fall within the prohibition. First, not all agreements fall under the prohibition in any case. For some agreements the effect upon competition is too small to justify prohibiting them. This exception is discussed in section 3.2.4 below. Further, there are agreements that fall under a block exemption or satisfy the conditions for an exemption. The rules on block exemptions are dealt with in section 3.4, while we consider the rules concerning exemptions in section 3.5. Then, in section 3.6, we discuss the position of a number of commonly encountered agreements *vis-à-vis* the prohibition.

3.1.2 The Structure of Section 2(1) CA 1998 and Article 101 TFEU. How Should They Be Applied?

Article 101 TFEU regulates agreements that affect competition. It may be useful for the reader to explain the structure of this complex provision before discussing the constitutive elements thereof. Article 101(1) TFEU only applies to an agreement when all constitutive elements of this provision are met. These elements are treated in section 3.2. However, an agreement can be exempted from Article 101(1) TFEU if it satisfies the conditions of Article 101(3) TFEU.[1] A major part of these exemptions come within the scope of the block exemptions. This is explained in section 3.4. There are also exemptions that do not follow from the block exemptions but follow from the application of Article 101(3) TFEU in individual cases. This is the subject of section 3.5.

It is up to the parties to a specific agreement to assess whether the conditions for this exemption provision are satisfied. In case of disputes this falls to national courts or arbiters. In view of its structure, Article 101 TFEU can be applied as follows. Does the conduct amount to an agreement between undertakings meeting all the criteria of Article 101(1) TFEU? If so, the next question is whether the agreement comes within the scope of a block exemption or can it be amended so as to come within the scope. If so the agreement does not infringe Article 101(1) TFEU. If it does not come within the scope of a block exemption, a careful analysis should be made whether the agreement satisfies the conditions of Article 101(3) TFEU. The agreement is compatible with the competition rules if and when, after ample analysis, it can be shown that the agreement comes within the scope of Article 101(3) TFEU. If the agreement does not fall within the scope of Article 101(3) TFEU it is, according to Article 101(2) TFEU, void.

3.2 The Prohibition of Cartels

3.2.1 Introduction

Article 101(1) TFEU provides:

> The following shall be prohibited as incompatible with the common market: all agreements between undertakings, decisions by associations of undertakings and concerted practices which may affect trade between Member States and which have as their object or effect the prevention, restriction or distortion of competition within the common market, and in particular those which:
>
> (a)   directly or indirectly fix purchase or selling prices or any other trading conditions;
> (b)   limit or control production, markets, technical development, or investment;
> (c)   share markets or sources of supply;
> (d)   apply dissimilar conditions to equivalent transactions with other trading parties, thereby placing them at a competitive disadvantage;
> (e)   make the conclusion of contracts subject to acceptance by the other parties of supplementary obligations which, by their nature or according to commercial usage, have no connection with the subject of such contracts.

---

[1] The equivalent exception under UK law can be found in s 9 CA 1998, schs 1–3 CA 1998 also exclude certain types of agreement from the scope of the Chapter I prohibition (see further, ch 2).

As a matter of UK law, according to section 2(1) CA 1998:

> Subject to section 3, agreements between undertakings, decisions by associations of undertakings or concerted practices which
>
> (a)   may affect trade within the United Kingdom [or a part thereof (section 2(7) CA 1998)], and
> (b)   have as their object or effect the prevention, restriction or distortion of competition within the United Kingdom,
>
> are prohibited unless they are exempt in accordance with the provisions of this Part.

As with Article 101 TFEU, each of the constituent parts of the test must be satisfied before the prohibition applies.

As can be seen from the above, the elements of Article 101 TFEU and the Chapter I prohibition are substantively very similar. The most significant difference is that for Article 101(1) TFEU to apply the conduct in question must be capable of having an effect on trade between EU Member States, whereas, for the purposes of the Chapter I prohibition, it is sufficient if there is an effect on trade in the UK or a part thereof. This distinction is logical given the different roles and jurisdiction enjoyed by the European Commission and the CMA.

Under the CA 1998 an agreement that satisfies both conditions of section 2(1) is then, in whole or in part, void in law (section 2(4) CA 1998) unless it falls under a parallel or block exemption or has been granted an individual exemption. Under EU competition law, the same result follows (as a result of Article 101(2) TFEU) so long as all three of the cumulative criteria are met.

For the combined system of competition law (at UK and EU levels) there is also a lower boundary. This is often called the *de minimis rule*, although its application in the UK is subsumed within the question of the appreciability of any restriction upon competition. We discuss this in section 3.2.4.

It is also important to note at the outset that there are certain exclusions from the application of the Chapter I prohibition in UK competition law. These are given effect by section 3 CA 1998 and their substance is to be found in the various schedules to the CA 1998. Thus, schedule 1 excludes agreements to the extent that they result in mergers and concentrations within the meaning of Part 3 of the Enterprise Act 2002 (EA 2002),[2] schedule 2 excludes situations subject to competition scrutiny under other enactments and schedule 3 covers exclusions for planning obligations as well as other general exclusions.

It should also be remembered that section 3 CA 1998 empowers the Secretary of State to make amendments to schedules 1 or 3 CA 1998 in certain circumstances, provided that an affirmative resolution is given by each House of Parliament. In this context, note that section 3(6) CA 1998 emphasises that schedule 3, paragraph 7 CA 1998 allows for certain agreements to be excluded from the Chapter I prohibition for 'exceptional and compelling reasons of public policy'.

Article 101 TFEU has direct effect[3] and section 2(1) CA 1998 is also capable of being relied upon by private individuals before the UK courts. Both provisions must

---

[2] See Chapter 5.3 below for our discussion of the UK merger control regime.
[3] Case 127/73 *BRT v SV Sabam (No 2)*.

be applied by the courts and the relevant authorities, and also by arbitrators in arbitral proceedings. In its *Eco-Swiss v Benetton* judgment, the ECJ held that the Dutch courts in that case were required to ensure that arbitrators applied EU competition law.[4] Where necessary, the national court must apply EU competition law *ex officio* whenever this has not been done during the arbitral proceedings. Since this decision concerned the application of Article 101 TFEU, the Court did not cover whether or not a similar duty was incumbent upon national courts if arbitrators fail to apply national competition law.[5]

3.2.2 Anti-competitive Practices: 'Collusion'

The prohibition on restrictions of competition under Article 101 TFEU and the Chapter I prohibition only applies where there is some collusion. In this book, we will use the collective term 'collusion' to cover an agreement, a decision of an association of undertakings or a concerted practice. It is sufficient if one of these forms of collusion is present. Naturally, the typical case will concern an agreement, because most matters are settled by written or oral agreements. Nevertheless, it is particularly the case in competition law that parties try to move to using other forms of collusion, in an attempt to escape its prohibition. This is thus the reason why most competition legislation includes, alongside agreements, decisions of associations of undertakings and concerted practices among those instances of collusion that will not be tolerated. It is not necessary for the competition authority or the courts to distinguish between whether conduct amounts to an agreement or a concerted practice.[6]

3.2.2.1 *Agreements*

The concept of an 'agreement' as used in the TFEU and the CA 1998 should be defined broadly.[7] The key element is the need for a concurrence of wills, but this agreement obviously need not necessarily be set down in writing. The concept also covers so-called 'gentlemen's agreements'. Generally speaking, in practice, proving the existence of such an agreement does not create too many problems, but there are exceptions to this.[8] Thus, there are some situations that appear at first sight not to count as

---

[4] Case C-126/97 *Eco-Swiss China Time Ltd v Benetton International NV*. For a helpful consideration of some of the practicalities arising in such situations, see R Nazzini, 'International Arbitration and Public Enforcement of Competition Law' (2004) *European Competition Law Review* 153.

[5] It is interesting that the *Hoge Raad* (Dutch Supreme Court), in its reference of the *Eco-Swiss* case (n 4, above) to the ECJ, highlighted that under Dutch law the mere fact that a prohibition decision under national competition law was not applied in the content or execution of an arbitral award was not sufficient to find that there was a conflict with the '*ordre public*' provisions in the sense of Art 1065(1)(e) of the Dutch Civil Procedure Code. In this connection, it should be noted that at the time of the *Eco-Swiss* case, the old Dutch law on Economic Competition was in force, which was an abuse-based system (unlike the new regime, which operates on a prohibition basis, as does the current UK system) (see Chapter 1.5 above for discussion of the distinction).

[6] See *JJB Sports v OFT* [2004] CAT 17. See Case T-551/08 *H&R ChemPharm*.

[7] See the CMA's Guidance in 'Agreements and concerted practices' (OFT 401).

[8] See the extensive discussion in Case T-551/08 *H&R ChemPharm*.

an agreement, yet *are* such on closer inspection. This relates in particular to situations where any connection between the parties appears to be only unilateral in character. For example, a situation where a document/receipt is sent after an order is placed and the supply conditions are set out on the reverse of the receipt will still be treated as a bilateral arrangement in law.[9] The buyer is treated as having accepted the stated supply conditions by tendering payment, which created a mutual connection between the parties. A one-sided refusal to supply right-hand drive cars was also treated as an agreement, because this action formed a part of the dealership agreement.[10] The ECJ's judgment in *Bayer-Adalat* has made clear that, in cases of apparently one-sided action, an express or silent assent must be shown if it is to be concluded that there has been a genuine concurrence of wills between the parties.[11]

3.2.2.2 *Decisions of Associations of Undertakings*

Many undertakings are organised in some form of (trade) association. In the EU there are many such associations. The MasterCard payment organisation is such an association. It is responsible for managing and coordinating the MasterCard and Maestro card payment systems.[12] Article 101 TFEU does not apply to EU associations that act under regulatory authority.[13] Acts of associations that do not fall within the remit of public authority are subject to Article 101 TFEU. In the UK, for example, there exists the Northern Ireland Livestock and Auctioneers' Association;[14] the Association of British Insurers;[15] and the National Farmers' Union[16] to name but a few of a myriad of such organisations.[17] These associations can take various decisions that directly affect competition, such as requiring their members to adopt uniform prices or levels of commission *vis-à-vis* their customers.[18] Decisions of associations of undertakings are formally legal acts of a single legal person. For competition law, the key issue is that such decisions can often have a significant impact upon the competitive process. The practice of competition authorities has experienced many examples of such decisions. Also, recommendations by associations of undertakings can in certain circumstances be treated as a decision.[19] A good example of this phenomenon is

---

[9] See the *Tipp-Ex* Decision of the Commission of 10 July 1987 [1987] OJ L222/1 and the subsequent ruling of the ECJ in Case C-279/87 *Tipp-Ex GmbH & Co KG v Commission*.

[10] Decision of the Commission of 24 November 1983, *Ford* [1983] OJ L327/31 and Case 25/84 *Ford v Commission*. This refusal was summarised by the Commission and the ECJ as dealing in the context of an ongoing dealership agreement, and was therefore viewed as a two-sided commercial relationship (see, eg, paras 20–22 of the ECJ's judgment).

[11] Cases C-2/01 P and C-3/01 P *Bundesverband der Arznemittel-Importeure eV and Commission v Bayer AG*.

[12] See Case T-111/08, *Mastercard*. Confirmed on Appeal C-382/12P.

[13] Case C-1/12 *OTOCAC;* Case T-90/11 *ONP*.

[14] DGFT Decision No CA/98/1/2003, 3 February 2003.

[15] OFT Decision No CA/98/04/2004, 22 April 2004.

[16] Short-form Opinion of 23 August 2012, *Rural Broadband Wayleaves*.

[17] See the CMA's Guideline, *Trade Associations, Professions and Self-regulating Bodies* (OFT 408) for the CMA's approach to these issues.

[18] As in the *Northern Ireland Livestock and Auctioneers' Association* Decision (n 14, above).

[19] See, eg, DGFT Decision, *Film Distributors' Association Ltd* (No CA/98/10/2002, 1 February 2002).

the decision in the *Sachversicherer* case.[20] The Association of Insurers had published a recommendation concerning a collective increase in insurance premiums. Both the Commission and the Court concluded from all the circumstances that the recommendation in fact operated as a compelling prescription of a certain type of behaviour and thus could be treated as a decision contrary to what is now Article 101(1) TFEU and Chapter I CA 1998.

3.2.2.3 Concerted Practices

It is regularly the case that undertakings coordinate their conduct among themselves without there being any question of a concurrence of wills.[21] Such coordination of behaviour can also restrict competition.

Examples of such behaviour are those meetings where information relating to cost calculations and other commercial data, and perhaps even prices, are exchanged. Knowledge of such important information gives the relevant undertakings the possibility to coordinate their commercial behaviour.

In the practical enforcement of competition law, proof of the existence of concerted practices can create difficulties. Therefore, the authorities will first look for forms of written evidence: letters, memos, faxes, emails, sms and the like. If no written evidence can be found, then the market behaviour of the undertakings concerned will be analysed, with the aim of proving that competition has been restricted. Parallel price movements form perhaps the most important indication in this regard. Nevertheless, to prove the existence of the concerted practice it must also be shown that the commercial behaviour at issue cannot be explained by the structure and particular characteristics of the relevant market.[22] This means that in some cases a thorough economic analysis of the market and the behaviour of the parties (and others) on that market must be made.

In its ruling in *Apex Asphalt and Paving Co Ltd v OFT*, the CAT, in reliance on the principles established by the case law of the EU Courts, concluded that a concerted practice can arise where there are reciprocal contacts between undertakings which remove or reduce uncertainty as to their future conduct. As an example, the CAT continued that reciprocal contacts are established where one competitor discloses its future intentions or conduct on the market to another when the latter requests it or, at the very least, accepts it.[23]

In addition, even indirect and isolated instances of contact between competitors may be sufficient to infringe Article 101, if their object is to promote artificial

---

[20] Case 45/85 *Verband der Sachversicherer v Commission*.

[21] Good examples of such practices are Case T-448/07, *YKK* and Case T-442/08, *CISAC*.

[22] This was made clear in the ECJ's *Woodpulp II* judgment: Case C-89/85 *Åhlström Osakeyhtiö and others v Commission*. In the *CISAC* judgment Case T-442/08, the GC held, in para 182, that: 'the Commission has not proved to a sufficient legal standard the existence of a concerted practice relating to the national territorial limitations, since it has neither demonstrated that the collecting societies acted in concert in that respect, nor provided evidence rendering implausible one of the applicant's explanations for the collecting societies' parallel conduct.'

[23] *Apex Asphalt & Paving Company Limited v Office of Fair Trading (OFT)*, Case No 1032/1/1/04, [2005] CAT 4.

conditions of competition in the market. Following its investigations into *Football Shirts*,[24] *Toys and Games*[25] and *Dairy Products*,[26] the OFT found a concerted practice as to the retail prices at which these consumer goods were sold to consumers. In each of these cases, the concerted practices had come about not, or not only, from direct contact between the retailers but also through the role played by the supplier in each case (so-called hub and spoke arrangements).

3.2.3 Restriction of Competition

3.2.3.1 Introduction

Article 101(1) TFEU prohibits agreements, decisions by undertakings and concerted practices that have as their object or effect the prevention or distortion of competition. In order to find an infringement of Article 101(1) there has to be either an agreement that has the object of preventing competition, or the effect of preventing competition. The anti-competitive object and anti-competitive effects constitute not cumulative but alternative conditions in determining whether a practice falls within the prohibition in Article 101(1) TFEU. The distinction between these two categories is important because in the case of object restrictions it is not necessary to prove anti-competitive effects. The distinction between these two types of restriction has been the subject of a lively debate.[27] In the *GlaxoSmithKline* case the Commission condemned the dual pricing system for drugs as an indirect export ban. Upon appeal the General Court (GC) disagreed with the Commission.[28] The ECJ overruled the GC, applying its traditional approach.[29] A 2014 judgment of the ECJ has helped to clarify matters.

According to the ECJ in the *Groupement de Cartes Bancaires* judgment:

> Certain types of coordination between undertakings can be regarded, by their very nature, as being harmful to the proper functioning of normal competition.[30]

The Court went on to say that:

> Consequently, it is established that certain collusive behaviour, such as that leading to horizontal price-fixing by cartels, may be considered so likely to have negative effects, in particular on the price, quantity or quality of the goods and services, that it may be considered redundant, for the purposes of applying Article 81(1) EC, to prove that they have actual effects on the market.[31]

---

[24] *Price-fixing of Replica Football Kit*, CA98 decision, Case CP/0871/01, Decision No CA98/06/2003, [2004] UKCLR 6, 1 August 2003.
[25] *Hasbro UK Limited and ors*, Decision No CA98/2/2003, [2003] UKCLR 553, 19 February 2003.
[26] *Dairy retail price initiatives, Arla Foods Limited and ors, Infringement decision*, Case CE/3094-03, No CA98/03/2011, 10 August 2011.
[27] See for a summary R Whish and D Bailey, *Competition Law*, 8th edn (Oxford, 2015) 120–145.
[28] Case T-168/01 *GlaxoSmithKline*.
[29] Case C-501/06 P *GlaxoSmithKline*.
[30] Case C-67/13 P *Groupement de Cartes Bancaires*, para 50.
[31] ibid, para 51.

The court gave the following guidelines for finding an object agreement:

> According to the case-law of the Court, in order to determine whether an agreement between undertakings or a decision by an association of undertakings reveals a sufficient degree of harm to competition that it may be considered a restriction of competition 'by object' within the meaning of Article 81(1) EC, regard must be had to the content of its provisions, its objectives and the economic and legal context of which it forms a part. When determining that context, it is also necessary to take into consideration the nature of the goods or services affected, as well as the real conditions of the functioning and structure of the market or markets in question.[32]

It should be noted that the reference to the economic and legal context in the above quote does not amount to an economic analysis. Such an analysis is only necessary for establishing that the agreement has an effect on competition.

Several subsequent judgments have followed this approach.[33]

As will be explained in section 3.4.3 below the Commission's position in its block-exemptions and guidelines provides considerable guidance. Both types of restrictions may be exempted under Article 101(3) although this will normally be very difficult for object restrictions.

There are agreements, whether they be object or effect agreements, that have an effect upon competition, but that effect is so slight that they are excluded from the reach of competition law. These will be discussed in section 3.2.4. There are also agreements where the effect on competition is ancillary to rules that serve objectives other than competition. The most prominent case is the *Wouters* judgment.[34] This will be addressed in section 3.2.4.1.

An infringement of Article 101 TFEU may take place for a prolonged period involving several participants. In such circumstances it may be artificial to treat each separate element of the conduct as a separate infringement. As a result, competition law has developed the concept of a single and continuous infringement (SCI), which allows competition authorities (or private litigants) to treat the conduct as a single overall agreement, while, at the same time, recognising that some participants may be more active than others—that is to say, that they are not involved in every single infringement.[35]

The following quotes from the *Verhuizingen Coppens* judgment[36] express this concept clearly. The Court held that:

> According to settled case-law, an infringement of Article [101(1) TFEU] can result not only from an isolated act, but also from a series of acts or from continuous conduct, even if one or more aspects of that series of acts or continuous conduct could also, in themselves and taken in isolation, constitute an infringement of that provision. Accordingly, if the different actions form part of an 'overall plan', because their identical object distorts competition within the common market, the Commission is entitled to impute responsibility for those actions on the basis of participation in the infringement considered as a whole...

---

[32] ibid, para 53.
[33] See Case C-281/13 P *Dole*; Case C-172/14 *ING Pensii*.
[34] Case C-309/99. See also Case T-90/11, *ONP.*
[35] See Case C-49/92 P *Commission v Anic.*
[36] Case C 441/11 P *Commission v Verhuizingen Coppens NV.*

An undertaking which has participated in such a single and complex infringement through its own conduct, which fell within the definition of an agreement or a concerted practice having an anti-competitive object for the purposes of Article [101(1) TFEU] and was intended to help bring about the infringement as a whole, may accordingly be liable also in respect of the conduct of other undertakings in the context of the same infringement throughout the period of its participation in the infringement. That is the position where it is shown that the undertaking intended, through its own conduct, to contribute to the common objectives pursued by all the participants and that it was aware of the offending conduct planned or put into effect by other undertakings in pursuit of the same objectives or that it could reasonably have foreseen it and was prepared to take the risk…

…In such cases, the Commission is also entitled to attribute liability to that undertaking in relation to all the forms of anti-competitive conduct comprising such an infringement and, accordingly, in relation to the infringement as a whole.

As can be seen, the application of the SCI allows the Commission, or any party challenging the conduct of cartelists, to bring one single action instead of several individual actions. The SCI concept alleviates the burden of proof considerably in complex cartel cases, by not requiring the competition authority (or private litigant) to demonstrate that each and every contact constitutes an infringement.

3.2.3.2 Object

Agreements that have an obvious anti-competitive object are enumerated in Article 101 (1)(a), (b), and (c) TFEU: price fixing, restrictions of output and market sharing.[37] As noted in the previous section the ECJ has clarified the concept of object restriction in the *Groupement de Cartes Bancaires* judgment. This approach was subsequently confirmed and applied in a case involving the Romanian private pension fund in the *ING Pensii* judgment.[38]

The Commission in its block exemptions and guidelines[39] refers to these restrictions as hardcore restrictions, they are prohibited per se. Further object restrictions are listed in Articles 4(a) and 4(b) of Regulation 330/220, the Block exemption on vertical agreements. These are further discussed in section 3.6.3.2. Such restrictions are presumed to fall under Article 101(1) TFEU although there may be exceptional cases where such a restriction falls outside the scope of this provision. The qualification whether an agreement has the object to restrict competition has to be analysed in the economic and legal context, as can be seen from the quote in section 3.2.3.1 above. It is possible that an agreement that has a prima facie anti-competitive object may nevertheless escape that qualification. Thus there is a need to examine the counterfactual and ask the question 'what would the position of the parties have been without the agreement?'. This is clearly demonstrated by the *O2* judgment.[40] The GC ruled that the roaming agreement on prices was necessary in order to create an effective roaming system.

---

[37] The restrictions listed under Art 101(1)(d) and (e) TFEU: discrimination and tie-in practices are less obvious anti-competitive.

[38] Case C-172/14 *ING Pensii*.

[39] See eg, Guidelines on Vertical Restraints, para 47.

[40] Case T-328/03, *O2 v Commission*. See R Whish and D Bailey, *Competition Law*, 8th edn (Oxford, Oxford University Press, 2015) 135.

Once it is established that an agreement has the object of restricting competition no further analysis as to the restrictive effect in the economic context is required. As the ECJ confirmed in the *GSK* case,[41] as well as in the Telecom operators case. In this judgment the ECJ held:

'Accordingly, contrary to what the referring court claims, there is no need to consider the effects of a concerted practice where its anti-competitive object is established.'[42]

Object or hardcore restrictions are not shielded by the Commission *De minimis* Notice (see below at section 3.2.4).

3.2.3.3 Effect

Many agreements that have a perfectly legitimate business purpose may nevertheless have an effect on competition. By their very nature agreements always exclude third parties from the deal. It is therefore important to keep the goal of competition law, the maintenance and promotion of competition between companies, in mind. Healthy competitive relations are good for economic development and also protect consumers. The effect upon competitive relationships is therefore the most prominent starting point for competition law. To be able to analyse this effect, it is necessary to determine the relevant product and geographic market (on which see Chapter 1.3.2 above). Competition can be restricted in various different ways. In the CA 1998, section 2(1)(b) refers to 'prevention, restriction or distortion'. If competition is prevented then it is excluded altogether. In practice, this will rarely be the case, because (for example) even where uniform prices are agreed upon it will still be possible to compete on matters such as the quality of the product or service. When we think of restrictions on competition, we are concerned with the curtailment of the normal commercial freedom of action held by market participants. As we shall see below, this can happen in many different ways. This can also occur by providing preferential tariffs or where governments offer subsidies. In what follows, we will use the shorthand term 'restriction of competition' to cover all three of these concepts. Collusion that *intends* to restrict competition but does not in fact lead to that intended result is prohibited in the same way as collusion that *does* achieve that result.[43] Equally, collusive behaviour that does not aim at restricting competition and yet does have that effect is also prohibited. The assessment of whether or not there has been a restrictive effect relates either to actual or potential competition: naturally, the exclusion of potential future competition is just as damaging as the elimination of the competition that already exists on the market.

Since almost every agreement in economic transactions has a certain limiting effect upon competition, it is necessary to establish which measure of competition is the proper subject of competition law. The ECJ has accepted that the principal issue is

---

[41] Case C-501/06 P *GlaxoSmithKline v Commission*. See also section 3.6.3 below.

[42] Case C-8/08 *T-Mobile Netherlands v Raad van Bestuur NMa*, para 30.

[43] Applying the terms of Art 101(1) TFEU and the Ch I prohibition that either the restrictive 'object or effect' of a collusive arrangement will be sufficient: see Cases 56 and 58/64 *Établissements Consten SARL and Grundig-Verkaufs GmbH v Commission*, and in the UK, eg, DGFT Decision, *Price Fixing Agreements involving John Bruce (UK) Limited, Fleet Parts Limited and Truck and Trailer Components* (No CA98/12/2002, 13 May 2002). See also Case C-38/12 *Mastercard*. The ECJ held that the multilateral interchange fees are a restriction since they limit the pressure which merchants can exert on acquiring banks when negotiating the costs charged by those banks.

the establishment and maintenance of 'workable competition'.[44] That is a measure of competition that is necessary to realise the goals of the EU Treaties. To be able to establish whether or not a particular collusive arrangement restricts competition, an analysis of the legal, economic and sometimes the technical effects of that arrangement is usually required.

In contrast to object restrictions, effect restrictions require an extensive economic analysis of the content and context of the agreements. Many agreements are concluded for perfectly legitimate business purposes yet they may harm the competition in the relevant market. In order to find such harm an extensive market analysis is required. A good example of such an analysis is provided in the *Delimitis* judgment.[45] In this case the ECJ had to answer the question whether the exclusive supply contract between the Brewery Henninger Brau and the publican Delimits infringed Article 101(1) TFEU. The ECJ answered as follows:

> A beer supply agreement is prohibited by Article 101(1) TFEU[46] if two cumulative conditions are met. The first is that, having regard to the economic and legal context of the agreement at issue, it is difficult for competitors who could enter the market or increase their market share to gain access to the national market for the distribution of beer in premises for the sale and consumption of drinks. The fact that, in that market, the agreement in issue is one of a number of similar agreements having a cumulative effect on competition constitutes only one factor amongst others in assessing whether access to that market is indeed difficult. The second condition is that the agreement in issue must make a significant contribution to the sealing-off effect brought about by the totality of those agreements in their economic and legal context. The extent of the contribution made by the individual agreement depends on the position of the contracting parties in the relevant market and on the duration of the agreement.

3.2.4 The *De Minimis* Rule

There are agreements that can have an effect upon competition, but that effect is so slight that they are excluded from the reach of competition law.[47] Thus, an agreement between a number of local cafés having the effect of distorting competition might be detrimental to the pocket of the socialising public, but it would have insufficient impact upon the relevant market to pay it much attention from the perspective of competition law. In the UK, the CMA covers this issue under the general heading of 'appreciability', drawing upon the case law of the Union Courts on the notion of a restriction of competition, as a result of section 60 CA 1998.[48] It should be noted, however, that the common law has long regulated certain contracts and covenants that

---

[44] This concept was commonly used in the early days of EEC competition law. It is referred to in case 26/76, *Metro Grossmarkte*. The concept was originally coined by the economist JM Clark, see Chapter 1.3.1.

[45] Case C-234/89, *Delimitis v Henninger Brau*. See also Case C-384/13, *Spanish Repsol*, Order of the court.

[46] Please note that we substituted the new TFEU numbers for the old EEC numbers. Please also note that the citation is a summary of the judgment in the dictum, a fuller analysis is provided in paras 28–32.

[47] See Order of 4/12/2014 in Case C-384/13 *Spanish Petrol Stations*.

[48] See *Agreements and Concerted Practices* (OFT 401), ss 2.18–2.22. See further our discussion of this issue of appreciability in s 3.2.4.1 below.

are said to be a 'restraint of trade' although this cannot be covered in any detail in this volume: the reader is referred to other works on this topic for details.[49]

In EU competition law, the Commission defines the lower limit of the effect upon competition in another way. The market share of the parties to the agreement is used to define what counts as a *de minimis* restriction: under the relevant Commission Notice,[50,51] these market shares must currently be under 10 per cent for horizontal agreements and under 15 per cent for vertical agreements.[52] Establishing these market shares in practice can cause some difficulty. It should be stressed that this European lower limit is only of importance in UK legal practice if there is an issue concerning the competence of the European Commission.[53] This will be discussed in Chapter 6. As a consequence of the basically identical substantive content of the major elements of UK and EU competition law, it is normally not necessary definitively to decide under which system agreements actually fall.[54] This is of great importance for legal practice, as the national judge no longer has to establish whether certain types of conduct fall under European or UK competition law by applying the difficult criterion of an 'effect upon trade between Member States'. Since the *Expedia* judgment it is clear that hardcore restrictions are not shielded by the *de minimis* rule. This is clarified in paragraph 13 of the Notice.[55]

---

[49] See, eg, GH Treitel, *The Law of Contract*, 11th edn (London, Sweet & Maxwell, 2003), 453–77; JD Heydon, *The Restraint of Trade Doctrine* (London, Butterworths, 1971); M Trebilcock, *The Common Law of Restraint of Trade: A Legal and Economic Analysis* (Toronto, Carswell, 1986); A Kamerling and C Osman, *Restrictive Covenants under Common and Competition Law*, 4th edn (London, Sweet & Maxwell, 2004); and R Whish and D Bailey, *Competition Law*, 8th edn (Oxford, Oxford University Press, 2015), ch 3.5.

[50] These details are to be found in a Notice of the European Commission of 30 July 2014, [2014] OJ C 291/1. See also 'Guidance on restrictions "by object" for the purpose of defining which agreements may benefit from the De Minimis Notice' published on the website of DG Comp. Note that these limits are provided in European law by pseudo-legislation in the form of a Notice (*cf* the position in Dutch law, where the Law on Competition, the *Mededingingswet* (*Mw*))—ie a statute—defines the relevant limits on the basis of annual turnover of the undertakings concerned and on how many undertakings were involved: the number involved must be eight undertakings or fewer, and for agreements relating to goods the turnover amount is less than €5,500,000 million, while service providers must turn over less than €1100,000 (see Art 7 *Mw*). The number of undertakings that can be involved is limited, so as to prevent small local markets from being taken over by extensive cartels). This Commission Notice only concerns the effect on competition. The Commission has also issued a further Notice giving guidance on the effect upon trade between Member States ([2004] OJ C101/81): this will be discussed in section 3.2.5 below.

[51] As the ECJ has observed, in its *Expedia* judgment C-226/11 para 27, the Commission's notice is not binding upon National Competition Authorities.

[52] Note that this Commission Notice is not treated as legally binding upon the Community judicature; rather, it acts as a clear policy statement by the Commission that it will apply these principles in its own decisional practice. The GC has held that the legal test is one of the appreciability of the restriction upon competition, which has also been called a '*de minimis*' rule: see, eg, the helpful judgment in Case T-374/94 *European Night Services Ltd v Commission*.

[53] Case C-226/11 *Expedia v Autorité de la concurrence*, concerned an exceptional case where the competence of French National Competition Authority to apply Art 101(1) and Art 3(2) of Regulation 1/2003 was challenged on the basis that agreement did not reach the thresholds of the *de minimis* notice.

[54] See, eg, the *Hendry v WPBSA* case in the UK ([2002] ECC 8, [2002] UKCLR 5), where both sets of rules were assumed to be relevant and were analysed, although the court acknowledged that the substantive consequences were largely the same and so did not rule finally on which system applied.

[55] In para 10 of the Notice the Commission states that the *de minimis* rule does not shield hardcore restrictions. Case law of the ECJ held that the *de minimis* rule is also applicable for restrictions that have the restriction of competition as their object, see Case 5/69, *Volk v Vervaeke* as well as case C-260/07 *Pedro IV Servicios SL v Total Espana SA*, para 82. The *Expedia* judgement C-226/11, para 37 seems to have changed this. See Faull and Nickpay (eds), *The EC Law of Competition*, 3rd edn (Oxford, Oxford University Press, 2014) para 3.209 at p 243 et seq.

The CMA has, by taking over the previous OFT guidance, (in OFT 401, paragraphs 2.19ff) confirmed that it will 'have regard to the European Commission's approach as set out in the Notice on Agreements of Minor Importance', while being careful to note that:

> The mere fact that the parties' market shares exceed the thresholds..., does *not* mean that the effect of an agreement on competition *is* appreciable.[56] Other factors will be considered in determining whether the agreement has an appreciable effect. Relevant factors may include for example, the content of the agreement and the structure of the market or markets affected by the agreement, such as entry conditions or the characteristics of buyers and the structure of the buyers' side of the market.[57]

The relationship between UK and EU competition law and the competences of the various supervisory bodies, as well as the role of the national courts, is illustrated in Fig 2.1 of Chapter 2, section 2.2.2.1 (above).

3.2.4.1 Wouters: *An Ancillary Restriction Not a Rule of Reason*

Apart from the collusive arrangements that *do* have a certain restrictive effect upon competition and yet still fall outside the prohibition on restrictions of competition as a result of their non-appreciable or *de minimis* effects, there are other agreements that fall outside the scope of the prohibition of Article 101(1) TFEU. It is not easy to deduce a clear category from the case law of the Union courts. According to some writers the case law of the ECJ can be interpreted as embodying a 'rule of reason'. The term 'rule of reason' has been developed in US antitrust law.[58] In this interpretation, the question turns on a market analysis to establish whether the arrangement concerned restricts or actually promotes competition. This interpretation of the concept of a restriction of competition should be clearly distinguished from the weighing of the advantages and disadvantages of agreements that restrict competition in connection with decisions whether or not to grant an individual exemption. In this latter case, it has always already been decided that there is a restriction of competition and thus a breach of the prohibition. It should be noted that the Union courts have never endorsed the concept of a 'rule of reason' and the GC has explicitly held that there is no place for it in EU law.[59]

In the UK this notion is covered by use of the appreciability criterion. In assessing the appreciability of the restriction upon competition caused by a particular arrangement, the prior question is whether or not there is a restriction of competition in the first place. In some cases the CMA has decided that arrangements could not be seen

---

[56] The correctness of this approach is reflected in Case C-384/13 *Spanish Petrol Stations*.

[57] This reflects observations made by the CFI in Joined Cases T-374, 375, 384 and 388/94 *European Night Services Ltd and others v Commission* (see especially paras 102–3) and picked up by the Commission in its Notice on the subject (n 50, above), para 2.

[58] See, eg, V Korah, 'The Rise and Fall of Provisional Validity: the Need for a Rule of Reason' (1981) 3 *Northwestern Journal of International Law & Business* 320, esp 354–55; IS Forrester and C Norall, 'The Laicization of Community Law' (1984) 21 *Common Market Law Review* 11; and R Whish and B Sufrin, 'Article 85 and the Rule of Reason' (1987) 7 *Yearbook of European Law* 1.

[59] Case T-112/99 *Métropole Télévision (M6) and others v Commission* (annotated by Odudu (2002) 27 *European Law Review* 1000).

as a restriction upon competition at all,[60] while in others the CMA has ruled that the arrangement concerned had no appreciable effect upon competition.[61]

In EU law not every agreement restricting the freedom of action of the parties falls within the prohibition of Article 101(1) TFEU. There are agreements that have an effect on competition but have as their object the promotion of principles that are endorsed or respected by EU law. In such cases the effect on competition is ancillary to the main objective of the agreement. This is well illustrated by the *Wouters* judgment.[62] The case dealt with a rule of the Dutch bar prohibiting partnerships between lawyers and registered accountants. *Wouters* claimed that this rule was contrary to Article 101(1) TFEU. The ECJ disagreed. It held that:

> not every agreement between undertakings or every decision of an association of undertakings which restricts the freedom of action of the parties or of one of them necessarily falls within the prohibition laid down in Article 85(1) of the Treaty. For the purposes of application of that provision to a particular case, account must first of all be taken of the overall context in which the decision of the association of undertakings was taken or produces its effects. More particularly, account must be taken of its objectives, which are here connected with the need to make rules relating to organisation, qualifications, professional ethics, supervision and liability, in order to ensure that the ultimate consumers of legal services and the sound administration of justice are provided with the necessary guarantees in relation to integrity and experience … It has then to be considered whether the consequential effects restrictive of competition are inherent in the pursuit of those objectives.[63]

3.2.5 Effect on Trade Between Member States

In EU competition law it is of importance to know where the competence of 'Brussels' arises to deal with anti-competitive agreements. The question, in other words, is: where does the scope of application of EU competition law begin? This demarcation is necessary to ensure that purely local conduct remains under the jurisdiction of national competition law. As we have shown in Chapter 2.2.2 above, the importance of establishing this boundary line is diminished for most of UK competition law, as a result of the adoption of UK national competition law that is closely modelled on (and connected to—see section 60 CA 1998) the EU competition rules.[64] This also applies

---

[60] See the summary released by the OFT of its various non-infringement Decisions in the *Anaesthetists' groups* case,. Most of the groups of anaesthetists were viewed as a single undertaking and thus not guilty of concluding agreements between separate economic entities. However, the individual members of the Guildford Anaesthetic Services group were found to operate as separate undertakings on the market, but no agreement between them was found that was restrictive of competition.

[61] See, eg, DGFT Decision, *Film Distributors' Association Ltd* (Case No CA/98/10/2002, 1 February 2002) (once amendments to the agreement had been made) and Oftel Decision, *Swan Solutions Ltd/Avaya ECS Ltd* (March 2001) (see paras 37 and 38).

[62] Case C-309/99, *Wouters v Nederlandse orde van advocaten* see also Case T-90/11 *ONP*.

[63] Para 97.

[64] One possible situation where the effect upon trade between Member States would make a difference concerns a case where a prosecution is brought for a breach of the (criminal law) cartel offence under UK law, whereas no such penalty is available under EU competition law. See Chapter 6.3.5.2 below for discussion of the cartel offence.

to the other EU Member States that have aligned their competition law with EU law. Naturally, agreements where the undertakings concerned together have a substantial turnover and are established in various Member States, will generally be subject to EU competition law in addition to UK law.

The criterion of an 'effect on trade between Member States' has from the beginning been interpreted extensively by the Commission, which has been supported in this approach by the ECJ.[65] It is sufficient that trade between Member States be potentially influenced. Moreover, it is sufficient if one of the clauses of the agreement in question can have this effect.[66] This concept was further widened when the ECJ decided that purely national agreements could fall under the prohibition of Article 101(1) TFEU.[67] According to the Court, such national cartels can raise barriers that prevent foreign companies from entering that national market to provide competition for those members of the cartel. The consequence of this ruling was that many more 'national' arrangements could be held to fall under the scrutiny of EU competition law than had first been thought.

In the context of the entry into force of Regulation 1/2003 from 1 May 2004, the Commission has developed further its understanding of the concept of an effect on trade between Member States in a Notice published on 27 April 2004.[68] According to the Commission, the issue turns upon identifying an appreciable influence upon inter-Member State trade. The criteria that the Commission provides for making this assessment are not easy to summarise. The most important criteria for establishing that there is an effect on trade between the Member States is that the total market shares of the parties should be more than 5 per cent and, in the case of horizontal agreements, the total turnover more than €40 million.

3.3 Voidness

In both the EU and UK systems, a breach of the prohibition leads to the voidness of the relevant agreements and decisions. This sanction does not always have the consequence that the agreement or decision *as a whole* is rendered void. It is up to the national court to decide whether or not the agreement or decision is to be held void in full. The court will declare the arrangement to be void as a whole if the clause (or clauses) of the agreement or decision that is (are) in conflict with the prohibition amounts (amount) to an essential part of the agreement or decision, without which the arrangement would not have been concluded. If this is not the case, then the

---

[65] Case 56/65 *Société Technique Minière (STM) v Maschinebau Ulm GmbH.*
[66] Case 193/83 *Windsurfing International Inc v Commission.*
[67] Case 8/72 *Vereniging van Cementhandelaren (VCH) v Commission.*
[68] Commission Notice, 'Guidelines on the 'effect on trade' concept contained in Articles 81 and 82 of the Treaty' [2004] OJ C101/81. For an interpretation of this notice see the opinion of Advocate General Kokott in Case C-439/11 P *Ziegler v Commission.*

agreement or decision will only be void in part.[69] Arbitrators can also declare such clauses to be void.[70] In practice, this last point is of great importance, because many commercial contracts contain an arbitration clause.

The declaration of voidness cannot be made by the CMA or the European Commission. These competition authorities must restrict themselves to establishing a breach of the prohibition on restrictions of competition. Such a finding of breach will bind the national court insofar as it has taken place in the form of an official decision. If such a finding was made in an informal context (such as by the use of comfort letters), then the national court is not formally bound by it. On this point, see, further, Chapter 6 (in particular, Chapter 6.2.2 on Article 4(3) TEU and cooperation between the Commission and national courts).

The CMA and the European Commission can impose other sanctions for breach of the prohibition. These include making directions, adopting interim measures, imposing fines for the CMA (as well as possibly facilitating the criminal prosecution of cartel activity; see Chapter 6.3.5.2 below), and the imposition of fines, the adoption of interim measures for the European Commission as well as accepting commitments under Article 9 of Regulation 1/2003. We provide a fuller discussion of these matters in Chapter 6.

3.4 Block Exemptions

3.4.1 Introduction

The system of block exemptions was not provided for in the EC Treaty. But, with the entry into force of the basic Regulation on the application of Articles 101 and 102 TFEU (Regulation 17),[71] it quickly became apparent that the number of notifications for an individual exemption was so large that the Commission could not deal with the flood of cases. At that point, the idea of the block exemption was born. Block exemptions provide that, for certain clearly defined groups of agreements, the prohibition of Article 101 TFEU does not apply. In competition practice, it had become clear that some sorts of agreements would always be granted an exemption, because the conditions for such an exemption were met. Instead of requiring the undertakings concerned to notify each new agreement for an individual exemption, it was more practical to provide in advance that for that particular sort of agreement the

---

[69] Cases 56 and 58/64 *Établissements Consten SARL and Grundig-Verkaufs-GmbH v Commission*.
[70] See for an extensive treatment of the issues related to the application of the competition rules by arbiters; G Blanke and P Landolt (eds), *EU and US Antitrust Arbitration* (Wolters Kluwer, 2011) 1–2211.
[71] Reg 17/62/EEC ([1962] OJ 13/204, [1959–62] OJ English Special Edition 87) will be discussed in Chapter 6.4 below.

prohibition of Article 101 TFEU would not apply. In the practice of EU competition law, such block exemptions have regularly been adopted, but only after sufficient
experience has been acquired in dealing with notifications for individual exemptions
for that particular type of agreement. Furthermore, the Commission often waited for
rulings of the Court of Justice on the validity of Commission decisions dealing with
such notifications for individual exemptions.

A good example is the block exemption for vertical agreements, Regulation
330/2010.[72] The block exemption is based upon the principle that everything that is
not forbidden is permitted. The Regulation prohibits the so-called 'hardcore restrictions', such as price-fixing agreements, market sharing and export restrictions. All
other forms of vertical agreements are permitted, on the condition that the market
share of the supplier on the relevant market where he sells goods or services does not
exceed 30 per cent. Above this market share, agreements are not automatically forbidden but need to be assessed on a case-by-case basis. This block exemption will be
discussed in section 3.6.3 below.

The system of adopting block exemptions brings with it the consequence that not
all practices that have an impact upon competition can be scrutinised fully and in
advance. True, the move to establish a block exemption is only made once sufficient
experience in that particular field has been gathered, but it remains possible that
exceptional market circumstances may be present that might change the assessment
of agreements that prima facie satisfy the criteria of the block exemption in question.
For these cases, the block exemptions offer the possibility that their exemption can
be withdrawn. In UK competition law this may be done by the CMA, on the basis of
the provisions adopted in any block exemption order (see section 6(5) and especially
(6)(c) CA 1998), and in EU competition law by the European Commission, on the
basis of Article 29(1) of Regulation 1/2003/EC. Article 29(2) of Regulation 1/2003/EC
offers the national competition authorities the same opportunity. This competence is
repeated in the block exemptions themselves eg, Article 6 of Regulation 330/2010/EC.
In practice, such a withdrawal has only occurred once.

3.4.2 Block Exemptions in UK Competition Law

3.4.2.1 UK Law Block Exemptions

Under section 6 CA 1998, the Secretary of State for Trade and Industry is empowered,
on the recommendation of the CMA, to adopt block exemptions; the procedure for
so doing is laid down by section 8 CA 1998.[73] Given the system of parallel exemptions
introduced by the CA 1998 (see section 3.4.2.2 below), it seems highly unlikely that
block exemptions will be adopted with any regularity under UK law; indeed, thus far

---

[72] [2010] OJ L102/1–7.
[73] The possibility of including an 'opposition procedure', used by some earlier EC block exemption
regulations and formerly included in s 7 CA 1998, was repealed in the UK's reforms to align the UK system
of competition law with the modernised EC regime (see the Competition Act 1998 and Other Enactments
(Amendment) Regulations 2004 (SI 2004, No 1261), Regs 1 and 4 juncto sch 1).

only one such exemption has come into force under UK law, concerning the system for public transport ticketing schemes.[74]

3.4.2.2 The System of 'Parallel Exemptions' in UK Law[75]

One of the more ingenious and practically significant devices introduced by the CA 1998 is the mechanism to allow UK law to take advantage of the substance of EU block exemption regulations even in situations falling wholly under UK law. Under section 10 CA 1998, a so-called 'parallel exemption' (section 10(3) CA 1998) from the application of the UK competition rules is afforded to undertakings by allowing any agreement that would benefit from an EU block exemption regulation to rely upon the substance of that regulation to be exempted from the Chapter I prohibition under UK law (ie, where it does not have an effect upon trade between Member States). Following the recent reforms to the UK regime for vertical agreements (see section 3.6.3.3 below, for discussion), section 10 CA 1998 assumes even greater importance, by allowing undertakings to rely upon important block exemption regulations concerning vertical restraints (Regulation 330/2010/EC) and (as previously) technology transfer agreements (Regulation 772/2004/EC).

For undertakings, this eases the compliance burden imposed by competition law considerably and is a further illustration of the closely combined nature of the UK and EU competition law systems. For example, it considerably alleviates the danger that the CMA may run into difficulties in attempting to apply stricter standards of compliance where an agreement satisfies Article 101(3) TFEU (as per Article 3(1) of Regulation 1/2003/EC). The limitations which apply to such parallel exemptions are similar to those applicable under EU law. Thus, such an exemption provides no protection from the application of either Article 102 TFEU or the Chapter II prohibition, and the CMA may:

(a) impose conditions or obligations subject to which a parallel exemption is to have effect;
(b) vary or remove any such condition or obligation;
(c) impose one or more additional conditions or obligations; or
(d) cancel the exemption (section 10(5) CA 1998).

Since this device makes the content of EU law block exemptions of the utmost importance for the application of UK competition law as well, it is to those rules that we now turn.

3.4.3 The European Block Exemptions

As noted above, a large number of block exemptions have been adopted in EU competition law. This has occurred through the adoption of Regulations, which have direct

---

[74] The Competition Act 1998 (Public Transport Ticketing Schemes Block Exemption) Order 2001, SI 2001 No 319.
[75] See OFT 401, paras 5.15 and 5.16.

application in all Member State legal systems. The EEC Treaty itself, however, did not provide for the adoption of such Regulations. As a result, the Council of Ministers, on the basis of what is now Article 103 TFEU, empowered the Commission to adopt block exemptions.[76] The Commission Regulations must thus remain within the limits set by the mandate given by the Council of Ministers.

A proper understanding of the relationship between block exemptions and individual cases where the Article 101(3) TFEU criteria can be satisfied is vital in this area. It should be appreciated that block exemptions, by their nature, only grant an exemption for cases that are 'safe' from a competition law point of view. And what counts as 'safe' here is closely based upon the decisional practice of the Commission and the case law of the ECJ. That means that not all agreements that do not fall under a block exemption are necessarily prohibited in the end. There are many situations where, on closer analysis, the granting of an individual exemption is in fact possible.

The following EU block exemption Regulations are currently in force:

Commission Regulations

(a)   Regulation 330/2010[77] on vertical agreements and concerted practices. [2010] OJ L 102/1-7.

(b)   Regulation 906/2009 on certain categories of agreements, decisions and concerted practices between liner shipping companies (consortia). [2009] OJ L256/31.

(c)   Regulation 1218/2010 on specialisation agreements. [2010] OJ L335/43.

(d)   Regulation 1217/2010 on research and development agreements. [2010] OJ L335/36.

(e)   Regulation 461/2010on vertical agreements and concerted practices in the motor vehicle sector. [2010] OJ L129/52-59.

(f)   Regulation 267/2010[78] on agreements, decisions and concerted practices in the insurance sector. [2010] OJ L33/8.

(g)   Regulation 316/2014[79] on technology transfer agreements. [2014] OJ L93/17.[80]

---

[76] Reg 19/65/EEC of the Council of 2 March 1965 concerning the application of Art 85(3) of the EC Treaty to groups of agreements and concerted practices [1965] OJ L36/633, as amended by Reg 1215/99/EC. The Council has also adopted further enabling Regulations: Reg 2821/71 for research and development and specialisation agreements [1971] OJ L285/46/EEC; Reg 487/2009 for certain groups of agreements in the air transport sector [2009] OJ L 148/1; Reg 1534/91/EEC for certain groups of agreements in the insurance sector [1991] OJ L143/1; and Reg 464/2009 for certain agreements between shipping line (consortia) [2009] OJ L 79/1; Reg. 169/2009 [2009] OJ L 61/1. See the following text for fuller details.

[77] In force until 31 May 2022.

[78] In force until 1 March 2010.

[79] In force until 30 April 2026. Repealing and replacing Reg 240/96 on the application of Art 81(3) EC to groups of agreements concerning technology transfer [1996] OJ L31/2.

[80] The Commission has also published Guidelines on the application of this Regulation: [2014] OJ C89/3.

Council Regulations

The following Council Regulations include both block exemptions and enabling measures that allow the Commission to adopt such block exemptions.

(a)   Regulation 26/62/EEC Application of certain rules concerning competition in the production and trade of agricultural products. [1962] OJ 30/693.
(b)   Regulation 19/65/EEC Application of Article 81(3) to groups of agreements (enabling Regulation). [1965] OJ 36/533. *Amended by Regulation 1215/1999/ EC [1999] OJ L148/1, by Regulation 1216/1999/EC [1999] OJ L148/15 and by Article 40 of Regulation 1/2003/EC [2003] OJ L1/1.*
(c)   Regulation 169/2009/EEC Application of the competition rules to transport by rail, road and inland waterways. [2009] OJ L61/1.
(d)   Regulation 2821/71/EEC Application of Article 81(3) EC to groups of agreements, decisions and concerted practices in research and development and specialisation (enabling Regulation). [1971] OJ L285/46.
       Amended by Article 40 of Regulation 1/2003/EC [2003] OJ L1/1.
(e)   Regulation 1534/91/EEC Application of Article 81(3) EC to groups of agreements in the insurance sector (enabling Regulation). [1991] OJ L398/7.
       Amended by Article 40 of Regulation 1/2003/EC [2003] OJ L1/1.
(f)   Regulation 264/2009 agreements, decisions and concerted practices between liner shipping companies (consortia). [2009] OJ L79/1.

Notices from the Commission concerning the Application of Block Exemptions

(a)   Guidelines on Vertical Restraints. [2010] OJ C130/1.
(b)   Commission notice—Supplementary guidelines on vertical restraints in agreements for the sale and repair of motor vehicles and for the distribution of spare parts for motor vehicles [2010] C138, p 16.
(c)   Guidelines on horizontal cooperation agreements. [2011] OJ C11/1.
(d)   Guidelines on the application of Article 101 of the Treaty on the Functioning of the European Union to technology transfer agreements [2014] C89, pp 3–50.

In general, block exemptions offer a framework for setting up agreements in the relevant sector. If the relevant block exemption offers too little room for manoeuvre, there always remains a limited possibility of satisfying the criteria for an exemption under Article 101(3) TFEU.[81] The great advantage of block exemptions is obviously their direct application. If an undertaking respects the conditions set out in the block exemption, there is no danger that the Commission, the CMA or a national court will consider that the arrangement is contrary to the competition rules.

   Judges or arbitrators can apply and interpret the criteria of block exemptions. The judge or the arbitrator must not extend the scope of the block exemption to cover arrangements that do not fall under it. Such an extension falls under the legislative

---

[81]   See section 3.5 below.

competence of the Commission. Thus, in cases of doubt in the interpretation of the criteria of a block exemption, the judge must make a reference to the ECJ under Article 267 TFEU.[82] The national court can also ask such questions where the EU rules apply due to a parallel exemption under UK law (see sections 10 and 60 CA 1998). It is clear that this is possible from the case law of the ECJ.[83] Arbitrators cannot ask such questions of the ECJ, however.[84] It is possible that a court may later have to rule upon such an arbitral award or may have to execute it, at which point questions of interpretation could be sent to the ECJ.[85]

Great care must be taken to ensure that the whole arrangement is in conformity with the block exemption. If the arrangement deviates from the conditions of the block exemption on even one point, then it no longer falls under that exemption.[86] If an agreement falls outside the scope of the block exemption this does not mean that it is automatically prohibited. Rather, it simply means that an individual assessment needs to be conducted to determine whether the agreement is prohibited. Arrangements that are thus within the prohibition of Article 101(1) TFEU can only be permitted if they satisfy the criteria under Article 101(3) TFEU.

Block exemptions are not an all-encompassing panacea to save undertakings from the prohibitions of competition law. There are three situations in which careful attention must be paid. First, some block exemptions are only operative if the undertakings connected to the relevant arrangement remain below a certain market share. For example, this is the case under Article 4(2) of Regulation 1217/2010/EC in the field of agreements for research and development: the block exemption is not applicable where the joint market share exceeds 25 per cent. The block exemption for vertical agreements only applies if the parties' market shares do not exceed 30 per cent in the relevant markets.

Secondly, it should be pointed out that block exemptions only exempt conduct from the prohibition of Article 101(1) TFEU. They do not provide relief from the application of the prohibition of the abuse of a dominant position, nor can they do so.[87] It

---

[82] The clarification of the criteria in a block exemption was the subject of the judgment of the ECJ in Case C-234/89 *Delimitis v Henninger Bräu*. See, also, the Commission 'Notice on Cooperation between the Commission and the Courts of EU Member States in the Application of Articles 81 and 82 EC' [2004] OJ C101/54; for further discussion, see Chapter 6 below.

[83] See Case C-28/95 *Leur-Bloem v Inspecteur der Belastingdienst/Ondernemingen Amsterdam 2*. See also Case C-7/97 *Oscar Bronner GmbH v Mediaprint*.

[84] Case 102/81 *Nordsee Deutsche Hochseefischerei GmbH v Reederei Mond Hochseefischerei Nordstern AG & Co KG and Reederei Friedrich Busse Hochseefischerei Nordstern AG & Co KG*.

[85] For an example, see Case C-393/92 *Municipality of Almelo v NV Energiebedrijf IJsselmij*. See further, on the role of the national court in executing an arbitral award, Case C-126/97 *Eco Swiss China Time Ltd v Benetton International NV*.

[86] This does not apply to the sales obligations that breach Art 5 of Reg 330/2010. Also, if these obligations run for more than the five years allowed, then it is only that obligation as to time that is void and not the whole agreement.

[87] In its *TACA* judgment, however, the CFI ruled that if an agreement has been notified then no fine can be imposed: Joined Cases T-191/98 and T-212 to 214/98, *Atlantic Container Line AB and others v Commission* paras 1603–33.

is thus possible that arrangements of undertakings that fall under a block exemption may still fall under the prohibition of the abuse of a dominant position, although this obviously can only occur insofar as the relevant undertaking holds a position of market dominance or is a part of a collective dominant position.[88]

Thirdly, it must be remembered that most block exemptions contain a provision under which the Commission can withdraw the benefit of the block exemption if competition is seriously threatened: on this, see section 3.4.1 above.

3.5 Other Exceptions from Article 101(1) TFEU and the Chapter I Prohibition

3.5.1 Introduction

Alongside the block exemptions discussed above, both UK and EU competition law offer the possibility in individual cases of granting an exemption from the prohibition on restrictions of competition. The relevant provisions in the two systems are section 9 CA 1998 and Article 101(3) TFEU. The criteria for the granting of such exemptions are substantially identical in both systems (although the UK regime refers to 'improving production and distribution' generally, rather than to 'production and distribution of goods' as under Article 101(3) TFEU, thus clearly allowing for the provision of services to be included). Such provisions have formed an essential part of competition law.

With the entry into force of Regulation 1/2003, the Commission's sole right to determine whether an agreement satisfies the Article 101(3) TFEU criteria has been removed. As such, undertakings are no longer under a duty to seek an exemption from the Commission as was the case under Regulation 17.

In view of its limited interpretation of Article 10 of Regulation 1/2003 this discretionary power of the Commission and (to some extent) the CMA is no longer wielded. The Commission and the CMA have taken up a more restrained position now that an important part of such exemptions 'business' is conducted through the national courts. However, it should be noted that the Commission has used its power to impose conditions under Article 9 of Regulation 1/2003 with similar objectives as its powers to grant individual exemptions in the past. Furthermore, the main thrust of its policy is now reflected in the block exemptions. Rather, according to Article 10 of Regulation 1/2003/EC, the Commission will only give an individual exemption or a negative clearance 'where the Community public interest relating to the application of Articles

---

[88] For an example of such a situation, see the judgment of the CFI in Case T-51/89 *Tetrapak Rausing SA v Commission* ('*Tetrapak II*').

101 and 102 TFEU so requires'. That is to say, there must be special circumstances, such as a new kind of agreement or practice in an unfamiliar area,[89] before the Commission will act in this way. The national competition authorities (such as the CMA) will also give an individual exemption or a negative clearance in exceptional circumstances. National courts can now at any time apply Article 101(3) TFEU if, during a proceedings under Article 101 TFEU, Article 101(3) TFEU is relied upon by either of the parties. We will discuss the implications of this development for EU competition law in Chapter 6.3.4 below, while the national law impact will be treated in Chapter 6.3.4 below. Briefly, the current UK position is now as follows:[90]

(a)   the CMA can no longer accept notifications for guidance or decision, but it can still offer informal advice and produce Opinions where novel questions of the application of EU or UK competition law are raised (see Part 7 of OFT 442 for a discussion);

(b)   agreements satisfying the section 9(1) CA 1998 criteria will not be prohibited, and no prior CMA decision to that effect will be required (this is basically equivalent to the direct effect of Article 101(3) TFEU following Regulation 1/2003/EC).

The criteria used in Article 101(3) TFEU (and, indeed, section 9 CA 1998) are broad and leave scope for interpretation as to how they may be satisfied in each individual case.

On the other hand it should be noted that Article 101(3) TFEU is an exception and therefore needs to be interpreted strictly in the sense that the burden is on the parties to show that Article 101(3) TFEU has been satisfied and this (because of the strict interpretation) is a difficult burden to discharge. The broad wording simply means that there is no prescribed manner in which the parties must satisfy Article 101(3) TFEU— the burden of showing that they have done this, however, is high. In this respect, the Commission and NCAs have discretion in determining whether the relevant criteria have been satisfied.

From the outset, the ECJ has stressed that in EU competition law the Commission has a wide discretion in such matters. In the ground-breaking judgment *Consten and Grundig*, the Court ruled that, in exercising its competence under Article 101(3) TFEU, the Commission is usually required to reach a judgement on questions of a complex economic nature.[91] Until not too long ago, the Commission decisions were subject to 'marginal review' by the Courts. This has now changed. There is a trend in the judgments of the GC, which can be seen particularly starkly in the area of merger control—see for example, the judgments in *Airtours*,[92] *Schneider Electric*[93] and *Tetra Laval*[94]—to increase the intensity of judicial review of the Commission's

---

[89]   See Recital 14 of the Preamble to Reg 1/2003/EC.

[90]   See the OFT's Guideline, *Modernisation* (OFT 442), para 3.5 and Pt 11. These changes were effected by the Competition Act 1998 and Other Enactments (Amendment) Regulations 2004 (SI 2004, No 1261), Regs 1 and 4 *juncto* sch 1, ss 2–7, 9 and 26. Their effect was to repeal ss 4, 5, 7, 12–16, 20–24 CA 1998, as well as also repealing s 41 and amending ss 9 and 10 CA 1998 to align with the new EC system.

[91]   Cases 56 and 58/64 *Établissements Consten SARL and Grundig-Verkaufs GmbH v Commission*.

[92]   Case T-342/99 *Airtours plc v Commission*.

[93]   Case T-310/01 *Schneider Electric SA v Commission*.

[94]   Case T-5/02 *Tetra Laval BV v Commission*.

decision making. The approach of the GC in *Tetra Laval* was confirmed by the ECJ on appeal.[95] This stricter approach has become the norm in recent case law.[96]

On this point, the position in the UK would seem to be that, in principle, the CAT has much wider powers when hearing appeals from a CMA decision: an appeal 'on the merits' is provided for in paragraph 3, schedule 8 of the CA 1998 and the CAT's powers include the power to confirm or set aside the CMA decision, to return the matter to the CMA, to impose, vary or revoke any penalty imposed and to grant or to cancel an individual exemption. In practice thus far, however, the CAT has taken care not to act in a heavy-handed way in this field, often preferring to remit cases to the OFT (and now the CMA) rather than substitute its own finding on the matter of law at stake.[97] This is because the CAT has not wished to convert itself from an appellate tribunal into a general court of first instance on such matters.[98]

In spite of the change in the system, some knowledge of the system of individual exemptions under Regulation 17 (and, to a lesser extent, section 9 CA 1998) is necessary to understand the current competition rules. This is because many decisions were taken under the old system of exemptions that provided interpretations of the criteria of Article 101(3) TFEU (and section 9 CA 1998). These sources will continue to have their uses under the new regime of Regulation 1/2003/EC and the amended provisions of the CA 1998. The next section draws upon examples from various individual exemption decisions to explain the operation of the relevant criteria.

3.5.2 The Article 101(3) TFEU and Section 9 CA 1998 Criteria

Arrangements that restrict competition can also play a useful role in the economy; therefore, in both the UK and EU systems there exists the possibility for the provisions of Article 101(1) and the Chapter I prohibition to be declared inapplicable, but only if the economic and social advantages outweigh the negative effect upon competition. The four conditions for an exemption laid down by section 9 CA 1998 and Article 101(3) TFEU aim to make this weighing up of the effects of various arrangements possible. These provisions can only be applied if all four conditions are satisfied. Conversely, if one of the four criteria is not fulfilled an exemption is excluded.

The criteria that must be fulfilled are as follows:

(a)   the arrangement must contribute to the improvement of production or distribution or to the promotion of technical or economic progress;

---

[95] Case C-12/03 P *Tetra Laval BV v Commission*.

[96] The stricter approach is justified by reference to the recognition of the quasi-criminal nature of competition law. see AG Sharpston's Opinion in Case C-272/09 P *KME Germany* (by contrast, however, see Case T-486/11 *Orange Polska*, which came out at the same time, but took a completely different position on the quasi-criminal nature of competition law).

[97] See, eg, *Aberdeen Journals Ltd v DGFT* [2002] CAT 4, [2002] Comp AR 167 and *Freeserve.com plc v DGT* [2003] CAT 5 (although cf *Napp Pharmaceutical Holdings Ltd v DGFT* [2002] CAT 1, [2002] Comp AR 13, [2002] ECC 177 and *Aberdeen Journals Ltd v OFT* [2003] CAT 11, where the penalty was changed, and *IIIB v DGFT* [2001] CAT 4, [2001] Comp AR 62, where the Tribunal held that the one of the rules at issue clearly breached the ch I prohibition).

[98] See *Freeserve.com plc v DGT* [2003] CAT 5, paras 111–13.

(b)   a fair share of the resulting benefit must be enjoyed by consumers;
(c)   the arrangement must not impose any restrictions upon the undertakings concerned that are not indispensable to the achievement of these goals;
(d)   the arrangement must not give the undertakings concerned the possibility of
eliminating competition in respect of a substantial part of the goods or services
in question.

3.5.2.1 Improvement in Production or Distribution, or the Promotion of Technical or Economic Progress

Cartels and other restrictive practices must offer a clear advantage for society if they
are to be tolerated. We are here concerned with an objective advantage. It will not suffice to show that the cartel creates advantages for the parties involved in it.

Production can be improved through agreements on specialisation. Each of the parties concerned concentrates on doing what it is good at. On the basis of this thinking,
the block exemption on specialisation agreements was adopted.[99] Before that Regulation, many individual exemptions were granted on such grounds. Today, specialisation
agreements that fall outside the scope of the Regulation will need to be assessed on a
case-by-case basis. If, following such an assessment, it is concluded that the agreement
in question would fall within the scope of Article 101(1) TFEU, then Article 101(1)
TFEU can only be disapplied if the agreement satisfies the Article 101(3) TFEU
criteria.

Improvements in distribution are a subject covered to some extent by the block
exemption Regulation 330/2010 for vertical agreements.[100] There is also a specific
block exemption for selective distribution agreements in the motor vehicle sector.[101]
The promotion of technical and economic progress is similarly of relevance in various
other block exemptions. Thus, the block exemptions for research and development
(R&D)[102] and for technology transfer (ie, patent and know-how licence agreements)
contain a concrete working-out of this concept. These block exemptions allow those
agreements that make such progress possible. The first of these (on R&D) is only
applicable where the market share of the undertakings concerned does not exceed 25
per cent. Individual exemptions can then be granted where agreements exceed this
market share level. In a similar vein, one can also consider the various joint venture
agreements that have made possible an important technical step forward. A good
example in this area is the Commission Decision in the case of *Pasteur Merieux*.[103]

Pasteur Merieux and Merck were both engaged in work producing and developing vaccines for humans. They set up a subsidiary company that was to focus upon
the development of specific immunologies (ie, vaccines). Both Pasteur Merieux and
Merck also transferred their patents and know-how in the relevant field to the joint
venture undertaking. Through this concentration of patents and know-how, the

---

[99] Reg 1218/2010/EC [2010] OJ L335.
[100] Reg 330/2010 [2010] OJ L 102/52–57.
[101] Reg 461/2010 [2010] L129.
[102] Reg 1217/2010 [2010] OJ L335.
[103] [1994] OJ L309/1.

subsidiary was in a much better position than either of its parents to develop the new vaccine. Furthermore, this transaction led to a situation where a better product could be developed. On this basis, the agreement setting up the joint venture in this way was granted an exemption, although there were obviously other conditions that had to be satisfied.

3.5.2.2 Fair Share of the Resulting Benefit for Consumers

It is of great importance for society that the advantages of any competition-restricting agreements are passed on to consumers. Where technical and economic progress is concerned this will usually rapidly be the case, while the benefits to consumers of improvements in production and distribution are far less (immediately) obvious. The term 'consumers' should be interpreted broadly, and thus should also include buyers at different levels of the distribution chain, in addition to final consumers. These producers must be able to show with reasonable certainty that the advantages of the agreement will be passed on to consumers. Often, competition ensures that this occurs. Examples of benefits to consumers include a better range or quality of products or services offered, the introduction of new products or lower costs resulting in lower prices.

3.5.2.3 The Restriction of Competition Must Be Indispensable

A basic rule of EU law is that all exemption and derogation provisions must be interpreted restrictively. Article 101(3) TFEU and section 9 CA 1998 are also derogating provisions. Thus, the only restrictions of competition that can be accepted are those that are genuinely indispensable for achieving the relevant goal. To put the matter another way: the parties must aim to achieve their goal in such a way that competition is restricted as little as possible. Thus, in a selective distribution system the clause that sales may not be made to those outside the system is accepted as indispensable. Similarly, when setting up a joint venture it is acknowledged as indispensable that the parent undertakings may not compete with the joint venture.

Territorial restrictions, however, will not usually be treated as indispensable under EU competition law. The same goes, for example, for vertical price-setting.

3.5.2.4 No Elimination of Competition

An exemption can only be granted if competition in the relevant market is not eliminated. This is a completely logical condition if one bears in mind the starting point of competition law. It is more difficult, however, to answer the question: how much competition must remain in any given case? Just as is the case when deciding whether or not an undertaking holds a dominant position, a diverse range of factors plays a role here. It is for the parties that seek to rely upon Article 101(3) TFEU to show that their agreement fulfils the four relevant criteria.

3.5.3 The Application of Article 101(3)

Since the enactment of Regulation 1/2003/EC the application of Article 101(3) TFEU is no longer the 'monopoly' of the Commission. It is now up to the parties to an agreement to assess its application. Subsequently national courts or arbiters may have to apply the provision. For their guidance the Commission has adopted its Guidelines.[104]

Further guidance may also be found from cases where the Commission brings infringement procedures. There are cases where the parties involved in infringement procedures will argue that Article 101(3) is applicable thus forcing the Commission to address the issue. A good example is the *Mastercard* case.[105] In this case the Commission had to provide a full Article 101(3) analysis in rebutting the arguments of the parties. The Commission's approach was accepted by the Courts. Another example is the *STIM* case.[106] In this case the Commission found that the restrictions relating to the national territorial limitations were not indispensable. Similarly, it found that the maintenance of the system of national one-stop-shops for the licensing of music rights does not require the presence of national territorial limitations.[107]

3.5.4 Commitments

Article 9 of Regulation 1/2003/EC offers the Commission the possibility of accepting commitments offered by the undertakings concerned where the Commission has indicated its intention to adopt a decision requiring that an infringement be brought to an end.

Under UK law, the CA 1998 provides a similar power for the CMA. This power exists 'where the [CMA] has begun an investigation under section 25 [CA 1998] but has not made a decision (within the meaning given by section 31(2) [CA 1998]' (section 31A CA 1998).[108] This procedure for accepting commitments allows arrangements, which would not otherwise pass muster under the Article 101(1) TFEU or Chapter I prohibition, to nevertheless be declared compatible with Article 101(1) TFEU. Such commitments have a substantive significance. Commitments can be connected both with particular forms of behaviour and with possible structural remedies. Thus, for example, a commitment could be made and accepted that requires that the parties should have access to certain technology.[109]

---

[104] Guidelines on the application of Art 81(3) of the Treaty, 2004 OJ C 101, 97–118.

[105] Case C-382/12 P, *MasterCard and others v Commission*.

[106] Case T-451/08 *STIM*.

[107] The Commission also did a full Art 101(3) analysis in the World Cup Decisions (Cases 33.384 and 36.888) and UEFA Champions League Decision (Case 37.398 respectively), where it analysed collective selling of broadcasting rights and ticket sales. It also analysed the collective purchasing of broadcasting rights under Art 101(3) in the Eurovision case (Case 32.150)—annulled on appeal in Case T-185/00 *M6*.

[108] See ss 31A–E CA 1998 and the OFT's Guideline *Enforcement* (OFT 407), paras 4.1–4.28 and annexe ('The OFT's guidance as to the circumstances in which it may be appropriate to accept commitments').

[109] Commission Decision, *Rockwell/Iveco* [1983] OJ L224/19. Compare the Commission's Decision in the *Microsoft* case (W2000, Comp/C-3/37.792, 24 March 2004).

3.5.5 An Example of an Article 9 of Regulation 1/2003 Decision[110]

The Commission carried out unannounced inspections in the ship classification market in January 2008. In the course of its investigation, the Commission came to the preliminary view that IACS may have reduced the level of competition in the ship classification market, notably by preventing classification societies which are not already members of IACS from joining IACS, from participation in IACS' technical working groups (which develop IACS' technical resolutions that lay down requirements and interpretations to be incorporated into the classification rules and procedures of individual classification societies) and from access to technical background documents relating to IACS' technical resolutions.

To address the Commission's competition concerns, IACS offered the following commitments:

(a)   To set up objective and transparent membership criteria and to apply them in a uniform and non-discriminatory manner. The commitments foresee detailed rules, including clear deadlines, for the different steps of the membership application, suspension and withdrawal procedure.

(b)   To ensure that classification societies which are not members of IACS will nonetheless be able to participate in IACS' technical working groups.

(c)   To put all current and future IACS resolutions and their related technical background documents into the public domain at the same time and in the same way as they are made available to IACS members.

(d)   To set up an independent appeal board to settle possible disputes about access to, suspension or withdrawal of membership of IACS, participation in IACS' technical working groups and access to IACS' resolutions and to their technical background documents.

3.5.6 A Practical Example of an Assessment under Section 9 CA 1998: The OFT's Decision in *Pool Reinsurance Co Ltd*[111]

It is useful to reproduce here an abbreviated version of an OFT Decision (*Pool Reinsurance Co Ltd*), both to illustrate the structure of reasoning applied when taking such decisions and to give a good example of the various factors relevant to the analysis under section 9 CA 1998 and Article 101(3) TFEU.

The case arose as a result of the IRA bombing in St Mary Axe in the City of London in 1992. Following the bombing, reinsurers withdrew their cover of insured terrorist risks for commercial property in mainland Great Britain. As a result, insurance against damage to commercial property caused by an act of terrorism became

---

[110]   The following summary is taken from Press release IP/09/1513 of 14 October 2009. A summary of the decision is published in 2010 OJ C2, pp 5–6.

[111]   OFT Decision No CA98/03/2004 (15 April 2004). The footnotes in the decision are renumbered from the original.

unavailable. In order to deal with the lack of insurance against risks of terrorism, the Reinsurance (Acts of Terrorism) Act 1993 was enacted. Pool Re was set up to act as a reinsurance pool in respect of Terrorism Cover, for all insurers wishing to become a member and which insure commercial property in the United Kingdom, with the UK Government being the insurer of last resort.

On 7 March 2003, the OFT received a request from Pool Re for a decision under the CA 1998 in relation to various Pool Re agreements which were entered into. Pool Re requested: (i) a decision that the notified arrangements are not caught by the Chapter I prohibition or, in the alternative, an individual exemption decision, and (ii) a decision that the notified arrangements do not infringe the Chapter II prohibition.

Under the terms of the agreements, Pool Re members were subject to a series of standard terms. Pool Re adopted a tariff structure[112] based on the geographic location of the risks held by insurers for the calculation of their reinsurance premiums. The Terrorism Cover provided by the members must be subject to the same terms and conditions as the relevant General Cover. Pool Re members were free to set their insurance premiums but the scope of the Terrorism Cover offered by Pool Re members to insureds needed to be at least as wide as that provided to the insurers by Pool Re under the Reinsurance Agreement. As such, the Pool Re agreements limited the terms on which Terrorism Cover was offered by Pool Re members. All members agreed to offer Terrorism Cover in line with the Pool Re terms.

The OFT first assessed whether the creation of a re-insurance pool was, in itself, contrary to the Chapter I prohibition. In reliance on the Commission's decision in *P&I Clubs*, the OFT concluded that the creation of a re-insurance pool was not, as such, anti-competitive because, in the absence of a co-reinsurance pooling arrangement such as Pool Re, insurers would not be able to offer insurance of terrorism risk for commercial properties in the UK at the level required (in terms of insured value). The aim of Pool Re was to 'plug the gap' in the reinsurance market for commercial property by ensuring that coverage was available for all commercial property, at affordable prices.

The OFT, however, continued its analysis to determine whether any of the specific terms of the Pool Re agreements were anti-competitive.

In this respect, the OFT concluded that the obligation that Pool Re members shall not offer insurance of Terrorism Cover, unless such cover attaches to the relevant insurance of General Cover, deprives insureds of their ability to purchase Terrorism Cover on a standalone basis; reduces competition between insurers as to the terms and conditions on which they supply insureds with Terrorism Cover for commercial property; and limits the scope for insurers which are not Pool Re members to offer General Cover.

In addition, the OFT also concluded that two rules that prevented insurers and insureds from selecting against Pool Re prevented, restricted or distorted competition. These rules were the 'cede all business' rule, which required Pool Re members and their group companies to reinsure all of their Terrorism Cover with Pool Re, and the 'all or nothing' rule, which meant that all of the insured properties must be covered by the

---

[112] The simple tariff structure sets out a single rate for 'business interruption' and two rates for 'property damage' (four zones based on GB postal codes are identified to which one of these two rates applies).

Terrorism Cover or none of them (ie, it was not possible to take out Terrorism Cover on only a select number of properties).

The OFT concluded that these two rules were anti-competitive for the following reasons. Concerning the 'cede all business' rule, the OFT considered that this rule amounted to an exclusivity agreement since pool members are under a contractual obligation to reinsure all of their insurance of Terrorism Cover for commercial property with the pool and this may have the effect of foreclosing the market for reinsurance of terrorism cover for commercial property in the UK. Regarding the 'all or nothing' rule, the OFT considered that this rule reduced competition between insurers as to the terms and conditions on which they supply insureds with Terrorism Cover for commercial property and deprives customers of their right to choose which properties to insure against terrorism risks.

Having concluded that the obligation to grant Terrorism Cover in conjunction with General Cover and the no adverse selection rules fell within the scope of the Chapter I prohibition, the OFT went on to examine whether the measures could nevertheless satisfy the cumulative criteria of section 9 CA 1998 (ie, the equivalent of the Article 101(3) TFEU criteria). In this respect, the OFT reasoned as follows:

Exemption criteria

IMPROVING PRODUCTION OR DISTRIBUTION OR PROMOTING TECHNICAL OR ECONOMIC PROGRESS

79. The overall objective of the notified arrangements is to ensure the continued availability of insurance cover for damage and loss which might be caused to commercial property in GB by acts of terrorism. Crucially, in the absence of the Pool Re scheme, it seems unlikely that this type of insurance would be widely available.

80. The contribution of insurance to economic progress has been described as follows: 'Through a reduction or absorption of some of the risks associated with the process of production, insurance enables risk-adverse entrepreneurs to take on entrepreneurial risks to a much greater extent than would be the case in the absence of insurance'.[113]

81. It seems likely that the availability of terrorism cover facilitates investment in business and construction, in particular by reducing the risks attached to such activities. Terrorism cover is in fact generally required to allow insureds to meet requirements set out in loan and tenancy agreements. Responses to the OFT enquiries indicate that terrorism insurance coverage is dictated by finance providers or lessors who insist that 'full' material damage cover is available on all locations to protect their financial interests.

82. In addition, terrorism cover ensures that businesses that suffer from a terrorist event are more likely to be able to survive, thus minimising the adverse economic impact of the event and improving economic progress.

83. Hence economic progress is enhanced by the availability of terrorism cover for commercial property. The OFT has concluded that the Pool Re scheme fulfils the first exemption criterion.

---

[113] Michael Wolgast, 'Global Terrorism and the Insurance Industry: New Challenges and Policy Responses' in Geneva Association, 'Insurance and September 11 One Year After—Impact, Lessons and Unresolved Issues' (2002), 248.

CONSUMERS ALLOWED A FAIR SHARE OF THE RESULTING BENEFIT

84. The Pool Re scheme enables its members to provide Terrorism Cover as part of a policy of general cover for commercial property.

85. The benefit of the notified arrangements to the end-consumer of the Pool Re scheme, i.e. the original insured, is the availability of terrorist coverage which, as indicated above, is often required for insureds to comply with financing or lease provisions as well as being desirable more generally. Terrorism cover is provided by general insurers on an annual basis with almost immediate cancellation conditions. In the absence of Pool Re, this can result in a high degree of volatility as reinsurers react quickly to changes in perceived terrorism threats. Hence, property owners would face price volatility and cover may not be available from one year to the next, which would make financial planning extremely difficult.

86. The existence of Pool Re provides insureds with greater certainty that terrorism cover will be available from one year to the next, at prices that are affordable, irrespective of the location of the property. The end-consumer benefits from the full extent of the reinsurance cover available to the insurer member within the Pool Re scheme as the member is required to provide the same scope of cover to the original insured and cannot exclude liability where Pool Re would otherwise meet the claim. In response to OFT enquiries insureds also indicated that a major benefit of Pool Re was the certainty afforded by the assurance that coverage will remain in place irrespective of whether there is heightened terrorist activity.

87. In light of the above, the OFT has concluded that the scheme fulfils the second exemption criterion.

INDISPENSABILITY OF THE RESTRICTIONS

— The rule requiring Pool Re members to offer Terrorism Cover only in conjunction with General Cover

88. The Pool Re scheme was established to 'plug the gap' that appeared in the market following the exclusion of cover in general policies of liabilities for losses arising from acts of terrorism. By providing Terrorism Cover through a mechanism of write-back into a policy of general cover, the scheme's aim is to restore the scope of general cover for commercial property provided to insureds In this, the rule reflects long-standing market practice: responses by insurers to the OFT enquiries suggest that it is market practice to offer coverage of a particular peril (eg caused by terrorism) alongside primary material damage cover.

89. Pool Re contends that the rule is indispensable to meet the Government's public interest objective of ensuring the widespread availability of Terrorism Cover and encouraging commercial insurers and reinsurers to reassume liability for terrorism risk. The rule has the effect of ensuring that Pool Re members are general insurers with a diverse portfolio of insured properties for which Terrorism Cover is available. To maintain their competitive position general insurers who are not in the Pool Re scheme are attracted to join to ensure that they too can offer their customers a comprehensive coverage of risks.[114] The fact that over 260 insurers have joined Pool Re indicates the strength of this incentive. Pool Re contends that such a wide distribution of the terrorism product could not be achieved through narrower distribution

---

[114] Pool Re members are required to provide Terrorism Cover when requested to do so by any insured already having or requesting General Cover. Although Pool Re members are subject to a 'must write' obligation in relation to Terrorism Cover, they are free to set their insurance premiums and the policy terms and conditions.

channels. Moreover there are benefits that flow from this in terms of the volume of premium and diversification which are important to the sustainability of the pooling arrangements. In addition, the rule results in the widespread familiarisation amongst general insurers with the provision of Terrorism Cover which is an essential component in encouraging commercial capacity back into the market.

90. The OFT accepts the arguments advanced by Pool Re and, for the reasons set out above, has concluded that the rule requiring Pool Re members to offer Terrorism Cover only in conjunction with General Cover satisfies the indispensability criterion.

— The 'no adverse selection' rules

91. With regard to the 'no adverse selection' rules, it is a normal principle of the (re)insurance business that (re)insurers will require or, at the very least, seek to ensure that they are not selected against, i.e. that risks presented to them are not atypical when compared with the assumptions they make in deciding the price and terms on which the business has been accepted.

92. This is particularly the case where the reinsurer is committed, as is Pool Re, to underwrite on standard terms all reinsurance (within a given definition) presented to it. Under a typical reinsurance agreement, a reinsurer would normally ensure a balanced portfolio by setting its reinsurance rate against the risks in the underlying portfolio of the insurer. However, in the case of terrorism risks, modelling is difficult and research suggests that underwriters are so averse to ambiguity that they tend to charge much higher premiums than if the risks were well specified.[115] For this reason, Pool Re has adopted a simple tariff structure for its reinsurance premium which sets out a single rate for 'business interruption' and two rates for 'property damage' (four zones based on GB postal codes are identified to which one of these two rates apply). The objective of this simple tariff structure is to determine, on a uniform basis, the cost of reinsurance objectively by reference to the risks introduced into the pool.

93. Without the 'adverse selection' rules, insurers could 'cherry pick' by choosing only to reinsure those risks that they consider are the greatest. The responses to the OFT enquiries indicate that Pool Re members acknowledge the need for Pool Re to retain a balanced portfolio of risk. They view the 'cede all business' rule as customary where there is a 'treaty arrangement', ie a form of reinsurance coverage in which there is an automatic reinsurance for an insurer against losses that exceed a predetermined loss limit. The 'all or nothing' rule also appears to be necessary to ensure a balanced portfolio of risk for Pool Re, in order to prevent insureds from insuring with Pool Re members only those risks that they consider are the greatest.

94. If insurers and insureds were able to select against Pool Re, this could significantly reduce the number of risks in the pool and threaten the sustainability of the pooling arrangements. It is possible, moreover, that HM Treasury may not be willing to provide unconditional backing to Pool Re in the absence of the 'no adverse selection' rules because the public purse would then be exposed to the risk of cherry picking.[116]

---

[115] Kunreuther, Meszaros, Hogarth and Spranca, 'Ambiguity and Underwriter Decision Process' (1995) 16 *Journal of Economic Behaviour and Organisation* 337–52.
[116] In this regard, see the statements made in the House of Commons debate on the Reinsurance (Acts of Terrorism) Bill, Hansard, 13 May 1993, cols 970–71.

95. In conclusion, if the reinsurer is prepared to carry a 'must write' obligation on standard terms, it must be protected from adverse selection. Hence, the 'no adverse selection' rules appear to be necessary to enable Pool Re to generate a wider and more balanced portfolio of business, capable of funding claims on a sustainable basis. For this reason, the OFT has concluded that the 'no adverse selection' rules satisfy the third exemption criterion.

NO ELIMINATION OF COMPETITION

96. The Pool Re scheme does not eliminate competition in the market for the provision of reinsurance of terrorism cover for commercial property and in the relevant markets at the insurance level, since:

(i)   there is no obligation on any insurer to join Pool Re;

(ii)   membership of Pool Re is open to any corporation authorised by the state in which it is resident to carry on general insurance business and which insures risks situated in GB, and to any underwriter of a Lloyd's syndicate which writes general insurance business in GB;

(iii) Pool Re applies standard non-discriminatory terms to its members for the provision of terrorism reinsurance;

(iv)   Pool Re members may withdraw from the Pool Re scheme on giving a notice period of 90 days and there are no significant barriers to withdrawal from Pool Re;

(v)   Terrorism Cover may be issued by members only for a period not exceeding 12 months;

(vi)   there is evidence that some (re)insurers which are not members of Pool Re participate, to a limited extent, in the market in competition with Pool Re and its members; and

(vii) the levels of the retentions to be borne by each member,[117] which will increase over time, aim at encouraging commercial capacity back into the market. Pool Re has indicated that the increase will be phased in, in order to allow the market to get used to the new arrangements gradually and to allow substantial time for the reinsurance market to re-establish terrorism capacity.

III. DECISION

97. The OFT has concluded that the rule requiring Pool Re members to offer Terrorism Cover only in conjunction with General Cover, the 'cede all business' rule and the 'all or nothing' rule satisfy the exemption criteria set out in section 9 of the Act.

98. On the basis of the facts and for the reasons set out above, the OFT has decided, pursuant to section 14 of the Act, to grant an individual exemption from the Chapter I prohibition in accordance with section 4 of the Act, for a period of three years from the date of this decision. However, the OFT considers that the grounds for exemption are likely to continue to exist after such date, unless there is a significant change in market circumstances, which might lead to the re-emergence of competing terrorism reinsurers at the level of cover required.

99. The OFT has decided also that the remainder of the notified arrangements do not contain restrictions that are likely appreciably to prevent, restrict or distort competition within the meaning of the Chapter I prohibition.'

---

[117] For a definition of the retention, see fn 5 of the original decision.

3.6 Some Important Types of Anti-competitive Agreements

3.6.1 Introduction

For a good understanding of competition law, it is useful to provide a short overview of a number of common types of agreement that may have an impact upon competition. This discussion does not aim to provide comprehensive coverage: for this, the reader must consult the specialist literature. Anti-competitive arrangements can be divided into horizontal and vertical arrangements. Horizontal arrangements concern dealings between parties at the same level of the production and distribution chain, for example an agreement among all bakers, or cement or bicycle dealers. Vertical arrangements are agreements (etc) reached between undertakings at different levels of the production and distribution chain. Agreements between producer and distributor are a good example of this type of arrangement.

Horizontal arrangements are generally seen by competition law as more suspicious than vertical arrangements. This is clear, for example, from the fact that the Commission Notice on Agreements of Minor Importance (that do not fall under the prohibition of Article 101(1) TFEU) sets a market share boundary of 10 per cent for horizontal arrangements and 15 per cent for vertical arrangements.[118]

3.6.2 Horizontal Agreements

Horizontal agreements are agreements between undertakings operating at the same level of the distribution chain (ie, direct competitors). Types of horizontal arrangement that are clearly prohibited by Article 101 and the Chapter I prohibition include agreements on price levels, production and sales quotas, and market-sharing agreements. Such agreements are expressly mentioned in Article 101(1) TFEU. They are almost always caught by its prohibition and will usually lack any possibility of exemption.

Such an agreement was in issue in the *Belasco* case.[119] Belasco is a cooperative association of Belgian manufacturers of bitumin roof coverings. The agreement that the members of Belasco had concluded entered into force on 1 January 1978. This agreement provided, inter alia, for the setting of prices and sales conditions for all deliveries of bitumin roof coverings in Belgium, the setting of a quota to decide how to share out the market among each of the members of the agreements, the production of collective advertising, the study and promotion of measures to standardise and rationalise production and sale, and a prohibition on giving gifts to clients and on selling at a loss. Furthermore, the agreement provided for protective measures to be taken

---

[118] [2001] OJ L368/13.
[119] Case 246/86 *SC Belasco v Commission*.

to face up to competition from various sources: foreign undertakings, newly created undertakings and as a result of the discovery of new replacement products. In taking its decision that this agreement was contrary to Article 101(1) TFEU, the Commission imposed fines on Belasco and its members.[120] The ECJ agreed with the Commission that the agreement breached Article 101(1) TFEU and rejected the application for annulment by Belasco.

In the UK, the OFT's *West Midlands flat-roofing* Decision[121] provides a good illustration of how horizontal agreements may operate to restrict competition. The parties colluded (using both individual agreements and concerted practices) in fixing the prices that they submitted in response to numerous invitations to tender for 'repair, maintenance and improvement' (RMI) services for flat roofs. This collusion was achieved via various means, including forwarding faxes to each other concerning the proposed tender prices, terms and conditions. This prevented the purchaser of those RMI services from generating competition between service providers in the tender process and thus made it unable to receive a competitive price for those services. The OFT examined a mass of evidence relating to many different tendering processes and found that the parties were involved to varying degrees depending upon the contract in question, and imposed fines on all of the perpetrators of varying amounts (save those that fell within its leniency policy, on which see Chapter 6.3.5.1(v) and 6.5 below). The CAT upheld the OFT's findings relating to the two undertakings that chose to appeal the OFT's Decision.[122]

Agreements between direct competitors to exchange information also create serious problems under competition law. In the *Dole* judgment the ECJ held that such conduct constitutes an object restriction of competition.[123] This is because such agreements make it possible for the parties to adopt their commercial behaviour on the basis of this extra information acquired. Without a clear objective justification such agreements are prohibited. An example of such an objective justification was found in the air transport sector: the exchange of commercial information was allowed here within the framework of tariff negotiations.[124] The justification for this was that airline companies 'interline' with each other, ie, they accept tickets issued by each other to allow the use of various connecting flights. But such tickets are only accepted if the official tariff adopted for a particular route has been paid. On cheaper tickets, it is always made clear that there are restrictions upon their use and transferability.

---

[120] [1986] OJ L232/15.

[121] OFT Decision, No CA98/1/2004, 16 March 2004. See also OFT 401, para 3.14 on 'bid-rigging'. See further OFT Decision, No CA98/08/2004, *Agreement between UOP Limited, UK ae Limited, Thermoseal Supplies Ltd, Double Quick Supplyline Ltd and Double Glazing Supplies Ltd to fix and/or maintain prices for desiccant* (8 November 2004), this cartel operated in the double glazing sector.

[122] See *Apex Asphalt and Paving Co. Ltd v OFT* [2005] CAT 4 and *Richard W Price (Roofing Contractors) Ltd v OFT* [2005] CAT 5 (although the CAT did reduce the fine imposed by the OFT in the latter case from £18,000 to £9,000).

[123] Case C-281/13 P, *Dole*. In doing so it confirmed the view of both the Commission and the General Court.

[124] See Art 2 of Reg 1617/93/EEC [1993] OJ L155/18, most recently amended by Reg 1324/2001/EC [2001] OJ L177/56. The regulation is no longer in force. Presently there are no block exemptions in force in this sector. The market conditions in this sector have changed dramatically after the entry into the market of the low cost carriers.

Crisis cartels form a separate category. Such cartels are above all focused upon regulating production capacity. In the past, the Commission has granted an exemption to two crisis cartels. One concerned an agreement between manufacturers of synthetic fibres.[125] This industrial sector had been in a worldwide crisis for many years. In this case, alongside agreements to restrict production capacity there were also agreements on production quotas and measures to protect the participants from competition from outside the EU. Taking the very exceptional circumstances into account, including the fact that many Member States were supporting the industry on a massive scale, after extensive negotiations the Commission approved the agreement. The other example concerned the Dutch *Stichting Baksteen* (Brick Association).[126] It is doubtful that this policy would still be adhered to today.

The assessment of joint ventures is generally much more positive. Many forms of joint venture allow important industrial cooperation that leads to technical and economic progress. It should be noted that nowadays many cases of the creation of a JV will fall under the EU or national merger regime.[127] Only where it falls outside the notification regime of the EUMR will Article 101 TFEU still apply. The example of *Pasteur/Merck* was given above. An important question in the assessment of joint ventures is whether or not the undertakings concerned would each have been in a position to set up the relevant production process on their own. If that is not the case then such joint ventures tend not to fall under the prohibition of Article 101(1) TFEU.

Such a positive assessment of a joint venture agreement can be found in the Commission's Decision in *P&I Clubs*.[128] P&I Clubs (Protection & Indemnity Clubs) are associations of ship owners in maritime transport that offer liability insurance to their members on a not-for-profit basis. These clubs were set up to deal with the potentially enormous damages that can flow from contractual liability and liability to third parties.[129] The associations thus amount to a form of risk sharing. The P&I Clubs and the ship owners together take on the risk of possible damage, so that if a catastrophe were to occur the relevant ship owner would not immediately go bankrupt. Under this regime, the P&I Clubs divided themselves into groups, of which the International Group (IG) of P&I Clubs were by far the most important. The IG is a worldwide association that includes 19 P&I Clubs and insures around 89 per cent of the worldwide maritime fleet and almost 100 per cent of the European fleet.

The problem arose in *P&I Clubs* due to the IG agreement to spread the risk of possible damage over all of its members. Was this agreement to spread the risk a horizontal agreement that impermissibly restricted competition or not? At first sight, such a worldwide conglomerate that organised insurance among its members naturally appears very restrictive. The Commission, however, came to a different conclusion, due to the very particular nature of the insurance and the very large amounts that were at stake.

---

[125] [1984] OJ L207/17: see the discussion by PVU van Grevenstein, 'Restructuring Arrangements under EEC Competition Law' [1985] *European Competition Law Review* 56.

[126] [1994] OJ L131/15.

[127] It should be noted that the decisions cited here all pre-date the latest EUMR Regulation.

[128] Decision 1999/329/EC of the Commission of 12 April 1999 [1999] OJ L125/12.

[129] Damage to ships (the hull, machinery and such like) is usually insured in the normal commercial way.

Such an agreement cannot be considered anti-competitive, at least when the claim sharing is necessary to allow its members to provide a type of insurance that they could not provide alone. Indeed, there cannot be a restriction of competition when the members of the pool are not actual or potential competitors, because they are unable to insure alone the risks covered by the pool. If anything, such claim sharing indeed strengthens competition since it allows several insurers which are not able to provide such cover to pool their resources and create a new player.[130]

If insurance can only be offered if all of the clubs in the world work together, then that insurance association cannot itself be restrictive of competition. If the association were not in existence, then the service itself could not exist, even though competition would be possible. Thus, the existence of the association in fact creates positive effects for competition.

The Commission researched the situation of the P&I Clubs and came to the conclusion that such substantial sums were at stake that they could only be insured through one insurer that provided insurance cover for more than 50 per cent of the global fleet. This conclusion had the logical consequence that there could only ever be one insurer for the risks that IG insured against, so that the agreements concluded within the IG could not restrict competition. Thus, those agreements did not fall within Article 101 TFEU.[131]

It is this reasoning that keeps many joint ventures outside the firing line of Article 101 TFEU.

For example, if a particular medicine can only be developed by cooperation between the three largest medicine producers in the world, then such a cooperation agreement cannot restrict competition. Such medicines would simply not be developed if these undertakings did not work together. If the product or service could be delivered or produced by the individual members of a joint venture, then assuming that the joint venture is not notifiable, the competition authority would need to assess whether the agreement has as its object or effect the distortion or restriction of competition and, if so, whether it could benefit from the Article 101(3) TFEU exemption, or equivalent national provision.

A further example of this can be found in the Decision of the Commission concerning *Elopak*.[132] Odin was a jointly owned company in which Elopak and Metal Box each owned half of the shares. Odin was intended to focus upon the research, development and possible exploitation (such as production and sale) of a new form of packaging. Elopak and Metal Box concluded a number of agreements concerning the functioning and use of their licences by Odin. The hot potato in the application of these agreements was the exclusive right of Odin to exploit the industrial property rights under licence from the parent undertakings, including any improvements and developments of such rights made by Odin. Through this provision, competition between the parent undertakings could be restricted, since in the packaging industry such licences to use packaging and packaging machinery are extremely important.

---

[130] Decision No 1999/329/[1999] OJ L125/12, s 66.
[131] ibid, para 68 (emphasis added).
[132] Decision No 90/410/EEC of the Commission of 13 July 1990 [1990] OJ L209/15.

Since Elopak and Metal Box were not direct competitors of each other, there was no danger in setting up the jointly owned company in itself. Rather, if they were to agree not to compete with each other on the basis of the new know-how developed by Odin, this could be a breach of Article 101 TFEU. In this connection, the Commission considered that cooperation was necessary in this field of research:

> Both Metal Box's and Elopak's experience and resources are necessary to develop the new product which will be a combination of their respective technical and commercial know-how. The technical risks involved in carrying out research for a brand new product yet to be proven and which involves a whole new area of technology for each partner, and the risks involved in developing the new filling, sealing and handling machinery necessary, would realistically preclude each party from attempting to carry out research and development on its own.[133]

Subsequently, the Commission investigated whether or not the conditions under which the cooperation was to take place were necessary or whether they went too far and unjustifiably restricted competition.

> The specific provisions of the agreement must however be examined to ascertain whether such provisions restrict competition within the meaning of Article [101(1)], or whether they are no more than is necessary to ensure the starting up and the proper functioning of the joint venture.[134]

Once again, we see here the same test as employed in the *P&I Clubs* decision: if an agreement is necessary for the development of a product that would not be achieved without the cooperation, there can be no talk of a restriction of competition in relation to that product. The cooperation must not, however, go further than is necessary to achieve that positive effect.[135]

The cooperation agreement between Elopak and Metal Box did not go too far, in the Commission's view. The agreed rights for Odin guaranteed the interests of both parties and left sufficient room for competition.

> As the success of Odin depends on such efforts these provisions will make each of them willing both to bear the financial, technical and commercial risks involved as well as to divulge secret know-how. This is particularly important in this case where a significant proportion of the proprietary know-how involved is not protected by patents. A similar analysis applies to the provisions relating to the non-exclusive licence of improvements which may be granted by Odin to its parents and to those limiting the use of such improvements. These ensure that Odin will be able to exploit exclusively the proprietary know-how in the field of the agreement.[136]

Since the boundaries of necessity had not been overstepped, the Commission came to the conclusion that the agreements did not tend to distort or have as their consequence that competition in the internal market was restricted to an appreciable extent. Thus, the agreements did not fall under Article 101 TFEU.

Because horizontal agreements can quickly lead to competition problems, it is difficult to adopt block exemptions in this area. Unlike in the vertical restraints field, there are no general block exemptions in force for horizontal arrangements. There are two particular

---

[133] ibid, para 24.
[134] ibid, para 29.
[135] Compare the conditions for an individual exemption under Art 81(3) EC.
[136] Decision 90/410/EEC, para 30.

block exemption regulations, however: Regulation 1217/2010/EC for research and development agreements[137] and Regulation 1218/2010/EC for specialisation agreements.[138] The stimulation of R&D is an important part of Commission policy and cooperation in this field is thus encouraged and promoted. The Commission takes a more critical view of cooperation if it leads to the joint exploitation of the results of such R&D.

Specialisation covers the situation where, for example, one car manufacturer produces the engine and another the chassis. Here, too, the Commission generally expects some form of technological progress to flow from such arrangements. Around the same time as these two Regulations were adopted, the Commission also issued Guidelines on acceptable forms of cooperation in horizontal agreements.[139] The Guidelines form a supplement to the two block exemptions but also give an insight into the Commission's general policy towards horizontal agreements. The Guidelines distinguish between those arrangements that almost always fall under the prohibition of Article 101(1) TFEU (as noted above, these include price and market-sharing agreements) and those agreements that may or may not fall thereunder depending on the specific terms of the agreement or the context in which it was made. The latter category includes agreements that fall under the block exemptions, as well as purchasing agreements, commercialisation agreements and agreements concerning standard setting and the environment. According to paragraph 5 of the Guidelines their purpose is:

> …to provide an analytical framework for the most common types of horizontal co-operation agreements; they deal with research and development agreements, production agreements including subcontracting and specialisation agreements, purchasing agreements, commercialisation agreements, standardisation agreements including standard contracts, and information exchange. This framework is primarily based on legal and economic criteria that help to analyse a horizontal co-operation agreement and the context in which it occurs. Economic criteria such as the market power of the parties and other factors relating to the market structure form a key element of the assessment of the market impact likely to be caused by a horizontal co-operation agreement and, therefore, for the assessment under Article 101.

The Guidelines set out criteria that apply to horizontal cooperation agreements concerning both goods and services. Subsequently, these criteria are applied to the agreements mentioned above. The Guidelines discuss examples for each type of agreement.

The CMA has also adopted a number of guidelines, parts of which are relevant to this area under UK competition law.[140]

Alongside these rules, there are also EU block exemption Regulations that apply to particular sectors:

(a) Regulation 267/2010/EC for the insurance sector;
(b) Regulation 169/2009 for road, rail and inland water transport;
(c) Regulation 906/2009 for liner shipping consortia;[141]
(d) Regulation 487/2009 for air transport.[142]

---

[137] [2010] OJ L335/36.
[138] [2010] OJ L335/43.
[139] [2011] OJ C 11/1-72.
[140] See, in particular, *Agreements and Concerted Practices* (OFT 401) (esp paras 3.1–3.27).
[141] See section 3.4.3 above.
[142] [2009] OJ L 148/1. This is the Council regulation authorising the Commission to issue block exemptions. So far the Commission has not adopted such block exemptions.

All of these block exemptions are particularly directed at horizontal arrangements, as is the UK block exemption, which covers public transport ticketing schemes.[143]

3.6.3 Vertical Agreements

3.6.3.1 Introduction

In contrast to horizontal agreements, vertical agreements concern agreements between undertakings that operate at different levels of the supply chain. Vertical agreements allow producers as well as distributors to focus their attention on their core business. If a producer had to develop its own distribution system this may take time and additional investments. Moreover, it may not lead to optimal service to the final consumer. Wholesalers and retailers may be better at serving consumers. Sophisticated products require extensive service for consumers which can often be best provided by specialised dealers. In paragraph 6 of the preamble to the Vertical Block Exemption Regulation the Commission writes: 'Certain types of vertical agreements can improve economic efficiency within a chain of production or distribution by facilitating better coordination between the participating undertakings. In particular, they can lead to a reduction in the transaction and distribution costs of the parties and to an optimisation of their sales and investment levels.'[144]

EU competition law had for a long time been relatively strict and very formalistic in its treatment of vertical arrangements. This approach was closely linked to the fear that such arrangements could lead to markets being partitioned and to the creation and maintenance of territorial restrictions. After the dismantling of the trade barriers put in place by national governments, such as customs rules and quotas, it was necessary to be particularly vigilant in the scrutiny of any possible re-erection of such barriers by private individuals. Gradually the Commission took a less formalistic approach. This was first reflected in Regulation 2790/99, the predecessor of Regulation 330/2010.

This section will first discuss the block exemption set out in Regulation 330/2010 (henceforth the VBER). Subsequently the situation in the UK will be addressed. The following sections will look at some specific vertical agreements, ie agency agreements and franchising agreements.

3.6.3.2 The Block Exemption

The VBER aims to provide a comprehensive system for the exemption of vertical arrangements. The Commission has also published extensive Guidelines, which explain and clarify the application of the Regulation.

The system of the VBER is relatively simple. Article 2 exempts vertical agreements from the prohibition of Article 101(1) TFEU. Article 2(3) exempts intellectual

---

[143] The Competition Act 1998 (Public Transport Ticketing Schemes Block Exemption) Order 2001 (SI 2001, No 319).
[144] Para 107 contains an extensive discussion of these advantages.

property agreements as well provided that those provisions do not constitute the primary object of such agreements and are directly related to the use, sale or resale of goods or services. If such agreements constitute the primary objective they have to be assessed under the block exemption for technology transfer agreements (which is discussed in section 3.6.4). Article 2(4) provides that the VBER does not apply to vertical agreements between competing undertakings.

According to Article 3(1), the block exemption only applies where the market share of the undertakings concerned, the supplier and the buyer, is not above 30 per cent in each of the relevant markets and provided that the agreement in question does not contain any restrictions of competition listed in Articles 4 and 5 of the VBER.

The hardcore restrictions are set out in Article 4 of the VBER. These include price-fixing: setting fixed or minimum prices, whether directly or indirectly is prohibited. The regulation allows the setting of maximum or recommended prices. Further, this category includes the creation of territorial restrictions or limits on delivery to certain customers, restrictions of active and passive sales to end users, as well as restrictions of cross-supplies by members of a selective distribution system. Arrangements that contain such restrictions are void in their entirety.

According to Article 5(1)(a) any direct or indirect non-compete obligation, the duration of which is indefinite or exceeds five years, is prohibited. According to Article 1(d) a '"non-compete obligation" means any direct or indirect obligation causing the buyer not to manufacture, purchase, sell or resell goods or services which compete with the contract goods or services, or any direct or indirect obligation on the buyer to purchase from the supplier, or from another undertaking designated by the supplier, more than 80 per cent of the buyer's total purchases of the contract goods or services.' Article 5(1)(b) excludes any direct or indirect obligation causing the buyer, after termination of the agreement, not to manufacture, purchase, sell or resell goods or services from the benefit of the block exemption. Article 5(1)(c) excludes any direct or indirect obligation causing the members of a selective distribution system not to sell the brands of particular competing suppliers. The clauses listed in Article 5 are prohibited but they do not lead to the entire agreement becoming void part. Article 5(2) provides that the time limitation of five years in Article 5(1)(a) shall not apply where the contract goods or services are sold by the buyer from premises and land owned or leased by the supplier.

It should be noted that the regulation only applies to clauses of agreements that meet the conditions of Article 101(1) TFEU. If not, market shares are not relevant. Therefore, the case law of the ECJ on the applicability of Article 101(1) TFEU remains important. According to the Commission, agreements falling within the scope of the *de minimis* notice are not normally prohibited by Article 101(1) TFEU. Similarly, agency agreements are not prohibited by this prohibition.

The regulation nowhere mentions the internet. However, the Commission in paragraph 52 of the guidelines notes that the internet is a powerful tool to reach a greater number and variety of customers. In view of its importance we reproduce this paragraph in full.

52) In principle, every distributor must be allowed to use the internet to sell products. In general, where a distributor uses a website to sell products that is considered a form of passive selling, since it is a reasonable way to allow customers to reach the distributor. The use of a website may have effects that extend beyond the distributor's own territory and customer

group; however, such effects result from the technology allowing easy access from everywhere. If a customer visits the web site of a distributor and contacts the distributor and if such contact leads to a sale, including delivery, then that is considered passive selling. The same is true if a customer opts to be kept (automatically) informed by the distributor and it leads to a sale. Offering different language options on the website does not, of itself, change the passive character of such selling. The Commission thus regards the following as examples of hardcore restrictions of passive selling given the capability of these restrictions to limit the distributor's access to a greater number and variety of customers:

(a) an agreement that the distributor shall prevent customers located in another territory from viewing its website or shall automatically re-rout its customers to the manufacturer's or other distributors' websites. This does not exclude an agreement that the distributor's website shall also offer a number of links to websites of other distributors and/or the supplier;

(b) an agreement that the distributor shall terminate consumers' transactions over the internet once their credit card data reveal an address that is not within the distributor's territory;

(c) an agreement that the distributor shall limit its proportion of overall sales made over the internet. This does not exclude the supplier requiring, without limiting the online sales of the distributor, that the buyer sells at least a certain absolute amount (in value or volume) of the products offline to ensure an efficient operation of its brick and mortar shop (physical point of sales), nor does it preclude the supplier from making sure that the online activity of the distributor remains consistent with the supplier's distribution model (see paragraphs (54) and (56)). This absolute amount of required offline sales can be the same for all buyers, or determined individually for each buyer on the basis of objective criteria, such as the buyer's size in the network or its geographic location;

(d) an agreement that the distributor shall pay a higher price for products intended to be resold by the distributor online than for products intended to be resold offline. This does not exclude the supplier agreeing with the buyer a fixed fee (that is, not a variable fee where the sum increases with the realised offline turnover as this would amount indirectly to dual pricing) to support the latter's offline or online sales efforts.

53) A restriction on the use of the internet by distributors that are party to the agreement is compatible with the Block Exemption Regulation to the extent that promotion on the internet or use of the internet would lead to active selling into, for instance, other distributors' exclusive territories or customer groups. The Commission considers online advertisement specifically addressed to certain customers as a form of active selling to those customers. For instance, territory-based banners on third party websites are a form of active sales into the territory where these banners are shown. In general, efforts to be found specifically in a certain territory or by a certain customer group is active selling into that territory or to that customer group. For instance, paying a search engine or online advertisement provider to have advertisements displayed specifically to users in a particular territory is active selling into that territory.

3.6.3.3 UK Law

Under UK competition law, section 50(1) CA 1998 gives the Secretary of State a power to exclude vertical agreements from the Chapter I prohibition. Following the adoption of Regulation 1/2003, however, it was considered expedient to align national UK competition law with the EU law system. As such, previous statutory instruments were repealed and the position is now that vertical agreements that affect trade between Member States are subject to Article 101 including, when applicable, the VBER. Agreements that do not affect trade between Member States are subject to the Chapter I prohibition, which is interpreted consistently with the case law of the EU Courts according to section 60(2) of the CA 1998, and the EU block exemption by virtue of section 10 of the CA 1998 which provides for parallel exemption. Consequently, many agreements are exempt from both EU and UK law, and there is no need for the UK to adopt a block exemption of its own for vertical agreements.[145] The CMA has adopted the OFT's Guidance on Vertical agreements, which discusses the application of Articles 101 and 102 TFEU and the Chapter I and Chapter II prohibitions to vertical agreements.[146]

3.6.3.4 Some Specific Forms of Vertical Agreements

The Commission Guidelines discuss several common vertical agreements. Some of them are discussed in this section.

Agency agreements are normally compatible with the competition rules:[147]

> An agent is a legal or physical person vested with the power to negotiate and/or conclude contracts on behalf of another person (the principal), either in the agent's own name or in the name of the principal, for the: purchase of goods or services by the principal, or sale of goods or services supplied by the principal. The determining factor in defining an agency agreement for the application of Article 101(1) is the financial or commercial risk borne by the agent in relation to the activities for which it has been appointed as an agent by the principal.[148]

Where the requirements are met, the principal can direct the commercial actions of the agent including, for example, setting resale prices—something that could not be done under a normal supplier/distributor agreement due to the resale price maintenance (RPM) rules—see the discussion above of Article 4(a) of the VBER.

An important category of vertical agreement is *selective distribution*. Here, the supplier selects retailers on the basis of certain criteria. If these criteria only demand that certain qualitative requirements are satisfied (such as the availability of attractive shop premises, trained staff and suchlike) then they will not breach Article 101(1) TFEU

---

[145] It is worth noting that vertical integration or vertical agreements may be investigated under the market investigation provisions in the Enterprise Act 2002. A market investigation might be appropriate, for example:

- where vertical agreements are prevalent in a market and have the effect of preventing the entry of new competitors (see, eg, the CMA's investigation into Private motor insurance (Private motor insurance market investigation, Final report, 24 September 2014)); or
- where vertical integration by a single undertaking may foreclose competitors and add to entry barriers within an industry (see, eg, the Monopolies and Mergers Commission's investigation into the Supply of Beer 'The Supply of Beer—A Report on the Supply of Beer for Retail Sale in the United Kingdom by Monopolies and Mergers Commission [Cm 651]').

[146] Vertical agreements and restraints (OFT Guideline 419).
[147] See paras 12–21 of the guidelines.
[148] See paras 12 and 13 of the guidelines.

at all, according to the case law of the ECJ.[149] Other criteria, particularly quantitative requirements (such as demanding a certain minimum turnover in the products in question or the holding of a minimum level of stocks of the product), can fall under the prohibition of Article 101(1) TFEU.[150] They will, however, benefit from the VBER provided that the relevant criteria are met (ie, less than 30 per cent market share on the relevant markets and that the agreement does not contain any hardcore restrictions or restrictions covered by Article 5 of the VBER).

Franchising is another important form of distribution, which operates by exploiting a particular product (and/or service) formula. The franchisee uses the name and the know-how of the franchisor. One of the best-known examples is McDonalds. The parent company gives the independent undertakings a franchise—a sort of licence—for the operation of a hamburger restaurant. This is accompanied by a duty to take supplies of certain basic products (such as the meat for the hamburgers and the potatoes for the French fries) from McDonalds. It must be possible to source goods that are not essential to the McDonalds formula (such as the napkins) from suppliers other than McDonalds. Further, the franchisee must comply with a certain formula in running the operation. Recommended or maximum prices are permitted, but fixed or minimum prices are not. The VBER also covers franchising. The provisions of Article 5(2) and (3) allow restrictions that are common in franchise contracts.

Export bans are prohibited under Article 4(b) of the VBER.[151] They are the classic examples of restrictions that are targeted by the prohibition of Article 101 TFEU. Thus it was no surprise that the Commission singled this practice out for one of its first decisions in the *Consten-Grundig* case.[152] Thereafter, backed by the Court, the Commission was able to develop its policy for vertical agreements. There are many examples of such cases in the practice of the Commission. In the *Nintendo* case the Commission imposed a fine of €167,8 million on the Japanese video games maker for preventing parallel trade of video games compatible with its consoles.[153] In the *GlaxoSmithKline* case the Commission condemned the dual pricing system for drugs as an indirect export ban and a by object restriction. Upon appeal the GC disagreed with the Commission holding that the system was not a by object restriction.[154] The ECJ overruled the GC applying its traditional approach thus finding for the Commission.[155]

3.6.3.5 Agreements Not Covered by the Block Exemption

Agreements between parties with market shares above 30 per cent do not automatically lead to the presumption that they cannot be exempted. Such agreements, if they are caught by Article 101(1) TFEU may, nevertheless, qualify for an exemption under

---

[149] See, eg, Case 26/76 *Metro SB-Großmärkte GmbH & Co KG v Commission (Metro I)*.
[150] See, eg, the Commission Decision in *Parfums Givenchy* [1992] OJ L236/11 for a good illustration of the Commission's practice, prior to the advent of Reg 2790/1999/EC.
[151] See para 50 of the Guidelines.
[152] Case 56 and 58/64.
[153] [2003] OJ L255/13.
[154] Case T-168/01 *GlaxoSmithKline v Commission*.
[155] Case C-501/06P *GlaxoSmithKline v Commission*.

Article 101(3) TFEU. Such was the view of the Dutch Competition authority (NMa) in the case of distribution agreements concluded by Heineken with its distributors.[156] Heineken had a market share approximately 60 per cent in the Netherlands and thus could not benefit from the exemption under Regulation 2790/99 (the predecessor of Regulation 330/2010). Nor could Heineken claim the presumption of validity for vertical agreements without 'hardcore' restrictions according to the guidelines. Nevertheless, Heineken's agreements did not, according to the NMa, infringe Article 101(1) TFEU. The contracts were all concluded for a short term and could be terminated upon two months' notice. Furthermore, a survey of the market showed that Heineken's competitors experienced no difficulties concluding contracts with the publicans notwithstanding the Heineken contracts.[157] In other words the market was contestable. Thus the fact that an undertaking has a market share of more than 50 per cent does not automatically lead to a prohibition of such vertical agreements.

The Commission provides a comprehensive analytical framework for answering the question whether an agreement that does not come within the scope of the block exemption can benefit from the exemption of Article 101(3) TFEU in paragraphs 96 et seq of the Guidelines. Paragraph 111 provides the following guidance:

> In assessing cases above the market share threshold of 30%, the Commission will undertake a full competition analysis. The following factors are particularly relevant to establish whether a vertical agreement brings about an appreciable restriction of competition under Article 101(1):

(a)   nature of the agreement;
(b)   market position of the parties;
(c)   market position of competitors;
(d)   market position of buyers of the contract products;
(e)   entry barriers;
(f)   maturity of the market;
(g)   level of trade;
(h)   nature of the product;
(i)   other factors.

The Commission Guidelines under point (6) note that:

> For most vertical restraints, competition concerns can only arise if there is insufficient competition at one or more levels of trade, that is, if there is some degree of market power at the level of the supplier or the buyer or at both levels.

Furthermore vertical restraints only lead to competition issues when there is insufficient interbrand competition. Restrictions of intra-brand competition do not normally lead to competition concerns. Intra-brand competition refers to sales of one product by different retailers, eg, the sales of Sony Playstation video game consoles by different department stores. Interbrand competition occurs when two producers offer similar products, eg, McDonalds and Burger King.

---

[156] Decision NMa nr. 2036, 28 May 2002. See RBB brief 04: 'Procompetitive exclusive supply agreements: How refreshing'.
[157] The NMa refused to grant the individual exemption because it was of the opinion that prohibition of the Dutch equivalent of Art 101(1) did not apply.

3.6.4 Agreements Concerning Intellectual Property (IP) Rights

An important category of agreements that can restrict competition consists of the various forms of agreements concerning intellectual property rights.

From the formative days of EU competition law, it has been debated whether or not agreements concerning intellectual property rights could be subject to the prohibition on agreements restricting competition. The same issue has also arisen in connection with the analysis of possible abuses of a dominant position (discussed in Chapter 4). The issue has arisen because IP rights can be seen as monopoly positions. In the early case of *Consten and Grundig*,[158] the ECJ ruled that (what are now) Articles 36[159] and 345[160] TFEU did not exclude the influence of EU law over the exercise of national industrial property rights (including intellectual property). In a series of subsequent judgments, the ECJ has developed and expanded upon the consequences of this basic proposition. In summary, this later case law comes down to the position that the *existence* of national industrial property rights is protected by Article 36 TFEU, but the *exercise* of those rights may be subject to certain limitations under EU law. The exemption granted by Article 36 TFEU only holds for the protection of the 'specific subject matter' of the relevant right—ie, the right to bring the discovery, the (trade)mark, etc to the market first (eg, via licences). Once the product has been put on the market with the permission of the right-holder, that right is thereby exhausted. Further restrictions upon (for our purposes) competition are then no longer tolerated. This prohibition on further restrictions holds good against national legislation as well as against agreements to transfer licences and trademark rights. The ECJ's judgment in *Windsurfing International*[161] is often seen as the key decision in this area.

Windsurfing International, the owner of a brand of rig for use with sailboards (to form the necessary equipment for windsurfing), obliged its licensees to sell that rig only in combination with sailboards that had been approved by Windsurfing International. In order to understand the effect of this clause it is important to know that Windsurfing International had a patent on the rig but not on the board. This clause enabled Windsurfing International to force its users of the patent to buy its board as well. The Commission and the ECJ both found this clause to be in contravention of the prohibition on anti-competitive agreements.[162]

Regulation 316/2014 the Technology Transfer Block Exemption Regulation (TTBER) provides a block exemption for agreements concerning the transfer of technology.[163] Article 1(1)(b) TTBER mentions the following technology: patents, utility models,

---

[158]   Joined Cases 56 and 58/64, *Établissements Consten SARL and Grundig-Verkaufs-GmbH v Commission*.

[159]   This Article provides for exceptions from the prohibition on quantitative restrictions upon the free movement of goods and any measures having an effect equivalent to such restrictions, insofar as those restrictions can be justified upon the ground of (inter alia) the protection of intellectual property rights.

[160]   This Article leaves the Member States free to regulate national systems of property rights.

[161]   Case 193/83 *Windsurfing International Inc v Commission*.

[162]   Because there was no evidence that Windsurfing's approval of such boards was granted according to any objective criteria that concerned the rig or the board; rather, the ECJ held that Windsurfing's real interest was held to lie 'in ensuring that there was sufficient product differentiation between its licensee's sailboards to cover the widest possible spectrum of market demand' (ibid, para 49).

[163]   [2014] OJ L93/17.

designs, topographies of semiconductor products, protection certificates for medicinal products and breeders' rights. Licensing means that the owner of such rights allows another person, usually an undertaking, to use the technology for the production of certain goods. The TTBER follows the model of the VBER. In other words, technology transfer agreements are in principle allowed, so long as the market share of the undertakings concerned does not exceed 20 per cent if they are competitors or 30 per cent if they are not. So-called 'hardcore' restrictions are not permitted. There are two lists of such restrictions, depending upon whether or not the parties are competitors.

The TTBER makes a distinction between restrictions that are agreed between competitors and those between undertakings that do not compete. For that the first category, Article 4(1) TTBER prohibits:

(a)   the restriction of a party's ability to determine its prices when selling products to third parties;
(b)   the limitation of output;
(c)   the allocation of markets or customers;
(d)   the restriction of the licensee's ability to exploit its own technology rights or the restriction of the ability of any of the parties to the agreement to carry out research and development, unless such restriction is indispensable to prevent the disclosure of the licensed know-how to third parties.

Article 4(2) lists the hardcore restrictions for licensing between non-competitors:

(a)   the restriction of a party's ability to determine its prices;
(b)   the restriction of the territory into which, or of the customers to whom, the licensee may passively sell the contract products;
(c)   the restriction of active or passive sales to end users by a licensee which is a member of a selective distribution system.

There is also a list of restrictions that are not automatically exempted and must therefore be tested under Article 101(3) TFEU. The Commission has also issued Guidelines to clarify the operation of the rules in the TTBER.[164]

---

[164] 'Guidelines on the application of Article 81 of the EC Treaty to technology transfer agreements' [2014] OJ C89/30.

4

The Prohibition of the Abuse of Positions of Dominance

4.1 Introduction

> What we are trying to do is use our server control to do new protocols and lock out Sun and Oracle specifically ... Now I don't know if we'll get to that or not, but that's what we are trying to do.

This the stuff competition lawyers' dreams are made of! It is an extract from a speech given by Mr Bill Gates, founder and former CEO and Chairman of Microsoft, in February 1997. It is quoted in the *Microsoft* judgment in the section that discusses Microsoft's plea for a substantial reduction of a fine of nearly €500 million.[1]

In both UK and European competition law, the abuse of a position of economic dominance (hereafter referred to as a 'dominant position') is prohibited. Simply holding such a position of dominance, however, is not prohibited. Nevertheless, it is wise to note at the outset that undertakings that hold such a dominant position find themselves in a kind of 'glass house' as far as competition law is concerned. As will become clear in the course of this chapter, the behaviour of undertakings with a dominant position is judged more strictly than that of undertakings that do not hold such economic power. The reason for this is that competition law seeks above all else to ensure that opportunities remain for competition on the relevant market. The prohibition on the abuse of a dominant position is not intended to operate as a punishment for an undertaking that has acquired that position by good and effective commercial practice and management. As was famously stated in the *Alcoa* case[2] in the United States, dominance resulting from 'superior foresight, skill and industry' is not the target of competition law. The word 'abuse', therefore, should be understood as relating to behaviour that: (i) has an influence upon the structure of the market, by which

---

[1] Case T-201/04, *Microsoft v Commission*.
[2] *United States v Aluminium Co. of America* 148 F.2d 416 (2nd Cir 1945), at 430 (*per* Judge Learned Hand).

the opportunities for other undertakings to compete on that market are reduced; and (ii) consists of the use of other devices than the performance of undertakings under normal conditions of competition.[3]

In this chapter, we will first discuss the Communication from the Commission: Guidance on its enforcement priorities in applying Article 82 of the EC Treaty (now Article 102 TFEU, hereinafter referred to as the Article 102 Enforcement Priorities) to abusive exclusionary conduct by dominant undertakings.[4] Thereafter, we will present and discuss the various general concepts relating to abuses of a dominant position. We will then move on to analyse the specific elements of this prohibition: positions of market power, the concept of 'abuse' and its various forms. After these elements have been treated, the chapter concludes by examining both the concept of 'objective justification' (which can provide an exemption for certain forms of behaviour and practice that would otherwise fall foul of the prohibition), the possible overlaps between Articles 101 and 102 TFEU and their consequences.

4.1.1 The Article 102 Enforcement Priorities

After a long gestation period and many years of discussion among practitioners and academics about the proper scope of Article 102 TFEU, the Commission has published its Article 102 Enforcement Priorities.[5] For a long time, the case law and decisional practice of the Union courts and the Commission have been criticised for having become inconsistent and unclear (eg, lacking a sense of possible business justifications for certain practices and failing to establish that deleterious effects would actually flow from allegedly 'abusive' conduct), making the job of advising companies on their commercial strategies increasingly difficult for practitioners.[6] The criticism was that the case law as well as the Commission's decisional practice did not incorporate an economics based approach—sometimes also referred to as an effects based approach. This led critics to claim that EU competition law protected competitors instead of competition.[7] The high profile Commission decisions in the *Microsoft* and

---

[3] Case 85/76 *Hoffmann-La Roche & Co AG v Commission*, which concerned loyalty rebates. See further section 4.2.4 below.

[4] [2009] OJ C 45/7–20.

[5] Communication from the Commission—Guidance on the Commission's enforcement priorities in applying Art 82 of the EC Treaty to abusive exclusionary conduct by dominant undertakings. [2009] OJC 45/7—20. See for a discussion of this document in Faull and Nickpay, *The EU Law on Competition*, 3rd edn (Oxford, Oxford University Press, 2014) 351–355.

[6] See B Sher, 'The Last of the Steam-powered Trains: Modernising Article 82' (2004) *European Competition Law Review* 243, M Furse, 'On a Darkling Plain: the Confused Alarms of Article 82 EC' (2004) *European Competition Law Review* 317 and T Eilmansberger, 'How to Distinguish Good from Bad Competition under Article 82 EC: In Search of Clearer and More Coherent Standards for Anti-competitive Abuses' (2005) 42 *Common Market Law Review* 129. For a brief summary, see R Whish and D Bailey, *Competition Law*, 7th edn (London, LexisNexis Butterworths, 2012) 175. For the developments post Enforcement priorities see P Ibanez Colom, '"Beyond the More Economics-based Approach": A Legal Perspective on Art 102 TFEU Case Law' (2016) 53 *Common Market Law Review* 709–740.

[7] See, eg, Eleanor M Fox, 'Abuse of Dominance and Monopolization: How to Protect Competition without Protecting Competitors', in *European Competition Law Annual: 2003 Fordham Corporate Law Institute Annual Proceedings*. The Commission acknowledges this criticism, indirectly, in para 6.

Intel cases,[8] which were originally initiated following complaints from competitors, resulted in the imposition of fines of nearly €500 million and €1.06 billion respectively, further fuelling the debate.

Greater clarity on the application of Article 102 TFEU is important particularly in the light of the consequences for the application and enforcement of Article 102 TFEU by national courts and national competition authorities. Further, in the UK, by virtue of section 60 CA 1998 and the link between the UK's national competition regime and with that of the EU (on which see Chapter 2.2.1 above), any such statements by the Commission concerning the application of Article 102 TFEU are of great significance for the development of the UK's own system of competition law. We will refer to the Article 102 Enforcement Priorities in this chapter wherever appropriate. There is, however, one general point about the Enforcement Priorities that should be noted here.

It is important to stress, that the Article 102 Enforcement Priorities is not a statement of law. The Commission does not have a mandate for defining the law under Article 102 TFEU. There is no authorisation to enact such rules as there is for issuing block exemptions under Regulation 19/65.[9] It is for the EU Courts to explain and define the rules.[10] Rather, the Article 102 Enforcement Priorities are a framework, which identifies the types of situations that the Commission is most likely to consider constitute abuses of Article 102 TFEU and that it will, therefore, treat as a priority in terms of enforcement. When formulating the Article 102 Enforcement Priorities, the Commission's focus was on identifying the types of conduct that are most harmful to consumers. At the same time the EU courts do not seem to feel constrained by the Article 102 Enforcement Priorities and continue to apply their own case law, as can be gleaned from the *Tomra* judgments.[11]

4.2 The Prohibition of the Abuse of a Dominant Position

4.2.1 Introduction

Article 102 TFEU provides:

Any abuse by one or more undertakings of a dominant position within the internal market or in a substantial part of it shall be prohibited as incompatible with the internal. market in so far as it may affect trade between Member States.

---

[8] Case COMP/C-3/37.792 confirmed in case T-201/04, *Microsoft v Commission*, (not appealed) and Case COMP/C-3/37.990 confirmed in Case T-286/09, *Intel v Commission*. Appeal before the ECJ, C-413/14 P.

[9] OJ 1965, L 36/533 as amended by Reg 1215/1999, OJ 1999, L 148/1.

[10] This was confirmed in Case C-360/09 *Pfleiderer*, paras 21–24.

[11] T-155/06 and C-549/10 P *Tomra Systems ASA and Others v Commission*.

Such abuse may, in particular, consist in:

(a) directly or indirectly imposing unfair purchase or selling prices or other unfair trading conditions;
(b) limiting production, markets or technical development to the prejudice of consumers;
(c) applying dissimilar conditions to equivalent transactions with other trading parties, thereby placing them at a competitive disadvantage;
(d) making the conclusion of contracts subject to acceptance by the other parties of supplementary obligations which, by their nature or according to commercial usage, have no connection with the subject of such contracts.

The equivalent provision under UK law is contained in Section 18 CA 1998 (known as 'the Chapter II prohibition'), which provides that:

(1) Subject to section 19,[12] any conduct on the part of one or more undertakings which amounts to the abuse of a dominant position in a market is prohibited if it may affect trade within the United Kingdom.
(2) Conduct may, in particular, constitute such an abuse if it consists in—
   (a) directly, or indirectly imposing unfair purchase or selling prices or other unfair trading conditions;
   (b) limiting production, markets or technical development to the prejudice of consumers;
   (c) applying dissimilar conditions to equivalent transactions with other trading parties, thereby placing them at a competitive disadvantage;
   (d) making the conclusion of contracts subject to acceptance by the other parties of supplementary obligations which, by their nature or according to commercial usage, have no connection with the subject of the contracts.

(3) In this section—

'dominant position' means a dominant position within the United Kingdom; and 'the United Kingdom' means the United Kingdom or any part of it.

(4) The prohibition imposed by subsection (1) is referred to in this Act as 'the Chapter II prohibition.'

It is clear that these provisions are largely identical in their wording and scope. From them, it is also clear that the prohibition applies only if the following conditions are satisfied:

(i) there has been some relevant conduct by one or more undertakings (see section 4.2.3 below as to the issue of collective dominance);
(ii) a position of *dominance* (market power) is held (see section 4.2.2 below);
(iii) *abuse* of that dominant position has taken place (see section 4.2.4 below).

Finally, it is important to note that Article 3(2) of Regulation 1/2003 lays down that:

Member States shall not under this Regulation be precluded from adopting and applying on their territory stricter national laws which prohibit or sanction unilateral conduct engaged in by undertakings.

---

[12] Section 19 details those cases excluded from the Ch II prohibition, which include mergers and concentrations (see sch 1 CA 1998) and other general exclusions (see sch 3, including, eg, planning obligations (para 1), EEA Regulated Markets (para 3) and services of general economic interest (para 4).

As noted in Chapter 2.2.2.2 above, this provision gives the UK the competence to adopt stricter national competition laws than those found in the TFEU. An example of unilateral behaviour that is caught under UK law that could be subject to stricter treatment than under Article 102 TFEU is the possibility for the CMA to take action under the market investigation provisions of the Enterprise Act 2002.

As with all competition law, an effect upon competition and upon trade (either within the UK[13] or between Member States, for UK and EU law respectively) must also be shown for the prohibition on the abuse of a dominant position to apply. These also apply in relation to the prohibition on anti-competitive agreements and arrangements—these matters have been discussed in Chapter 3 (see Chapter 3.2.5). These requirements will usually be satisfied as a matter of course under Article 102 TFEU if it can be established that the undertaking concerned holds a dominant position on the EU market or a substantial part thereof. The question under EU law of whether or not there is an effect on inter-Member State trade falls analytically to be considered together with the delimitation of the relevant geographic market (on which see Chapter 1.3.2.2 above). This geographic market analysis will therefore often be decisive of the jurisdictional question whether or not a particular case falls under the Chapter II prohibition or that of Article 102 TFEU.[14] However, as a result of the introduction of the Chapter II prohibition in substantially identical terms to those of Article 102 TFEU and the advent of Regulation 1/2003 (which empowers National Competition Authorities (NCAs) to enforce EU competition law), drawing the jurisdictional dividing line in such matters is unlikely to be of great significance in the vast majority of cases.[15]

While discussing the criterion of an effect upon trade, it should be noted that there is an important difference between the text of section 18 CA 1998 and Article 102 TFEU: the former concerns a dominant position within the UK or a part thereof (section 18(3)) while the latter refers to a dominant position within the internal market or substantial part thereof. Under EU law, a substantial part of the internal market can consist of a national market or even a part thereof, where that part is important from the perspective of the EU.

---

[13] As the case law in the UK currently stands, there is no requirement under UK competition law to show that any effect upon trade within the UK is appreciable: see *Aberdeen Journals Ltd v OFT (No 2)* [2003] CAT 11, paras 459–62. The CAT's reasoning in Aberdeen Journals was that the appreciability criterion was required under EU law so as to distinguish the scope of EU law from that of domestic competition law. Such justification was not required under domestic law and, as such, there was no need to read the appreciability criterion into UK competition law. It should be noted, however, that the High Court has expressed 'considerable misgivings' on the correctness of this position in a number of subsequent cases: see *P&S Amusements v Valley House Leisure* [2006] EWHC 1510 (Ch), paras 21, 22 and 34; and *Pirtek v Joinplace* [2010] EWHC 1641 (Ch), paras 61–67.

[14] For a rare case where it was held that the conduct of an undertaking did not have an effect upon trade between Member States, see Case 22/78 *Hugin Kassaregister AB and Hugin Cash Registers Ltd v Commission*. In this judgment, the ECJ did not go into the issue of the definition of the relevant geographic market, but instead declared straight away that there was no question that the relevant conduct could have an effect upon cross-border trade.

[15] Most UK court judgments applying competition law since the advent of the CA 1998 have explicitly stated that they were not definitively ruling upon whether UK or EU competition law was applicable, but also that this was not important given the substantively identical provisions in play: see, eg, *Hendry v WPBSA* [2001] *Eur LR* 770, [2002] ECC 8.

In its *Michelin*[16] judgment, the ECJ accepted that the Dutch market could amount to a substantial part of the common market, while in the *Merci*[17] case the ECJ agreed that the Port of Genoa also satisfied that criterion. In that regard, the ECJ emphasised the 'volume of traffic in that port and its importance in relation to maritime import and export operations as a whole in the Member State concerned', which justified its finding in the case.[18]

Thus, although the Chapter II prohibition is aimed at the UK geographic market, it can be seen that a degree of overlap is possible between the relevant geographic markets at issue under section 18 CA 1998 and Article 102 TFEU respectively. The example of the Port of Genoa illustrates that in such a case it is possible that both EU and UK competition law may be applicable in an individual case.[19] In the UK context, it is clear that the Ports of Felixstowe and Southampton (the first and second largest container ports in the UK) would each be regarded as a relevant geographic market under both EU and UK competition law.[20] Since the substance of UK and EU competition law is largely identical, this overlap will not usually cause any difficulty. The CMA and UK courts have jurisdiction to apply both sets of competition rules. At worst, problems of overlapping competence could develop between the Commission and the CMA. These problems must be solved by means of the duty of cooperation between the Commission and national competition authorities. Article 11 of Regulation 1/2003 provides the detailed rules for this cooperation. The Commission adopted a Notice on cooperation between national competition authorities and the Commission in handling cases falling within the scope of Articles 85 or 86 of the EC Treaty Such cooperation is also fostered through the European Competition Network discussed in Chapter 8 below.[21] The most important of these duties are that the CMA must keep the Commission informed of any formal investigative measures that it intends to take or has taken (Article 11(3) Regulation 1/2003), and that the CMA must notify the Commission of any proposed formal decision (whether requiring that an infringement be brought to an end, accepting commitments or withdrawing the benefit of a block exemption) 30 days before its formal adoption by the CMA.[22]

The structure of both section 18 CA 1998 and Article 102 TFEU clearly departs from that of the prohibition on anti-competitive agreements laid down in section 2 CA 1998 and Article 101 TFEU. Here, instead of forbidding practices (agreements, concerted practices, etc), it is the *abuse* of a dominant position that is not permitted. Further, there is no mechanism for obtaining exemptions from the prohibition of such abuses: an abuse is always prohibited. The only exception to this proposition is to be found in section 19 in conjunction with schedule 1 CA 1998—which excludes conduct resulting in a merger subject to either the UK or EU merger regime; or schedule 3 CA 1998. While not all of the provisions of schedule 3 CA 1998 apply

---

[16] Case 322/81 *Michelin v Commission*.

[17] Case C-179/90 *Merci convenzionali porto di Genova SpA v Siderurgica Gabrielli SpA*.

[18] ibid, para 15.

[19] Like the UK's legislation, the Italian competition rules are strongly influenced by EU competition law: in Italy, just as under Art 102 TFEU, the abuse of a dominant position is also prohibited.

[20] See further, eg, Commission Decision 98/190/EC *FAG—Flughafen Frankfurt-Main AG* [1998] OJ L72/30, paras 54–58.

[21] See Commission Notice on cooperation within the Network of Competition Authorities, [2004] OJ C 101, 43–53.

[22] See further Chapter 6.9 below.

to the Chapter II prohibition, an undertaking's conduct will be excluded from the Chapter II prohibition if it falls within the scope of the following paragraphs of schedule 3 CA 1998: paragraph 4 (services of general economic interest—see further Chapter 7); paragraph 5 (compliance with legal requirements): paragraph 6 (avoidance of conflict with international obligations); and paragraph 7 (exceptional and compelling reasons of public policy). It is possible to apply for a declaration that the prohibition on such abuses is not applicable to a particular case, as provided for by Article 10 of Regulation 1/2003. The ECJ has ruled that NCAs do not have the power to take such a decision.[23] While there is no specific provision for such a procedure in the UK legislation,[24] there would seem to be nothing to prevent an undertaking going to court and applying for such a declaration under normal administrative law procedures.[25] Equally, it remains open to the CMA to provide confidential informal advice to undertakings and to provide non-statutory opinions 'in specific cases that raise novel or unresolved questions of law'.[26]

Article 102 TFEU, like Article 101 TFEU, has been held to have direct effect and this finding has now been enshrined in Article 6 of Regulation 1/2003/EC. Thus, Article 102 TFEU must be applied by national courts. The same applies to the Chapter II prohibition in the UK. Similarly, the prohibition of Article 102 TFEU/Chapter II CA 1998 must also be applied by arbitrators in arbitration proceedings. As was discussed in Chapter 3.2.1 (above), in the *Eco-Swiss v Benetton* case[27] the ECJ held that national courts were required to ensure that arbitrators applied EU competition law. Where necessary, this required the national court to apply EU competition law if it had not been applied during the arbitration proceedings. In this context it should be noted that the ECJ held in the *Nordsee* judgment that arbitrators were not entitled to refer preliminary questions to the ECJ.[28] Since the *Eco-Swiss* case concerned litigation over Article 101 TFEU, the ECJ did not presume to provide an answer to the question of whether or not a similar duty applied to national courts where an arbitrator failed to apply *national* competition law. In our view, given that the goal of the UK legislation is to secure alignment of the UK system with EU competition law and in the light of the 'governing principles' clause in section 60 CA 1998, it would seem strongly arguable that a similar duty should be incumbent upon national courts where the non-application of UK competition law is concerned.

---

[23] Case C-375/09 *Prezes Urzędu Ochrony Konkurencji i Konsumentów v Tele2 Polska*.

[24] The possibility to notify conduct to the CMA for an assessment of whether or not it was caught by the Ch II prohibition used to exist under s 20 CA 1998, but this was repealed along with the notification system as a whole (by the Competition Act 1998 and Other Enactments (Amendment) Regulations 2004 (SI 2004, No 1261), sch 1, para 9).

[25] This would seem to be the case even in the absence of any clear dispute at the time that a declaration was sought: see, eg, *R v Secretary of State for Health ex p British American Tobacco (Investments) Ltd & Imperial Tobacco Ltd*, where the companies sought judicial review of the 'intention and/or obligation' of the UK government to implement the Tobacco Advertising Directive. For further, purely UK law, examples, see *R (on the application of Rusbridger) v Attorney-General* [2004] 1 AC 357 at [22]–[24] and *R (on the application of Pretty) v Director of Public Prosecutions* [2002] 1 AC 800. For general discussion, see PP Craig, *Administrative Law*, 5th edn (London, Sweet & Maxwell, 2003) 775–77 and Lord Woolf, J Jowell and AP Le Sueur, *De Smith, Woolf & Jowell's Principles of Judicial Review* (London, Sweet & Maxwell, 1999) paras 15-043 and 15-044.

[26] See the OFT Guidance (OFT 442) Modernisation, s 7.

[27] Case C-126/97 *Eco-Swiss China Time Ltd v Benetton International NV*.

[28] Case C-102/81 *Nordsee*.

4.2.2 A Dominant Position

The concept of a 'dominant position' forms the core of the Article 102 TFEU/ Chapter II prohibition. It is closely related to the existence of the possibility for entities to compete on the relevant market.[29] It is important to recognise that the concept of a dominant position does not correspond exactly to that of 'monopoly'. Where a monopoly exists, there will of course be a dominant position; where a company holds 100 per cent of the market there is naturally no competition.[30]

The classic definition of the concept of a dominant position in EU competition law is provided by the judgment of the ECJ in *Hoffmann-La Roche*:

> [A] dominant position ... relates to a position of economic strength enjoyed by an undertaking which enables it to prevent effective competition being maintained on the relevant market by affording it the power to behave to an appreciable extent independently of its competitors, its customer and ultimately of the consumers. Such a position does not preclude some competition, which it does where there is a monopoly or a quasi-monopoly, but enables the undertaking which profits by it, if not to determine, at least to have an appreciable influence on the conditions under which that competition will develop, and in any case to act largely in disregard of it so long as such conduct does not operate to its detriment.[31]

Under UK law, the CMA's guidance on the Assessment of Market Power, indicates that the concept of market power arises where an undertaking does not face effective competitive pressure and can be thought of as the ability profitably to sustain prices above competitive levels or to restrict output or quality below competitive levels.[32] The guidance also draws heavily on EU law, citing the ECJ's ruling in *United Brands*,[33] the ability to 'prevent effective competition being maintained on the relevant market'. The CAT has also adopted virtually identical language in determining the existence of dominance in multiple UK cases.[34] In addition, in its decision in *Cardiff Bus* the OFT (as it was at the time) clarified that market power is a question of degree and that it is not necessary for a finding of dominance that an undertaking has eliminated all opportunity for competition in the market.[35] In *Albion Water*[36] the CAT confirmed that when assessing dominance, it was not for the competition authority to investigate distant or theoretical possibilities that could conceivably be imagined.

As we have discussed in Chapter 1.3.3 above, the market share of the undertaking concerned is the starting point for the analysis of the existence of a dominant position.

---

[29] This is also reflected in the Art 102 Enforcement Priorities of the Commission where paras 9–18 are devoted to a discussion of this issue.

[30] Often, this situation will be due to legislation that reserves a particular market to one operator for other reasons of public policy: see, eg, Case C-189/95 *Criminal proceedings against Franzén*, concerning the Swedish alcohol monopoly. See further Chapter 7.2.1.3 (below) and the references therein.

[31] Case 85/76 *Hoffmann-La Roche & Co AG v Commission*, paras 38 and 39.

[32] OFT Guideline (OFT 415) Assessing Market Power, paras 1.3–1.4.

[33] Case 27/76 *United Brands v Commission*.

[34] See, eg, *Napp Pharmaceutical Holdings Ltd v Director General of Fair Trading* [2002] CAT 1, paras 153–69; *Aberdeen Journals Ltd v Director General of Fair Trading* [2002] CAT 4, paras 86–97 and (after being remitted to the DGFT) *Aberdeen Journals Ltd v OFT (No 2)* [2003] CAT 11, paras 119–22; and *Genzyme Ltd v OFT* [2004] CAT 4, paras 188–89.

[35] OFT decision *Cardiff Bus*, 18 November 2008, paras 5.6–5.7.

[36] *Albion Water v Water Services Regulation Authority* [2006] CAT 36.

As the ECJ stated in the *AKZO* case, the first threshold is a 50 per cent market share.[37] If a company has a market share of over 50 per cent then it is presumed that it holds a dominant position. This is a rebuttable presumption, however. The undertaking concerned can attempt to show, with the help of other factors, that despite its large market share it does not in fact hold a position of dominance on that market. The factors relevant to this analysis will be discussed in the subsequent text in this section. In the context of EU merger control, just such a situation has been held to exist. The merger between Alcatel and Telettra[38] resulted in a market share of more than 80 per cent, but since that market also contained a very strong player that represented almost the whole of the demand for the relevant product, the Commission decided to clear the merger.[39] Meanwhile, in the UK an attempt to make out this claim (in the face of a finding that a 100 per cent market share had been held during most of the infringement period) met with rather less success. In *Genzyme*,[40] the pharmaceutical company appealed against a fine levied by the OFT for various abuses of its dominant position in the market for the drug Cerezyme. The company argued that the immense power held by the National Health Service (NHS) as the monopoly purchaser of the drug meant that any power held by Genzyme was so strongly counterbalanced by the strength of the NHS that Genzyme could not be said to be dominant. After careful assessment of this argument, the CAT rejected Genzyme's assessment, finding that the absence of any real alternative product was such a significant reduction of any buyer power that the NHS might have held it showed that Genzyme *was* dominant in the relevant market.[41]

Where the market share is below 50 per cent, recourse must be had to other factors to assess whether or not the undertaking concerned holds a dominant position. In the case law a great number of such factors have been discussed and applied:

(a)   First, it is important to establish the *market shares* of the undertakings operating on the market and assess how they relate to each other. In assessing the competitive environment on any given market it is of great significance to discover what the market shares of the other players on the market are. If the next largest competitor has a market share of 40 per cent or more, the position of the largest company with a 50 per cent share is naturally far less strong than if the number two company holds only a 4 per cent market share. The CMA considers that it is unlikely (although not impossible) that dominance will be shown to exist

---

[37]   Case C-62/86 *AKZO Chemie BV v Commission*; in the UK, see OFT 415, para 2.12. In the *Kali + Salz* judgment (Case C-68/94), the ECJ seems to have ruled that, in cases of collective dominance, the threshold on this point must be put at 60% market share.

[38]   [1991] OJ L122/48.

[39]   Although the assessment criterion under the Merger Control Regulation is not based upon market share alone (but instead upon whether or not the merger would create an unacceptable impediment to competition—see ch 5, for detailed discussion), this example is an appropriate one to illustrate this point with regard to a dominant position.

[40]   *Genzyme Ltd v OFT* [2004] CAT 4.

[41]   ibid, paras 249–58; and see paras 259–89, where the CAT also gave detailed consideration to possible statutory and other means of constraining Genzyme's market power, and concluded that such mechanisms were ineffective on the facts. See, also, the arguments made by Napp relating to the UK's Pharmaceutical Price Regulation Scheme and its alleged constraint upon Napp's dominance in *Napp Pharmaceutical Holdings Ltd v Director General of Fair Trading* [2002] CAT 1, paras 161–68.

where the allegedly dominant undertaking holds a market share of less than 40 per cent.[42]

(b) A further factor is the extent of the undertaking's *financial resources*. If a company with an extensive share is also a part of a large and financially powerful undertaking, such a company can invest much more easily so as to face up to (and face down) the competition than if the resources at its disposal were far more limited. This is often known as the 'deep pockets' point.[43]

(c) Alongside this, there may also be certain *commercial advantages* in the hands of the undertaking concerned.

    (i) The fact that a company offers a large *product range* may give it a competitive advantage in the market.[44] For many years it was said that Boeing-McDonnell Douglas had an advantage over Airbus Industrie because it offered Jumbo Jets as well as smaller aircraft. For an air transport company it is attractive to be able to source the full range of aircraft needed to run an airline from just one manufacturer: it offers advantages in stocking and ordering spare parts and in the training of pilots. The key point to remember in using this argument is that its persuasiveness is strongly dependent upon the factual situation prevailing in the individual case at hand. In some areas, the wide product or service portfolio may be a key consideration, while in others it may be easy to source the range of products or services from a variety of undertakings with little extra difficulty or cost.[45]

    (ii) Another commercial advantage may be found in the undertaking holding a *well-known mark or brand*. Everyone knows Chiquita bananas and thus they are easy to sell. The same goes for Coca-Cola.

    (iii) The fact that an undertaking is vertically integrated can also offer it certain commercial advantages.[46] The firm United Brands, the owner of the Chiquita banana brand, controls all of the facilities relevant to the production and transportation of bananas, from plantations to the market itself.[47] Similarly, to have a complete network of service centres is an important advantage where the product in questions is technically complicated and in need of regular and careful maintenance.

(d) A dominant position can also arise where *technical advantages* are present. These advantages are usually found in the form of patents, know-how licences

---

[42] DGFT Decision *DSG Retail and others* CA98/3/2001 of 6 April 2001, itself citing the predecessor to OFT 415, para 2.12; and see Pt 4 of OFT 415 for further discussion of market shares and their significance in the context of time factors and barriers to entry, as well as guidance on the calculation of market shares.

[43] OECD Glossary of statistical terms.

[44] Note that the ECJ rejected this argument (rather summarily, it must be said) in Case 85/76 *Hoffmann-La Roche & Co AG v Commission*; however, the Commission later used the point in its *Aérospatiale–Alenia Espace/de Havilland* Decision (Case No IV/M053, 2 October 1991, [1991] OJ L334/42).

[45] ibid.

[46] Vertical integration involves a company setting up and controlling all (or a large proportion) of the resources necessary to bring a product from its creation all the way to delivering the final product to the relevant market. Shell and BP prospect for oil and gas, produce it, transport it, refine it and sell it via their own petrol pumps on garage forecourts. Such companies are not (or are only to a small extent) reliant upon independent distributors to get their products to the customer.

[47] See Case 27/76 *United Brands Co v Commission*, esp paras 69ff.

and copyrights. In this connection, a distinction must be drawn between, on the one hand, situations where the whole product falls under a patent, a know-how licence or a copyright and, on the other hand, the situation in which only a part of the production process falls under such right(s). In the former case, the exclusive right in itself creates a dominant position if the product concerned cannot be replaced by any competing substitute product. Think of a patent on a drug for which there is no effective replacement, such as Zantac.[48] If an alternative does exist, or if the exclusive right covers only a part of the production process, the market position of the right-holder is nevertheless strengthened by virtue of that right.

(e) A dominant position can also come about due to certain specific factual circumstances. An example can be found in the agreements concerning the Formula 1 motor racing championships.[49] These agreements were concluded between the Fédération International de l'Automobile (FIA), Formula 1 Management Ltd (FOM, owned by Mr Bernie Ecclestone, which controls the broadcasting rights concerning the Grand Prix), the Formula 1 teams and the national broadcasting organisations. The FIA is a non-profit-making body consisting of 162 members organised on a national basis and entrusted with the organisation and regulation of motor sports in their respective national territories.

It is clear, by virtue of the Statute of FIA, the International Sporting Code of the FIA and its Appendices, the General Prescriptions applicable to all FIA championships, challenges, trophies and cups as well as the Regulations of FIA International Championships, that the FIA is the central regulatory body for motor sports in the EU. During its investigation, the Commission came to the preliminary view that the FIA's various activities in connection with motor sports[50] formed the relevant markets and that the combination of the FIA's elaborate network of rules and the *de facto* regulatory role that resulted therefrom established the dominant position of the FIA.

In its statement of objections of June 1999, the Commission came to the provisional conclusion that the FIA had a conflict of interests between, on the one hand, its task as the regulatory body for that branch of the sport and, on the other hand, its activities as an organiser of motor races and the claims it made to the television rights regarding those races. The Commission preliminarily considered that it was possible that the FIA had for some time been abusing its dominant position within the meaning of Article 102 TFEU. The Commission took the view that other provisions in the relevant agreements were incompatible with EU competition law. Its objections focused upon the prohibition on Formula 1 teams taking part in competitions that were comparable to Formula 1, the ban on local promoters making available circuits used for Formula 1 for other races

---

[48] A drug for treating and preventing stomach ulcers, which operates by reducing the amount of acid produced by the stomach. There has been much litigation surrounding the scope of the Zantac patent in the USA (see, eg *Glaxo Inc v Novopharm Ltd* 34 USPQ 2d 1565 (Fed Cir, 1993)) and the patent has been an incredible money-earner for its owner over the years.

[49] Commission Notice [2001] OJ C169/5.

[50] These include: the organisation of cross-border motor sport series; the promotion of such series; the certification/licensing of motor car sport events' organisers and participants; the broadcasting rights of the FIA Formula 1 Championship.

which could compete with Formula 1 for a period of 10 years and the prohibition on the television companies broadcasting pictures that competed with those of the Formula 1 races. As a result of the Commission's objections, the parties gave notice that they were prepared to make significant amendments to the agreements. The FIA was to pull back from the commercial side of the operation, so as to protect its independence and neutrality as a regulatory body. So far as the award of FIA-licences to sporting events and participants was concerned, clear and objective criteria were to be adopted that were to be applied in a transparent and non-discriminatory manner. Where those conditions were satisfied, the FIA would not be able to make any objection to the organisation of new events. Also, in the contracts between FOM and the national television companies concerning the broadcasting rights, the sanctions provisions were to be scrapped. In the Commission's view, these amendments offered adequate structural solutions to ensure that the danger of abuse in the future had been limited sufficiently. As a result, the Commission accepted the notified agreements, as amended.

(f)   The presence of statutory monopolies and exclusive rights will automatically create a dominant position. In the *Merci* case (discussed in section 4.2.1 above), the ECJ made it clear that an undertaking that held a statutory monopoly in a substantial part of the market (the Port of Genoa) could be treated as occupying a dominant position. In such a case, an extended analysis of the relevant market is not necessary to establish dominance: it was sufficient to point to the market over which the statutory monopoly operates. 'Special rights', however, do not create a similarly unambiguous indication of the existence of a dominant position. A special right may well secure a favourable position for the undertaking concerned on the relevant market but that advantage is shared with its competitors.[51]

(g)   A final category of the elements that are relevant in establishing the existence of a dominant position consists of supply-side factors. The basic idea here is that if it is difficult to begin to produce a particular product, then the undertakings already in the market hold an advantage. In practice there are a large number of factors that can influence the available supply of products on the market. In the economic literature, these factors are usually known as 'barriers to entry':[52]

(i)   The fact that there are advantages of scale in certain industries forms such a barrier. In the automobile industry, for example, it costs billions to develop a completely new model. The investments that are involved in this process can only be recouped by the sale of a sufficient quantity of cars. If too few are made then the price of each car will be much too high. In most cases this is a definite disadvantage for producers. The only case where it

---

[51] The term 'exclusive rights' is used where only one undertaking is granted the right to operate on a particular market. In the case of 'special rights', however, access to the market is restricted but there is more than one participant. eg, on the UK telecoms market, British Telecom was an exclusive right-holder prior to liberalisation, whereas it may now be viewed as the holder of a special right, alongside a variety of other telecoms undertakings.

[52] For helpful discussion of these factors, see OFT 415 Assessment of Market Power, para 5, which identifies six different types of barrier to entry: sunk costs; poor access to key inputs and distribution outlets; regulation; economies of scale; network effects; exclusionary behaviour, such as predation, margin squeezing and refusals to supply.

can be an advantage is in markets for luxury and thus expensive cars, such as Ferraris: here there is an attractive, but very small, so-called 'niche' market. For most car producers, however, significant production capacity and subsequent turnover will be required to balance the books.

(ii)   Further barriers to entry can be created by very high investment costs. To launch a new aircraft, whether civil or military, demands very high development costs. Only a few very large undertakings are in a position to incur such costs.

(iii)   Patents, a limited number of good locations (eg, location of a sea port on an island), environmental restrictions and legal and technical limitations can also lead to barriers to entry. In the *United Brands* judgment, it was explained that United Brands was the only undertaking that possessed 'ripeners' (facilities where green bananas were made ready for final market sale to consumers) and it is clear from the judgment that this was an important factor in assessing United Brands's dominance on the market.[53] Equally, a previously held advantage due to patent protection may endure even after the expiry of that protection by cementing a 'first-mover' advantage for the former patent-holder. This was one of the factors relied upon by the DGFT and upheld by the CCAT in the *Napp Pharmaceuticals* case: by being the first product on the market and by developing a reputation for having been an innovative method of pain relief for severe intractable pain (particularly among cancer sufferers), the first-mover advantage (originally established and protected by the patent) had acquired such a strong reputational effect that subsequent entry into that market by new products was rendered very difficult.[54]

Thus, to answer the question whether or not there is a dominant position in any given case, the matter turns on the identification of which factors in the relevant market cause competition to be restricted. These factors are necessary to be able to show that, despite the fact that the undertaking concerned does not have a very high market share, it nevertheless occupies a dominant position or, vice versa, that despite a high market share the undertaking is in fact not dominant in that market. Sometimes other factors will also be used in making this assessment.[55] The charging of high prices even where costs are very low (ie, making very substantial profits) may be an indication that the market in question is suffering from a lack of effective competition. The same point can be made about the imposition of unreasonable terms and conditions.

Although in practice most positions of dominance concern the supply side of a market (ie, an undertaking that offers for sale goods or services), it is also possible to identify a dominant position on the demand side. The *Alcatel/Telettra* example[56]

---

[53]   Case 27/76 *United Brands*, paras 69ff.

[54]   In particular in relation to the non-hospital purchasing sector of the market for oral sustained release morphine, because of the strong reputation of the drug among general practitioners: see *Napp Pharmaceutical Holdings Ltd v Director General of Fair Trading* [2002] CAT 1, para 160 and DGFT Decision CA98/2/2001 of 30 March 2001, paras 104–13.

[55]   On these matters, see OFT 415, Pt 6.

[56]   Cited above, n 38.

concerned a dominant buyer—the Spanish national telecoms company Telefonica. Before the liberalisation of the telecoms market (as of 1 January 1998),[57] this company clearly held a dominant position as supplier of telephone services over fixed lines. This position also resulted in a dominant position as purchaser of telecoms equipment, as discussed and found in the Commission's Decision on the approval of the merger. There are also other practical examples of dominant positions held by buyers.[58] The criteria for determining the existence of such a dominant position are largely the same as those discussed in the foregoing text.

Sometimes, it is very easy to establish the existence of a dominant position. This was the case in the *GVL* Decision,[59] where the Commission asserted that GVL was the only company (known as a 'collecting society') in Germany that was concerned with the representation of the interests of performers in the 'secondary exploitation' of their copyrights and related rights. Thus, it followed that GVL was dominant in that market: this was an example of dominance due to factual circumstances (as GVL held no statutory monopoly over the provision of such services).[60]

Finally, it should be noted that there have been some indications in the case law of the ECJ that a category of so-called 'super-dominance' may exist, where a stricter approach might be taken to the dominant undertaking's conduct in the light of the particular circumstances of the case, ie, conduct that might not be abusive by a dominant undertaking may be held to be an abuse if practised by a 'super-dominant'[61] undertaking. While the phrase has never been used by the EU courts, it may provide an explanation for such judgments as *Compagnie Maritime Belge*, where conduct aimed at eliminating competitors from the market that would not seem to have been abusive on a standard analysis (here, of predatory pricing, because the prices charged *did* cover costs sufficiently) was held to have been contrary to Article 102 TFEU. The judgment of the GC in the *Microsoft* case[62] may also be interpreted in this way. Microsoft's marketshare in the client PC operating market was over 90 per cent world-wide. According to the Commission the abuse consisted first of a refusal to supply and authorise interoperability information, and secondly the tying of the Windows client PC operating system and Windows Media Player. The GC found for the Commission on both counts. The Court's judgment was met with a substantial amount of criticism.[63] The UK's CAT does seem to have acknowledged this concept explicitly and has held that holding such a position of super-dominance may impose a 'special responsibility' upon such undertakings.[64] This is another illustration of the point that

---

[57] On the basis of Art 1 of Directive 97/13/EC of the European Parliament and Council of 10 April 1997 on a common framework for general authorisations and individual licences in the field of telecommunications services [1997] OJ L268/37, which required the telecoms market to be liberalised by 1 January 1998.

[58] See, eg, the Commission's *Twenty-First Report on Competition Policy* (1991), para 107, where it was explained that in the coal industry in England the British Coal Board occupied the position of a dominant purchaser *vis-à-vis* the small mines.

[59] [1981] OJ L370/49.

[60] ibid, paras 18–32 and 45.

[61] See Case T-83/91 *Tetra Pak*; and Case T-228/97 *Irish Sugar*.

[62] Case T-201/04 *Microsoft v Commission*.

[63] The judgment has generated an impressive flow of case notes and articles. The website of the Court lists, as of December 2015, 61 contributions.

[64] See *Napp Pharmaceutical Holdings Ltd v Director General of Fair Trading* [2002] CAT 1, paras 219, 343 and 352. See on these issues: E Szyszczak, 'Controlling Dominance in European Markets' (2011) 33(6) *Fordham International Law Journal* 1738.

the nature of a given abuse may be relevant to establishing whether or not there is a position of dominance, but is also relevant because it shows that a quantification of the *extent* of dominance in a given situation may have implications for the types of conduct that may amount to an abuse. Clearly, the issues of dominance and abuse are in theory capable of being analytically distinguished, but in practice there are obviously significant overlaps.

4.2.3 Behaviour of More than One Undertaking (Collective Dominance)

The prohibition on the abuse of a dominant position concerns only the activities of undertakings. The concept of an 'undertaking' has been discussed in Chapter 2.1.1 above.

It is important to note that both EU and UK competition law in this area are directed towards the activities of one or more undertakings: this much is clear from the relevant provisions reproduced above. Where two or more undertakings are involved, this is known as a 'joint' or 'collective' dominant position. It should also be emphasised that there can be no such collective dominance within a single concern, eg, where the two entities involved are a parent company and its subsidiary. Such a situation falls, as discussed in Chapter 2.1.1 (above), to be considered as the behaviour of a single undertaking for these purposes.

In the EU competition case law, the concept of a collective dominant position has been discussed on a number of occasions in the context of Article 102 TFEU. More case law was developed under the merger control rules. From earlier case law, it can be stated that such a position can be established where the undertakings involved are connected by such links that they are able to coordinate their conduct on the market.[65] In its *Almelo* judgment, the ECJ held that such structural links between undertakings could consist of the joint setting up and operation of the same standard contracts.[66] In the Dutch electricity sector (at issue in *Almelo*) all electricity supplies were made by regional energy companies, which all used the same standard form contracts that contained the same individual terms and conditions. Thus, for an individual electricity purchaser it was not possible to buy electricity on any terms other than those in the standard contracts. In the *CMB* judgment, the ECJ provided further guidance on this point.[67] In this case, the ECJ ruled that the execution of an agreement could have the incontrovertible consequence that the undertakings concerned, so far as their behaviour on a particular market was concerned, were linked to each other sufficiently

---

[65] Case 30/87 *Bodson v Pompes funèbres de régions libérées*, Case T-68/89 *Società Italiana Vetro v Commission* ('*Italian Flat Glass*') and Case C-393/92 *Gemeente Almelo v Energiebedrijf IJsselmij*.

[66] In that regard, it should be noted that the *Almelo* case (ibid) was argued in the context of the Dutch Electricity Act 1989. The factual situation was therefore strongly influenced by the relevant regulatory regime in operation under that Act.

[67] Joined Cases C-395 and 396/96 P *Compagnie Maritime Belge Transports SA v Commission*. Earlier, in its judgment in *Kali + Salz* (Joined Cases C-68/94 and 30/95 *France v Commission* the ECJ had provided an extensive analysis of the relevant structural links between various undertakings, which (according to the Commission's merger decision in the case) would acquire a collective dominant position as a result of the proposed deal.

closely that they operated as a single, collective unit vis-à-vis their competitors, business partners and consumers. According to the ECJ, a collective dominant position can also be identified by examining the nature and terms of an agreement, the manner of implementation of that agreement and the resulting links or connections between undertakings. However, it is not a necessary condition of such a collective dominant position that there must be some (formal) legal links: such a position can also be established by showing other links between undertakings and depends upon an economic assessment. For example, such links could exist as a result of the structure of the relevant market.

In the absence of such structural or contractual links between the parties, the question arises whether or not a collective dominant position may be established by examining the prevailing conditions on the relevant market. In the *Airtours* decision, the GC laid down a number of criteria by which to judge whether or not a collective dominant position can be said to exist.[68] Airtours, a UK-based tour and package holiday company, intended to take over First Choice (one of its competitors) by acquiring the entire share capital of First Choice. This 'concentration' (see Chapter 5 for discussion) was referred to the Commission under Article 4 of Regulation 4064/89 (now Regulation 139/2004). The Commission declared the concentration to be incompatible with the common market because it would lead to a collective dominant position, with the result that competition on the EU market for such services would be significantly hindered.[69] Airtours took the view that the Commission had made an error of assessment in its decision to prohibit the concentration agreed. According to the GC, the Commission in its Decision had failed to prove to the requisite legal standard that the merger would lead to a collective dominant position that could create significant restrictions upon practical competition on the relevant market. The GC thus annulled the Decision and emphasised that it was vital that the Commission made a careful assessment of whether or not the merger created or strengthened a collective dominant position, as a result of which competition on the relevant market would be restricted in a significant and lasting way, and that it be shown that this collective dominant position was the direct consequence of the merger.[70] In essence, a collective dominant position exists where multiple undertakings, together, in particular because of factors giving rise to a connection between them, without reaching an agreement or concerted practice for the purposes of Article 101 TFEU, are able tacitly to adopt a common policy on the market and act to a considerable extent independently of their competitors and customers.[71]

In the *Airtours* judgment, the GC set out three conditions that must be satisfied for a collective dominant position to be established.[72] These criteria can be summarised as follows:

(a)   Each member of a collective dominant position must know or have the ability to discover the behaviour of the other members. In that regard, each member must

[68]   Case T-342/99 *Airtours plc v Commission*.

[69]   Commission Decision 2000/276/EC of 22 September 1999 [2000] OJ L93/1.

[70]   Case T-342/99 (see above), para 69. See (and compare) our discussion of the *Airtours* case and the new EC merger control regime under Reg 139/2004/EC [2004] OJ L24/1 in Chapter 5.2.5 and the new test requiring that a 'significant impediment to effective competition' be shown.

[71]   Case T-342/99 (see above), para 59.

[72]   ibid, para 62. These criteria have been adopted by the Commission in its Guidelines on the assessment of horizontal mergers [2004] OJ C31/5.

have the means at its disposal to know whether or not other market participants are following and maintaining the same strategy.

(b)   The situation of tacit coordination between these undertakings must be capable of being sustained over time. This means that there must be a sufficient and enduring incentive not to depart from this policy of maintaining common market behaviour. Each member of the collective dominant position must thus give up the possibility of unleashing a competitive policy in an attempt to increase its market share, knowing that such means are also available to the other members and so its unilateral action would not garner any advantage for it. Other members of the collective dominant position must have sufficient deterrent means to discourage the other members from departing from the tacit collusion.

(c)   The foreseeable reactions of current and potential future competitors and consumers would not be such as to cause the members of that dominant position to waver in holding their common line as to market behaviour.

In the *Impala* judgment[73] the ECJ supplemented and clarified the *Airtours* conditions. It stressed the importance of 'correlative factors' which exist between the collectively dominant firms, which must enable them to adopt a common policy on the market and profit from a situation of collective economic strength without actual or potential competitors, let alone customers or consumers, being able to react effectively.

Such 'correlative factors' include, in particular, the relationship of interdependence existing between the parties to a tight oligopoly within which, on a market with the appropriate characteristics, in particular in terms of market concentration, transparency and product homogeneity, those parties are in a position to anticipate one another's behaviour and are therefore strongly encouraged to align their conduct on the market.

The ECJ stressed that: 'it is necessary to avoid a mechanical approach involving the separate verification of each of those criteria taken in isolation, while taking no account of the overall economic mechanism of a hypothetical tacit coordination'.

For discussion of the overlap between collective dominant positions and Article 101(1) TFEU, see section 4.2.6 below.

For the remainder of this chapter, for ease of analysis, we will start from the assumption that we are dealing with the situation where only one undertaking is alleged to hold a dominant position on the relevant market.

4.2.4 Abuse

When examining the connection between the various elements of the prohibition on the abuse of a dominant position, it is useful to remember that it is not essential that the abuse takes place on the same market as that in which a dominant position has been

---

[73] Case C-413/06P *Bertelsmann and Sony v Independent Music Publishers (Impala)*, paras 120–126.

established. Where it does not take place in the same market, however, it must at least occur on an adjacent market. This means an 'upstream', or 'neighbouring' market to 'downstream' that on which the dominant position is held. Such adjacent markets are those markets on which the main elements of the first market have undergone an earlier process (upstream) or will be subjected to a further process (downstream). The oil industry provides a good illustration of this phenomenon: extracting oil from the ground is generally known as the upstream market and refining that oil as the downstream market.

In the *Télémarketing* judgment,[74] the ECJ held that there had been an abuse of a dominant position by the Luxembourg television company CLT, which held a statutory monopoly, when CLT refused access to the television network to CBEM, a company that wanted to carry out telemarketing.[75] As the facts of the case made clear, CLT was using its dominant position on the television market to protect its own position on the market for telemarketing from competition from the likes of CBEM. Similarly, in the *AKZO* judgment, the ECJ ruled that AKZO had abused its dominant position on the peroxide market, but had done so through its activities on the market for baking products.[76]

4.2.4.1   Various Types of Abuse

As discussed in section 4.2.1 above, Article 102 TFEU contains a non-exhaustive list of forms of abuse. In practice, many other forms of abuse have been alleged and held to have been committed. Although it is not necessary for competition authorities to pigeon-hole conduct as constituting a specific type of abuse, the literature generally distinguishes between exploitative, exclusionary and discriminatory abuses.[77] Under the 'exploitation' heading, one finds such practices as very high pricing and other unfavourable terms and conditions, such as 'long-term exclusive purchasing contracts'. 'Exclusion' mainly concerns instances of refusals to supply and refusals to grant access to certain facilities. In addition, some types of abuse are 'structural.'[78] Such abuses consist of the acquisition of another company by which a dominant position is strengthened[79] or of taking over a patent licence through which the last possibility of any competitor entering the relevant market is removed.[80]

---

[74] Case 311/84 *CBEM v CLT and IPB*.

[75] A practice whereby the advertiser places an advertisement in the media including a telephone number, which the customer can then call to obtain further information on the product or to respond to the advertising campaign.

[76] Case C-62/86 *AKZO Chemie BV v Commission*; this was possible because certain flour additives and bleaching agents for flour are created using compounds based upon peroxides.

[77] See, J Faull and A Nickpay, *The EC Law of Competition*, 3rd edn (Oxford, Oxford University Press, 2014) 348, 412.

[78] L Ritter, WD Braun and F Rawlinson, *European Competition Law*, 3rd edn (The Hague, Kluwer Law International, 2004) ch V.

[79] Case 6/72 *Continental Can v Commission*.

[80] Case T-51/89 *Tetra Pak Rausing SA v Commission ('Tetra Pak II')*.

4.2.4.2   Unfair Prices or Other Conditions

The first category of abuses listed in Article 102 TFEU is that of unfair prices or other conditions. Unfair prices can be either unfairly high or unfairly low. In the latter case, this usually concerns 'predatory pricing'.[81]

4.2.4.2.1 Predatory Pricing

Predatory pricing is where an undertaking has as its goal the removal of a competitor from the market.[82] This occurs by offering products at a price below the cost price, so that the competitor must also offer his products at a price that forces him to make a loss. This principle may seem quite simple but its application has led to extensive discussions in EU competition law, US antitrust law and UK law. There are two difficulties. First, different cost concepts may be used and the application of these concepts is not easy. Secondly, even if upon the proper application of cost concepts a presumption of predation is established, the dominant undertaking may have good reasons for its pricing policy.

Let us start with the cost concepts.[83] The Commission in its Article 102 Enforcement Priorities Article 102[84] uses the following concepts:

> Average avoidable cost (AAC) is the average of the costs that could have been avoided if the company had not produced a discrete amount of (extra) output. In most cases, AAC and the average variable cost (AVC) will be the same, as it is often only variable costs that can be avoided. Long-run average incremental cost is the average of all the (variable and fixed) costs that a company incurs to produce a particular product. LRAIC and average total cost (ATC) are good proxies for each other, and are the same in the case of single product undertakings. If multi-product undertakings have economies of scope, LRAIC would be below ATC for each individual product, as true common costs are not taken into account in LRAIC. In the case of multiple products, any costs that could have been avoided by not producing a particular product or range are not considered to be common costs. In situations where common costs are significant, they may have to be taken into account when assessing the ability to foreclose equally efficient competitors.[85]

The identification of these types of costs is by no means easy and it will be a rare occasion to have the economists agree.

---

[81]   Note that excessively low prices could also be at issue where excessive buyer power (tending towards a monopsony) leads to the buyer demanding unfairly low prices: see, eg, Case 298/83 *CICCE v Commission* (where, however, the claim was not found to have been proved sufficiently to require the Commission to intervene on behalf of the disgruntled sellers). For a UK example with a similar result, see DGFT Decision *The Association of British Travel Agents and British Airways plc* CA98/19/2002 of 11 December 2002, where the DGFT rejected the allegation that British Airways had used its dominant buyer position to extract excessively low prices in return for travel agents' services (see paras 28–37 of the Decision).

[82]   For an excellent treatment see the International Competition Network study: *Unilateral Conduct Workbook. Chapter 4: Predatory Pricing Analysis*. Prepared by The Unilateral Conduct Working Group. Presented at the 11th Annual ICN Conference Rio de Janeiro, Brazil April 2012, pp 1–63 http://www.internationalcompetitionnetwork.org/uploads/library/doc828.pdf. See also Faull & Nickpay, *The EU Law of Competition*, 3rd edn (Oxford, Oxford University Press, 2014), paras 4.298–4.396.

[83]   See the Art 102 Enforcement priorities, p 7.

[84]   Para 26 and n 2. Other cost concepts are marginal cost: the cost of producing an additional unit and variable costs, the costs that vary with output, increasing when output increases and falling when output decreases (for instance, raw material or energy costs).

[85]   It adds the following note: 'In order to apply these cost benchmarks it may also be necessary to look at revenues and costs of the dominant company and its competitors in a wider context. It may not be sufficient to only assess whether the price or revenue covers the costs for the product in question, but it may

Second, the pricing behaviour may be justified, ie, there may be good business reasons for it. Similarly, undertakings may have to adjust their prices during a recession.

Because of these difficulties, additional elements have been developed to establish predation. Thus the literature and the case law have looked at whether there was an intent to hurt competitors. It should be stressed that Article 102 remains an objective concept and in most cases it is not necessary to have intent although it might be one additional factor to assist in classifying conduct as abusive. In its case law on predatory pricing, the court has held that it is necessary for the Commission to demonstrate an intention to foreclose competition where the dominant undertaking's costs are below its Average Total Cost (ATC), but remain above its Average Variable Cost (AVC).[86]

Moreover, proving intent has not been easy. The speech by Bill Gates quoted above is a rare example of intentions being expressed so blatantly. It served the GC well when rejecting Microsoft's plea for a reduction of the fine. Another element that has been coined in the US case law is that of recoupment. The idea is that if the undertaking had the expectation that it could recoup the losses incurred by predation, that would be proof of predation.[87]

4.2.4.2.2 The EU Case Law

In the *AKZO* judgment, which at the time was considered a landmark decision, the ECJ held that charging prices below the average variable cost of a product amounts to an abuse; in such a case there is no good justification for such sales at a loss.[88] The Court followed the test formulated by Areeda and Turner in the context of US antitrust law.[89]

Subsequent cases in the EU have followed the AKZO test.[90]

The Article 102 Enforcement Priorities discuss predation and introduced a fresh element.[91] The Commission indicates that it will generally intervene when there is evidence showing that the dominant undertaking deliberately incurs losses (referred to as sacrifice). The benchmark for such sacrifice is pricing below average avoidable cost. According to the Commission this benchmark is to be preferred over the average variable cost which was employed by the ECJ in the *AKZO* case.[92]

The Court made an important contribution in the *Post Danmark* judgment nuancing the law on predation.[93] The judgment of the Court answered preliminary questions from the Danish Supreme Court. Post Danmark enjoyed a monopoly in the delivery of

---

be necessary to look at incremental revenues in case the dominant company's conduct in question negatively affects its revenues in other markets or of other products. Similarly, in the case of two sided markets it may be necessary to look at revenues and costs of both sides at the same time.'

[86] Case C-202/078 *France Telecom v Commission*, para 109.

[87] The ICN study at p 44 puts this as follows: 'A recoupment analysis asks whether the dominant firm will be able to recoup its short run "investment in predation" by raising prices over the longer run. If recoupment is likely, competitive harm is also likely. If recoupment is not likely, competitive harm may be considered also unlikely.'

[88] Case C-62/86 *AKZO v Commission*.

[89] See R Whish and D Bailey, *Competition Law*, 8th edn (Oxford, 2015) 740. Interestingly, the judge drafting the judgment was Rene Joliet, a well known expert in US Antitrust law.

[90] eg, the *Wanadoo* Case C-2002/07P *France Telecom*, in which the ECJ confirmed both CG judgment T-340/03 and the Commission decision.

[91] Paras 63–74.

[92] See n 94.

[93] Case C-209/10 *Post Danmark*.

addressed letters and parcels. As a result it had a network that covered the national territory in its entirety. This network was also used for the distribution of unaddressed mail. In 2003, Post Danmark concluded contracts with three supermarket groups for the distribution of their unaddressed mail. Before that date this mail was distributed by Forbruger-Kontakt, the second largest undertaking in the unaddressed mail sector. The Coop group had conducted negotiations both with Post Danmark and with Forbruger-Kontakt. The offers made by those two operators were comparable in terms of price, Post Danmark's being only marginally lower. Forbruger-Kontakt lodged a complaint with the National Competition Authority which held inter alia that Post Danmark had abused its dominant position by practising a targeted policy of reductions designed to ensure its customers' loyalty. According to the Authority the abuse consisted of first, not putting its customers on an equal footing in terms of rates and rebates and, secondly, charging Forbruger-Kontakt's former customers rates different to those it charged its own pre-existing customers without being able to justify those significant differences. According to the referring court the price offered to the Coop group did not allow Post Danmark to cover its 'average total costs', but it did allow it to cover its 'average incremental costs.' Post Danmark argued that the contract made it possible to achieve considerable economies of scale. The Competition Authority was of the opinion that economies of scale were not listed in the general conditions of Post Danmark. The Court hearing the appeal of the decision of the Authority held that it could not be established that Post Danmark had intentionally sought to eliminate competition and that, accordingly, it had not abused its dominant position. Before the Danish Supreme Court Post Danmark claimed that an abuse can only be established when there is an intention to drive a competitor from the market. The Competition Authority defended the opposite opinion.

The ECJ ruled that:

> Article [102 TFEU] must be interpreted as meaning that a policy by which a dominant undertaking charges low prices to certain major customers of a competitor may not be considered to amount to an exclusionary abuse merely because the price that undertaking charges one of those customers is lower than the average total costs attributed to the activity concerned, but higher than the average incremental costs pertaining to that activity, as estimated in the procedure giving rise to the case in the main proceedings. In order to assess the existence of anti-competitive effects in circumstances such as those of that case, it is necessary to consider whether that pricing policy, without objective justification, produces an actual or likely exclusionary effect, to the detriment of competition and, thereby, of consumers' interests.

The Court also noted that:

> 41. In particular, such an undertaking may demonstrate, for that purpose, either that its conduct is objectively necessary (...), or that the exclusionary effect produced may be counterbalanced, outweighed even, by advantages in terms of efficiency that also benefit consumers (...).

> 42 In that last regard, it is for the dominant undertaking to show that the efficiency gains likely to result from the conduct under consideration counteract any likely negative effects on competition and consumer welfare in the affected markets, that those gains have been, or are likely to be, brought about as a result of that conduct, that such conduct is necessary for the achievement of those gains in efficiency and that it does not eliminate effective competition, by removing all or most existing sources of actual or potential competition.

As can be gleaned from these quotes, the Court incorporates the standard of the Commission formulated in its Article 102 Enforcement Priorities. But it adds an important reference to the detriment to competition as well as to consumers' interest. In shorthand, the test of the Court is the following: There is no presumption of an exclusionary abuse merely because the price that the dominant undertaking charges one of those customers is lower than the average total costs attributed to the activity concerned, but higher than the average incremental costs. In such a case, the competition authority needs to show that the conduct will have the actual or likely effect of excluding competitors from the market. If such effects are demonstrated, then the dominant undertaking can seek to escape Article 102 TFEU by showing either that the conduct is objectively justified or outweighed by advantages in terms of efficiency that also benefit consumers. According to Faull and Nickpay the Court had in mind the exclusion of an equally efficient competitor:[94] 'the judgment is crystal clear that competitors which are less efficient than the dominant undertaking are not entitled to protection from competition through Article 102.' It is also interesting to note that the Court did not get embroiled in the different cost concepts that the Danish Authority and government presented. It simply stated at paragraph 38:

> Indeed, to the extent that a dominant undertaking sets its prices at a level covering the great bulk of the costs attributable to the supply of the goods or services in question, it will, as a general rule, be possible for a competitor as efficient as that undertaking to compete with those prices without suffering losses that are unsustainable in the long term.

As noted above, EU law has not accepted the recoupment requirement.

4.2.4.2.3 UK Law

The area of predation is one that has received significant attention in the UK.[95] Although the UK regime follows closely the position taken in the EU and regularly draws reference from EU case law and decisional practice, the UK case law has also provided some very helpful analysis of detailed issues relating to the analysis of costs for the purpose of proving an allegation of predatory pricing,[96] while also clarifying

---

[94] Faull and Nickpay at p 408. The notion of equally efficient competitors is designed to restrict the protection of Article 102 to hypothetical competitors that are equally efficient.

[95] See *Napp Pharmaceutical Holdings Ltd v Director General of Fair Trading* [2002] CAT 1 (discussed by S Kon and S Turnbull, 'Pricing and the Dominant Firm: Implications of the Competition Commission Appeal Tribunal's Judgment in the *Napp* Case' (2003) 70 *European Competition Law Review* and *Aberdeen Journals Ltd v Director General of Fair Trading* [2003] CAT 11 (*Aberdeen Journals (No 2)*). Other regulators, besides the CMA have also had occasion to review pricing conduct that is potentially predatory. See, eg, the ORR's decision in English Welsh & Scottish Railway, in which it found that EW&S had abused its dominant position in several ways, including by predatory pricing (ORR decision of 17 November 2006). Similarly, in *Severn Trent Laboratories* (OFWAT decision of 17 January 2013), OFWAT investigated whether Severn Trent had abused its dominant position by pricing below cost to win contracts to provide water-analysis services. Unusually, Severn Trent managed to avoid a formal finding of an infringement, by offering commitments to divest the affiliated company, which OFWAT accepted under s 31A CA 1998. While commitments are not normally considered to be appropriate in predatory pricing cases, OFWAT noted that the structural remedy given by Severn Trent removed its ability to leverage its market power in the future. In *Complaint against BT's pricing of digital cordless phones* (OFCOM decision of 1 August 2006) OFCOM rejected a complaint about BT's pricing of digital cordless telephones because BT was neither dominant nor guilty of predatory pricing.

[96] *Aberdeen Journals (No 2)*, above, n 95, esp paras 380 and 411 (warning the OFT not to apply the cost-based rules on predation in a mechanistic manner) and 353–56 and 382–87 (emphasising that careful attention had to be paid to the time-frame within which cost calculations were made). Similarly, see also the CAT's criticism of the OFT in *Claymore Dairies v OFT* [2005] CAT, in which it annulled the OFT's finding of predation on the basis that the OFT had failed to investigate sufficiently whether the undertaking's prices were above ATC.

that there may be objective justifications for differences in the prices charged even if those prices were below cost.[97] On the question of objective justification, see section 4.2.5 below.

4.2.4.2.4 Excessive Pricing

Proving that a price is too high as a result of an abuse of a dominant position has not proved an easy task in competition law practice over the years. Most procedures that have been commenced by competition authorities on this basis have not reached a successful conclusion.[98] However, the early UK practice saw the DGFT succeed in bringing such a case against Napp Pharmaceuticals: the prices charged by Napp for the sale of its sustained release morphine products to the 'community' market (ie, not to hospitals) were analysed by the DGFT and found in most cases to be over 10 times higher than those charged to the hospitals market. In assessing such prices as excessive, comparisons were made between the profit margins secured by Napp in the hospital and non-hospital markets, and between the prices actually charged to the non-hospital sector and what a 'competitive' price might have been.[99] These methods and the Decision itself were upheld by the CCAT on appeal, although the fine levied was reduced from £3.21 million to £2.2 million to reflect mitigating circumstances and the rather uncertain state of the law in this area (in the absence of any prior ECJ decision or practice of the UK authorities on the point).[100]

4.2.4.2.5 Sharing of Markets

The sharing of markets is another example of abuse that is explicitly mentioned in Article 102 TFEU. This is most often practised by cartels, but individual companies with a dominant position[101] (or a number of companies holding a collective dominant position) can also avail themselves of similar practices. This can take place through the conclusion of contracts that prohibit exports or the selling on of the products.

4.2.4.3 Margin Squeeze

Margin squeeze is a specific form of pricing abuse. So far, one of the sectors where this has occurred most frequently is the telecom sector. This sector is characterised by

---

[97] ibid, paras 357–58 and 371. See also, the OFT's decision in *Alleged abuse of a dominant position by Flybe* (OFT 1286). Although the OFT ultimately concluded that FlyBe could not have breached the Art 102 TFEU and/or Chapter II prohibition on the basis of predatory pricing, because it did not hold a dominant position on the relevant route, the OFT also stated that there was an objective justification for Flybe to expect to and to incur initial losses on entering a new route.

[98] See, in particular, Case 27/76 *United Brands v Commission*, paras 248–68: the Commission failed to provide adequate proof that its allegations of unfair pricing were established.

[99] Decision CA98/2/2001 of 30 March 2001, paras 203–34.

[100] *Napp Pharmaceutical Holdings Ltd v Director General of Fair Trading* [2002] CAT 1, paras 497–541, esp 535–41.

[101] For an example of such a practice by a company that was held not to be dominant, see Case T-102/92 *Viho Europe BV v Commission* (esp paras 47–55) and, on appeal, Case C-73/95 P, (including the Opinion of AG Lenz, paras 31ff): Parker distributed its pens via a network of its wholly owned subsidiaries, one in each Member State, by which it managed to divide national markets. In the absence of any collusion between independent economic units and of any dominance, the practice survived a challenge under EC competition law.

a very capital intensive infrastructure which only few companies can afford to build. Therefore, liberalisation of this market is only possible if the incumbents allow the use of their infrastructure by new entrants. Sometimes vertically integrated incumbents charge prices for the use of the infrastructural facilities or inputs (in the upstream market) that do not enable the new entrants to compete in the downstream markets. The incumbents themselves do not have to pay similar prices for the upstream market products, which allows them to charge lower prices in the downstream markets. Because the incumbents are operating at all levels of the industry chain, they are able to allocate costs in the sectors where the market can bear relatively high costs. Unlike the incumbents the new entrants cannot allocate their costs in such a way.[102] In plain terms you charge the competitors higher prices for the infrastructure than you have to pay yourself. That gives you a cost advantage when competing on the market for end products. There have been two important ECJ judgments where the abuse of margin squeeze was the central issue: *Deutsche Telekom v Commission*[103] and *TeliaSonera v Konkurrensverket*.[104] Both judgments formulate the same standards for this type of abuse. In the *TeliaSonera* case the Swedish national court asked the ECJ: 'Under what conditions does an infringement of Article [102 TFEU] arise on the basis of a difference between the price charged by a vertically integrated dominant undertaking for the sale of ADSL input products to competitors on the wholesale market and the price which the same undertaking charges on the end-user market?' The ECJ held that:

31 A margin squeeze, in view of the exclusionary effect which it may create for competitors who are at least as efficient as the dominant undertaking, in the absence of any objective justification, is in itself capable of constituting an abuse within the meaning of Article 102 TFEU (…).

32 In the present case, there would be such a margin squeeze if, inter alia, the spread between the wholesale prices for ADSL input services and the retail prices for broadband connection services to end users were either negative or insufficient to cover the specific costs of the ADSL input services which TeliaSonera has to incur in order to supply its own retail services to end users, so that that spread does not allow a competitor which is as efficient as that undertaking to compete for the supply of those services to end users.

33 In such circumstances, although the competitors may be as efficient as the dominant undertaking, they may be able to operate on the retail market only at a loss or at artificially reduced levels of profitability.

34 It must moreover be made clear that since the unfairness, within the meaning of Article 102 TFEU, of such a pricing practice is linked to the very existence of the margin squeeze and not to its precise spread, it is in no way necessary to establish that the wholesale prices for ADSL input services to operators or the retail prices for broadband connection services to end users are in themselves abusive on account of their excessive or predatory nature, as the case may be (…).

---

[102] Para 80 of the Art 102 Enforcement Priorities states: 'Finally, instead of refusing to supply, a dominant undertaking may charge a price for the product on the upstream market which, compared to the price it charges on the downstream market, does not allow even an equally efficient competitor to trade profitably in the downstream market on a lasting basis…'.

[103] Case T-271/03 *Deutsche Telekom v Commission*; Case C-280/08P *Deutsche Telekom v Commission*.

[104] Case C-52/09 *Konkurrensverket v TeliaSonera Sverige AB*. See also the *Telefónica* case (Case T-336/07 *Telefónica and Telefónica de España v Commission*; Case C-202/07 P France Telecom. And Commission decision AT.39523 *Slovak Telekom* (currently before the GC).

35 In addition, as maintained by TeliaSonera, before the spread between the prices of those services can be regarded as squeezing the margins of competitors of the dominant undertaking, account must be taken not only of the prices of services supplied to competitors which are comparable to the services which TeliaSonera itself must obtain to have entry to the retail market, but also of the prices of comparable services supplied to end users on the retail market by TeliaSonera and its competitors. Similarly, a comparison must be made between the prices actually applied by TeliaSonera and its competitors over the same period of time.

Some additional points need to be mentioned. The first is whether Article 102 TFEU can be applied in a situation where the question of access to the infrastructure facilities is regulated. In the *Deutsche Telekom* judgment the ECJ held the presence of regulation does not exclude the possibility of applying Article 102. The Court stated: 'that notwithstanding such legislation, if a dominant vertically integrated undertaking has scope to adjust even its retail prices alone, the margin squeeze may on that ground alone be attributable to it.'[105] In *TeliaSonera* the ECJ held that in absence of regulation: 'where an undertaking has complete autonomy in its choice of conduct on the market, Article 102 TFEU is applicable to it.' The second point is that at §§74–75 of *TeliaSonera* that the ECJ explicitly recognised that margin squeeze can exist even where the margin remains positive.

A third point concerns the standard of proof for an abuse or the benchmark for exclusionary effects. In both judgments the ECJ stressed that when assessing whether prices are abusive it has to be examined whether the effect of the dominant undertaking's pricing practice was likely to hinder the ability of *competitors at least as efficient as themselves*[106] to trade on the retail market for broadband connection services to end users. Thus the benchmark for establishing an abuse is the cost level of an efficient producer. This also clearly stated in the Article 102 Enforcement Priorities.[107]

The issue of margin squeeze has been examined by the UK authorities on a number of occasions.[108] One of the most notable cases concerns the pharmaceutical company Genzyme, which the OFT fined £6.8 million for abusing its dominant position, including by way of margin squeeze practices.[109] The OFT's investigation concerned Genzyme's pricing practices with respect to the drug Cerezyme, which is used in the treatment of Gaucher's disease. Genzyme was found to have squeezed the margins

---

[105] *Deutsche Telekom v Commission*, para 85 and *TeliaSonera*, para 5.1.

[106] Emphasis supplied.

[107] In paras 23–27.

[108] See, eg, *Albion Water* (OFWAT decision of 26 May 2004), in which OFWAT originally concluded that Albion Water had not abused a dominant position by way of margin squeeze. This decision was, however, overturned by the CAT (*Albion Water Ltd v Water Services Regulation Authority* [2006] CAT 36), and subsequently upheld by the Court of Appeal (*Dŵr Cymru Cyfyngedig v Water Services Regulation Authority* [2008] EWCA Civ 536). With respect to the telecoms sector, OFCOM has investigated potential margin squeeze practices on a number of occasions. Each time, however, OFCOM has concluded either that there a breach has not been committed or that there were insufficient grounds for action (see, eg: *Suspected margin squeeze by Vodafone, O2, Orange and T-Mobile, OFCOM* decision of 26 May 2004; *Complaint from Gamma Telecom against BT about reduced rates for Wholesale Calls from 1 December 2004*, OFCOM decision of 16 June 2005; *Complaint from THUS plc and Gamma Telecom Limited against BT about alleged margin squeeze in Wholesale Calls pricing*, OFCOM decision of 20 June 2013; *Complaint from TalkTalk Telecom Group against BT*, OFCOM decision of 21 October 2014. The OFT also investigated whether BSkyB had engaged in abusive margin squeeze practices. However, after an extensive economic analysis, the OFT concluded that there were insufficient grounds to establish an abuse (OFT decision of 17 December 2002).

[109] *Genzyme*, OFT decision of 27 March 2003. Subsequently upheld by the CAT in *Genzyme Ltd v OFT* [2004] CAT 4.

of its downstream competitor Healthcare at Home, which purchased Cerezyme from Genzyme for the purposes of delivering the drug to patients in their homes—in competition with a similar service provided by Genzyme.

It is also worth noting that, in 2012, OFGEM (the UK energy regulator) accepted commitments to address concerns that Electricity North West had imposed a margin squeeze when charging for connections to its network.[110] This stands in contrast to the position adopted at the EU level, which is yet to accept commitments for margin squeeze practices.

4.2.4.4 Various Forms of Contracts

Long-term supply contracts often provide for exclusive purchasing or purchasing of an extensive proportion of the buyer's future demand for the relevant product(s). According to the Article 102 Enforcement Priorities the Commission will focus its attention on those cases where it is likely that consumers as a whole will not benefit.[111] Another well-known example of a potentially abusive contract is one that allows for 'loyalty rebates'. In various industries it is customary for suppliers to seek to bind customers to themselves by the use of loyalty rebates. Such contracts can take many different forms. Yet another type of contract is one that offers so-called 'postponed' or 'delayed' discounts, whereby the discount is only given if the customer concerned buys a large part of its needs from the dominant undertaking. Still another form of contract is the 'English clause', on the basis of which the seller agrees to equal any better offer received by the buyer from the seller's competitors. To take advantage of this, the buyer must report any such offer to the seller and the buyer can only accept the offer if the seller fails to match it.

All of these contracts lead to customers having to place orders either for the whole or a substantial part of their requirements with the dominant undertaking. As a consequence, competitors are then deprived of any opportunity to supply such customers. In the case of the English clause, the restrictive effect upon competition is still greater, because the operation of such clauses leads to the acquisition by the dominant undertaking of perfect information about the commercial behaviour of its competition.[112] Such clauses may increase the transparency of oligopolistic markets and facilitate coordination. These discounting and similar practices have been analysed by the GC in the cases of *Michelin II*[113] and *British Airways*.[114]

In the Intel case the Commission found that Intel had granted conditional discounts to its customers.[115] The Commission also found that Intel had engaged in a form of exclusionary abuse, termed 'naked restrictions', by paying computer manufacturers for their support in preventing or delaying the launch of products of its competitors.

---

[110] *Electricity North West*, OFGEM decision of 24 May 2012.
[111] Para 34.
[112] See, eg, the Commission's *Guidelines on Vertical Restraints* [2010] OJ 2010 C130/1, para 129.
[113] Case T-203/01 *Manufacture française des pneumatiques Michelin v Commission* (*Michelin II*). For an economic analysis from a UK perspective, see the economic discussion paper published by the OFT, *Selective price cuts and fidelity rebates* (29 July 2005, OFT 804).
[114] Case T-219/99 *British Airways plc v Commission*.
[115] Case COMP/C-3/37.990. Case T-286/09 *Intel v Commission*. Appeal before the ECJ, C-413/14 P.

Intel disagreed, claiming that the Commission failed to establish that the restrictions had an actual capability to foreclose competition. The GC found for the Commission and rejected the argument that the Commission should have applied the principles of the Article 102 Enforcement Priorities. The GC stated that it did not apply to proceedings that had already been initiated before it was published. Thus there was no need for the Commission to apply the 'As Efficient Competitor' test as explained in the Article 102 Enforcement Priorities. This test is formulated as follows in the Article 102 Enforcement Priorities: 'With a view to preventing anti-competitive foreclosure, the Commission will normally only intervene where the conduct concerned has already been or is capable of hampering competition from competitors which are considered to be as efficient as the dominant undertaking.'[116]

In the *Orange Polska* case the Commission bases the refusal to supply abuse on the grounds that the addressees were under a pre-existing national law obligation to grant access and engaged in a constructive refusal to supply.[117] Although the breach of Article 102 TFEU consisting in the use of a margin squeeze is an infringement of a different nature than *Orange Polska's* infringement, which is a refusal to provide services, that infringement was considered to be a serious abuse.

In *Telefónica and Telefónica de España v Commission*, the classification of the infringement as very serious was founded, in essence, on three elements, namely the fact that the applicant could not ignore the illegality of its conduct, the intentional nature of that conduct, and the fact that the incumbent operator had a virtual monopoly on the wholesale market for broadband access and a very strong dominant position in the retail markets.

4.2.4.5 Refusals to Supply

A further form of abuse is a refusal to supply. An undertaking with a dominant position cannot simply and without good reason refuse to continue to supply goods and/or services to an established customer. Such a refusal can have a seriously harmful effect upon the independence of small and medium-sized undertakings. Furthermore, it is a disproportionate response to an alleged attack upon the position of the dominant undertaking.[118]

The classic EU law example in this field is the *Commercial Solvents* case.[119] Commercial Solvents was the dominant supplier of amino-butanol, which was a raw material vital to the manufacture of Ethambutol, an anti-tuberculosis drug produced by Zoja in Italy. Commercial Solvents refused to continue to supply Zoja with the raw material, while at the same time bringing its subsidiary into the market for

---

[116] Paras 23–27 of the Article 102 Enforcement Priorities.

[117] Case AT.39525 *Telekomunikacja Polska* (upheld by GC in Case T-486/11, *Orange Polska v Commission*, on appeal C-123/16 P, and Case AT.39523 *Slovak Telekom* (currently before the GC).

[118] Case 27/76 *United Brands v Commission* and Joined Cases 6 and 7/73 *Instituto Chemioterapico Italiano SpA and Commercial Solvents Corp v Commission* (typically known as *Commercial Solvents*).

[119] Joined Cases 6 and 7/73, see above.

anti-tuberculosis drugs. The Commission ordered Commercial Solvents to resume supplies to Zoja,[120] and the ECJ upheld its Decision.

> [A]n undertaking being in a dominant position as regards the production of raw material and therefore able to control the supply to manufacturers of derivatives cannot, just because it decides to start manufacturing the derivatives (in competition with its former customers) act in such a way as to eliminate their competition which in the case in question would amount to eliminating one of the principal manufacturers of Ethambutol in the common market. [Such action by a dominant undertaking] ... is abusing its dominant position within the meaning of Article [102 TFEU].

In the UK, this issue has received attention since the entry into force of the CA 1998. The courts have also heard a number of claims on this basis. The majority have been rejected (usually summarily),[121] but there have been occasions where claimants have secured an interim injunction preventing such refusal, pending the trial of the matter.[122] The case of *Network Multimedia Television Ltd v Jobserve Ltd*[123] serves as a good example. The claimant (NMT) argued that Jobserve had acted in breach of the Chapter II prohibition in the terms it imposed for access to its website, which provided a means (known as 'job boards') for information technology recruitment agencies to advertise various job vacancies to the relevant community. Jobserve would not post advertisements on its website if the advertiser had any interest in other internet-based job boards, and when it sought to extend this refusal to cover any advertising on the site of a rival, ATSCo (a trade association in the field), NMT complained since it had been engaged by ATSCo to design, develop, establish and operate a similar job board for it. It sought an injunction:

> 9. ... Network's case is that, if Jobserve is not restrained from so acting, Network will be prevented from competing with Jobserve: if forced to make a choice, members of ATSCo will stay with the site which dominates the market rather than opt to use a new site attempting to compete with Jobserve.

Given that the claim required more detailed factual analysis, the Court of Appeal refused to dismiss it summarily and granted an injunction restraining Jobserve from denying access to its website to such 'dual users' pending trial. As Mummery LJ explained:

> 12. ... Network's complaint is about the detrimental effects suffered by it as a result of Jobserve's treatment of its existing ATSCo customers. It requires them to make a choice under threat of refusing to continue to supply them with an existing service. The choice presented by Jobserve to members of ATSCo is between continuing to use Jobserve's facility, which enjoys a dominant position in the relevant market, and using the new competing facility, which

---

[120] [1972] OJ L299/51.
[121] See, eg *Claritas (UK) Ltd v Post Office* [2001] UKCLR 2, [2001] ECC 12, [2001] ETMR 63.
[122] See, eg, *Intel Corp v Via Technologies Inc* [2003] UKCLR 106, [2003] ECC 16, [2003] Eu LR 85, [2003] FSR 33, concerning patent licensing and computer processor chips (noted by A Toutongi, '*Intel v Via*: Holding Back the Tide of Compulsory Licensing' (2002) *European Intellectual Property Review* 548 (on the first instance judgment) and D Curley, 'Eurodefences and Chips: "A Somewhat Indigestible Dish": the UK Court of Appeal's Decision in *Intel Corp v Via Technologies*' (2003) *European Intellectual Property Review* 282 (on the Court of Appeal's ruling)). See also, *Software Cellular Network Ltd v T-Mobile (UK) Ltd*, (2007) EWHC 1790; and *Dahadshill Transfer Service Ltd v Barclays Bank* [2013] EWHC 3379 (Ch).
[123] [2002] UKCLR 184, [2001] EWCA Civ 2021.

Network wishes to establish in the same market. Jobserve has not refused to allow Network to use essential facilities. Jobserve's action against ATSCo members is aimed at destroying, distorting or restricting competition from Network. The action involves Jobserve's use of its dominant position in order to stop its existing ATSCo customers from using a competing service. By that means Jobserve hopes to perpetuate its existing dominance of the relevant market.

Another interesting example is the CAT judgment[124] that overturned an OFT Decision concerning the Harwood Park Crematorium and (inter alia) a refusal by its owner, Austins, to supply crematorium services to Burgess. In *JJ Burgess & Sons v OFT*,[125] the CAT concluded, contrary to the OFT's finding,[126] that Austins' refusal constituted an abuse of a dominant position. The case before the CAT turned mainly on the appropriate geographic market definition (on which aspect see Chapter 1.3.2.2 above), but once this had been established, the CAT found that Austins' refusal to allow Burgess access to the Harwood Park Crematorium amounted to an abuse of a dominant position under the Chapter II prohibition. In discussing the relevant standard for establishing whether an undertaking's refusal to supply is abusive, the CAT summarised the legal position as follows:[127]

(1) An abuse of a dominant position may occur if a dominant undertaking, without objective justification, refuses supplies to an established existing customer who abides by regular commercial practice, at least where the refusal of supply is disproportionate and operates to the detriment of consumers: United Brands at paragraphs 182 to 183, and also at 189 to 194; Advocate General Jacobs in Bronner, at paragraph 43.

(2) Such an abuse may occur, in particular, if the potential result of the refusal to supply is to eliminate a competitor of the dominant undertaking in a neighbouring (eg downstream) market where the dominant undertaking is itself in competition with the undertaking potentially eliminated, at least if the goods or services in question are indispensable for the activities of the latter undertaking, and there is a 81 potential adverse effect on consumers: see Commercial Solvents, at paragraph 25; Télémarketing at paragraphs 26 to 27; Advocate General Jacobs in Bronner at paragraphs 43, and 58 to 61; and the judgment of the Court in Bronner at 38 and 41.

(3) It is not an abuse to refuse access to facilities that have been developed for the exclusive use of the undertaking that has developed them, at least in the absence of strong evidence that the facilities are indispensable to the service provided, and there is no realistic possibility of creating a potential alternative: the opinion of Advocate General Jacobs at paragraphs 56 to 66: the judgment of the Court in Bronner, at paragraphs 41 to 46.[128]

The CAT's analysis in the *Burgess* case provides a good illustration of how the duty imposed upon the CAT under section 60 CA 1998 to use the EU materials to inform the development of UK competition law in this field is respected by the CAT in

---

[124] See also *Attheraces Ltd v BHB Ltd* [2005] EWHC 1553 (Ch), in which Sir Andrew Morritt V-C refused to strike out Attheraces's application to amend its statement of claim to include allegations of breach of Art 102 TFEU and/or Ch II CA 1998 by the BHB: various breaches were alleged, including an abusive and unjustified cessation of supply of pre-race data to bookmakers.

[125] *JJ Burgess & Sons v OFT* [2005] CAT 25.

[126] Decision No CA98/06/2004, *Refusal to supply JJ Burgess & Sons Limited with access to Harwood Park Crematorium* (29 June 2004).

[127] *JJ Burgess & Sons v OFT* [2005] CAT 25, para 311.

[128] See [2005] CAT 25, paras 291–345, for the full analysis of the CAT on this point.

practice. Finally, it shows that the principles of the Chapter II prohibition under the CA 1998 are equally applicable to markets of a very local nature (on this point, see further section 6.3.5.3 below).

The *Microsoft* case is another seminal case of the refusal to supply abuse. In this case the refusal was largely analysed from the perspective of the essential facilities doctrine, hence it will be discussed below in the following section.

In the Article 102 Enforcement Priorities the Commission stresses that the existence of an obligation to supply may undermine undertakings' incentives to invest and innovate. Therefore intervention has to be considered carefully.[129]

4.2.4.6 Essential Facilities

Matters become even more nuanced where the refusal concerns a future competitor. In this area, the debate surrounding the concept of 'essential facilities' has come to the fore. The basic idea behind this doctrine is that essential facilities—such as harbours and ports for shipping lines, computer reservation systems for airlines, and high voltage electricity transmission lines and gas transmission pipelines for energy companies—must be made available for use by competitors where those competitors cannot, or can only by incurring very high costs, build their own 'version' of such facilities. The doctrine has not generated warm support from captains of industry proud of their audacious investments opening new market horizons.[130] In the *Bronner* judgment, the ECJ ruled that before this doctrine could be applied it must first be shown that there is no real or potential alternative that would allow competition on that 'secondary' market.[131] Providing the claimant with access to the facility must be seen, as it were, as a last resort. It is not sufficient that it would be expensive and/or difficult for the claimant to provide itself with similar facilities. It must also be considered whether there were alternatives open to the claimant (even if they were less advantageous than securing access to the facility in question). In the *IMS Health* case,[132] the ECJ emphasised that there can only be an abuse due to refusal of access where the undertaking that sought a licence to use the facility (here, a copyright) intended to offer a *new* product or service that was not offered by the facility's owner and for which there was potential customer demand.[133]

---

[129] Para 75.

[130] See Case T-301/04, *Clearstream v Commission*.

[131] Case C-7/97 *Oscar Bronner GmbH & Co KG v Mediaprint Zeitungs- und Zeitschriftenverlag GmbH & Co KG*.

[132] Case C-418/01 *IMS Health GmbH & Co OHG v NDC Health GmbH & Co KG*, discussed by D Geradin, 'Limiting the Scope of Article 82 EC: What Can the EU Learn from the U.S. Supreme Court's Judgment in *Trinko* in the Wake of *Microsoft*, *IMS* and *Deutsche Telekom*?' (2004) 41 *Common Market Law Review* 1519. On the specific question as to whether or not there were 'exceptional circumstances' (such that refusal to licence an IP right amounts to an abuse) within the meaning of the *Magill* case (Joined Cases C-241/91 P and C-242/91 P *RTE and ITP Ltd v Commission* (often known as *Magill* or *TV Guides*)), the ECJ held that the result of the refusal to grant access must be such as to exclude all competition on a secondary market but also noted that such a secondary market could be potential or even hypothetical (paras 40–47). This is precisely the issue upon which the Court of Appeal in the UK case of *Intel Corp v Via Technologies Inc.* (above, n 122) felt that there was sufficient uncertainty to hold that Via might have an arguable case at trial.

[133] For a UK case that discusses this question of the emergence of a new product, see *The Racecourse Association and the British Horseracing Board v OFT* [2005] CAT 29; see also the OFT Decision from which

In the *Microsoft* judgment the essential facilities doctrine played a major part in the reasoning of the GC. The GC applied this doctrine in order to assess the legality of the Commission's argument that Microsoft's refusal to supply and authorise the use of interoperability information constituted an abuse. Microsoft maintained that the requirement to disclose such information would amount to an interference with its intellectual property (IP) rights.[134] The Commission disagreed but argued that even under the stricter standard of the doctrine as applied to IP rights the conditions for its application were satisfied.[135] The CG proceeded to assess the case on the assumption that Microsoft's rights were protected as IP rights. Thus the GC analysed the issue as a question of the application of the doctrine to intellectual property rights.[136] The GC proceeded from a summary of the case law of the ECJ in paragraphs 331–333.

332 It also follows from that case-law that the following circumstances, in particular, must be considered to be exceptional:

—   in the first place, the refusal relates to a product or service indispensable to the exercise of a particular activity on a neighbouring market;
—   in the second place, the refusal is of such a kind as to exclude any effective competition on that neighbouring market;
—   in the third place, the refusal prevents the appearance of a new product for which there is potential consumer demand.

333 Once it is established that such circumstances are present, the refusal by the holder of a dominant position to grant a licence may infringe Article [102 TFEU] unless the refusal is objectively justified.

334 The Court notes that the circumstance that the refusal prevents the appearance of a new product for which there is potential consumer demand is found only in the case-law on the exercise of an intellectual property right.

335 Finally, it is appropriate to add that, in order that a refusal to give access to a product or service indispensable to the exercise of a particular activity may be considered abusive, it is necessary to distinguish two markets, namely, a market constituted by that product or service and on which the undertaking refusing to supply holds a dominant position and a neighbouring market on which the product or service is used in the manufacture of another product or for the supply of another service. The fact that the indispensable product or service is not marketed separately does not exclude from the outset the possibility of identifying a

---

the appeal was made (No CA98/2/2004 *Attheraces*. The CAT quashed the OFT's Decision on the ground that it had failed accurately to define the relevant market (itself an interesting analysis: see paras 135–50), but went on to consider the OFT's approach to the substantive analysis of the media rights agreement between, on the one hand, the 49 racecourses and, on the other, Attheraces plc. While the case was considered by the OFT and the CAT under the Ch I prohibition, the analysis concerning the emergence of a new betting product bears a degree of similarity to considerations of access to information and the *IMS Health*-style analysis: see, eg, paras 160–76 of the judgment of the CAT.

[134]   Para 267 et seq. See also the ECJ's ruling in Case C-170/13 *Huawei Technology Co Ltd v ZTE Corp and ZTE Deutschland GmBH*, para 53—where the ECJ acknowledges that a failure to licence SEPs on FRAND terms could amount to an abusive refusal to supply.

[135]   Case T-201/04 *Microsoft v Commission* para 313.

[136]   Para 334. It may be noted that the GC considered that it was possible that the conduct might still be abusive even if the Bronner criteria were not met (see para 336 in conjunction with para 317). Ultimately, the GC did not have to look at this question because, on the facts, the Bronner criteria had been satisfied.

separate market (…). Thus, the Court of Justice held, at paragraph 44 of IMS Health (…) that it was sufficient that a potential market or even a hypothetical market could be identified and that such was the case where the products or services were indispensable to the conduct of a particular business activity and where there was an actual demand for them on the part of undertakings which sought to carry on that business. The Court of Justice concluded at the following paragraph of the judgment that it was decisive that two different stages of production were identified and that they were interconnected in that the upstream product was indispensable for supply of the downstream product.

After extensive reasoning, the General Court, in a very exceptional composition of 13 judges, concluded that the Commission had sufficiently established that the exceptional circumstances enumerated in paragraphs 331 et seq were present in this case.[137] The GC also held that Microsoft had not demonstrated the existence of any objective justification for its refusal to disclose the interoperability information.[138]

To the surprise of many Microsoft watchers the company did not appeal the judgment. In a press release Microsoft and the Commission announced that the decision would be implemented. Nevertheless, the implementation proved to be wrought with failed attempts by Microsoft to meet the concerns of the Commission.

In the absence of an appeal to the ECJ it is difficult to express an opinion on the interpretation of the GC of the law. Some findings of the GC seem to be tainted by the very exceptional circumstances of the case.[139] It is interesting to note that proceedings against Microsoft in the US[140] led to a somewhat similar settlement.

The case continued because Microsoft did not fulfill the obligations imposed on it in the Commission decision according to which Microsoft was required to grant access to, and authorise the use of, the interoperability information on reasonable and non-discriminatory terms. The negotiations did not produce any results even though Microsoft proposed some 13 successive versions of the agreements containing remuneration schemes. Finally, the Commission adopted a fresh decision on 27 February 2008 imposing a periodic penalty payment of € 899 million.[141] On 27 June 2012 the GC largely dismissed the action seeking an annulment of the decision.[142] The Court did, however, lower the payment to € 860 million. Microsoft did not appeal the judgment. In 2009 Microsoft offered commitments offering users a browser choice enabling them to easily choose their preferred web browser. On 6 March 2013, the Commission fined Microsoft again for non-compliance with its browser choice commitments.[143]

The *IMS Health* as well as *the Microsoft* judgment raise the question of whether or not the condition—that a new product must be prevented from emerging as a result of the refusal to grant access—also applies in cases concerning access to network facilities.[144] It should be noted that this requirement has never been a condition in

---

[137] Para 712.

[138] Para 711.

[139] The judgment has generated an impressive number of comments and articles. The website of the Court lists 54 contributions.

[140] Summarised in paras 51–58 and 838 of the GC judgment.

[141] Decision C (2005) 4420 final (Case COMP/C-3/37.792-Microsoft).

[142] Case T-167/08, *Microsoft v Commission*. Not appealed.

[143] IP 13/196, 6 March 2013, case COMP/39.530.

[144] While one might seek to confine the case to the IP field, it should be noted that the ECJ in *IMS Health* (above, n 132) specifically drew upon the *Bronner* judgment (above, n 131) to develop its reasoning on the assessment of access to the copyright at issue in *IMS Health*.

non-IP cases. In this connection, it is interesting to note that where the EC legislator has wanted clearly to protect access to particular types of facility, it has done so by adopting directives requiring that such access is secured by national law. Thus, in the telecommunications sector interconnection or access to the local loop has been laid down in Directive 97/33/EC.[145] The same basic concepts of access can also be found in the Directives on the internal market for electricity[146] and natural gas.[147] Nevertheless, it is clear that there remains a supplementary role for competition law, even in the context of sector-specific legislation and regulation.[148] This supplementary role has been confirmed in the *Deutsche Telekom* and the *TeliaSonera* judgments of the ECJ discussed in section 4.2.4.3 above.[149]

4.2.4.7 Abuse in Relation to IP Rights

Patents and other intellectual property rights are an essential feature of the economy. They stimulate innovation and technological development. Because IP rights confer an exclusive advantage on the holders they may lead to dominant positions. And hence there is a possibility that the owners abuse their rights. Thus a conflict may arise between the protection of IP rights on the one hand and undistorted competition on the other hand. In the *Huawei* judgment the Court observed that it:

> must strike a balance between maintaining free competition—in respect of which primary law and, in particular, Article 102 TFEU prohibit abuses of a dominant position—and the requirement to safeguard that proprietor's intellectual-property rights and its right to effective judicial protection, guaranteed by Article 17(2) and Article 47 of the Charter, respectively.[150]

In some sectors of the economy, IP rights are particularly important, notably the pharmaceutical sector and the IT sector. It is therefore not surprising that disputes about the abuse of IP rights have arisen in these sectors. The question whether Microsoft's refusal to licence an IP right constitutes an abuse is discussed in the above section on essential facilities. It may be recalled that both the Commission and the GC assessed the Microsoft's refusal on the assumption that Microsoft's rights were

---

[145] Directive 97/33/EC on interconnection in Telecommunications with regard to ensuring universal service and interoperability through application of the principles of Open Network Provision (ONP) [1997] OJ L199/32.

[146] Originally Directive 96/92/EC [1997] OJ L27/20; subsequently Directive 2003/54/EC [2003] OJ L 176/37; now Directive 2009/72 concerning common rules for the internal market in electricity and repealing Directive 2003/54 [2009] OJ L211/55.

[147] Originally Directive 98/30/EC [1998] OJ L204/1; subsequently Directive 2003/55/EC [2003] OJ L 176/57; now Directive 2009/73 concerning common rules for the internal market in natural gas and repealing Directive2003/55 [2009] OJ L211/94.

[148] On this point, see the relevant OFT Guidelines: *Concurrent Application to Regulated Industries* (OFT 405) (on which see generally the Competition Act 1998 Concurrency Regulations (SI 2004, No 1077)) and *Application in the Energy Sector* (OFT 428). For an intriguing US perspective on these matters, see the judgment of the US Supreme Court in *Verizon Communications Inc v Law Offices of Curtis V Trinko LLP* 540 US 682 (2004).

[149] See Case AT.39525 *Telekomunikacja Polska* (upheld by GC in Case T-486/11, *Orange Polska v Commission* appeal C-123/16 P and Case AT.39523 *Slovak Telekom* (currently before the GC) which are right on point in this respect.

[150] Case C-170/13, *Huawei*, para 42.

protected by IP rights and hence both institutions applied the test of whether the refusal prevented the appearance of a new product for which there is potential consumer demand. The fact that this condition for the applicability of the essential facilities doctrine only applies for IP rights is a reflection of the special position of IP rights.

In this section we discuss some other forms of abuse that have arisen in the context of IP rights in the pharmaceutical and the IT sector,[151] in particular the supply of misleading information and the patent hold-up in the case of standard-setting organisations.

In the *AstraZeneca* case the Commission found that the undertaking had abused its IP rights by supplying the patent authorities with misleading information with the purpose of having the patent on the highly successful drug Losec extended.[152] The second abuse consisted of the requests for the surrender of its market authorisations for Losec capsules and the launch of Losec tablets. As a result, the sellers of generics could no longer market their capsules. Upon appeal the GC found for the Commission for the first abuse and for Astra for the second abuse.[153] The GC held that, in the light of the appellant's argument that the reduction in parallel imports was due to the success of Losec MUPS, that institution had not shown to the requisite legal standard that the withdrawal, in Denmark and in Norway, of the marketing authority for Losec capsules was liable to prevent parallel imports of those products. The ECJ confirmed the judgment of the GC.[154]

Another abuse consists of pay for delay settlements. In such cases the patent holder pays the producer of generics to delay the production and marketing of off-patent drugs. The Commission is keen to avoid such settlements.

Licensing patents is common practice in the IT industry. It allows the patent holder to make additional profits without having to incur expenses for increasing the production of the patented products. Licensing is only successful if both parties can agree on proper remuneration. Asking excessive royalties frustrates licensing and may constitute an abuse. This is especially the case in the context of standard setting. A particular form of abuse is the patent ambush. This may occur when the holder of a patent participates in industry-wide Standard-Setting Organisations (SSOs). Participants are required to disclose their interest when they hold essential patents likely to be incorporated in industry wide standards. Not disclosing an interest would give them an unfair advantage and allow them to secure high royalties. The Commission has challenged such behaviour in the *Rambus* decision.[155] The case concerned standards for DRAM memory chips. The Commission closed the investigation after it secured commitments designed to avoid unfair competitive pressure.

The *Huawei* judgment provides a good example of the issues involved in the context of industry wide standard setting.[156] The case concerned a patent said to be

---

[151] For a good overview of the relationship between IP rights and abuse see: Faull & Nickpay, *The EU Law of Competition*, 3rd edn (Oxford, Oxford University Press, 2014), paras 4.694–4.814. See also the annotation on the Huawei judgment by T. Koerber, 53 *CMLRev.* 2016, 1107–1120

[152] Case COMP/A.37.507/F3—*AstraZeneca*, OJ 2006 L 332/24.

[153] Case T-321/05, *AstraZeneca v Commission*.

[154] Case C-457/10 P, *AstraZeneca v Commission*.

[155] Case COMP/38.636 *Rambus*.

[156] Case C-170/13, *Huawei*. This summary is a shortened version of the opinion of the AG. The Commission provided guidance on this issue in Cases AT.39985 *Motorola—Enforcement of GPRS standard essential*

'essential to a standard developed by a standardisation body' (a standard-essential patent (SEP)) and, for the first time, the Court was called upon to analyse whether—and, if so, in what circumstances—an action for infringement brought by the SEP-holder against an undertaking which manufactures products in accordance with that standard constitutes an abuse of a dominant position. The infringement concerned a European patent held by Huawei. The patent is 'essential' to the Long Term Evolution (LTE) standard developed by the European Telecommunications Standards Institute (ETSI). This means that anyone using the standard inevitably uses the teaching of that patent. The patent was notified to ETSI by Huawei which gave ETSI a commitment to grant licences to third parties on fair, reasonable and non-discriminatory terms—commonly referred to as 'FRAND terms'. After the 'breakdown' of the negotiations for the conclusion of a licensing agreement on FRAND terms, Huawei brought an action for infringement before the Landgericht Düsseldorf against ZTE in order to obtain an injunction prohibiting the continuation of the infringement and an order for the rendering of accounts, the recall of products and the assessment of damages. According to ZTE, that action for a prohibitory injunction constituted an abuse of a dominant position, since ZTE was willing to negotiate a licence. Advocate General Wathelet observed that the conduct of SEP-holders who have given a commitment to grant licences to third parties on FRAND terms has given rise to a plethora of actions before the courts of several Member States and third countries.

The Court's ruling clearly addresses the questions raised by the FRAND standard. In doing so it was greatly assisted by the pertinent preliminary questions. It ruled that:

> Article 102 TFEU must be interpreted as meaning that the proprietor of a patent essential to a standard established by a standardisation body, which has given an irrevocable undertaking to that body to grant a licence to third parties on fair, reasonable and non-discriminatory ('FRAND') terms, does not abuse its dominant position, within the meaning of that article, by bringing an action for infringement seeking an injunction prohibiting the infringement of its patent or seeking the recall of products for the manufacture of which that patent has been used, as long as:
>
> — prior to bringing that action, the proprietor has, first, alerted the alleged infringer of the infringement complained about by designating that patent and specifying the way in which it has been infringed, and, secondly, after the alleged infringer has expressed its willingness to conclude a licensing agreement on FRAND terms, presented to that infringer a specific, written offer for a licence on such terms, specifying, in particular, the royalty and the way in which it is to be calculated, and
> — where the alleged infringer continues to use the patent in question, the alleged infringer has not diligently responded to that offer, in accordance with recognised commercial practices in the field and in good faith, this being a matter which must be established on the basis of objective factors and which implies, in particular, that there are no delaying tactics.
>
> 2. Article 102 TFEU must be interpreted as not prohibiting, in circumstances such as those in the main proceedings, an undertaking in a dominant position and holding a patent essential

patents; AT.39939 *Samsung Enforcement of UMTS standard essential patents*, decisions of 29 April 2014, see Commission Staff Working Document accompanying Report Competition Policy 2014, at p 36. See also the annotation on the Huawei judgment by T. Koerber, 53 CMLRev. 2016, 1107–1120

to a standard established by a standardisation body, which has given an undertaking to the standardisation body to grant licences for that patent on FRAND terms, from bringing an action for infringement against the alleged infringer of its patent and seeking the rendering of accounts in relation to past acts of use of that patent or an award of damages in respect of those acts of use.

4.2.4.8 Market Division

Although this form of restriction upon competition is most commonly practised by cartels, it is possible for undertakings with a dominant position to attempt to compartmentalise markets. Dominant undertakings are particularly interested in such market division so as to prevent or restrict parallel importation.[157] By appointing an exclusive seller in each geographical area, the undertaking can effectively divide markets and separate them from each other. In practice, this approach is a more obvious one in the context of collective dominant positions.[158]

4.2.4.9 Discrimination

The application of dissimilar conditions to various clients is not permitted according to Article 102(c) TFEU. In a market where an undertaking holds a dominant position, those who take supplies of goods or services from it are strongly dependent upon that undertaking; thus, it is not allowed to discriminate between its clients. In this context, it must be remembered (as will be discussed further in section 4.2.5 below) that objectively justified differences in the treatment of such clients do not lead to abusive discrimination within Article 102 TFEU. The addition of the words 'thereby placing them at a competitive disadvantage' raises the question of whether or not this means that there can only be such prohibited discrimination where the unequal treatment concerns companies that are in competition with each other. To date there have been no cases in which this question has been answered specifically.

In the *GVL* case[159] the issue of discrimination upon grounds of nationality was relevant. Over a long period of time, GVL (a collecting society) had refused to represent the rights of those foreign artists who lacked any place of residence in Germany. As a result, those artists were unable to extract from their copyrights in Germany the return to which they were justly entitled. A further example in this vein may well be the series of cases on discounts on landing charges at various EU airports.[160]

In the UK, competition authorities have consistently taken the view that great care must be taken before characterising discrimination in prices or other conditions as

---

[157] Case 26/75 *General Motors Continental NV v Commission*, paras 11–24 and Case 27/76 *United Brands Co v Commission*, paras 151–62 (concerning the prohibition on sale of green bananas; in practice, this operated as an export ban, since bananas that were already ripe would be far too fragile to transport for sale).

[158] See also Case C-486/06 *Sot Lelos Kai*—which concerned a case of prevention of parallel trade through refusal to supply.

[159] Commission Decision [1981] OJ L370/49.

[160] See Case C-163/99 *Portugal v Commission*.

abusive. The example is given of an industry with 'high fixed costs, where customers can be split up into groups according to their willingness to pay, and where groups with low willingness to pay would not buy in the absence of price discrimination', such as the rail industry, where the time of travel may allow higher prices to be charged (eg, to commuters) so as to maximise output and even allow the emergence of new segments of the market. Cases brought under this heading in the UK have met with mixed success: in the *BT–BSkyB broadband promotion* Decision,[161] for example, the Director General of Telecommunications ruled that while price discrimination did appear to be taking place, it had not had a material effect on competition upon the market.[162] In *English Welsh & Scottish Railway*, however, the ORR did find that EW&S had abused its dominant position by discriminating between customers.[163] Similarly, in *Purple Parking v Heathrow Airport*[164] the High Court concluded that Heathrow Airport was guilty of discrimination in relation to the provision of access to the forecourts of Terminals 1, 3 and 5, and in *Arriva The Shires v Luton Airport*[165] the High Court held that the terms of a concession granted by Luton Airport unlawfully discriminated in favour of one coach operator over another.

4.2.4.10 Tying Practices[166]

In the *Microsoft* case in the USA, Microsoft used all manner of means to deny its competitor Netscape (which also offered an internet browser programme) access to the market. One important method was the practice of 'tying'. This form of abuse, listed in Article 102(d) TFEU, concerns the fact that the basic product—the Microsoft operating system for PCs—was only sold in combination with Microsoft's own internet browser (Internet Explorer), while these products did not necessarily have to be tied together. Microsoft's main argument was that such tying was necessary, or at least that it was strongly in the interest of technological progress. The judge did not accept this argument. In the course of the court proceedings, it had become clear that it had been Microsoft's express intention to bankrupt Netscape and other competitors. Judge Jackson concluded his judgment in the *Microsoft* case as follows:

> Most harmful of all is the message that Microsoft's actions have conveyed to every enterprise with the potential to innovate in the computer industry. Through its conduct towards Netscape, IBM, Compaq, Intel, and others, Microsoft has demonstrated that it will use its

---

[161] Decision of 19 May 2000 and see also *BT TotalCare* (Decision of 10 June 2003) (both available from http://www.oft.gov.uk).

[162] In this regard, he placed reliance upon paras 3.1 and 3.2 of OFT 414, which specifically referred to the 'effect of any discrimination on the market' and the need to show that 'the discrimination was used to reduce competition significantly'. It is noteworthy that these two paras have been removed from the new draft Guideline, OFT 414a.

[163] ORR decision of 17 November 2006.

[164] *Purple Parking v Heathrow Airport* [2011] EWHC 987 (Ch).

[165] *Arriva The Shires v Luton Airport* [2014] EWHC 67 (Ch). See M Farley and N Pourbaix, 'The EU Concessions Directive: Building (Toll) Bridges between Competition Law and Public Procurement?' (2015) *Journal of European Competition Law and Practice* 15.

[166] See generally D Waelbroeck, 'The Compatibility of Tying Agreements with Antitrust Rules: A Comparative Study of American and European Rules' (1987) 7 *Yearbook of European Law* 39 and B Nalebuff, 'DTI Economics Paper No 1' *Bundling, Tying, and Portfolio Effects* (2003).

prodigious market power and immense profits to harm any firm that insists on pursuing initiatives that could intensify competition against one of Microsoft's core products. Microsoft's past success in hurting such companies and stifling innovation deters investment in technologies and businesses that exhibit the potential to threaten Microsoft. The ultimate result is that some business innovations that would truly benefit consumers never occur for the sole reason that they do not coincide with Microsoft's self-interest.[167]

The EU Commission as well as the GC found that Microsoft's practice of supplying its Windows client PC operating system bundled with Windows media player to be an instance of the unlawful tying of products.[168] In 2008 the Commission initiated fresh proceedings against Microsoft upon a complaint about the introduction of new technologies alleged to reduce the compatibility with internet standards.[169] The case was settled with commitments under Article 9 of Regulation 1/2003.[170] First, Microsoft agreed to make available a mechanism in Windows that enables OEMs and users to turn Internet Explorer off and on. Second, OEMs will be free to pre-install any web browser(s) of their choice on PCs they ship and set it as default web browser. Microsoft offered to distribute a choice screen software update to users of Windows PCs by means of Windows Update. Windows XP, Vista and 7 users who have Internet Explorer set as their default web browser (no matter how this setting came about) and who subscribed to Windows Update. They will be prompted with this choice screen, which will offer them a choice of web browsers, and present them with links where they can find more information about the web browsers presented on the screen.

Tying questions have also arisen before the EU courts on a number of occasions. In *Hilti*, the GC accepted the Commission's argument that there were separate markets for nail guns, the nails themselves and the cartridge strips by which the nails were fed into the guns. Thus, Hilti's requirement that customers using its patented cartridges must only use its nails was an abusive tying of the nails product market to that of the cartridges, and other producers ought to be able to make and sell nails for use with Hilti's cartridges.[171] Similarly, in *Tetra Pak II* the ECJ upheld the Commission's finding that Tetra Pak's tying practices had been an abuse under Article 102 TFEU. Tetra Pak required customers acquiring its packaging machines (used for packaging liquids) also to acquire the cartons for use in those machines from Tetra Pak itself. In the absence of any objective justification for requiring those cartons to be purchased with the machines, Tetra Pak had been guilty of trying to drive competitors from the separate market for cartons (having also committed other abuses—discrimination and predatory pricing).[172]

---

[167] Section 412 of the judgment. The judgment has been affirmed in its key elements on appeal, although the Court of Appeals required that the finding of tying be reassessed under the rule of reason standard: 253 F 3d 34 (DC Cir), *cert. denied*, 120 S Ct 350 (2001), esp pp 87–88 on the nature of tie-ins. Finally, the case was settled: *United States v Microsoft Corp* F Supp.2d 144 (DDC 2002).

[168] Case T-201/04 *Microsoft Corp v Commission* para 1229. For a more extensive discussion of the case see section 4.2.4.6.

[169] COMP 39530.

[170] A summary of the commitment is found in [2010] OJ C 36/7-8.

[171] Case T-30/89 *Hilti AG v Commission*, esp paras 64–68.

[172] Case C-333/94 P *Tetra Pak International SA*, paras 34–38. See the discussion by V Korah of the Commission's Decision in this case in 'The Paucity of Economic Analysis in the EEC Decisions on Competition: *Tetra Pak II*' (1993) 46 *Current Legal Problems* 148, at 156–72.

The treatment of tying in the Article 102 Enforcement Priorities does not introduce novel ideas or concepts.[173]

In UK law, there still remains relatively limited guidance on questions of tying. In one of the few cases addressing the question of tying, OFCOM investigated a complaint that BT was abusing a dominant position by tying a billing analysis product, BT Analyst, to the provision of business telephony services. OFCOM ultimately concluded that the billing product was part of the telephony service, and that therefore there was no tie.[174] In *Genzyme*, the OFT concluded that Genzyme had abused its dominant position in respect of the drug Cerezyme, inter alia, by bundling the drug and homecare services for patients, and imposed a fine of £6.8 million on Genzyme.[175] However, on appeal, the CAT annulled the OFT's decision on the basis that the OFT had failed to demonstrate that the bundling had sufficiently adverse effects for it to be considered abusive.[176]

4.2.5 Objective Justification

The different forms of abuse discussed in section 4.2.4 above will only amount to an abuse if, in the final analysis, there is no objective justification for such behaviour in the circumstances. This is an important development given the absence of any express exemption mechanism in Article 102 TFEU. This issue concerns the question of whether or not a particular course of action is justified by considerations of a commercial, technical or industrial organisational nature.[177] Thus, for example, discounts are allowed where they amount to something given in exchange for genuinely saved costs. In this way, the supply of large quantities of goods at one time can generate savings in transport costs for the producer of those goods in delivering them to clients. Similarly, the production of a large series of products can also allow savings to be made. In such circumstances, discounts are permitted. Another example is long-term exclusive supply contracts. Where large investments must be made to construct infrastructure, it may be that such long-term contracts (which guarantee a source of revenue for recoupment of those costs) can be justified objectively.

In *European Night Services* (ENS),[178] for example, the GC had to rule on an application seeking annulment of a Decision in which the Commission had (inter alia) found that an agreement between the parties concerning the exploitation of the Channel Tunnel was contrary to Article 101 TFEU. On the basis of that agreement,

---

[173] Paras 47–58.

[174] *Pricing of BT Analyst* (OFCOM decision of 27 October 2004). See also the earlier OFTEL decisions in *Swan Solutions/Avaya Ltd*, 6 April 2001 and the DGFT's decision in *ICL/Synstar*, 26 July 2001. In both of these cases, however, OFTEL concluded that the products in question formed part of a single market, and therefore, did not give rise to a tie.

[175] *Genzyme*, OFT decision of 27 March 2003.

[176] *Genzyme Ltd v OFT* [2004] CAT 4.

[177] This is clearly formulated by the GC in the *Microsoft* case in para 333 cited above in section 4.2.4.6. See TDO van der Vijver: 'Objective Justification and *Prima Facie* Anti-Competitive Unilateral Conduct. An Exploration of EU Law and Beyond' *PhD Leiden* 2014, 1–327.

[178] Joined Cases T-374, 375, 384 and 388/94 *European Night Services Ltd and others v Commission*, paras 230–34.

the founders of ENS (the national railway operators in the UK, France, Germany and the Netherlands) had each bound themselves to supply ENS with the necessary services, including traction over their respective networks (locomotive, train crew and slots in the timetable), cleaning services on board, servicing of equipment and passenger-handling services. According to the Commission, the agreement led to a situation in which only ENS could purchase railway services to provide to passengers for the use of the Channel Tunnel, with the result that it was very difficult for other potential competitors to enter the market for providing such railway services. Nevertheless, since the exploitation agreement contributed to the financing of the investments made for the benefit of the Channel Tunnel and investments in the development of a completely new service of a high standard, the Commission cleared the agreement subject to certain conditions. These included the proviso that the agreement could only run for a limited period. In setting the duration of the exemption, the Commission took into account any reasonably foreseeable changes in the market in the future, balancing realistic economic projections with the need for both the parties and potential competitors to have an acceptable degree of legal certainty as to their position. The GC held that the duration of the exemption granted by the Commission had not put the undertakings in a position from which they could earn back the cost of their investment through the supply of rail transport services. Furthermore, according to the GC, in assessing the justifiable duration of the exemption, account had to be taken of how long it would take before the parties' investment was profitable. The GC referred to the parties making a 'satisfactory' or 'proper' return on the investment. While the case concerned Article 101 TFEU, the reasoning process is clearly transplantable to situations under Article 102 TFEU.[179]

In the *Tetra Pak II* judgment,[180] the GC agreed with the Commission's Decision that no objective justification could be made out. Tetra Pak took the view that its imposition of an obligation upon purchasers of its packaging machines only to use Tetra Pak's own cartons (and to acquire those cartons only from Tetra Pak)[181] was objectively justified. It argued that without these tying practices the quality of the products made using those machines could not be sufficiently guaranteed. The GC was not impressed with this argument. In the analysis of the case it is important to note that Tetra Pak held 90 per cent of the market for aseptic and 78 per cent of the market for non-aseptic packaging of liquid foods in the EU. Research showed that packaging produced by other manufacturers could also be used reliably and without problems on Tetra Pak's machines. As a result, there was no objective justification for Tetra Pak's tying practices and the GC thus held that Tetra Pak had abused its dominant position. Similarly, the Court held in its *Hilti* judgment[182] that safety concerns are not an

---

[179] Not least given that the parties to the agreement were all dominant players on their own national rail services markets.

[180] Commission Decision [1992] OJ L72/1, upheld by both the CFI (Case T-83/91 and then on appeal by the ECJ in Case C-333/94 P *Tetra Pak International SA v Commission*.

[181] Note that the supply contracts that Tetra Pak concluded with these purchasers also contained numerous further conditions of at least dubious status, such as Tetra Pak's right to inspect the wording to be used on the cartons and the condition that any improvements and innovations made by the purchaser relating to the cartons had to be notified to Tetra Pak and any resulting intellectual property rights in that connection had to be transferred to the ownership of Tetra Pak.

[182] Case T-30/89 *Hilti v Commission*.

objective justification for abusing a dominant position. The Court said that this was not Hilti's responsibility, but rather that of the relevant safety authority.

4.2.6 Overlap Between the Prohibition of the Abuse of a Dominant Position and Other Competition Law Provisions

4.2.6.1 Abuse of Dominant Position and Anti-competitive Agreements

It is possible that certain behaviour or dealings of an undertaking with a dominant position may amount both to a breach of the prohibition on anti-competitive agreements and to an abuse of a dominant position. This can only be the case where *all* of the elements of *both* prohibitions are satisfied.[183] It is not sufficient simply to 'recycle' the facts that prove a breach of *one* of these prohibitions to substantiate an allegation of a breach of the other prohibition.[184] Thus, in *Hoffmann-La Roche* the undertaking held a dominant position, on the basis of which its loyalty rebates could be treated as an abuse under Article 102 TFEU. At the same time, these contracts could also have been assessed under Article 101 TFEU.

As a result, it is open to the Commission and the CMA to choose the legal basis that appears to them to be the most opportune, and the same goes for private parties aiming to rely upon competition law before the national courts. In that connection, it is of particular importance that a duty to supply can be ordered if an abuse of a dominant position can be shown, whereas this is not possible as a response to a breach of Article 101(1) TFEU. Thus, the relevant competition authorities cannot force undertakings that have participated in anti-competitive collusion to enter into a particular contract so as to effect that supply (unless the relevant undertakings agree to do so in the context of commitments offered under Article 9 of Regulation 1/2003). Further, it is vital to appreciate that a finding that the exemption of Article 101(3) TFEU is applicable does not amount to an exemption from Article 102 TFEU. Nevertheless, it is unlikely that an agreement that has passed the test of Article 101(3) TFEU would at the same time be contrary to Article 102 TFEU, since one of the conditions under Article 101(3) TFEU is that the agreement must not give the undertakings concerned the possibility of eliminating competition in respect of a substantial part of the goods or services in question.[185] Finally, the GC has made clear in *Tetra Pak I* that the applicability of a block exemption to an agreement does not amount to an exemption from Article 102 TFEU: such exemptions are not subject to individual examination and thus cannot be equated to a Decision granting a negative clearance under Article 102 TFEU. As a result, conduct amounting to an abuse of a dominant position is abusive, even prior to the Commission taking a decision to withdraw the benefit of the block

---

[183] Case 85/76 *Hoffmann-La Roche & Co. AG v Commission*, para 116; see also Case T-51/89 *Tetra Pak Rausing SA v Commission ('Tetra Pak I')*, para 22.
[184] Cases T-68, 77 and 78/89 *Società Italiana Vetro SpA and others v Commission (Italian Flat Glass)*, para 360.
[185] See, eg, Commission Decision, *Decca Navigator System* [1989] OJ L43/27, where no exemption was granted because the agreement amounted to an abuse under Art 82 EC.

exemption.[186] This point was also of importance in *Compagnie Maritime Belge*[187] and emphasises the need to conduct a careful investigation of the market context of such practices to ensure that the obligations imposed by *both* Article 101 *and* Article 102 TFEU are being respected by the undertakings concerned.[188]

4.2.6.2 Market Studies and Market Investigations Under UK Competition Law[189]

For the sake of completeness, it is important to note that the Chapter II prohibition is not the only mechanism available under UK competition law for addressing positions of dominance on a market. When the CMA[190] identifies a problem within a market, in addition to opening an investigation on the basis of Article 101 or 102 TFEU and/or Chapters I or II of the CA 1998, it can choose to conduct either a market study, or a market investigation pursuant to the Enterprise Act 2002 (EA 2002).[191]

Market studies are conducted under the CMA's general review function in section 5 EA 2002.[192] The CMA uses these studies as a means of examining why particular markets may not be working well, taking an overview of regulatory and other economic drivers and patterns of consumer and business behaviour. Market studies may lead to a range of outcomes, including: declaring that the market is working well; adoption of measures to improve the quality and accessibility of information to consumers; adoption of measures seeking to encourage businesses in the market to self-regulate; making recommendations to the Government to change regulations or

---

[186] Case T-51/89 *Tetra Pak Rausing SA v Commission ('Tetra Pak I')*. It should be noted that since the entry into force of Reg 1/2003 individual exemptions are no longer a condition for the validity of agreements therefore the situation described in the text will only rarely occur.

[187] Cases C-395 and 396/96 P *Compagnie Maritime Belge Transports SA and others v Commission* (see esp para 130), where the relevant block exemption Regulation (Reg 4056/86/EC) gave extensive exemptions to (inter alia) price-fixing in the context of shipping liner conferences, but the characterisation of the liner conference as holding a collective dominant position allowed those practices to be attacked by the Commission. On 7 July 2016 the Commission accepted commitments offered by 14 container liner shipping companies. The commitments aim to increase price transparency for customers and to reduce the likelihood of coordinating prices.

[188] In UK law, a similar point was made clear by the way in which the exclusion of vertical agreements from the Ch I prohibition was specifically stated to apply only to Ch I and not to potential abuses of a dominant position under Ch II: see s 50 CA 1998. This exclusion of vertical agreements was ended as of 1 May 2005 by the Competition Act 1998 and Other Enactments (Amendment) Regulations 2004 (SI 2004, No 1261), Regs 1 and 4 *juncto* sch 1, para 50(a).

[189] See generally *Market Investigation References* (OFT 511), *Market Investigation References: Competition Commission Guidelines* (CC3), Pt 4 of *General Advice and Information* (CC4) and R Whish, *Competition Law*, 5th edn (2003) ch 11. For further commentary, see B Sufrin and M Furse, 'Market Investigations' (2002) *Competition Law Journal* 244 and D Morris, 'The Enterprise Act 2002: Aspects of the New Regime' (2002) *Competition Law Journal* 318.

[190] The relevant sector regulators, such as OFGEM, OFWAT, ORR etc. also have the power to conduct market studies or market investigations.

[191] The EA 2002 was amended by the Enterprise and Regulatory Reform Act 2013 (ERRA 2013). The reforms amended the procedure for conducting market studies and market investigations to take account of the institutional reforms and replacement of the OFT and Competition Commission with the CMA.

[192] The Enterprise and Regulatory Reform Act 2013 (ERRA 2013) introduced a formal requirement for a market study to be commenced by the issuing of a market study notice and laid down specific timetables and investigative powers for conducting market studies.

public policy; begin competition or consumer enforcement action; conducting a market investigation reference, or accepting undertakings in lieu of making a reference.[193]

Market investigations are more detailed examinations, conducted under Part 4 of the EA 2002, into whether there is an 'adverse effect on competition' (AEC) in the market(s) for the goods or services referred.[194]

The CMA or any of the sector regulators may make a reference where it has reasonable grounds for suspecting that any feature, or combination of features, of a market or markets in the UK for goods or services prevents, restricts or distorts competition in connection with the supply or acquisition of any goods or services in the UK or a part of the UK.[195]

Two principal types of market investigation reference may be made by the CMA are:[196]

(a)   ordinary references: these are references which are not cross-market references and do not raise public interest issues); and
(b)   cross-market references: this is a new type of reference, introduced by the ERRA 2013, in respect of specific features or combinations of features that exist in more than one market.

When the CMA Board considers that a market investigation is required, it will make a reference to a group drawn from the CMA's panel of members. The CMA's panel comprises individuals from a variety of backgrounds (economics, law, public sector, business), all eminent in their field and the market investigation is undertaken independently of the CMA Board. The CMA panel group are the sole decision-makers in the investigation.

Following the adoption of the Enterprise and Regulatory Reform Act 2013 (ERRA 2013), the CMA group must conclude the market investigation within 18 months from the date that the reference is made. This is extendable by six months in exceptional circumstances. Within that timescale, there are a number of stages to the investigation, including the publication of an early issues statement, setting out the proposed scope of the investigation and specific questions it will be addressing, evidence gathering including a series of site visits and hearings with parties and other interest groups, publication of a provisional findings decision (after approximately 12 months), further

---

[193] Further information on the management of market studies is contained in ch 4 of *Market Studies: Guidance* on the OFT approach (OFT 519); and *Market Studies and Market Investigations: Supplemental guidance on the CMA's approach* (CMA 3), s 2.

[194] The CMA has taken over a considerable amount of guidance from the OFT and Competition Commission concerning market investigations as well as publishing its own guidance. The principal guidance documents include: *Market studies: Guidance on the OFT approach* (OFT 519); *Market investigation references* (OFT 511), *Guidelines for market investigations* (CC3 (revised)); and *Market Studies and Market Investigations: Supplemental guidance on the CMA's approach* (CMA 3).

[195] Section 131(1) EA 2002 (moving away from the old test under the Fair Trading Act 1973, which operated on the basis of whether or not it such features operated in a manner contrary to the 'public interest'). Often, this will become apparent after the OFT has conducted a market study into a particular sector: on market studies, see s 5 EA 2002 and the OFT's Guidance *Market Studies* (OFT 519). This occurred in the case of store cards. Equally, such a study could lead to enforcement action under the CA 1998.

[196] The Secretary of State can also make either restricted or full market investigation references in cases that raise defined public interest issues. See further the CMA's guidance, *Market Studies and Market Investigations: Supplemental guidance on the CMA's approach* (CMA 3), s 1.14.

hearings and then the provisional decision on remedies (if required) before publication of the final report.

Following a reference, the market reference group is required to decide whether there is an adverse effect on competition (AEC) in the market(s) referred. In the event that the reference group does identify an AEC it needs to determine whether, and what, remedial action is appropriate. Such action can include price regulation; preventing the completion of acquisitions; and even divestiture of elements of an undertaking.[197] The wide range of remedies available to the CMA group renders the market investigation route particularly attractive where serious structural changes are required to facilitate competition in particular markets.

As can be seen from the above, the market study and market investigation regime is an important feature of the UK system of competition law, which recognises that not every market failure can be cured through the application of Articles 101 and 102 TFEU and the Chapter I and Chapter II prohibitions in the CA 1998. In this regard, the market study and market investigation regime focuses on markets rather than on the behaviour of individual firms, and enables the CMA to investigate whether features of the market have an adverse effect on competition, without the imposition of sanctions on market actors for past behaviour.

---

[197] See ch 8 to the EA 2002, paras 8, 12 and 13 respectively.

5

Control of Concentrations

5.1 Introduction

One major consequence of the realisation of the EU's internal market was that many undertakings that wanted to internationalise their activities began to look for possible commercial partners for joint operations, to take over or with which to merge. At the start of this development there was no effective regulation of this process at the Community level. Simply put, the EU Treaty had made no provision for merger control. At that stage, the most important instrument for achieving some degree of merger control was Article 102 TFEU, but that control had its limitations. It was control 'after the fact' and always required that one undertaking connected with the merger (also known as a 'concentration') held a dominant position.[1]

Since many Member States viewed merger control as the key instrument of national industrial policy, the negotiations that were ultimately to lead to a form of Community-level merger control were lengthy and laborious. A compromise was finally reached, and at the end of 1989 the text of Regulation 4064/89/EEC ('on the control of concentrations between undertakings') was published.[2] This Regulation provided for prior control of concentrations with a Union dimension by the European Commission. On 1 May 2004, Regulation 4064/89/EEC was replaced by Regulation 139/2004/EC[3] (hereafter, the 'EU Merger Regulation', or EUMR). Shortly afterwards, Regulation 447/98/EC,[4] which laid down the detailed procedural framework for the application of Regulation 4064/89/EEC, was replaced by Regulation 802/2004/EC.[5]

The EUMR has made a number of important changes to the EU's merger control regime. Thus, the European Commission need no longer examine whether or not a

---

[1] In this connection, see Case 6/72 *Continental Can v Commission*.
[2] [1989] OJ L395/1. For the corrected text, see [1990] OJ L257/14, as amended by Reg 1310/97/EC [1997] OJ L180/1.
[3] Reg 139/2004/EC of the Council of 20 January 2004 on the control of concentrations between undertakings [2004] OJ L24/1.
[4] [1998] OJ L61/11, as amended by the Act of Accession of 2003.
[5] Reg 802/2004/EC of the Commission of 7 April 2004 implementing Council Reg (EC) No 139/2004 on the control of concentrations between undertakings [2004] OJ L133/1. Lastly amended by Reg 1269/2013, OJ 2013, L 336/1. Consolidated version 2004R0802—EN—01.01.2014—003.001—1.

concentration will create or strengthen a dominant position, but instead must assess whether or not that concentration will give rise to a significant impediment to effective competition. A further innovation under the EUMR was that it is possible, before a proposed concentration has been notified to any particular competition authority, for the undertakings concerned to submit that it should be referred by the Commission to one or more Member States' national competition authorities (NCAs) (Article 4(4) EUMR). Equally, this referral process can operate in the other direction (ie, referral *to* the Commission) where the concentration would need to be notified to three or more individual Member State NCAs (even where no 'Union dimension' is present: Article 4(5) EUMR). In addition, the EUMR also established (inter alia):

(a) a binding notification and review timetable (Article 10 EUMR);
(b) the possibility to notify on the basis of a so-called 'concept agreement' (where no final agreement on merger has been reached but the parties can show that this is intended and/or has been publicly announced) (Article 4(1) EUMR, second paragraph); and
(c) rules on how the parties should conduct themselves where the Commission's decision has been annulled by the GC or the ECJ (Article 10(5) EUMR).

Merger control is actually carried out within the European Commission by the Merger Network consisting of five units and a Task Force. The latter is charged with the ex post supervision of the financial crisis decisions. The Commission is assisted by the 'Chief Economist Team'.[6] In order to ease the understanding of the application of the EUMR, the Commission has also published a number of detailed Notices. In practice, these Notices play a very important role in the application of the EUMR and will be discussed in this chapter. Since 2010 the Commission has published a handbook with the relevant rules in the area of merger control, which it updates on a regular basis.[7]

The European Commission has exclusive competence to scrutinise and reach decisions on concentrations with a Union dimension. The various national merger control regimes of the Member States are in principle inapplicable to such concentrations. Indeed, at the start of the EU merger control era, many undertakings, particularly multinational companies, had hoped that in the course of time the quantitative thresholds for showing a Union dimension for a concentration would be lowered considerably. This would have had the effect of further extending the competence of the Commission at the expense of the influence of national merger control regimes. For many companies, this would have been a desirable outcome as it would have simplified the merger notification and clearance process still further, requiring only one approval for the whole of the EU.

In the context of UK Competition Law, merger control has existed since the Monopolies and Restrictive Practices (Inquiry and Control) Act 1948. However, this legislation only provided for investigations after a merger had been completed, and it also lacked any measures to enable the Monopolies and Restrictive Practices Commission

---

[6] The organisation can be gleaned from the website of DG COMP.
[7] European Commission, EU competition law, rules applicable to EU merger control, situation as at 31 July 2013, http://ec.europa.eu/competition/mergers/legislation/merger_compilation.pdf.

(the forerunner of the OFT and CMA) to prevent mergers from being put into effect or to reverse such mergers by requiring structural changes (eg, divestitures) to be made. Since that legislation was introduced, many reform proposals have been made and a number of amendments to the legislative framework have entered into force. Developments in decisional practice during the mid-1980s led to the regime becoming increasingly 'competition'—rather than more broadly 'public interest'—based, and this trend was given explicit recognition with the introduction of the Enterprise Act 2002 (EA 2002), and was recently amended by the Enterprise and Regulatory Reform Act 2013 (ERRA 2013). A fuller introduction to the various procedural and substantive changes made to the UK regime is provided in section 5.3 below.

5.2 The Key Elements of the EU Merger Regulation

5.2.1 Introduction[8]

The EUMR only applies to transactions that bring about a concentration, that is, according to Article 3 EUMR, a transaction whereby one undertaking acquires control of another undertaking. This is discussed in section 5.2.3. The EUMR provides for the prior notification of concentrations with a 'Union dimension' and also lays down the procedural steps that must be followed (section 5.2.2). It lays down a system with two different investigative procedures: the initial or 'first' phase and a second phase, which is necessary where, following the first phase investigation, it appears that the concentration gives rise to serious doubts as to its compatibility with the internal market and, as such, a more detailed investigation is required. In principle, the EUMR applies to all concentrations that satisfy the criterion of possessing a Union dimension (section 5.2.4). The European Commission is exclusively competent to assess whether this group of concentrations is compatible with the internal market (section 5.2.5). In making this assessment, any relevant so-called 'ancillary restraints' are also analysed (section 5.2.6).

5.2.2 Prior Notification and Procedure

5.2.2.1 Prior Assessment

As mentioned above, the supervision exercised by the European Commission under the EUMR is by assessment and decision prior to the implementation of the concentration concerned. Only the EUMR is applicable to concentrations with a

---

[8] For in general Michael Rosenthal, Stefan Thomas *European Merger Control* (CH Beck, 2010); John Cook, Christopher Kerse *EC Merger Control* (Sweet & Maxwell, 2009).

Union dimension and the Commission is exclusively competent to adopt decisions on the basis of the EUMR (see Article 21(1) and (2) EUMR). This system has often been called a 'one-stop shop'. Whenever a transaction has a Union dimension, the undertakings concerned need notify only one authority to receive a decision that will cover all of the EU Member States.

Under Article 7(1) EUMR, a concentration with a Union dimension cannot, in principle, be implemented either before it has been notified or until it has been declared compatible with the internal market or deemed to be so compatible (as a result of the Commission's failure to take a decision within the relevant time limits).[9] Article 7 EUMR does, however, provide certain exceptions allowing for (inter alia) the implementation of a public bid and a series of transactions in securities admitted to trading that result in a transfer of control (provided that a notification of the concentration is made to the Commission forthwith and that the voting rights under the shares are not exercised pending clearance). This provision also empowers the Commission to grant a derogation from this standstill obligation (Article 7(3) EUMR).[10] Undertakings that do not observe this obligation and 'jump the gun' can be fined by the Commission, according to Article 14(2) EUMR.[11]

5.2.2.2 Putting the 'One-stop Shop' System into Perspective

While it is accurate to view the system of the EUMR as a 'one-stop shop' for the great majority of concentrations, the EUMR also contains provisions that allow deviations from this system in particular cases. On the basis of Article 9 EUMR, the Commission can, under certain conditions and on the express request of a Member State, refer a notified merger, wholly or partially, to the competent authorities of that Member State for assessment (Article 9 EUMR).[12] The Commission may also ask a Member State to submit such a reference request. This procedure must be carried out under strict time limits, to ensure that the notifying parties receive the legal certainty of a ruling on the concentration as quickly as possible. Article 9 EUMR distinguishes between two types of concentrations:

(a) concentrations within a Member State that present all the characteristics of a distinct market; and

---

[9] There have been disputes about the question when a merger is actually implemented, *cf* the decision of the President of the GC in the Aer Lingus case. The President ruled that a partial implementation of the merger did not contravene the standstill obligation: *Aer Lingus Group Plc v Commission*, T-411/07 R.

[10] In case of urgency the Commission may take such a decision at very short notice. In the Bradford & Bingley Assets, Comp/M.5363 decision the Commission granted a derogation within 24 hours.

[11] Such cases are, however, rare. The only cases involving gun jumping are: M.7184 *Marine Harvest/Morpol*; M.4994 *Electrabel/Compagnie nationale du Rhône*; M.969 *AP Møller*; M.920 *Samsung/AST*.

[12] For the most recent UK-related example, see the OFT's Decision on the *Completed acquisition by the Blackstone Group of NHP plc* (5 April 2005) after the Commission had agreed to refer the whole matter to the OFT: for details, see the Commission's Decision referring Case No COMP/M.3669 *Blackstone (TBG CareCo)/NHP* to the competent UK authorities pursuant to Art 9 of Council Reg No 139/2004 (1 February 2005). Subsequently the OFT has requested that the Commission refer the proposed acquisition of Exeter Airport from Devon County Council by Macquarie Airports Ltd and Ferrovial Aeropuertos SA to the UK competition authorities under Art 9 of the EC Merger Regulation: see OFT Press Release 132/05 (22 July 2005). See also Commission decision *Buitenfood/Ad van Geloven Holding/JV* (Comp/M.6321) in which the Commission approves the merger for the parts that do not relate to the Dutch market.

(b)   concentrations within a Member State that present all the characteristics of a distinct market *and which do not constitute a substantial part of the common market.*

In the first case the Commission has discretion whether or not to refer. In the latter case it must refer the merger to the NCA concerned.

On the basis of Article 22(3) EUMR, meanwhile, the reverse process is also possible: a Member State can (again, under certain conditions) request that the Commission rule on a concentration that lacks a Union dimension.[13] This procedure is also subject to strict time limits.

Under the EUMR, the parties concerned can also ask for a referral before the concentration has been notified to any particular competition authority. This request must be made by a reasoned notification using the Form RS, which must be submitted to the Commission. The information required by the Form RS and its format are laid down in Regulation 802/2004/EC. The parties can request that a concentration with a Union dimension should nevertheless be referred to one or more NCAs (Article 4(4) EUMR) and, vice versa, the parties can request that a concentration should be handled by the Commission where it might instead be notified to three or more EU Member State NCAs (Article 4(5) EUMR). In both cases, the Commission must consult the relevant NCAs before reaching its decision on such a request. Once again, both of these procedures are subject to strict time limits. Even though referrals often take more time the procedure by which parties ask that the case be handled by the Commission has gained importance.

In 2014 there were 35 requests for such referrals, all of which were granted.

The Commission has clarified the nature and operation of these four referral possibilities in its 'Notice on Case Referral in Respect of Concentrations'.[14]

5.2.2.3 Notification

According to Article 4(1) EUMR, a concentration with a Union dimension must be notified to the European Commission. Notification may also be made before an agreement has been concluded. In such a case the undertakings have to demonstrate to the Commission a good faith intention to conclude an agreement. Similarly, notification may be made in the case of a public bid, where an undertaking has publicly announced an intention to make such a bid. In both cases the intended agreement or bid should result in a concentration with a Union dimension.

Notification must be made using the 'Form CO' (as it is known). This form has been published by the Commission as Annex I to Regulation 802/2004/EC.[15] This Regulation contains rules and instructions on how the form must be completed, information about time limits, rules relating to conducting hearings for the concerned undertakings and third parties, and procedures for undertakings to make, and the Commission to accept, commitments relating to the concentration, so as to render it compatible with the internal market.

---

[13] The Commission does not examine mergers without a Community dimension when Member States have not requested it to apply Art 22 EUMR, even though the text of the article does not seem to exclude it do so, see decision (Comp/M.5282 *P&G/Sara Lee Air Care*).

[14] [2005] OJ 56/2.

[15] [2004] OJ L133/1.

It should be noted that in practice it is often the case that 'pre-notification discussions are conducted with the European Commission, so as to prevent possible problems (such as submission of an incomplete or unclear notification) from occurring later. In its document on 'Best Practices on the Conduct of EC Merger Control Proceedings',[16] the Commission also strongly recommends that pre-notification discussions be held.

The notification must be made by the undertaking or undertakings acquiring control over one or more undertakings (or a part thereof). Practice has shown that where one of the parties has refused to cooperate in the notification process, the Commission has also been willing to accept notifications made by just a single party.

If the parties provide incorrect and misleading details in the notification or if incorrect information is given in response to a request for information, the Commission can impose a fine on the basis of Article 14(1)(a), (b) and (c) EUMR.

Where the Commission rules that the notified concentration falls under the EUMR, the fact of the notification must be published, along with the relevant business sector concerned. This publication is made in the Official Journal, according to Article 4(3) EUMR, which also provides that the 'Commission shall take account of the legitimate interest of undertakings in the protection of their business secrets'.

The Commission's publication of the fact of the notification also invites comments from interested parties on the merger in question. This invitation is repeated when the Commission opens the second phase of its investigations (see section 5.2.2.6 below). The participation of these third parties is extremely important in the Commission's merger control practice. An excellent illustration of this point is provided by the intense third-party activity surrounding the Commission's investigation of the proposed *GE/Honeywell* merger, even though little of this is reflected in the Commission's formal Decision on the merger.[17]

Finally, the participation of third parties also allows the Commission to test the likely impact upon the market of any proposal to accept commitments from the undertakings involved to close the procedure. Third parties play an important role in developing the Commission's assessment of whether or not the undertakings offered by the parties are adequate to remove the competitive concerns raised by the proposed merger (see section 5.2.2.7 below).

5.2.2.4 Time Limits

Under the EUMR, the Commission is required to observe strict time limits in completing its procedures. First of all, in the first phase the Commission is obliged by Article 6 EUMR to examine the notification as soon as it is received, and must notify any decision that it takes to the undertakings concerned and to the competent competition authorities of the Member States without delay. This underlines the fact that the Member States also play a role in this procedure, inter alia via the Advisory Committee on Concentrations (Article 19 EUMR).

---

[16] See: ec.europa.eu/competition/mergers/legislation/proceedings.pdf.

[17] Case COMP/M.2220, *GE/Honeywell* (3 July 2001), available at http://ec.europa.eu/competition/mergers/cases/decisions/m2220_en.pdf: see, for the faintest trace of this point, para 565.

Alongside this, Article 10(1) EUMR requires that in the first phase a decision must be taken within 25 working days of the day after the receipt of (the full details concerning) the notification. This period may be extended to 35 working days where the Commission receives a request for a referral from a Member State or where undertakings offer commitments.

Where the Commission has seen fit to commence the second phase investigation, Article 10(3) EUMR requires a decision to be reached within 90 working days of the date on which the proceedings are initiated. This period can be extended to 105 working days under certain circumstances.[18] The notifying parties can themselves also ask for an extension of the time limit in the second phase. This request must be submitted within 15 working days of the initiation of the procedure and can only be made once. Equally, the Commission can itself come forward with a proposal to extend the time period applicable, though this will only succeed if the notifying parties agree to the extension proposed. The total duration of any extension at the request of the parties and on the proposal of the Commission cannot exceed 20 working days. This means that the maximum duration of the second phase, without suspension, is 125 working days.

Article 10(6) EUMR lays down that, where no decision has been delivered within the applicable time limits, the concentration is deemed to have been declared compatible with the internal market.

The time limits can only be suspended on the basis of Article 10(4) EUMR, which applies where, owing to circumstances for which one of the undertakings involved in the concentration is responsible, the Commission has had to request information by decision pursuant to Article 11 or to order an inspection by decision pursuant to Article 13 (Article 10(4) EUMR).

Within these time periods and in certain circumstances, the Commission is also obliged to hear the views of the undertakings concerned and third parties with a 'sufficient interest' (Article 18 EUMR). The details concerning how this right to be heard can be exercised are now laid down in Chapter IV of Regulation 802/2004/EC (Articles 11–16).

The strict time limits of the EUMR are very important for the mergers and acquisition practice. For mergers effected by way of a public bid for all or part of the (outstanding) shares of the target undertaking, in several Member States, such a public offer must be unconditional and has to be completed within a certain time. Moreover, the bid cannot be subjected to the condition that approval of the merger will be forthcoming. Thus the parties have no choice but to implement the merger. Article 7(2) EUMR allows for this possibility as an exception to the standstill requirements provided that the transaction comes within the scope of Article 7(2) EUMR[19] and that: (i) the concentration is notified to the Commission in accordance with Article 4(1) EUMR; and (ii) the acquirer does not exercise the voting rights attached to the securities in question pending receipt of clearance from the Commission. However, such exception does not prevent the Commission from ordering the merger to be broken up

---

[18] Namely where the parties offer commitments at a point after 55 working days have elapsed since the initiation of the procedure.

[19] Case COMP/M.7184—Marine Harvest/Morpol.

if it cannot approve the merger. This was the result of the Commission's Decision on the *Tetra Laval/Sidel* merger.[20]

Even if national law does not require the public bid to be implemented, the very fact that the Commission may open the second phase may lead the acquirer to offer a higher price for the outstanding shares of the undertaking being acquired. This is what happened in the *Blackstone/Celanese* merger.[21] Furthermore, many acquisitions are financed by short-term credits provided by banks. It is not unusual for such credits to be interest free or subject to a very low interest charge for an initial period. If, however, the transaction takes longer then interest will be due or the interest rate will be increased.

5.2.2.5 Decision by the Commission in the First Phase

According to the EUMR, there are three basic possible situations in the first phase. First, the Commission can consider that the notified concentration does not fall within the scope of application of the EUMR. In that case, the Commission must find as such by formal decision (Article 6(1)(a) EUMR).

Secondly, the Commission can take the view that the notified concentration does indeed fall within the scope of the EUMR, but that it does not raise any serious doubts as to its compatibility with the internal market. In such a case, the Commission adopts a decision clearing the concentration as compatible with the internal market (Article 6(1)(b) EUMR).

Thirdly, after investigating the notified concentration the Commission can come to the conclusion that there are serious doubts as to its compatibility with the internal market. In this scenario, the Commission will take a decision to open the second-phase procedure (Article 6(1)(c) EUMR). However, if the undertakings concerned have

---

[20] On 27 March 2001, Tetra Laval SA announced a public bid for all outstanding shares in Sidel. Tetra Laval SA is a privately held company established under French law for the purpose of holding Sidel's shares acquired through the public bid. It is a wholly owned subsidiary of Tetra. Tetra Laval SA's bid for Sidel was for cash at a price of €50 per share. This represented a 32% premium to the 3-month average share price and a 52% premium on the 21 March 2001 share price but was significantly lower than the average Sidel share price over a period of 3 years. The bid valued Sidel at approximately €1.9 billion and was financed through the existing credit lines and internal resources of Tetra. The board of directors of Sidel unanimously recommended the acceptance of the bid. In accordance with French law, the bid was unconditional. Pursuant to the bid, approximately 27.1 million shares, or 81.3% of the outstanding Sidel shares, were tendered to Tetra Laval SA. In addition to those shares, Tetra Laval SA has also acquired approximately 3.5 million shares in Sidel either on the open market or in individual purchases from major shareholders. As a result, Tetra currently holds 92% of Sidel's shares. Pursuant to the Art 7(2) EUMR exception, Tetra Laval implemented the proposed concentration, despite the fact that the Commission issued a Prohibitive decision, declaring that concentration incompatible with the internal market (Commission Decision 2004/124/EC). The implementation of the concentration, despite the Prohibitive Decision, prompted the Commission to issue the Divestiture Decision (Commission Decision 2004/103/EC, [2004] OJ L38/1), ordering Tetra Laval to unscramble the implemented concentration. See further Table 5.1 for details on this series of Decisions. See also the Commission's decision in Case M.7184 *Marine Harvest/Morpol*, in which Marine Harvest implement a concentration prior to notification to, and clearance by, the Commission in reliance on Art 7(2) EUMR. The Commission considered that Art 7(2) EUMR did not apply and fined Marine Harvest €20 million for failing to respect its notification and standstill obligations under Arts 4(1) and 7(1) EUMR.

[21] Case No COMP/M.3371, Decision of 10 March 2004 (an Art 6(1)(b) non-opposition decision). In this case the shareholders that held out until the very last moment before accepting the offer by Blackstone received a premium on their shares of some €20.

made changes to the notified transaction to such an extent that the Commission no longer entertains such doubts about the concentration, then the Commission (by virtue of Article 6(2) EUMR) may declare the concentration after all to be compatible with the internal market, in the sense of Article 6(1)(b) EUMR.

The Commission will formalise its assessment that a concentration is compatible with the internal market in a decision, to which it may in some cases also attach certain conditions and obligations to the clearance (Article 6(2), second sentence, EUMR), these conditions must be satisfied by the undertakings concerned. The Commission in certain circumstances can revoke such a clearance decision. Under Article 6(3) EUMR, this would be the case where the decision has been based upon incorrect information for which one of the undertakings is responsible or which has been obtained by deceit, or where the undertakings concerned breach any of the conditions attached to the clearance decision.

5.2.2.6 Decision by the Commission in the Second Phase

Every second phase procedure must be closed with a decision finding the concentration to be either incompatible or compatible with the internal market (Article 8 EUMR).[22] A decision finding compatibility can include certain conditions and obligations for the parties. Here, too, such decisions can be revoked where the decision has been based upon incorrect information for which one of the undertakings is responsible or which has been obtained by deceit, or where the undertakings concerned breach any of the conditions attached to the clearance decision (Article 8(6) EUMR).

A Commission prohibition can have an enormous impact. This was illustrated by the *Schneider/Legrand* case. The Commission declared the merger incompatible with the internal market but because the merger had already been implemented it took a second decision ordering Schneider to divest Legrand. The GC annulled the Commission decision but, in line with Article 10(5) EUMR, the Commission pursued its procedure after the decision of the GC. Schneider divested Legrand losing €1.7 billion and subsequently brought a claim for damages against the Commission. In the end the ECJ accepted Schneider's claim but only for a minor part, that is the damages related to the loss Schneider incurred as a result of the continuation of the procedure by the Commission.[23] The ECJ annulled the judgment of the GC awarding damages compensating two thirds of the damages claimed by Schneider.[24]

5.2.2.7 Remedies and Amendments of the Notification

The Commission may harbour serious doubts whether the notified merger is compatible with the internal market. It may express these doubts during the pre-notification discussions or following the notification. Parties may also have second thoughts about the compatibility of the planned merger. In such a situation parties may decide not to

---

[22] The exception is Art 10(6) EUMR where clearance is deemed in the absence of a decision.
[23] Case C-440/07 P *Commissie v Schneider Electric SA*.
[24] Case I-351/03 *Schneider v Commission*.

proceed with the merger as originally contemplated. They will carefully study the possibilities on how to amend the proposed transaction in order to make it compatible. This may take the form of structural adjustments, such as a divestiture of parts of the undertakings concerned or behavioural commitments. It is common that this process of adjustment of the transaction takes place in close contact with the Commission.

5.2.2.8 Decisions Subject to Conditions

In both the first and second phases of the EU merger control procedure, a concentration can be declared compatible with the internal market subject to certain conditions and obligations imposed by the Commission upon the undertakings concerned. The Commission published a 'Notice on remedies' to assist parties when considering submitting commitments.[25]

In this Notice, the Commission explains how it will judge whether or not a particular measure will or will not resolve the competition problems in issue.

> Under the Merger Regulation, the Commission only has power to accept commitments that are deemed capable of rendering the concentration compatible with the internal market so that they will prevent a significant impediment of effective competition. The commitments have to eliminate the competition concerns entirely and have to be comprehensive and effective from all points of view. Furthermore, commitments must be capable of being implemented effectively within a short period of time as the conditions of competition on the market will not be maintained until the commitments have been fulfilled.[26]

The Commission has also published standard models for Divestiture Commitments as well as Trustee Mandates. Both are explained in the 'Best Practice Guidelines Explanatory Note on the Commission's Model Texts for Divestiture Commitments and the Trustee Mandate under the EC Merger Regulation'.[27] These publications are designed to help parties in their efforts to clear the proposed merger.

Commitments of a structural nature (such as a commitment to sell a subsidiary undertaking) are typically the preferred remedy. The Notice goes on to discuss a number of other measures that are in principle acceptable to the Commission, as well as detailing the formal requirements for the submission of commitments by the parties to the Commission.

The discussion about the possible conditions that may be imposed by the Commission regularly gives rise to heated debates between the parties to the merger, the Commission and third parties.

A good illustration of the way in which the Commission may attach conditions to merger clearance and accept commitments in lieu of a prohibition decision is provided by its *Exxon/Mobil* Decision.[28]

> 4. Exxon Corporation (Exxon) is a diversified company active worldwide in the exploration, development, production and sale of crude oil and natural gas; the refining and sale of refined

[25] [2008] OJ C 267/1.

[26] ibid, para 9.

[27] http://ec.europa.eu/competition/mergers/legislation/divestiture.html.

[28] Case No IV/M.1383, 29 September 1999. All confidential information that has been deleted from the subsequent extracts from the Commission's Decision and the conditions imposed is marked as follows: [*]. The following parts are excerpts from the decision.

petroleum products; the development, production and sale of various chemical products; the production and sale of coal and minerals; and power generation. Mobil Corporation (Mobil) is a diversified company active worldwide in the exploration, development, production and sale of crude oil and natural gas; the refining and sale of refined petroleum products; and the development, production and sale of various chemical products. Mobil and British Petroleum (BP) regrouped all their refining and retailing activities in Europe into a jointly controlled joint venture, BP/Mobil.[29]

5. This notification concerns a full merger ... Exxon and Mobil signed an Agreement and Plan of Merger on December 1, 1998. Pursuant to this agreement, Mobil will merge with a wholly owned subsidiary of Exxon, with Mobil as the surviving corporation. As a result, Exxon will hold 100 percent of Mobil's issued and outstanding voting securities.

823. Exxon currently enjoys significant [market] shares in the supply of jet fuels to Gatwick. As a result of the merger, this position will be further enhanced. Exxon has up to 1.1 million tonnes spare capacity on its own pipelines. It could use this extra capacity to capture any incremental growth in demand at Gatwick. Other suppliers have no spare refining or pipeline capacity to exploit any further market growth.

It is the Commission's view that the operation will result in the creation of a dominant position in the market for the supply of aviation fuels to Gatwick airport, in the UK.

As a result of this assessment, the parties offered a range of commitments to the Commission, to address the competition concerns. These were reproduced in the Annex to the Commission's Decision, and we highlight some of those commitments here:

28. Within [*] from the Effective Date, unless extended by the Commission in accordance with paragraph 65 of this Undertaking, the Parties shall reach binding agreement for the sale of aviation fuel pipeline capacity from the Coryton refinery to Gatwick airport equivalent to Mobil's 1998 sales volume at Gatwick (ie, [*]), subject to the appropriate pipeline co-shareholder consents and preemptive rights and any government approvals.

29. Accordingly, the Parties shall sell such interest in the West London Pipeline Company Limited as necessary to reduce Mobil's interest in that pipeline to [*]%, and a [*]% interest in the Walton Gatwick Pipeline Company Limited to third parties approved by the Commission. The Parties' [*]% interest in United Kingdom Oil Pipelines Limited (UKOP) shall be sold with the Coryton Refinery upon dissolution of the BP/Mobil JV.

30. If within [*] from the Effective Date, the Commission has not approved a potential purchaser for Mobil's rights in the West London and Walton Gatwick pipelines, the Parties shall appoint an independent and experienced trustee with an irrevocable mandate to carry out such divestiture within the remainder of the divestiture period.

31. To assist the Commission in determining whether any proposed purchaser is suitable, the Parties shall submit a fully documented and reasoned proposal enabling the Commission to verify that (i) the Parties do not own a material direct or indirect interest in the purchaser; (ii) the purchaser is a viable existing or potential competitor with the ability to supply aviation fuels at Gatwick airport as an active competitive force; and (iii) at the time of completion of the purchase, the purchaser has, or reasonably can obtain, all necessary approvals for the purchase from the relevant competition authorities in the European Community.

---

[29] Case IV/M.727 *BP/Mobil* of 7 August 1996 (OJ C 381, 17.12.1996, 8). The activities of the joint venture do not include marine and aviation lubricants.

It should be noted that the time limit allowed for the sale of the assets is a crucial element in the divestiture operation. Too short a time limit will normally reduce the price the divesting company will get for its assets. The Commission practice is to allow a six-month period with the possibility of an extension for another six months. After the lapse of the 12-month period, a trustee will be appointed who will carry out the divestiture. There are also: (a) up-front buyer scenarios—where the parties cannot complete the transaction until they have found a new buyer which has been approved by the Commission; and (b) fix-it first scenarios—in which the parties find a buyer and enter into an agreement prior to clearance, so that the clearance decision already takes this sale into account when assessing whether the concentration is compatible with the internal market.

5.2.2.9 Commission Enforcement

The Commission has far-reaching powers to deal with any concentration that has been implemented and which has subsequently been found to be incompatible with the internal market. Under Article 8(4) EUMR, the Commission may:

> require the undertakings concerned to dissolve the concentration, in particular through the dissolution of the merger or the disposal of all the shares or assets acquired, so as to restore the situation prevailing prior to the implementation of the concentration.

In essence, this is a process of trying to 'unscramble the egg'. There are very few illustrations of where the Commission has tried to impose divestiture. However, a somewhat acrimonious example is provided by its series of Decisions concerning *Tetra Laval/Sidel*.[30] The Commission took the view that Tetra Laval's acquisition of Sidel would create a dominant position in one market and strengthen it in another, with the consequence that the only way of restoring conditions of effective competition to these markets was to require Tetra Laval to separate itself from Sidel.

> (9) Tetra has ... already implemented a concentration which has been declared incompatible with the common market and the functioning of the EEA Agreement.

> (10) This Decision is a consequence of and gives effect to the Prohibition Decision which found that the notified concentration would create and strengthen dominant positions as a result of which effective competition would be significantly impeded in the common market and declared the concentration incompatible with the common market. Where concentrations prohibited by the Commission have already been implemented, the Commission may, pursuant to Article 8(4) of the Merger Regulation, 'require the undertakings or assets brought together to be separated ... or any other action that may be appropriate in order to restore conditions of effective competition'.

> (11) Restoration of conditions of effective competition is the primary concern in proceedings pursuant to Article 8(4) of the Merger Regulation. Both the text and the scheme of

---

[30] See Table 5.1. See the second page hereafter for the references to the various Decisions, subsequent appeals to the CFI and ECJ and the final Decision closing the file. For our purposes here, the Decision in which the Commission required Tetra Laval to divest itself of Sidel was Decision 2004/103/EC of 30 January 2002 [2004] OJ L38/01.

the Merger Regulation indicate that this requires the removal of any residual structural impediments to effective competition on the relevant markets arising from the prohibited concentration.[31] Article 8(4) envisages that, in situations where concentrations prohibited by the Commission have already been implemented, the restoration of effective competition must, in principle, be effected by means of a separation of the undertakings or assets brought together through the prohibited transaction.

(12) In applying Article 8(4) of the Merger Regulation the Commission has regard to the principle of proportionality. This principle dictates that, when the Commission is faced with different possible options, such as divestiture structures, which could restore conditions of effective competition as required by Article 8(4), the Commission should allow a choice or should adopt the least restrictive option.

(13) Having regard to proportionality, the Commission considers the legitimate interests of the undertakings concerned, when pursuing the primary Community interest of restoring conditions of effective competition by giving effect to its prohibition decision. This should include not only the interests of the acquiring undertaking, Tetra, which naturally wants to preserve as much of the value of its investment as possible, but also of the acquired undertaking, Sidel, which wants to minimise the period of uncertainty it faces and to continue its operations as an independent entity without the imposition of unduly disruptive or onerous measures.[32]

(14) In the light of the above and in order to restore conditions of effective competition pursuant to Article 8(4) of the Merger Regulation, under the particular circumstances of the present case, it is necessary to order the separation of Tetra and Sidel on the basis of the following principles:

(1)   the separation should be by means of an effective and final divestiture of such part of Tetra's shareholding in Sidel as will ensure that conditions of effective competition are restored by retaining Sidel as an independent and viable competitor;

(2)   the divestiture should result in Sidel regaining its full independence from Tetra and Tetra not retaining any minority stake or interest in Sidel which could impede the restoration of conditions of effective competition;

(3)   the divestiture should take place promptly within a period of not more than [...]*[33] in order to safeguard Sidel's viability and effectiveness and thus to ensure the restoration of conditions of effective competition;

(4)   during the transitional period pending divestiture Tetra should appoint a Trustee to monitor the divestiture process and minimise Tetra's influence in Sidel.

---

[31] See the seventh and ninth recitals in the preamble to the Merger Regulation.

[32] It is important to note in this respect that not only Tetra but also Sidel is an undertaking concerned by these proceedings with specific rights granted under the Merger Regulation and Reg (EC) No 447/98 (the Implementing Regulation). For example, Sidel is an 'involved party' within the meaning of Art 13 of the Implementing Regulation. This imposes an obligation on the Commission to inform Sidel of the content of these proceedings and to allow Sidel to express its views in writing and orally. In this respect, the management of Sidel has a specific right to be heard by the Commission pursuant to Art 18(4) of the Merger Regulation.

[33] Parts of this text have been edited to ensure that confidential information is not disclosed; these parts are enclosed in square brackets and marked with an asterisk.

Table 5.1: Chronology of the *Tetra Laval* saga

Commission Decision 2004/124/ EC of 30 October 2001 declaring a concentration to be incompatible with the common market and the EEA Agreement (Prohibition Decision) [2004] OJ L43/13	The Commission concluded that the notified concentration would create a dominant position in the market for PET packaging equipment (in particular SBM machines used for the 'sensitive' product segments) and would strengthen a dominant position in aseptic carton packaging equipment and aseptic cartons in the EEA, as a result of which effective competition would be significantly impeded in the common market and in the EEA.
Commission Decision 2004/103/ EC of 30 January 2002 setting out measures in order to restore conditions of effective competition pursuant to Article 8(4) of Council Regulation (EEC) No 4064/89 (Divestiture Decision) [2004] OJ L38/01	In order to restore conditions of effective competition, the Commission ordered Tetra Laval BV to separate itself from Sidel SA in accordance with the provisions of the Annex to this Decision ('to unscramble the eggs'), since the concentration deemed incompatible with the common market had nevertheless already been carried out.
Case T-5/02 *Tetra Laval BV v Commission* [2002] ECR II-4381	The CFI annulled Commission Decision C (2001) 3345 final of 30 October 2001 declaring a concentration to be incompatible with the common market and the EEA Agreement.
Case T-80/02 *Tetra Laval BV v Commission* [2002] ECR II-4519	Since the illegality of the Prohibition Decision led to the illegality of the Divestiture Decision, the CFI ruled that the present action for annulment of the divestiture decision must be upheld and annulled the Divestiture Decision.
Case C-12/03 P *Commission v Tetra Laval BV* [2005] ECR I-987	The ECJ upheld the CFI's judgment annulling the Prohibition Decision.
Case C-13/03 P *Commission v Tetra Laval BV* [2005] ECR I-1113	The ECJ upheld the CFI's judgment annulling the Divestiture Decision.

As is clear from Table 5.1, however, the GC (the CFI as it was at the time) and ECJ held that the Commission's original Prohibition Decision could not stand, meaning that the Decision ordering the divestiture of Sidel fell with it. Nevertheless, the Commission's approach to the appropriate remedies in the *Tetra Laval/Sidel* Decision illustrates that it will not shy away from ordering divestiture where this is the only appropriate means of returning the relevant market(s) to a situation of effective competition (albeit subject to the requirements of proportionality, as noted in paragraphs 12 and 13 of its Divestiture Decision, reproduced above).

Where such divestiture is not possible (or would be a disproportionate reaction in the circumstances), the Commission may then take any other appropriate measures to restore the pre-existing situation as far as it is possible to do so.

Furthermore, under certain circumstances the Commission has the power to impose financial penalties upon the undertaking(s) concerned in the form of fines or periodic penalty payments (Articles 14 and 15 EUMR, respectively). If an undertaking takes the view that the Commission has unjustly imposed such a penalty, an application for judicial review of the Commission's decision can be made before the GC and the validity of the decision may ultimately be decided on appeal to the ECJ (Article 16 EUMR).

The EUMR also offers the Commission the possibility of adopting interim measures. In order to restore or maintain the conditions of effective competition, the Commission is empowered to adopt interim measures in three situations:

(a)   where the standstill obligation of Article 7 EUMR has not been respected by the undertakings concerned and the Commission has yet to adopt a formal decision on the compatibility of the concentration with the common market (Article 7(5)(a) EUMR);
(b)   where a condition or obligation imposed as part of a clearance decision has not been followed (Article 7(5)(b) EUMR); and
(c)   where the standstill obligation has not been respected and the concentration has been implemented, and a final decision has been taken that the concentration is incompatible with the common market (Article 7(5)(c) EUMR).

5.2.2.10 Simplified Procedure

In practice, it has become clear that concentrations between undertakings that are not active in the same markets or whose combined market share, or shares in vertically related markets, are sufficiently small, or where the joint venture has negligible activities within the EEA, rarely raise competition concerns.

In its 'Notice on a Simplified Procedure for Treatment of Certain Concentrations',[34] the Commission outlines a simplified procedure that it uses to accelerate and facilitate the merger transactions in cases such as these. According to the Notice five categories qualify for such a procedure:

(a)   where there are no or negligible activities within the Community under certain turnover thresholds;
(b)   where no horizontal or vertical anti-competitive effects occur due to the parties being active in different markets;
(c)   where the proposed transaction falls below *de minimis* market share thresholds (20 per cent for horizontal concentrations and 30 per cent for vertical mergers);
(d)   where a party is to acquire sole control of an undertaking over which it already exercised joint control.

---

[34] [2013] OJ C336/5.

(e)   mergers where the combined market share of the parties that are in a horizontal relationship to a transaction is less than 50 per cent and the increment of the Herfindahl-Hirschman Index (HHI)[35] transaction is below 150.[36]

There are also certain safeguard methods for the operation of the procedure and exclusions therefrom, which are discussed in the Notice. The Commission's Notice also strongly recommends that the parties concerned make a point of contacting the Commission prior to formal notification of a concentration, particularly where the parties intend to claim that they should only have to submit a short-form notification using the abbreviated version of the Form CO.[37] Where the various procedural and substantive criteria are satisfied, the Commission will issue a simplified decision declaring the concentration compatible with the internal market within 25 working days of the date of formal notification.

5.2.3 'Concentration'

5.2.3.1 General

The key concept for defining the scope of the EUMR is the definition of a concentration in Article 3 EUMR. This concept is further explained in the Commission Consolidated Jurisdictional Notice.[38] According to Article 3(1) EUMR, a concentration occurs where:

(a)   two or more previously independent undertakings (or parts of undertakings) merge; or
(b)   direct or indirect control of the whole or parts of one or more undertakings is acquired, whether by purchase of securities or assets, by contract or by any other means, by
  —   *either* one or more persons already controlling at least one undertaking;
  —   *or* one or more undertakings.

The merger of undertakings includes mergers in the legal sense and de facto mergers.[39] Examples of the former are where A and B merge into C, as a result of which A and B cease to exist; or where A and B merge into A, when B ceases to exist. The latter is the

---

[35] According to fn 15 of the Notice: 'The HHI is calculated by summing the squares of the individual market shares of all the firms in the market: see Commission Guidelines on the assessment of horizontal mergers under the Council Regulation on the control of concentrations between undertakings (OJ C 31, 5.2.2004, p 5), point 16. However, in order to calculate the HHI delta resulting from the concentration, it is sufficient to subtract from the square of the sum of the market shares of the parties to the concentration (in other words, the square of the merged entity's market share post-concentration) the sum of the squares of the parties' individual market shares (since the market shares of all other competitors in the market remain unchanged and thus do not influence the result of the equation). In other words, the HHI delta can be calculated on the basis of only the market shares of the parties to the concentration, without a need to know the market shares of any other competitors in the market.'
[36] For the simplified procedure: the short version of Form CO for notification of a concentration (Annex II to Reg 802/2004/EC [2004] OJ L133/1, at 22).
[37] ibid.
[38] [2008] OJ C 95/1.
[39] See para 10 the Jurisdictional Notice.

case where, in the absence of a legal merger, the combination of the activities of previously independent undertakings results in a single economic unit. The acquisition of control, meanwhile, is determined on the basis of qualitative rather than quantitative criteria, focusing on the concept of control, including both legal and de facto situations.[40]

The acquisition of control is thus a central issue in the application of the EUMR. What is 'control'? Article 3(2) EUMR provides:

Control shall be constituted by rights, contracts or any other means which, either separately or in combination and having regard to the considerations of fact or law involved, confer the possibility of exercising decisive influence on an undertaking, in particular by:

(a)   ownership or the right to use all or part of the assets of an undertaking;
(b)   rights or contracts which confer decisive influence on the composition, voting or decisions of the organs of an undertaking.

This control will be found to have been acquired by the persons or undertakings that (are able to) exercise these rights, whether directly or indirectly. The Consolidated Jurisdictional Notice[41] also contains a detailed discussion of the various forms of concentration and the circumstances in which exclusive or joint control will be found to exist. The Notice expressly states that a concentration may be found to have occurred where one shareholder has veto rights or where a change has been brought about in the structure of control of the undertaking (eg, a shift from joint to sole control).[42]

A good example of a situation in which a concentration is created through the acquisition of joint control is provided by the Commission's *Newspaper Publishing* Decision.[43] This case concerned the joint acquisition (by way of public bid) of Newspaper Publishing by three other undertakings: PRISA, Espresso and MGN. According to the Commission, if the public bid succeeded, Newspaper Publishing would be jointly controlled by PRISA, Espresso and MGN as the result of the following circumstances:

8. ... PRISA, Espresso and MGN ... together will control the majority of the share capital of NP and have the right to appoint 6 directors (2 directors each) out of a total of seven.

9. The decisions of the Board will be taken by simple majority. PRISA and Espresso have a separate agreement which provides that the two groups will vote together as regards the decisions of the Board of NP; this would effectively give them joint control in the absence of other considerations. However, MGN will have not only the right to propose the business plans and the budget of NP but also a veto right in the event that the NP Board votes against its proposals, in which case the contested matters will be settled by an independent expert agreed by all parties ...

...

11. ... Moreover, it is very unlikely that a risk of coordination of the competitive behaviour either between the JV and its parents or between the parents themselves will exist. In view of the above, the notified operation is a concentration within the meaning of the Merger Regulation.

---

[40] See para 7 of the Jurisdictional Notice.
[41] [2008] OJ C 95/1.
[42] Para 12 of the Jurisdictional Notice.
[43] Case No IV/M.423 (14 March 1994).

5.2.3.2 Joint Ventures

As set out above, a change from sole to joint control over a pre-existing undertaking, or part thereof, constitutes a concentration under Article 3(1)(b) EUMR. In addition, the creation of a joint undertaking—usually known as a 'joint venture'—can also qualify as a concentration under the EUMR (eg, in a situation where there is no acquisition of control over an existing undertaking, but a structural change in the market because two or more independent companies will exercise joint control over a new undertaking). Article 3(4) EUMR provides that the

> creation of a joint venture performing on a lasting basis all the functions of an autonomous economic entity shall constitute a concentration within the meaning of [Article 3(1) (b) EUMR].

Only the creation of a full-function joint venture falls under the scope of Article 3(4) EUMR.

It must be emphasised here that if the joint venture intends to coordinate, or in fact brings about the coordination of, the competitive behaviour of undertakings that remain independent, then this element of the transaction also falls to be assessed under the criteria of Article 101(1) and (3) TFEU (as discussed in Chapter 3): this is made clear by Article 2(4) EUMR. In such a case, the markets upon which the undertakings setting up the joint venture, and the joint venture itself, are and will remain (or become) active will have to be examined. Thus, the possibility that the undertakings setting up the joint venture will be able, as a direct result of the joint venture, to eliminate competition in respect of a substantial part of the goods or services concerned (as per Article 101(3) TFEU) will have to be assessed. Such transactions are normally not cleared by way of a Commission decision declaring compatibility with Article 101 TFEU because, according to Article 10 of Regulation 1/2003/EC, the Commission will only take such decisions where the Community interest so requires. The same applies to the so-called 'guidance letters'.[44]

Joint ventures that lack a Union dimension but which have the object or effect of coordinating of the competitive behaviour of the independent 'parent' undertakings fall outside the EUMR and within the procedures of (inter alia) Regulation 1/2003/EC. In this connection, the reader should note that the Commission Jurisdictional Notice provides 'Information on the Assessment of Full-function Joint Ventures Pursuant to the Competition Rules of the European Community',[45] in which this procedural distinction is discussed briefly.

The Commission has clarified the position in this area in its 'Jurisdictional Notice'.[46] The relevant part of the Notice begins by making general introductory observations regarding the nature of a joint venture: a joint venture involves an undertaking that

---

[44] Commission Notice on informal guidance relating to novel questions concerning Arts 81 and 82 of the EC Treaty that arise in individual cases (guidance letters) [2004] OJ C101/78. Point 8.b, third indent reads: 'the extent of the investments linked to the transaction in relation to the size of the companies concerned and the extent to which the transaction relates to a structural operation such as the creation of a non-full function joint venture.'

[45] [2008] OJ C95/1, para 91 et seq.

[46] [2008] OJ C95/1.

is under the joint control of two or more other undertakings. The Notice goes on to provide some detail on the characteristics of joint ventures in the sense of Article 3 EUMR. In summary, there must be joint control by two or more (so-called 'parent') undertakings and 'the joint venture must perform, on a lasting basis, all the functions of an autonomous economic entity'.[47] This last point implies that there must be some form of board to carry out the day-to-day business functions of the joint venture and that the joint venture must have sufficient personnel and assets at its disposal so to operate.

Article 3(5) EUMR lays down a limited number of exceptions from the concept of a 'concentration'. Thus, there will be no 'concentration' for the purposes of the EUMR where:

(a)   credit institutions or other financial institutions or insurance companies, the normal activities of which include transactions and dealing in securities for their own account or for the account of others, hold on a temporary basis securities which they have acquired in an undertaking with a view to reselling them …;

(b)   control is acquired by an office-holder according to the law of a Member State relating to liquidation, winding up, insolvency, cessation of payments, compositions or analogous proceedings;

(c)   [acquisitions] by … financial holding companies … provided however that the voting rights in respect of the holding are exercised … only to maintain the full value of those investments and not to determine directly or indirectly the competitive conduct of those undertakings.

In the Commission's 'Jurisdictional Notice' these exceptions are discussed in more detail (see its Part VII, paragraphs 206 et seq) and their application is explained further.[48] Their basic thrust is to avoid accidentally fixing normal commercial activities, which do not aim at the acquisition of commercial control under normal circumstances, with an obligation to notify innocuous transactions under the EUMR.

5.2.4 Thresholds: The Union Dimension

5.2.4.1 General

One of the key attractions of the EU's merger control regime is the centralisation of notifications for clearance with the European Commission, which can save time and resources when compared with multiple procedures in different Member States. At the same time, it is important to ensure that only those concentrations that are of significance for the interests of the Union are subjected to EU-level scrutiny: concentrations with a national dimension are the responsibility of the relevant national NCA(s), in accordance with the general EU law principle of subsidiarity (see Article 5(3) TEU). Thus, the concept of the 'Union dimension' was developed, which aimed to reflect these goals and delimit which concentrations required notification to the Commission. It should be noted that satisfying the Union dimension test is a jurisdictional

---

[47] ibid, para 92.
[48] Part VII, para 206 et seq.

question only: it does not direct itself to the substantive analysis of the position of the undertaking(s) on the relevant market(s) and the likely effects of the concentration on competition thereon. We will return to this (vitally important) latter issue in section 5.2.5 below.

According to the provisions of Article 1 EUMR, a concentration will have a Union dimension in the following two cases:

(a)   Concentrations where the undertakings concerned have a combined, aggregate worldwide turnover of more than €5 000 million (Article 1(2) EUMR): and
    —   where the total aggregate turnover of each of at least two of the undertakings concerned exceeds €250 million;
    —   *unless* each of the undertakings concerned achieves more than two-thirds of its total EU-wide turnover in a single Member State.
(b)   Concentrations where the undertakings concerned have a combined, aggregate worldwide turnover of more than €2 500 million (Article 1(3) EUMR): and
    —   where the total aggregate turnover of all the undertakings concerned is more than €100 million in each of at least three EU Member States; and
    —   in each of at least three of the Member States used to satisfy the previous condition the aggregate turnover of at least two of the undertakings concerned exceeds €25 million; and
    —   the aggregate EU-wide turnover of each of at least two of the undertakings concerned is greater than €100 million;
    —   *unless* each of the undertakings concerned achieves more than two-thirds of its EU-wide turnover in a single Member State.

From these provisions, it is clear that an accurate assessment of which undertakings are 'concerned' and the scope of their turnover will be of crucial importance for the determination of whether or not there is a Union dimension to any given concentration. Note that the conditions under Article 1(3) EUMR may only be applied to obtain jurisdiction under the EUMR where those under Article 1(2) EUMR are not met by the concentration in question. Note also that the EU assumes jurisdiction over mergers between two undertakings headquartered outside the EU if and when the Union-wide turnover exceeds €250 million. Thus the merger between Lenovo (an undertaking with its main seat in China) and the PC division of IBM came within the scope of Article 1(2) EUMR.[49]

5.2.4.2 Turnover

The exact calculation of the relevant turnover is often very complicated and the Commission has devoted a section of the Jurisdictional Notice to the topic.[50] According to Article 5(1) EUMR, aggregate turnover

shall comprise the amounts derived by the undertakings concerned in the preceding financial year from the sale of products and the provision of services falling within the undertakings'

---

[49] Nevertheless, this merger does not seem to have been notified.
[50] [2008] OJ C95/1 paras 209 et seq.

ordinary activities after deduction of sales rebates and of value added tax and other taxes directly related to turnover.

Thus, sales are the essential criterion here. Where only one part of an undertaking is being acquired then the calculation of turnover must only take into account the turnover attributable to the part of the undertaking that is the subject of the transaction. Special rules are provided for calculating the turnover of credit and other financial institutions and insurance undertakings (Article 5(3) EUMR). Article 5(4) EUMR makes it clear that the relevant turnover includes not only that of the undertaking concerned but also the turnover of (in summary) the whole corporate group of which that undertaking is a part. As a result, the calculation of turnover for these purposes often requires an extensive 'organogramme' showing the structure of the whole group of companies. In principle, the turnover obtained *within* a group need not be taken into account in making this calculation. These principles are illustrated in the Commission's *Boeing/Hughes* merger Decision:[51]

III COMMUNITY DIMENSION

(9) The notifying party considers that the present transaction does not have a Community dimension and therefore falls outside the jurisdiction of the Commission because HSC does not meet the EEA turnover thresholds laid down in the Merger Regulation. According to the notifying party, HSC's Community-wide turnover amounted to EUR [...]* million in 1999 and EUR [...]* million in 1998.

(10) However, HSC had significant turnover (approximately EUR [...]* million in 1999) with ICO Global Communications (Holdings) Ltd. ('ICO'). ICO was established to provide global mobile personal communication services by satellite. The ICO company filed for Chapter 11 protection (US procedure for companies facing bankruptcy) in August 1999 and has recently been reorganised. Boeing submits that the only way that HSC might be considered to exceed the EEA turnover threshold would be if its sales to ICO were to be included in its EEA turnover.

(11) Given that ICO is registered in the Cayman Islands but is actually managed in London, whether ICO should be seen as a Community company is decisive in determining whether or not the proposed transaction has a Community dimension. If HSC's turnover with ICO is allocated to the EEA, then the transaction falls under the Merger Regulation. The notifying party however maintains that HSC's turnover with ICO should be allocated to the Cayman Islands.

(12) On that basis, the Commission requested further information from ICO, which replied on 29 February 2000. It appears that ICO was formed as a result of a project established by Inmarsat (an international organisation based in London, which has now become a UK-listed company) to offer world-wide data and voice communication services through the use of a satellite-based telecommunication network. For that purpose, ICO was incorporated in 1994 in England and Wales. This company was subsequently liquidated and the assets were transferred to a Cayman Island company, which itself was changed into a Bermuda Company. However, these changes, which seem to have primarily been made for tax purposes, have not altered the management structure of the company. As ICO has formally stated, its principal place of business is in London, where all ICO's day-to-day management is carried

---

[51] Case No COMP/M.1879, Decision of 29 September 2000. Where a figure in the extract has been removed by the Commission for reasons of commercial confidentiality, it is marked as follows: '[...]*'.

out and where 73% of ICO's personnel is located, the remainder being spread in several locations around the world.

In the light of the foregoing, it appears that, formally speaking, the parties are correct in claiming that ICO is a Cayman Islands (or more precisely a Bermuda Islands) registered company but that, economically speaking, ICO is still clearly a United Kingdom based company.

(13) In the calculation of turnover for the purposes of the Merger Regulation, it is the economic reality of a situation that should be taken into account. Indeed, paragraph 7 of the Commission Notice on calculation of turnover states that 'the set of rules [concerning the calculation of turnover] are designed to ensure that the resulting figures are a true representation of economic reality'. In this case, therefore, HSC's turnover with ICO should be allocated to the United Kingdom.

(14) Furthermore, it appears that, although the satellite contract between HSC and ICO is formally placed with the Cayman Islands company, it was finally negotiated by ICO's London staff, and that any important modifications to this contract would be negotiated in London. If account is also taken of the place where the transaction was in reality carried out, and therefore where competition between HSC and other satellite prime contractors took place, it clearly points to the United Kingdom.

(15) Following the guidelines in paragraph 7 of the Notice on the calculation of turnover, HSC's turnover with ICO should therefore be allocated to the United Kingdom and included in its EEA turnover.

(16) Boeing and HSC have a combined aggregate world-wide turnover of more than EUR 5 000 million (EUR 53403 million for Boeing in 1999 and EUR 2136 million for Hughes in 1999). They each have an aggregate Community wide turnover in excess of EUR 250 million (EUR [...]* million for Boeing in 1999 and EUR [...]* million for Hughes in 1999) and neither of the undertakings concerned achieves more than two-thirds of its aggregate community-wide turnover within one and the same Member State. The notified operation therefore has a Community dimension within the meaning of Article 1(2) of the Merger Regulation.

5.2.4.3 Undertakings Concerned

The Commission has also devoted a chapter of the Jurisdictional Notice to the Concept of 'Undertakings Concerned'[52] to clarify the meaning of the concept and to provide illustrations of the typical situations that have arisen in the Commission's practice. The Jurisdictional Notice is an extremely important document as it puts flesh on the bare bones of the EUMR in an area of great significance for establishing whether or not the thresholds of the EUMR have been met. In the Jurisdictional Notice, the Commission makes clear in all illustrative cases which undertakings it considers are 'concerned' for these purposes. Thus, it is obvious that on the acquisition of an undertaking, both the acquiring and the acquired undertakings are 'undertakings concerned'. Where only one part of another undertaking is to be acquired, then only the acquiring undertaking and the acquired part amount to 'undertakings concerned'.

A useful example of the fact that it is only the acquiring and the acquired undertaking that are considered to be the 'undertakings concerned', and the consequences

[52] [2008] OJ C95/1 Chapter C.II.

of such a rule, can be seen in the Commission's Decision in *Phillips/Grundig*.[53] This case concerned an operation through which Philips Electronics would acquire 60 per cent of the shares in Grundig Verwaltungs GmbH (GVG), which in turn controlled Grundig AG. The shares subject to the acquisition were held by three banks (the Dresdner Bank, the Frankfurt, Bayerische Vereinsbank and the Munich and Schweizerische Bankgesellschaft, Zurich). As the Commission noted, the three banks had always acted together in exercising their rights in GVG, forcing Philips always to consider their common position when deciding on central GVG financial matters and thus ensuring that GVG remained subject to joint control.

With the acquisition, however, Philips—which prior to the deal owned 40 per cent of GVG—would obtain sole control of GVG and thereby also the controlling majority of the shares and sole control over Grundig AG.

In determining the Union dimension of this concentration, the Commission proceeded as follows:

> The worldwide turnover of the undertakings concerned exceeds 5,000 million ECU. The combined turnover of Philips/Grundig in 1992 was 25,783 million ECU. With regard to the aggregate Community-wide turnover each of the two undertakings exceed the 250 million ECU threshold laid down in the Regulation. Philips has a Community-wide turnover on 12,077 million ECU and Grundig 1,589 million ECU. And none of the undertakings achieves two-thirds of its turnover within one and the same Member State.

It is clear from this wording that the Commission considered only Phillips and Grundig AG to be the 'undertakings concerned' whose turnover was of relevance to the Commission in the procedure, leaving the three banks outside the scope of its analysis. This illustrates the importance of properly determining the 'undertakings concerned'.

The acquired part can be a separate legal entity, but can also be simply a particular activity within a company. The condition is that one must clearly be able to assign a turnover to that activity. The Jurisdictional Notice also gives guidance as to which are the undertakings concerned where a subsidiary company in a group makes an acquisition; where a joint venture is set up; and where the relationship between shareholders in a joint venture is amended.

Further, it should be noted that where two or more transactions take place within a two-year period between the same persons or undertakings, they will be treated as one and the same concentration that has arisen on the date of the last of these transactions (second sentence of Article 5(2) EUMR).

5.2.5 Substantive Assessment

According to Article 2(1) EUMR, all qualifying concentrations must be assessed to determine whether or not they are compatible with the internal market. In making this assessment, the Commission takes into account a variety of factors, including the necessity to ensure that effective competition is maintained and developed in the

---

[53] Case No IV/M.382 (3 December 1993).

internal market, the position of the undertakings concerned on the market, their economic and financial strength, and the options available to suppliers and consumers. This analysis often seems very similar to that applied when assessing whether or not a dominant position has been established, as discussed in section 4.2.2 above. However, there are also important differences between the approach under the EUMR and that concerning alleged abuses of positions of dominance.

The Commission has given further guidance in its guidelines for horizontal and non-horizontal mergers.[54]

What is meant by the phrase '(in)compatible with the internal market'? Article 2(2) EUMR provides that

> A concentration which would not significantly impede effective competition in the common market or in a substantial part of it, in particular as a result of the creation or strengthening of a dominant position, shall be declared compatible with the common market.

Article 2(3) EUMR, meanwhile, lays down that, where such a significant impediment would be created, the relevant concentration must be declared incompatible with the internal market. According to Article 8(1), (2) and (3) EUMR, this declaration shall take place by the issue of a decision by the Commission. For completeness, it should be remembered here that, in certain situations, joint ventures will also be assessed for their compatibility with the internal market by reference to the criteria of Article 101 TFEU. Thus, in assessing the compatibility of a qualifying concentration with EU law it must be examined whether or not a significant impediment to effective competition would be created thereby. This test was introduced in the 2004 EUMR and replaced the old approach under Regulation 4064/89/EEC, which focused upon the creation or strengthening of a dominant position that would impede competition in the EU.[55] Following the introduction of the EUMR, the creation and strengthening of a dominant position are simply two ways in which a concentration can result in a significant impediment to effective competition.

The European Commission has explained its approach to horizontal mergers by publishing a further set of Guidelines.[56] 'Horizontal mergers' are mergers between actual or potential competitors operating in the same relevant market. The Guidelines set out how the Commission views questions of market structure in cases of concentrations (market shares and market concentration); the effects that are generally considered to be restrictive of competition that may arise in the context of horizontal mergers (coordinated and non-coordinated (also called 'unilateral') effects) and those elements that need to be weighed against the potentially anti-competitive effects (countervailing buyer power, market entry, efficiency improvements or where the merger amounts to the rescue of a failing firm by the other party).[57]

---

[54] Guidelines on the assessment of horizontal mergers under the Council Regulation on the control of concentrations between undertakings [2004] OJ C31/ 5–18; Guidelines on the assessment of non-horizontal mergers under the Council Regulation on the control of concentrations between undertakings [2008] OJ C265/6-25.

[55] See for a summary of the debate about the different approaches R Whish and D Bailey, *Competition Law*, 8th edn (London, LexisNexis Butterworths, 2015) 906–910. See also European Commission: *White Paper Towards more effective EU merger control* Brussels, 9.7.2014 COM (2014) 449 final, p 5.

[56] Guidelines on the assessment of horizontal mergers under the Council Regulation on the control of concentrations between undertakings [2004] OJ C31/5.

[57] An example of such a situation is the merger of Shell with Nynas M 6360, [2014] OJ C 368.

It is clear from the formulation of the test in Article 2(3) EUMR ('significantly imped[ing] effective competition, in the internal market or in a substantial part of it, in particular as a result of the creation or strengthening of a dominant position') that the Commission considers the creation of a dominant position a particularly clear example of a significant impediment to effective competition. As a result of this, when assessing the compatibility of a concentration with the internal market it is still possible to fall back upon the earlier decisional practice of the Commission and the case law of the GC and the ECJ concerning such dominance. It is thus still vital first to determine the relevant market. Only then is it possible to examine the market shares of the undertakings concerned and the other relevant factors. On an examination of the decisions of the Commission, it emerges that we can in general speak of the creation or strengthening of a dominant position—and thus also of a significant impediment to effective competition—where the concentration results in a market share in excess of 50 per cent.[58] The EUMR not only catches dominance cases, but also so-called 'gap cases' where there is no creation/strengthening of dominance, but the transaction nevertheless results in a Significant Impediment to Effective Competition (SIEC).[59] The Commission has published a Notice on how the relevant market is to be determined.[60] The case law of the GC and the ECJ has clarified that it may also necessary to examine whether or not a collective dominant position has been created (for discussion of this area, see section 4.2.3 above).

The Guidelines for horizontal mergers show that under the EUMR the Commission will take efficiencies into account.[61] Such efficiencies have to benefit consumers, be merger-specific and be verifiable. These conditions are cumulative.

The judgments of the GC in the *General Electric* and *Honeywell* appeals against the Commission's Decision to prohibit the *GE/Honeywell* merger add a new chapter to the Commission's approach of conglomerate mergers. They provide a critical assessment of some of the Commission's theories applied in this case.[62] The Commission argued that the merged entity would engage in so-called mixed bundling whereby complementary products—GE's engines and Honeywell's avionics—would be sold together at a price lower than the price charged when they are sold separately. The Commission was also afraid that GECAS, GE's leasing subsidiary, would only offer deals for aircraft with GE engines and Honeywell avionics. The judgments show that the Commission's approach concerning the bundling effects as well as the argument about GE's financial strength has not received the endorsement of the Court.[63] Similarly, the

---

[58]   *cf* the AKZO presumption discussed in Chapter 4.2.2 Case C-62/86 *AKZO Chemie v Commission*.

[59]   See, eg, Commission decisions in UPS/TNT, COMP/M.6570; *Telefónica Deutschland/E-Plus*, COMP/M.7018; *Liberty Global/Base* COMP/M.7637.

[60]   [1997] OJ C372/5.

[61]   Paras 76–88.

[62]   Cases T-209/01 *Honeywell v Commission* and T-210/01 *General Electric v Commission*.

[63]   "As for the conglomerate effects resulting from the merger owing to GE's financial strength and vertical integration: The Court held that the Commission did not establish to a sufficient degree of probability that the merged entity would have extended to Honeywell's markets (avionics and non-avionics products) GE's practices on the market for large commercial jet aircraft engines, by which GE used the financial and commercial strength it derived from its subsidiaries. In any event, the Commission did not adequately establish that those practices, assuming that they had been put into effect, would have been likely to create dominant positions on the various avionics and non-avionics markets concerned. Consequently, the Commission made a manifest error of assessment."

Commission's assessment of the vertical overlap between Honeywell's engine start-ers and GE's engines as a result of the merger was found to be vitiated by a manifest error.[64] Nevertheless, the GC upheld the Commission's prohibition because it found that its findings on three markets (jet engines for large regional aircraft, engines for corporate jet aircraft and small gas turbines) would create or strengthen dominant positions. The Commission subsequently published guidelines for non-horizontal mergers.[65] According to the Commission:

> Non-horizontal mergers are generally less likely to significantly impede effective competition than horizontal mergers. First, unlike horizontal mergers, vertical or conglomerate mergers do not entail the loss of direct competition between the merging firms in the same relevant market. As a result, the main source of anti-competitive effect in horizontal mergers is absent from vertical and conglomerate mergers. Second, vertical and conglomerate mergers provide substantial scope for efficiencies. A characteristic of vertical mergers and certain conglomerate mergers is that the activities and/or the products of the companies involved are complementary to each other....[66]

The Commission subsequently, notes:

> There are two main ways in which non-horizontal mergers may significantly impede effective competition: non-coordinated effects and coordinated effects. Non-coordinated effects may principally arise when non-horizontal mergers give rise to foreclosure. In this document, the term 'foreclosure' will be used to describe any instance where actual or potential rivals' access to supplies or markets is hampered or eliminated as a result of the merger, thereby reducing these companies' ability and/or incentive to compete. As a result of such foreclosure, the merging companies—and, possibly, some of its competitors as well—may be able to profitably increase the price charged to consumers. These instances give rise to a significant impediment to effective competition and are therefore referred to hereafter as 'anticompetitive foreclosure'. Coordinated effects arise where the merger changes the nature of competition in such a way that firms that previously were not coordinating their behaviour, are now significantly more likely to coordinate to raise prices or otherwise harm effective competition. A merger may also make coordination easier, more stable or more effective for firms which were coordinating prior to the merger.[67]

The Commission analyses both input and customer foreclosure of conglomerate and vertical mergers by asking three questions. The guidelines state that the likelihood

As for the conglomerate effects resulting from bundling: the Court held that the Commission did not sufficiently establish that the merged entity would have bundled sales of GE's engines with Honeywell's avionics and non-avionics products. In the absence of such bundled sales, the mere fact that the merged entity would have had a wider range of products than its competitors was not sufficient to establish that dominant positions would have been created or strengthened for it on the different markets concerned. Consequently, the Commission also made a manifest error of assessment in this respect' (summary in the Press Release).

[64] 'The Court held that the pillar of the contested decision relating to the strengthening of GE's pre-merger dominance on the market for jet engines for large commercial aircraft, resulting from that vertical overlap, was unfounded. More specifically, the Court held that the Commission failed to take into account the deterrent effect of Art 102 TFEU, despite its relevance, and that the Commission's analysis was, as a result, vitiated by a manifest error of assessment' (summary in the Press Release).

[65] Guidelines on the assessment of non-horizontal mergers under the Council Regulation on the control of concentrations between undertakings; [2008] OJ C265/6-25.

[66] Paras 11, 12 and 13.

[67] Paras 17, 18 and 19.

of an anticompetitive input and customer foreclosure scenario, will be examined as follows:

> First, whether the merged entity would have, post-merger, the ability to substantially foreclose access to inputs, second, whether it would have the incentive to do so, and third, whether a foreclosure strategy would have a significant detrimental effect on competition downstream. In practice, these factors are often examined together since they are closely intertwined.

First, do parties have the ability to foreclose access. Such an ability only arises when parties have a significant degree of market power.[68] Input foreclosure may happen in several ways: the merged entity may decide not to deal with its actual or potential competitors in the vertically related market or the merged firm may decide to restrict supplies and/or to raise the price it charges when supplying competitors and/or to otherwise make the conditions of supply less favourable than they would have been absent the merger. Further, the merged entity may opt for a specific choice of technology within the new firm which is not compatible with the technologies chosen by rival firms.[69]

Customer foreclosure may occur when a supplier merges with an important customer in the downstream market.[70]

Secondly, the incentive to foreclose depends on the degree to which foreclosure would be profitable. The vertically integrated firm will take into account how its supplies of inputs to competitors downstream will affect not only the profits of its upstream division, but also of its downstream division.[71]

Thirdly, in general, a merger will raise competition concerns because of input foreclosure when it would lead to increased prices in the downstream market thereby significantly impeding effective competition.[72] As for customer foreclosure, the guidelines note that: foreclosing rivals in the upstream market may have an adverse impact in the downstream market and harm consumers. By denying competitive access to a significant customer base for the foreclosed rivals' (upstream) products, the merger may reduce their ability to compete in the foreseeable future. As a result, rivals downstream are likely to be put at a competitive disadvantage, for example in the form of raised input costs. In turn, this may allow the merged entity to profitably raise prices or reduce the overall output on the downstream market.[73]

Both horizontal and non-horizontal mergers may create efficiencies.[74] If such efficiencies outweigh the anti-competitive effects the Commission will approve the merger.[75]

5.2.6 Ancillary Restrictions

Under the EUMR, the Commission declares that any particular concentration is compatible with the internal market by adopting a formal decision. Such a decision 'shall be deemed to cover restrictions directly related and necessary to the implementation of

---

[68] Paras 33–39.
[69] Para 33.
[70] Para 58.
[71] Para 40.
[72] Para 47.
[73] Para 72.
[74] Paras 10–14.
[75] Para 21.

the concentration': this is laid down by Article 6(1)(b) EUMR for first phase decisions and by Article 8(1) and (2) EUMR for second phase decisions (respectively without and with modifications to the notified concentration by the undertakings). A form of ancillary restriction commonly encountered in practice is a non-compete obligation. Under such a clause, the seller may promise to the buyer that the seller will, for a certain period, refrain from competing in the market where the acquired undertaking is active. In this way, a justifiable attempt is made to prevent the seller from making use of its established commercial relationships and know-how in the field so as itself to recommence the activity that was sold to the buyer in the form of the undertaking acquired. Otherwise, the economic value of the acquired undertaking would be affected. Other examples of such restrictions that occur regularly include purchasing and supply obligations undertaken by the parties to the concentration.

Recital 21 to the EUMR explains that such ancillary restrictions should normally automatically receive clearance as a result of the Commission's clearance decision without the Commission being obliged to examine each restriction individually. Instead, the negotiation and assessment of such restrictions are in the first instance the task of the parties to the concentration. However, 'in cases presenting novel or unresolved questions giving rise to genuine uncertainty',[76] and at the request of the undertakings concerned, the Commission should expressly assess such restrictions and their necessity for the concentration and must rule thereupon.

The Commission has adopted a 'Notice on Restrictions Directly Related and Necessary to Concentrations',[77] which explains how the Commission will approach ancillary restrictions under the EUMR. Thus, for example, a general principle for determining whether a particular restriction qualifies under this heading is that it must be a restriction entered into by agreement between the parties to the concentration that restricts their own freedom to act on the market. Restrictions to which third parties may also be party cannot in principle qualify as ancillary restrictions under the EUMR. Further, the Notice requires that the restriction must be one that aims to achieve a goal subordinate to the main goal of the concentration. At the same time, the restriction must be one that is *necessary* for the implementation of the concentration. This necessity is to be tested upon the basis of a number of economic justificatory grounds, namely: the protection of the value of the acquired undertaking against 'free-riding'; the maintenance of continued supply relationships after the break-up of what used to be a single economic entity; and the facilitation of the start-up of a new economic entity. The duration of any such restriction must also be assessed for its justifiability. Reaching a decision as to whether or not these criteria are met depends upon the concentration concerned and the nature of the claimed ancillary restraints. The Notice provides more detailed discussion of certain types of acceptable ancillary restraints, including non-competition clauses, licences concerning intellectual and commercial property rights and know-how, and sales and supply agreements.

In summary, ancillary restrictions fall within the scope of the EUMR. It falls to the parties to assess whether or not a particular restriction qualifies to be treated as an ancillary restriction and thus to benefit from the deemed clearance granted to the

---

[76] Recital 21 explains that '[a] case presents a novel or unresolved question giving rise to genuine uncertainty if the question is not covered by the relevant Commission notice in force or a published Commission decision'.

[77] [2005] OJ C56/24.

concentration itself (unless the restriction raises novel or unresolved questions, when the parties should request the Commission to examine the matter for itself).

5.2.7 The Nature of the Judicial Review and the Standard of Proof Applied by the Union Courts

Traditionally, the Community courts have applied only a limited or marginal judicial review of the Commission's merger decisions.[78] Such an approach, however, has since given way to a much more comprehensive standard of judicial review.[79] In the *Tetra Laval* judgment the ECJ has endorsed this approach in the following terms:[80]

> (39) Whilst the Court recognises that the Commission has a margin of discretion with regard to economic matters, that does not mean that the Community Courts must refrain from reviewing the Commission's interpretation of information of an economic nature. Not only must the Community Courts, *inter alia*, establish whether the evidence relied on is factually accurate, reliable and consistent but also whether that evidence contains all the information which must be taken into account in order to assess a complex situation and whether it is capable of substantiating the conclusions drawn from it. [...].

> (41) Although the Court of First Instance stated, in paragraph 155, that proof of anti-competitive conglomerate effects of a merger of the kind notified calls for a precise examination, supported by convincing evidence, of the circumstances which allegedly produce those effects, it by no means added a condition relating to the requisite standard of proof but merely drew attention to the essential function of evidence, which is to establish convincingly the merits of an argument or, as in the present case, of a decision on a merger.

> (42) A prospective analysis of the kind necessary in merger control must be carried out with great care since it does not entail the examination of past events—for which often many items of evidence are available which make it possible to understand the causes—or of current events, but rather a prediction of events which are more or less likely to occur in future if a decision prohibiting the planned concentration or laying down the conditions for it is not adopted.

> (43) Thus, the prospective analysis consists of an examination of how a concentration might alter the factors determining the state of competition on a given market in order to establish whether it would give rise to a serious impediment to effective competition. Such an analysis makes it necessary to envisage various chains of cause and effect with a view to ascertaining which of them are the most likely.

> (44) [...] That being so, the quality of the evidence produced by the Commission in order to establish that it is necessary to adopt a decision declaring the concentration incompatible with the common market is particularly important, since that evidence must support the Commission's conclusion that, if such a decision were not adopted, the economic development envisaged by it would be plausible.

It is clear from the above that the Union courts review the Commission's merger decisions rather closely because they involve a prospective analysis. However, with respect

---

[78] The origins can be found in the great classic judgment of EC competition law in Cases 56 and 58/64 *Établissements Consten SARL and Grundig-Verkaufs GmbH v Commission*.

[79] Case T-342/99 *Airtours v Commission*, Case T-310/01 *Schneider Electric v Commission*, Case T-5/02 *Tetra Laval v Commission*.

[80] Case C-12/03 P *Tetra Laval v Commission*. A similar summary is given by the ECJ in Case C-67/13 P *Groupement des cartes bancaires v Commission* paras 43–54.

to the Commission's duty to state reasons under Article 296 TFEU, the Union Courts have recognised that under the EUMR the Commission is obliged to work under very strict time limits. As such, the Union Courts have held that the Commission does not infringe its duty to state reasons if, when exercising its power to examine transaction, it does not include precise reasoning in its decision as to the appraisal of a number of aspects of the Transaction which appear to it to be manifestly irrelevant or insignificant or plainly of secondary importance to the appraisal of the transaction—nor is the Commission obliged to anticipate potential objections.[81] The Union Courts have explicitly stated that this position is particularly justified in the case of decisions taken pursuant to the EUMR, where the degree of precision of the statement of the reasons for a decision must be weighed against practical realities and the time and technical facilities available for making the decision.[82]

5.3 Merger Control in the UK System

5.3.1 Introduction

The Government White Paper that led to the Enterprise Act 2002 (the 'EA 2002') was entitled *Productivity and Enterprise—A World Class Competition Régime*[83] and it sought to address various criticisms levelled at UK competition law in general, with a particular focus on the reform of the merger control system. As a result of the rather stuttering (and even haphazard) previous development of UK competition law throughout the twentieth century, the various persons and institutions involved in the assessment of mergers and the substantive test applied in making that assessment had come in for serious criticism.[84] The Secretary of State for Trade and Industry held the exclusive power to refer mergers to the Competition Commission (CC) (and the Monopolies and Mergers Commission (MMC) before the advent of the CC), and it was commonly argued that this led to excessive politicisation of the UK merger regime,

---

[81] Joined Cases C-465 and 466/02 *Germany and Denmark* v *Commission*, para 106.

[82] Case C-413/06 P *Bertelsmann and Sony Corporation of America* v *Impala*, para 167 and case law cited.

[83] Cm 5233, 31 July 2001. This was the result of a consultation process started by the DTI back in the summer of 1999 (see DTI, *Mergers: A Consultation Document on Proposals for Reform* (URN 99/1028, 6 August 1999) and *Mergers: The Response to the Consultation on Proposals for Reform* (URN 00/805, 26 October 2000)).

[84] For background and history, see S Wilks, *In the Public Interest* (Manchester, Manchester University Press, 1997) (concerning the history of the MMC); Celli and Grenfell, *Merger Control in UK and the EU* (The Hague, Kluwer Law International, 1997 (updated, 1999)) (Pt I on UK merger control); B Rodger, 'UK Merger Control: Politics, the Public Interest and Reform' (2000) *European Competition Law Review* 24; R Whish, *Competition Law*, 4th edn (2001) ch 22; D Morris, 'The Enterprise Act: Aspects of the New Regime' (2002) *Economic Affairs* 15; and C Graham, 'The Enterprise Act 2002 and Competition Law' (2002) 67 *Modern Law Review* 273.

raising suspicions among companies of political interference and increasing the uncertainty of the process. Further, the rather vague 'public interest' test of section 84 of the Fair Trade Act 1973 was long argued to place insufficient emphasis upon genuine economic analysis of competition issues arising from mergers and thus to allow too much discretion to the Secretary of State in taking the decision whether or not to refer any given merger. It should be noted, however, that the consistent policy adopted by successive Secretaries of State from the mid-1980s onwards had been 'to make references primarily on competition grounds',[85] illustrating that the shift towards a purer 'competition-based' assessment had commenced many years before the EA 2002 found its way on to the statute book.

Nevertheless, these aims of increasing certainty in the application of these provisions, of reducing the overt scope for political involvement and (consistent with the adoption of the Competition Act 1998 (the 'CA 1998')) of effecting a shift to an obviously competition-based system were felt to be of sufficient significance to introduce substantial changes to the UK merger control regime. This new regime entered into force on 20 June 2003, and remains the fundamental basis for merger control in the UK.[86] The EA 2002 was amended by the Enterprise and Regulatory Reform Act 2013 (the 'ERRA 2013'), which further strengthened the Competition and Markets Authority's (CMA) investigative powers; established a regulatory timetable for completing Phase I investigations and implementing Phase II remedies; and strengthened the CMA's ability to adopt interim measures. These amendments will be discussed in further detail below.

To the extent that the UK merger control regime applies to any transaction, this grants the transaction an exclusion from the application of the Chapter I prohibition. This covers any agreement that constitutes a 'relevant merger situation' (see section 5.3.2 below), as well as any ancillary restrictions contained in those agreements, so long as they are 'directly related and necessary to the implementation of the merger' (all as per paragraph 1, schedule 1, CA 1998).

Finally, it should be noted that UK legislation makes special provision for mergers in certain sectors: at present, newspapers[87] and water and sewerage undertakings.[88]

---

[85] Known as the 'Tebbitt doctrine' after Norman (now Lord) Tebbitt, the Minister who first announced this approach: DTI Press Notice, 5 July 1984. For discussion, see (eg) Rodger, above n 83: in conjunction with the subsequent reform of allowing undertakings to be offered in lieu of a reference (see ss 75G-K FTA 1973, as inserted by s 147 of the Companies Act 1989 and amended by s 9 of the Deregulation and Contracting Out Act 1994), the UK approach to merger control had shifted significantly away from any generalist public interest approach. The ability for the CMA to accept such undertakings in lieu of a reference is retained in ss 73–75 EA 2002: see the discussion in s 5.3.4.1 below.

[86] Thanks to the Enterprise Act 2002 (Commencement No 3, Transitional and Transitory Provisions and Savings) Order 2003 (SI 2003, No 1397), which brought the major provisions of the EA 2002 into force.

[87] The new Communications Act 2003 has amended the regime of the FTA 1973 on newspaper mergers, substantially including these within the normal provisions and procedures of the EA 2002, although certain special elements remain and these will be dealt with under the general public interest provisions.

[88] Regulated by the Water Industry Act 1991 (as amended by s 70 of the EA 2002). See further J Hurdley and P Price, in P Freeman and R Whish (eds), *Butterworths Competition Law* (London, Butterworths, loose leaf, 1994 and updates), Div IX, paras [1420]–[1463.7], and CM Weir, 'Comparative Competition and the Regulation of Mergers in the Water Industry of England and Wales' (2000) XLV *Antitrust Bulletin* 811.

The reader should consult more specialist works for coverage of these matters, but should also note here that where a merger involves a regulated sector (such as electricity or gas (Ofgem), telecommunications (Ofcom) or rail (ORR)), the CMA will cooperate closely with the sectoral regulator in assessing the merger.[89]

In addition, the CMA has published (or taken over from the OFT/CC) a number of very informative guidelines on the application of the UK merger control regime. The publications include:

(a) Mergers: Guidance on the CMA's approach to jurisdiction and procedure (CMA 2).
(b) Merger Assessment Guidelines (OFT 1254).
(c) Mergers—Exceptions to the duty to refer and undertakings in lieu of reference guidance (OFT 1122).
(d) Merger Remedies: Competition Commission Guidelines (CC 7).
(e) A Quick Guide to UK Merger Assessment (CMA 18).
(f) Administrative penalties: Statement of policy on the CMA's approach (CMA 4).

5.3.2 Procedural Stages

Essentially, the CMA is tasked with obtaining and reviewing information relating to merger situations (essentially, pre-notification enquiries and the Phase I investigation), and has a duty to refer mergers to an independent CMA Phase II Inquiry Group for further investigation where it believes that it is or may be the case that the merger gives rise to a 'relevant merger situation' and may (or may be expected to) result in a substantial lessening of competition (SLC) in a UK market.

Following referral, it is up to the independent Inquiry Group, selected from members of the CMA Panel, to conduct further investigations (the Phase II investigation) and determine whether the referred merger has resulted, or may be expected to result, in a substantial lessening of competition. The Inquiry Group determines the outcome of merger cases referred to it by the CMA.

Thus, the CMA acts as a filter in UK merger control and performs a first check upon the applicability of the rules of the EA 2002, while the Inquiry Group's role is one of more detailed investigation and analysis of the impact that any merger referred to it may have upon competition in the UK. In practice, the vast majority of cases are dealt with in Phase I, while only a small number are referred to the Inquiry Group for further investigation. As such, the procedure under the UK merger control regime is similar to that under the EUMR to the extent that cases of 'serious doubts' as to the compatibility of a merger with the internal market are taken to an in-depth Phase II investigation (on which see sections 5.2.2.5 and 5.2.2.6 above). However, unlike the system under the EUMR, in the UK system, the Phase II investigation is conducted by a separate group from Phase I.

---

[89] See, eg, the cooperation between the CMA and Ofcom during the *BT Group/EE* merger inquiry, Final Report issued 15 January 2016.

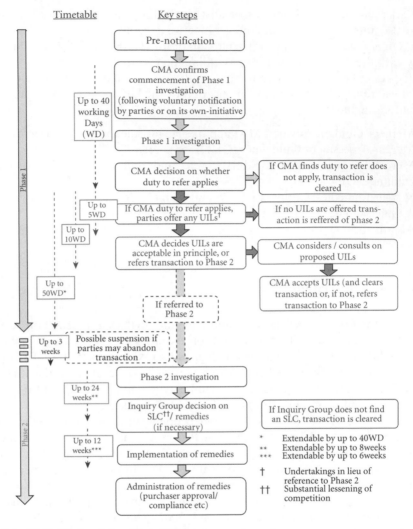

Figure 5.1: CMA 18. A quick guide to UK merger assessment

Naturally, in practice, matters are slightly more complex than this outline, as both Figure 5.1 and our subsequent discussion will make clear.

Figure 5.1 provides an outline of the operation of the merger control procedure under UK competition law. In what follows, we will outline the roles, functions and powers of the CMA and the Inquiry Group in UK merger control. Then, in section 5.3.3, we will provide a brief discussion of the elements of the substantive assessment of mergers under the UK regime. Finally, in sections 5.3.4 and 5.3.5 we discuss some of the tools for securing the enforcement of the UK competition law regime for mergers, including the role of the courts in this field.

5.3.2.1 The Phase I Procedure and the Role of the CMA

When examining the role played by the CMA in the UK merger control regime, it is important to appreciate that, unlike under the EU merger control regime, there is no legal duty imposed upon companies by UK merger law to notify a deal prior to the completion of a merger. Notification under the UK system is voluntary. However, many companies involved in mergers and joint ventures nevertheless choose to notify their proposed or completed deals to the CMA, either for guidance or to pre-empt the risk of subsequently being ordered to unwind the deal after investigation and potential regulatory action by the CMA.

In the absence of a notification, the CMA has other methods at its disposal for acquiring information on particular cases, including conducting its own research of the media, liaising with other public bodies and receiving information from third parties.

In cases where a merger is not notified but the CMA learns about it by other means, it will send an 'enquiry letter' if there is a reasonable prospect that it is under a duty to make a reference to the Inquiry Group.

In certain circumstances, the CMA is also prepared to provide informal advice to companies on substantive and, where relevant, jurisdictional questions concerning the merger control regime. The CMA will consider providing informal advice if:

(a)   the party seeking advice has demonstrated a good faith intention of proceeding with a confidential transaction; and
(b)   the party has explained why there is a genuine competition issue, that is to say that there is a theory of harm that the CMA might reasonably rely upon as a credible reason for a Phase II reference.

In a similar way to the European Commission, the CMA encourages parties—prior to submitting a formal notification—to approach it so as to engage in pre-notification discussions. As with the system under the EUMR, the benefit of such pre-notification discussions is that it enables the CMA to familiarise itself with the relevant markets which, oftentimes are complex, and help identify the information needed by the CMA, without triggering the formal process under which the CMA is required to operate within fixed statutory time limits.

Where the CMA begins an investigation of its own initiative, it will not have the opportunity to conduct pre-notification discussions. The Phase I timetable will start in such cases on the working day after the CMA confirms that it has sufficient information to enable it to begin its investigation.[90] The CMA can, and often does, seek information by sending an 'enquiry letter' to the parties or by issuing a formal notice under section 109 EA 2002, which carries financial penalties in the case of non-compliance.

In its guidance on jurisdiction and procedure under the merger regime,[91] the CMA sets out its approach to Phase 1 investigations. In this regard, the CMA's decision-making process differs depending on whether a merger raises 'no serious competition issues' or raises 'more complex or material competition issues'. In cases that do not

---

[90] Mergers: Guidance on the CMA's jurisdiction and procedure, paras 6.19 and 6.59.
[91] Mergers: Guidance on the CMA's jurisdiction and procedure, paras 7.32–7.59.

raise any competition concerns, the decision to clear the merger is taken by a director of mergers.

In more complex or problematic cases, a 'state-of-play' meeting will be held between the parties and officials from the CMA. The purposes of the state-of-play meeting is to inform the parties of the CMA's possible competition concerns and whether the CMA intends to hold a 'Case Review Meeting' (CRM).[92] If the CMA intends to hold a CRM, it will send an 'issues letter' setting out the relevant evidence and the core arguments for a Phase II reference and giving the parties an opportunity to respond in writing and/or at an 'issues meeting'. Once the issues meeting has been held, a CRM will usually take place within the CMA with the purpose of discussing the case and testing the soundness of the case team's assessment.

After the CRM a separate so-called 'SLC decision meeting' is held, at which the Phase I decision-maker hears a report on the discussions at the CRM and the overall recommendation following the CRM. A provisional decision on whether to refer the merger for a Phase II investigation is then taken. If an issues letter has been sent, but the CMA decides not to make a Phase II reference, the Court of Appeal has said that the CMA must show that, on the basis of the material relied upon, the likelihood of an SLC and the uncertainties highlighted by the issues letter have been removed.[93]

(i) Procedural Timetable

Following the adoption of the ERRA 2013, section 34ZA of the Enterprise Act now sets out time limits within which the CMA must complete its Phase I investigations. In general, Phase I decisions must be made within 40 working days from the first working day after a satisfactory merger notice has been filed, or, in the absence of a merger notice, the first working day after the CMA has informed the merging parties that it has sufficient information to begin its investigation.

Section 34ZB provides that the CMA may extend the initial period of 40 working days if it considers that a relevant person has failed, with or without a reasonable excuse, to comply with the CMA's powers of investigation. The CMA may also extend the initial period by no more than 20 working days where an intervention notice is in force (section 34ZC(2) EA 2002).

Sections 22(3)(za) and 33(3)(za) EA 2002 provide that, subject to minor exceptions,[94] if the CMA fails to reach a decision within the prescribed time limits, it is no longer able to make a Phase II reference.

In addition, in respect of completed mergers, section 24 EA 2002 provides that a reference to the Inquiry Group for a Phase II investigation cannot be made if the enterprises ceased to be distinct more than four months prior to the Phase II reference or, if later, more than four months before notice was given to the CMA of the merger or the fact of the merger was made public. In certain circumstances these time limits can be extended.[95]

---

[92] Mergers: Guidance on the CMA's jurisdiction and procedure, paras 7.33–7.34.

[93] *OFT v IBA Health Ltd* [2004] EWCA Civ 142, paras 73 and 100.

[94] For example, if the parties provide false or misleading information in a merger notice (see s 100(1) EA 2002; Mergers: Guidance on the CMA's jurisdiction and procedure, Annex A, para A.9.

[95] See ss 25 and 122 EA 2002. For the interplay between these time limits and investigations being carried out by the Commission, see the rulings of the CAT ([2011] CAT 23) and the Court of Appeal ([2012] EWCA Civ 643) in respect of Ryanair.

(ii) Referral to the CMA Phase II Inquiry Group?

References to the CMA Phase II Inquiry Group can be made both for completed (section 23 EA 2002) and anticipated mergers (section 33 EA 2002). The criteria to be applied by the CMA in determining whether or not to refer in either situation are essentially identical.

When deciding whether or not to refer, the CMA must consider the following issues:

(a) the *applicability of the EUMR*: this is an important factor to consider, because (as discussed in section 5.2.2.1 above) the Commission is the clear first port of call for notifications of mergers that have a 'Union dimension' (on which see section 5.2.4 above). Thus, the CMA must determine whether the transaction in question is one to which the EUMR applies and, if so, then the UK merger regime cannot, in the first instance, claim to regulate it (see section 5.2.2.2 above);

(b) has a *'relevant merger situation'* arisen (section 23 EA 2002)? This occurs where:
 — two or more enterprises cease to be distinct enterprises (on which see sections 26 (on how this might occur) and 27 (on the time at which this takes place) EA 2002); and
 — *either* the UK turnover of the acquired enterprise exceeds £70 million (section 23(1)(b) EA 2002; on calculation of turnover, see section 28 EA 2002 and the order adopted thereunder)[96] *or* 25 per cent or more of the relevant goods or services are supplied in the UK (or a substantial part thereof) by one and the same person (section 23(2)(b) EA 2002);

(c) the *substantive test* requires that a 'substantial lessening of competition' (SLC) is likely to result from the merger (on which see section 5.3.3 below): at the Phase I stage of the process, the CMA needs to consider whether, objectively, and on the basis of the relevant facts before it, there is a realistic prospect of an SLC due to the merger.

(d) if criteria (a), (b) and (c) are satisfied, then the CMA has a *duty to refer* the merger to the Phase II Inquiry Group, *unless*:[97]
 — the market involved is not sufficiently important to warrant such a reference under the EA 2002 (section 22(2)(a) EA 2002);[98]
 — sufficient 'customer benefits' can be identified (section 22(2)(b) EA 2002: see the discussion of SLC below (section 5.3.3)); or
 — the CMA considers it appropriate to accept undertakings from the companies involved in lieu of a reference (see section 5.3.4.1 below).

---

[96] Enterprise Act 2002 (Merger Fees and Determination of Turnover) Order 2003 (SI 2003, No 1370).

[97] See also s 22(3) EA 2002 for a limited list of situations in which a merger reference *cannot* be made by the CMA.

[98] See, eg, the OFT's Decision on the *Anticipated acquisition by Johnston Press plc of Thorne and District Gazette and associated titles* (13 May 2005). Here, the OFT found that although the 25% threshold was met by the merger, the geographical area involved was not considered to be 'of sufficient size, character and importance as to be worthy of consideration for the purposes of' the EA 2002'. However, note that this conclusion was expressed by the OFT as meaning that the 25% share was not held in a sufficiently 'substantial part of the United Kingdom' for the purposes of s 23 EA 2002. This relies upon the important ruling of the House of Lords in case of *R v Monopolies and Mergers Commission ex p South Yorkshire Transport Ltd* [1993] 1 WLR 23, decided under the previous merger regime but with reference to the question of 'a substantial part' of the UK.

Concerning the CMA's duty to make a reference to the Inquiry Group, we should dwell for a moment upon the importance of the *IBA Health* case.[99] This case concerned the proposed merger between iSoft and Torex,[100] and is relevant to the question of the scope of the (at the time) OFT's discretion in deciding whether or not to make a reference to the CC (the equivalent of what is now the Inquiry Group). This is important, due to the legal duty imposed upon the CMA to refer a merger to the CC where an SLC has been shown (see sections 22 and 33 EA 2002: 'the [CMA] shall … make a reference'). When the OFT decided not to refer the proposed merger between iSoft and Torex (two direct competitors on the particular market) to the CC, IBA Health (a rival company) made an application before the CAT under section 120 EA 2002 for judicial review of the OFT's Decision. The CAT took the view that section 33 EA 2002 required the OFT to satisfy a two-part test where the merger in question involved 'grey issues' upon which views might differ as to their significance in establishing an SLC. The OFT was required to:

> satisfy itself not only (i) that in its own mind there was no significant prospect of a substantial lessening of competition, but also (ii) there was no significant prospect of the Competition Commission reaching an alternative view on the basis of a fuller investigation.[101]

This was due to the CAT's interpretation of the significance of the OFT's role as the first filter in the merger control process: where a case raised difficult and complex matters, the nature of the system must be taken to have intended them to be resolved after more detailed investigation, on a reference to the CC.[102]

The result of this approach would have been to remove much of the discretion that the OFT had assumed under sections 22 and 33 EA 2002, requiring a much wider range of merger cases to be referred to the CC (with a concomitant reduction in the power of the OFT to act as the filter in this process). Further, the interaction between the CAT's judgment and the OFT's power to accept undertakings in lieu of making a reference to the CC was also unclear and unsatisfactory (seeming, as it did, to render this OFT power similarly impotent in cases involving any degree of controversy). From a business perspective, the increased uncertainty that would result from this approach, not to mention the greater delays involved (both generally and if the CAT's judgment encouraged challenges to OFT non-referral decisions by competitors) before a merger would be cleared (if at all) after a CC investigation, aroused many misgivings.

Happily, from these perspectives at least, the Court of Appeal did not follow the approach taken by the CAT in its construction of the scope of the duty to refer imposed upon the OFT. The Court of Appeal confirmed that the relevant belief was that of the OFT as to whether the merger may be expected to result in an SLC. There is no second part to this assessment, contrary to the approach of the CAT (above).[103]

---

[99] *OFT v IBA Health Ltd* [2004] EWCA Civ 142, [2004] ICR 1364, [2004] 4 All ER 1103, [2005] ECC 1 (noted by E Hardwick, 'The Court of Appeal's *IBA Health* Ruling: Victory for the OFT?' [2003/2004] *Utilities Law Review* 153 and A Scott, 'The Cutting of Teeth: *IBA Health v Office for Fair Trading*' (2004) *Journal of Business Law* 672).

[100] See OFT Decision, *Anticipated acquisition by iSoft Group plc of Torex plc* (6 November 2003).

[101] *IBA Health v OFT* [2003] CAT 27, para 228.

[102] See, ibid, paras 198, 199, 213 and 267.

[103] *OFT v IBA Health Ltd* [2004] EWCA Civ 142, [2004] ICR 1364, [2004] 4 All ER 1103, [2005] ECC 1, paras 35 and 38–39.

The Court of Appeal also provided guidance as to the requisite standard to which the OFT (and now, by analogy, the CMA) must establish that belief:

> the words 'may be the case' exclude the purely fanciful because OFT acting reasonably is not going to believe that the fanciful may be the case. In between the fanciful and a degree of likelihood less than 50 per cent there is a wide margin in which OFT is required to exercise its judgment. I do not consider that it is possible or appropriate to attempt any more exact mathematical formulation of the degree of likelihood which OFT acting reasonably must require ...[104]

This formulation does much to restore a fair range of discretion[105] for the OFT (and now the CMA) in conducting its first-look assessment of mergers and deciding whether or not to refer them to the CC (and now the Inquiry Group) for further scrutiny. However, it should be noted that the Court of Appeal nevertheless upheld the CAT's judgment on the substance of the reasoning provided by the OFT in justifying its refusal to refer the merger to the CC.[106] We will return to this point below (section 5.3.5) when discussing the framework for judicial review of CMA decisions in this area.

5.3.2.2 The Phase II Procedure and the Role of the CMA Phase II Inquiry Group

On receipt of a reference from the CMA, a Phase II Inquiry Group is set up, which consists of at least three members of the CMA Panel appointed by the Secretary of State. It is their job to conduct the Phase II merger inquiry.

An overview of the key milestones and steps in the Inquiry Group's investigation are set out at pages 95–98 of the CMA's Guidelines on jurisdiction and procedure (CMA 2). It should be noted that the Inquiry Group already has at its disposal any information gathered by the CMA during the Phase I examination of the merger. The investigation process exists to acquire deeper and more detailed knowledge of the merger and the likely results that it will have. This acquisition can be by way of issuing questionnaires, hearing witnesses and requesting evidence, both from the main parties to the merger and from all other relevant parties (including competitors, customers, government departments and trade associations).

To facilitate this investigation and information gathering process, the Inquiry Group has been granted a range of investigatory powers by the EA 2002 (see its sections 109–117 for details). The Inquiry Group may (by issuing a notice) oblige private individuals to attend its hearings as witnesses and to produce documents to aid the Inquiry Group in its investigation (section 109 EA 2002). Failure by any private party to comply with these obligations may lead to the imposition of penalties by the Inquiry Group (section 110 EA 2002). These may be either a fixed sum or periodic

---

[104] ibid, para 48.

[105] Note, however, that the CAT itself is not enamoured of the use of the term 'discretion' in this context, preferring to refer to the OFT's 'margin of judgment or evaluation of the facts': *UniChem Ltd v OFT* [2005] CAT 8, para 172 (and see, generally, the discussion of the *IBA Health* case in paras 158–75 of the *UniChem* judgment).

[106] ibid, paras 71–75 and 105–6.

in nature (or a combination of the two: section 111(2) EA 2002), ceasing only where compliance with the original obligation has been secured. An appeal may be lodged against the imposition of any such penalty before the CAT, covering the imposition or nature of the penalty, its amount or its timing (section 114 EA 2002). Any person who 'intentionally alters, suppresses or destroys any document which he has been required to produce by a notice under section 109' commits an offence, which can be punished by a fine or imprisonment for up to two years (section 110(7) EA 2002).[107] For guidance on how the CMA intends to use its powers in this area, see its *Statement of policy on administrative penalties* (CMA 4).

Once the Group has completed its investigations, it will notify the parties of its provisional conclusions and possible remedies that it is minded to impose.[108] As the *Interbrew* case[109] shows, it is important that the parties be given a genuine opportunity to comment upon these proposed remedies; failure to do so may render any final remedies decision vulnerable to challenge by way of judicial review.

(i) Report

Once representations have been heard on any proposed remedies, the Inquiry Group's final position on the merger must be adopted in a formal report. The report must record the Inquiry Group's reasons for reaching its decisions on the competition and remedies questions, as well as providing sufficient information to facilitate a proper understanding of the Inquiry Group's decisions and its reasons therefor (sections 38 and 136 EA 2002). This information and analysis may be published in annexes to the report,[110] which may also include a dissenting opinion from a Group member not in agreement with the final position on the merger (sections 119 and 178 EA 2002).

The time limit within which the merger report must be produced is 24 weeks from the date of the reference beginning the Phase II procedure—which is a longer period than the 90 working days available to the European Commission in a Phase II case under the EUMR. The 24-week time limit can only be extended where there are 'special reasons why the report cannot be prepared and published within that period'. In such a case, an extension of up to eight weeks is available. Notice of any such extension must be published.[111]

---

[107] Similar penalties apply where false or misleading information is knowingly or recklessly submitted to the CMA in response to a notice requiring information: s 117 EA 2002.

[108] Note that the Group must reach an adverse finding that there will be an SLC by a two-thirds majority if it is to move to the stage of considering remedies: sch 11, para 11 EA 2002. For an example of proposed remedies, published for consultation, see the CC's Notice of 11 November 2004, relating to the *Acquisition by Emap plc of ABI Building Data Ltd*. This case was finally resolved by the CC's acceptance of Emap's final undertakings in its Remedies Notice No 2 of 2005 (published on 3 March 2005). For an example of a Report where the Group split 3:2 in its finding of no SLC, see the CC's *Report on the acquisition by Arriva plc of Sovereign Bus & Coach Company Ltd* (7 January 2005).

[109] *Interbrew SA v Competition Commission* [2001] UKCLR 954 (a case decided prior to the EA 2002, but the import of the reasoning is equally applicable under the EA 2002 regime).

[110] See, eg the Competition Commission's Notice of Acceptance of Undertakings No 6 of 2004 (*First-Group plc acquisition of the ScotRail franchise*) (15 October 2004) and the maps relating to Annex E, illustrating the various bus and rail routes where competition concerns might be raised and how the undertakings offered responded to these concerns.

[111] Sections 38 and 39 EA 2002.

5.3.2.3 A Role for the Secretary of State?

While it is clear that one of the major motivations for the introduction of the new UK merger regime was the de-politicisation of the merger control process,[112] it must be acknowledged that there remain some areas in which the Secretary of State for Trade and Industry retains a role in respect of 'public interest' mergers.

The thinking behind the retention of this limited category of public interest considerations in the hands of the Secretary of State was to ensure coverage of those exceptional areas where a purely competition-based analysis would not permit scrutiny of a merger and yet important public interest questions might be at stake.[113] This is made clearer when we consider what currently counts as a 'public interest' for these purposes. Under the original wording of the EA 2002, section 58(1) EA 2002 specified 'national security' as a public interest matter for these purposes. Beyond this, section 58(3) EA 2002 allows the Secretary of State to add to the list of such public interests 'by order'. This would require the adoption of a statutory instrument and the approval of Parliament. Subsequently, the Communication Act 2003 has inserted a range of other, media-related public interest considerations (see section 58(2A), (2B) and (2C) EA 2002).[114] The need to maintain the stability of the UK financial system has also been designated as a matter of public interest[115] for these purposes.

The legislation imposes duties upon CMA to inform the Secretary of State of certain proposed decisions where relevant public interest considerations are at stake. Thus, when considering making a reference to the Inquiry Group, the CMA must inform the Secretary of State of any case raising a public interest matter specified under section 58, while CMA is required to pass on any representations made to it where they concern the use of the Secretary of State's powers (under section 58(3) EA 2002) to add to the list of public interest considerations.

Armed with this information, the Secretary of State may then give an 'intervention notice' to the CMA[116] where the Secretary of State considers a specified public interest consideration to be relevant for the examination of a merger situation. This requires the CMA to produce a report for the Secretary of State on the matter, covering both competition and public interest matters. Once transmitted, this transfers the question

---

[112] See, eg, various DTI publications: *Mergers: A Consultation Document on Proposals for Reform* (DTI/ Pub 4308; URN 99/1028, 6 August 1999) and the accompanying press release (P/99/690, 6 August 1999), *Mergers: The Response to the Consultation on Proposals for Reform* (URN 00/805, 26 October 2000), esp paras 4.1–4.12; and, finally, the Government's White Paper, *Productivity and Enterprise—A World Class Competition Regime* (Cm 5233, 31 July 2001), ch 5.

[113] As acknowledged by Art 21(3) EUMR.

[114] As inserted by s 375 of the Communications Act 2003. These new public interest considerations include: 's. 58(2A) The need for (a) accurate presentation of news; and (b) free expression of opinion in newspapers[;] s. 58(2B) The need for, to the extent that it is reasonable and practicable, a sufficient plurality of views in newspapers in each market for newspapers in the United Kingdom or a part of the United Kingdom is specified in this section [and] s. 58(2C) … (a) the need, in relation to every different audience in the United Kingdom or in a particular area or locality of the United Kingdom, for there to be a sufficient plurality of persons with control of the media enterprises serving that audience.'

[115] Inserted by the Enterprise Act 2002 (Specification of Additional Section 58 Consideration) Order 2008 (SI 2008, No 2645), adopted under s 58(3) and (4) of the Enterprise Act 2002. See the CMA Guidance on the CMA's jurisdiction and procedure (CMA 2), para 16.6.

[116] Under s 42(2) EA 2002.

of whether or not to make a reference to the Inquiry Group into the hands the of the Secretary of State. In making this decision, the Secretary of State is bound by the CMA's assessment of competition matters, but he may intervene and base his decision upon public interest grounds.[117]

If a reference is made to the Inquiry Group, it must issue a report, examining all of the usual questions as well as the public interest considerations.[118] This report functions as a series of recommendations to the Secretary of State as to the remedies or other action that should be taken. Again, the Secretary of State is bound by the Inquiry Group's assessment of any competition matters,[119] but not so far as the Inquiry Group's position on public interest issues is concerned.

In addition, sections 59–66 of the EA 2002 sets out provisions relating to a further, exceptional, category of 'special public interest' mergers. Such 'special public interest' mergers can be referred for investigation on public interest grounds, even though they do not meet either the turnover or the share of supply thresholds for reference contained in section 23 of the Act.

Two types of merger may be considered under the 'special public interest' provisions:

(a)   mergers involving certain government contractors or sub-contractors who may hold or receive confidential information or material relating to defence; and

(b)   certain mergers in the newspaper and broadcasting sectors that do not qualify for investigation under the general merger rules because they fall below the turnover or share of supply tests.

Such cases are not scrutinised on competition grounds, but against public interest considerations only. At the time of writing, there have been two cases under these provisions: *Insys Group Ltd/Lockheed Martin UK Ltd*;[120] and *Atlas Elektronik UK Ltd/QinetiQ*.[121]

The relevant procedure relating to special public interest mergers is set out at paragraphs 16.23–16.27 of the CMA's guidance: *Mergers: Guidance on the CMA's jurisdiction and procedure* (CMA 2).

5.3.3 Substantive Assessment

When determining, first, whether the CMA needs to make a reference to the Inquiry Group, and, secondly, whether the Inquiry Group should prohibit or clear a merger, the question that the relevant branches of the competition authority need to ask themselves is whether the merger is likely to result in a 'substantial lessening of competition' (an 'SLC'). It should be noted that the SLC test is not identical to that of a Significant Impediment to Effective Competition (SIEC) which applies under the EUMR,

---

[117] By virtue of s 46(2) EA 2002.
[118] See s 47 EA 2002.
[119] By virtue of s 54(7) EA 2002.
[120] A report to the Secretary of State for Trade and Industry, 19 September 2005.
[121] A report to the Secretary of State for Trade and Industry, 25 June 2009.

although it is clear that there are likely to be very strong similarities between the two approaches in practice.

The EA 2002 does not include a definition of a SLC. Both the CMA and the CAT, however, have offered guidance as to what is meant by a SLC.

In its ruling in *Global Radio Holdings Ltd v Competition Commission*[122] the CAT held that a 'substantial' lessening of competition does not mean that the reduction in the level of competition needs to be 'large', 'considerable' or 'weighty'. Rather, the 'significance' of the lessening of competition is a relative concept that is a finding that there is a 'significant lessening of competition', without there being a requirement for that lessening to be large in absolute terms.

The Merger Assessment Guidelines (OFT 1254), which were adopted by the OFT and CC in September 2010, but which have since been confirmed by the CMA, explain that a merger gives rise to an SLC when it has a significant effect on rivalry over time, thereby reducing the competitive pressure on firms to improve their offer to customers or become more efficient or innovative. A merger that gives rise to an SLC will be expected to lead to an adverse effect for customers.[123]

In this respect, the CMA and Inquiry Group, need to carry out a forward-looking, predictive analysis to establish what the likely level of competition will be on the relevant market post-transaction, as compared to the level of competition that exists pre-transaction. This analysis is often referred to as a 'counterfactual' assessment. For the purposes of Phase I, the CMA will usually accept the prevailing conditions of competition as the framework for conducting the counterfactual analysis. In Phase II, however, Inquiry Group will often select the most likely future situation in the absence of the merger.[124] In its ruling in *Stagecoach Group*,[125] the CAT highlighted the importance of ensuring that the assessment is conducted against an appropriate counterfactual where it held that a decision finding that a merger would create a monopoly for local buses in Preston as the choice of counterfactual was not supported by the evidence.

Paragraph 4.3.6 of the Merger Assessment Guidelines sets out three situations in which the CMA may use a counterfactual other than the prevailing conditions of competition:

(a)   'the exiting firm scenario': where a firm is likely to exit the market in the near future regardless of whether the merger takes place;

(b)   'the loss of potential entrant scenario': that is, whether the counterfactual situation should include the entry by one of the merger firms into the market of the other firm or, if already within the market, whether the firm would have expanded had the merger not taken place; and

(c)   the situation where there are competing bids and parallel transactions: where there is more than one bidder for a target business, the CMA will examine each competing bid separately and will consider whether each proposed merger

---

[122]   Case No 1214/4/8/13 [2013] CAT 26.
[123]   Merger Assessment Guidelines (OFT 1254), para 4.1.3.
[124]   Merger Assessment Guidelines (OFT 1254), paras 4.3.5–4.3.6.
[125]   *Stagecoach Group v Competition Commission*, Case No 1145/4/8/09 [2010] CAT 14.

would create a realistic prospect of a SLC as against prevailing conditions of competition.[126]

Although not binding on the CMA and the Inquiry Group, the Merger Assessment Guidelines provide a detailed summary of the major issues that will be considered by the CMA and the Inquiry Group when determining whether a merger is likely to give rise to a SLC. The Merger Assessment Guidelines address the following aspects of the SLC assessment: first the Merger Assessment Guidelines address the question of market definition and measures of concentration in the market; secondly, they examine the principal theories of harm that can potentially arise from a merger, that is: unilateral and coordinated effects of horizontal mergers; vertical effects; and conglomerate effects. The Merger Assessment Guidelines then set out (what are now) the CMA's views on efficiencies; barriers to entry and expansion; and countervailing buyer power.

The following paragraphs will touch briefly on each of the above-mentioned topics. The reader, however, is referred to the Merger Assessment Guidelines for a more detailed explanation of how the CMA treats each of these aspects in practice.

5.3.3.1 Market Definition

It will be recalled from our discussion in Chapter 1.3 (above) that defining the relevant market is an important element of competition law. The market definition exercise, however, plays an especially important role in the merger control assessment, as it forms the framework for analysing the competitive effects on the merger, and an initial proxy for indicating whether a merger is likely to result in a SLC. The process of market definition has been discussed in some detail in Chapter 1.3 above and its application in UK merger control is further examined in section 5.2 of the Merger Assessment Guidelines. The market definition exercise is key to assessing the effects of a merger because it is only once the relevant market has been defined that one can measure the degree to which the merger will result in a concentration of the market.

5.3.3.2 Measures of Concentration

As set out above, the underlying purpose of the CMA's and Inquiry Group's assessment is to determine what the market will look like after the transaction. Because a relevant merger situation arises when two enterprises cease to become distinct, UK merger control invariably applies to situations in which the number of actors on a market will be reduced as a result of the transaction—that is, the market becomes more concentrated. There are several measures that the CMA and Inquiry Group will use to assess the degree to which a merger results in greater concentration of the market: market shares; number of firms; concentration ratios; and the Herfindahl-Hirschman Index (HHI).[127]

---

[126] Merger Assessment Guidelines (OFT 1254), paras 4.3.8–4.3.27.
[127] Merger Assessment Guidelines (OFT 1254), paras 5.3.1–5.3.6.

During its Phase I investigation, when determining whether it is under a duty to refer the merger to the Inquiry Group, the CMA will generally base its decision on whether to refer a merger to the Inquiry Group on how the merger compares to the following concentration thresholds:[128]

(a)   markets where products are undifferentiated suggest that combined market shares of less than 40 per cent will not often give rise to concern over unilateral effects;

(b)   a merger is unlikely to raise concerns if, post-transaction, four or more firms remain in the relevant market;

(c)   any market with a post-merger HHI exceeding 1,000 may be regarded as con-centrated and any market with a post-merger HHI exceeding 2,000 as highly concentrated. In a concentrated market, a horizontal merger generating a delta of less than 250 is not likely to give cause for concern. In a highly concentrated market, a horizontal merger generating a delta of less than 150 is not likely to give cause for concern.

The HHI thresholds may be most informative at Phase 1 for mergers in a market where the product is undifferentiated and where firms compete on output; this is, based on the insights of an economic model of oligopolistic markets.

5.3.3.3 Horizontal Mergers

Horizontal mergers involve firms that operate in the same economic market: in such cases, issues of market share and concentration will be very important to assist any assessment of the likely effects of the merger on the competitive rivalry that would remain in the market thereafter. Thus, the CC took the view that the proposed acqui-sition by FirstGroup of ScotRail's Scottish Passenger Rail Franchise would result in significant overlaps between FirstGroup's existing bus services and the relevant rail services, leading to reductions in competition between the two transport types which might 'be expected to have the further adverse effects of higher bus fares, poorer ser-vices on overlapping bus routes and reduction in choice of services available to pas-sengers on overlap routes'.[129]

The types of effects likely to result from horizontal mergers fall into two broad categories: unilateral (or non-coordinated) and coordinated effects.

With respect to unilateral effects, the CMA's and Inquiry Group's analysis focuses on whether the elimination, as a result of the merger, of a competitor that was pre-viously acting as a competitive constraint, will enable the merged entity to raise prices on its own and without needing to coordinate with its rivals.[130] The Merger Assessment Guidelines discuss four principal potential theories of harm that could result from a merger: the loss of existing competition;[131] the loss of potential

---

[128] Merger Assessment Guidelines (OFT 1254), para 5.3.5.

[129] CC Report on FirstGroup plc and Scottish Rail Franchise (28 June 2004), paras 7–13 and more detailed discussion in the body of the Report.

[130] Merger Assessment Guidelines (OFT 1254), para 5.4.1.

[131] Merger Assessment Guidelines (OFT 1254), paras 5.4.4–5.4.12.

competition;[132] increased buyer power;[133] and the vertical effects arising from horizontal mergers.[134]

With respect to coordinated effects, the CMA and Inquiry Group will assess whether following the merger, the remaining firms in the market will be in a position of inter-dependence and that they can reach a more profitable outcome if they coordinate to limit their rivalry.[135]

In determining whether a merger is likely to result in coordinated effects, the author-ities will assess whether the remaining firms:

(a)   will be able to reach and monitor the terms of coordination;
(b)   have the incentive to coordinate and the existence of an effective mechanism to punish and deter cheating (so-called 'internal sustainability'); and
(c)   the absence of effective competitive constraints (so-called 'external sustainability')—that is, whether there exist third parties (actual or potential competitors) who are in a position to disrupt the coordination.

These conditions mirror the conditions set out by the GC in its ruling in *Airtours*, which the Commission applies for the assessment of coordinated effects under the EUMR.[136]

5.3.3.4 *Non-horizontal Mergers*

Non-horizontal mergers cover situations where enterprises that do not operate in the same market merge. For example, vertical mergers and conglomerate mergers.

Vertical mergers concern firms that operate on different, but often complementary, levels of the production and distribution chain. It is generally accepted that such mergers often enhance efficiency, rather than raising competition concerns. However, where market power is present (or is created) at one or more points along the sup-ply chain then the CMA will remain vigilant as to the possible detrimental effects of such mergers upon competition. Key among these effects is the danger of the merger foreclosing access to such markets for other competing parties; for example, if the merged entity would acquire control over an important distribution resource, then it might be in a position to prevent competitors from accessing downstream markets. In such circumstances, strong countervailing buyer power might act as a brake on such control held by the merged entity, as could the fact that new entry into the market for that distribution resource might be straightforward.

Conglomerate mergers are typically regarded as those involving firms that operate in different product or service markets. In most cases, such mergers raise no competition concerns, but where such a merger would lead to the merged entity acquiring 'portfo-lio power' then a SLC might result. This issue relates to the merged entity holding a

---

[132] Merger Assessment Guidelines (OFT 1254), paras 5.4.13–5.4.18.
[133] Merger Assessment Guidelines (OFT 1254), paras 5.4.19–5.4.21.
[134] Merger Assessment Guidelines (OFT 1254), paras 5.4.22–5.4.23.
[135] Merger Assessment Guidelines (OFT 1254), paras 5.5.1–5.5.19.
[136] T-342/99 *Airtours v Commission*.

wide range (or portfolio) of complementary products, which may allow it to exercise market power in the markets for the individual products more effectively. This can occur where a customer's ability to purchase that range of products from one supplier leads to reduced transaction costs; this could facilitate tying of products across that range or predatory behaviour by the merged entity (for example, by cross-subsidising attacks in one product market from receipts earned in another part of the portfolio). In addition, such mergers may increase the risk of coordination between the merged entity and other players left on the relevant markets, particularly 'if the merged firm's rivals in one market are also rivals in at least one of its other markets and if other factors facilitating collusion are also present in these markets'.

When conducting its assessment of non-horizontal mergers, the relevant parts of the CMA will typically frame their analysis by reference to the following three questions:

(a) *Ability*: Would the merged firm have the ability to harm rivals, for example through raising prices or refusing to supply them?
(b) *Incentive*: Would it find it profitable to do so?
(c) *Effect*: Would the effect of any action by the merged firm be sufficient to reduce competition in the affected market to the extent that, in the context of the market in question, it gives rise to an SLC?[137]

Section 5.6 of the Merger Assessment Guidelines provides a detailed explanation of the manner in which the CMA will assess each of these elements.

5.3.3.5 Countervailing Factors

Assessing whether a merger results in a SLC is not a unidirectional assessment. It may be that, following a transaction, the merged entity will have high market shares, or the transaction will result in a high(er) degree of concentration within the market. These factors clearly constitute significant indicators that the merger could generate competition concerns. This result is not, however, automatic. An equally important element of the assessment is to identify whether any countervailing factors exist, which could limit or offset the potential anti-competitive effects of the transaction. The principal countervailing factors that the CMA and Inquiry Group will examine in their assessments are: (i) the potential efficiencies generated by the merger, including customer benefits; (ii) barriers to entry and expansion; and (iii) countervailing buyer power.

(i) Efficiencies and Customer Benefits

The analysis of the potential efficiencies that might be generated by a merger plays a role at two distinct stages of the assessment: first, when assessing whether a merger gives rise to an SLC; and secondly, when assessing whether a merger generates 'relevant customer benefits' for the purpose of section 30 EA 2002 to offset an SLC.

According to the Merger Assessment Guidelines, for efficiencies to be considered as part of the competitive assessment of whether there is an SLC, such efficiencies

---

[137] Merger Assessment Guidelines (OFT 1254), para 5.6.6.

must increase rivalry among the remaining firms in the market. Such efficiencies might include, for example, cost savings or as pricing effects which arise when lowering the price of one product increases demand for it and other products that are used with it.[138] For the purposes of Phase I this requires the parties to prove, on the basis of compelling evidence, that the efficiencies are timely, likely and sufficient to prevent an SLC from arising and are merger-specific. In Phase II, the Inquiry Group will expect the parties to demonstrate that the same criteria are met on the balance of probabilities.[139]

With respect to customer benefits, section 30 EA 2002 specifically empowers the CMA and the Inquiry Group to have regard to 'any relevant customer benefits', even where the competition assessment of the merger has shown that an SLC would result. The matter to be determined is whether or not these 'customer benefits' would outweigh the detrimental effects of the SLC established. If so, then the CMA has the discretion not to make a reference to the Inquiry Group, while the Inquiry Group has the discretion to modify the remedies that it might otherwise have imposed (even to the extent of permitting the merger to proceed without imposing any remedies at all).

It must be clear that any such benefits identified are not merely theoretical: the parties must have sufficient incentive to pass them on to customers. Examples may include lower prices through marginal cost savings in production, increased innovation levels (for example, where large fixed costs are involved) and improved choice or quality being made available to customers due to an increase in the size of a network.

(ii) Barriers to Entry and Expansion

Even if, following a transaction the merged entity enjoys a large market share, it is unlikely to enjoy actual market power where there are low barriers to entry into and exit from the market, because an increase in prices to anti-competitive levels is likely to attract new competitors into the market, which will constrain prices. In deciding whether entry or expansion might prevent an SLC the CMA will consider whether it would be likely, timely and sufficient.[140] The Merger Assessment Guidelines highlight the following potential barriers to entry and expansion:[141]

(a)   absolute advantages for current market players, which include legal advantages— such as government regulations that limit the number of market participants; and technical advantages, such as preferential access to essential facilities or intellectual property rights, which make it difficult for any new entrant to compete effectively;

(b)   intrinsic or structural advantages arising from the technology, production methods or other factors necessary to establish an effective presence in the market (for example, initial set-up costs, costs associated with investment in specific assets, research and advertising). Such costs are more likely to deter entry or expansion

---

[138] See, eg, *Asda Stores Ltd/Netto Foodstores Ltd*, OFT decision of 23 September 2010, paras 65–76; *Global Radio UK Ltd/GCap Media plc*, OFT decision of 8 August 2008; and *Tradebe Environment Services Ltd/Sita UK Ltd*, Final Report of 28 March 2014.

[139] Merger Assessment Guidelines (OFT 1254), para 5.7.4.

[140] Merger Assessment Guidelines (OFT 1254), para 5.8.3.

[141] Merger Assessment Guidelines (OFT 1254), para 5.8.5.

where a significant proportion of them cannot be recovered when exiting from the market (that is, are 'sunk' costs);.

(c)   economies of scale, which arise where average costs fall as the level of output rises. Such a situation may prevent small-scale entry from acting as an effective competitive constraint in the market;

(d)   strategic advantages, which arise where the incumbent has an advantage over new entrants because of its established position (sometimes called 'first-mover advantages'). These advantages can flow, for example, from the experience and reputation which incumbents have built up, or from the loyalty which they have attracted from customers and suppliers.

With regard to the way in which the CMA will assess the likelihood, timeliness and sufficiency of entry or expansion, the Merger Assessment Guidelines provide that, although the assessment needs to be carried out on a case-by-case basis, the CMA will generally consider that entry or expansion within two years is timely.[142]

(iii) Countervailing Buyer Power

The Merger Assessment Guidelines consider that it is less likely that a SLC will exist where one or more customers are able to use their negotiating strength to constrain the ability of a merged firm to increase prices.[143] The higher the proportion of customers that are able to exercise significant buyer power, the lower the risk of the merger resulting in a SLC. Were only a limited number of customers are able to exercise buyer power, the CMA will assess the extent to which that power can be relied on to protect all customers. The Merger Assessment Guidelines set out various factors that affect the ability of buyers to constrain the power of a supplier, such as their ability to switch, the existence of alternative suppliers and the ability of buyers to either sponsor new entry or enter the supplier's market itself. Any buyer power must remain effective following the merger.[144]

5.3.4 Enforcement and Remedies

There are two principal means by which the UK merger rules can be enforced: regulatory enforcement and enforcement by third parties.

5.3.4.1 Regulatory Enforcement

The presentation of the options open to the CMA will be made here, so far as possible, in chronological order: that is, in the order in which such remedial measures might be adopted in any given case. We will not provide any detailed discussion here of the

---

[142] Merger Assessment Guidelines (OFT 1254), paras 5.8.8–5.8.13. See, eg, Zipcar/Streetcar, Final Report of 22 December 2010, paras 7.29–7.57.

[143] Merger Assessment Guidelines (OFT 1254), para 5.9.1.

[144] Merger Assessment Guidelines (OFT 1254), paras 5.9.2–5.9.8.

procedural requirements imposed upon the CMA by schedule 10 EA 2002, which apply to the adoption of any orders or decisions by the CMA apart from initial and interim orders.

(i) The Role of the CMA in Phase I

At the initial stage of considering a merger, the CMA may have concerns that steps may be taken to move forward with the merger in such a way that any subsequent reference to the Inquiry Group (or, indeed, remedies adopted by the Inquiry Group thereunder) might be frustrated or obstructed in practice. Thus, the CMA may, under section 71 EA 2002 and subject to certain conditions, accept an 'initial undertaking' from the merging parties that they will not take such 'pre-emptive action'. A similar power exists under section 72 EA 2002 to make an 'initial enforcement order' where the CMA has reasonable grounds to believe that such pre-emptive action might be contemplated or even underway (section 72(3B) EA 2002). Such orders can cover a wide range of activities, including requiring the provision of information, the prohibition of certain activities considered to be pre-emptive action and obliging the merging parties to safeguard assets (see section 72(2) and schedule 8, paragraph 9 EA 2002 for full details).

It is also possible for the CMA to accept undertakings from the merging parties in lieu of making a reference to the Inquiry Group (section 73 EA 2002).[145] The details concerning how and in which circumstances such undertakings might be accepted are discussed in some detail in the Guideline: *Mergers—Exceptions to the duty to refer and undertakings in lieu of a reference* (OFT 1122). In deciding whether or not to accept such undertakings in lieu, the CMA is required to consider any relevant customer benefits (section 73(4) EA 2002)[146] and must have regard to the need to achieve as comprehensive a solution as is reasonable and practicable to the SLC and any adverse effects resulting from it. (section 73(3) EA 2002).

Acceptance of undertakings prevents any reference from being made by the CMA to the Inquiry Group (section 74(1) EA 2002), unless material facts about relevant arrangements or transactions, or relevant proposed arrangements or transactions, were not notified to the CMA or made public before an undertaking has been accepted (section 74(2) EA 2002).

Such undertakings may be broader in scope than the order-making powers contained in schedule 8 EA 2002 (see section 89 EA 2002). Finally, the CMA is empowered by section 75(1) EA 2002 to make an order where it finds that any undertaking is not being fulfilled. It is clear that the CMA does not envisage that the acceptance of undertakings in lieu of a reference to the Inquiry Group will be a remedy for any but those cases where the competition concerns raised by the merger and the remedies proposed to address them are clear cut, and those remedies are capable of ready implementation.

This will usually involve cases where clear structural remedies can be formulated.

---

[145] See, eg, the case of *Blackstone Group/UGC Cinemas Holdings Ltd* (OFT Decision of 28 April 2005), in which the OFT decided to consider whether or not to accept undertakings in lieu.

[146] See section 5.3.3.5 above for discussion of this concept.

(ii) Statutory 'Restrictions on Certain Dealings' Once a Merger Has Been Referred

The specific statutory restrictions laid down by sections 77 and 78 EA 2002[147] exist to ensure that, once a reference has been made to the Inquiry Group, the merging parties are formally and clearly legally prevented from pursuing any further steps toward the completion of the merger. This prohibition can only be avoided where the Inquiry Group gives its consent to any further steps, actions or transactions. The key question is likely to be when any particular action amounts to the acquisition of shares, and section 79 EA 2002 provides detailed provisions covering how this notion should be interpreted.

(iii) The Role of the Inquiry Group on Receipt of the Reference

As with the CMA in Phase I, the Inquiry Group is also empowered to accept interim undertakings[148] and make orders in order to prevent pre-emptive action from being taken by the merging parties (sections 80 and 81 EA 2002). This can include simply adopting an undertaking (section 80(3) and (4) EA 2002) already given to the CMA[149] or an order (section 81(3) EA 2002) already made by the CMA. These measures serve to preserve the position while the Inquiry Group conducts its investigation of the merger referred to it.

When that investigation is complete and where an SLC has been found to exist by at least a two-thirds majority of the Inquiry Group,[150] the Inquiry Group has a range of 'final powers' of which it can make use. Only a small number of Phase II merger cases have been resolved by way of a final order.[151] In the majority of cases, the CMA prefers to resolve an investigation by accepting undertakings rather than by making final orders.

The final powers at the CMA's disposal are laid down in sections 82 to 84 EA 2002 and the range of orders that may be made by the Inquiry Group is specified in schedule 8 EA 2002. The range and strength of remedies available to the Inquiry Group under the UK merger control regime is noteworthy. Schedule 8 contains an extensive list of possible remedies that may be adopted in a final order (under section 84 EA 2002). These include: 'general restrictions on conduct' (paragraphs 2–9), 'general obligations to be performed' (paragraphs 10–11), acquisitions and divisions (paragraphs 12–14) and the 'supply and publication of information (paragraphs 15–19). Licences of regulated undertakings may be revoked (section 86(5) together with schedule 9, Part 1 EA 2002) and the parties may be prevented from performing an agreement already in existence (section 86(3) EA 2002).

---

[147] Which deal with completed (s 77) and anticipated (s 78) mergers respectively.
[148] See, eg, the Competition Commission's Acceptance of Interim Undertakings in its investigation of the *Completed acquisition by Somerfield plc of 114 stores from Wm Morrison Supermarkets plc* (13 May 2005).
[149] See, eg, the Competition Commission's Adoption of Undertakings in its investigation of the *Completed acquisition by British Salt Ltd of New Cheshire Salt Works Ltd* (1 June 2005).
[150] Sch 11, para 11 EA 2002.
[151] See, eg, *Tesco/Co-op Store*, Final Report of 28 November 2007 and Final Order of 23 April 2009; *Eurotunnel SA/SeaFrance SA*, Final Report of 6 June 2013 and Final Order of 18 September 2014; *Ryanair Holdings PLC/Aer Lingus Group PLC*, Final Order of 11 June 2015.

(a) General Restrictions on Conduct

With respect to the CMA's power to impose general restrictions on conduct, paragraphs 2 to 9 of Schedule 8 provide that the CMA may make an order prohibiting the making or performance of an agreement or require the termination of an agreement (paragraph 2); may forbid refusals to supply (paragraph 3), tie-ins (paragraph 4), discrimination (paragraph 5), preferential treatment (paragraph 6) and deviation from published price lists (paragraph 7). It is also possible for the CMA to regulate prices by way of a final order under paragraph 8. An order may prohibit the exercise of voting rights attached to shares, stocks or securities (paragraph 9).

(b) General Obligations to be Performed

Conversely, paragraphs 10 and 11 of Schedule 8 enable the CMA to make orders which positively oblige a party to take certain steps (rather than simply refraining from certain conduct). Paragraph 10 provides that an order may require a person to supply goods or services, and it can be specified that they should be of a particular standard or that they should be applied in a particular manner. Paragraph 11 enables the CMA to order that certain of a party's activities should be carried on separately from other activities.

(c) Acquisitions and Divisions

Paragraphs 12–14 of Schedule 8 concern divestiture and non-acquisition obligations. Paragraph 12 enables the CMA to prohibit or restrict the acquisition of the whole or part of an undertaking or the assets of another person's business. Paragraph 13 provides for the division of any business, whether by sale of any part of an undertaking or assets or otherwise.[152] Provision is made for the buyer of a business to be approved by the CMA and for the appointment of a trustee to oversee the divestment of a business.[153]

(d) Supply and Publication of Information

Following the entry into force of the ERRA 2013, paragraph 17 of Schedule 8 now enables the CMA to require parties to publish non-pricing information without also having to require parties to publish pricing information (previously an obligation under paragraph 15 of Schedule 8, which was repealed by the ERRA 2013). Paragraph 16 allows the CMA to impose a prohibition on providing recommended resale prices to dealers. Paragraph 17 enables an order to be adopted requiring a person to publish accounting, pricing and/or non-pricing information. Paragraph 18 provides that orders can specify the manner in which information is to be published. There is a general power in paragraph 19 to require a person to provide the competition authorities with information, and for that information to be published.

---

[152] See, eg, *Somerfield plc/Wm Morrison*, in which the CC ordered the divestiture of four supermarkets, Final Report of 2 September 2005, paras 11.9–11.23.
[153] Sch 8, paras 13(3)(k) and 13(1) of the EA 2002 respectively.

(iv) The Overall Monitoring and Enforcement Role of the CMA

Under the UK merger control regime introduced by the EA 2002, the CMA is entrusted with the function of monitoring the proper respect by the merging parties of undertakings and orders (section 92(1) EA 2002). This includes monitoring compliance with the statutory restrictions imposed by sections 77 and 78 EA 2002. Another part of this role involves keeping undertakings and orders under review, so as to be able to consider whether or not they need to be varied or even released in the light of changing circumstances (section 92(2) EA 2002). For example, in March 2016, the CMA completed its review of 71 old structural merger remedies given by companies prior to 1 January 2005. In April 2016, the CMA launched a subsequent consultation in respect of a further 38 merger remedies that were more than 10 years old, and decided to launch a review into 12 of these merger remedies, to determine whether the remedies were still necessary.

   Since undertakings and orders can be enforced in the civil courts (section 94 EA 2002), the CMA may secure compliance therewith by seeking an injunction (section 94(6) and (7) EA 2002, respectively).

5.3.4.2 Third Parties

It should not be forgotten that third parties also have a role to play in enforcing the UK merger regime. This involves two main elements. First, third parties may bring an action for judicial review of decisions by the CMA and/or the Inquiry Group: this possibility is discussed in section 5.3.5 below. Secondly, the introduction of sections 94 and 95 EA 2002 allows third parties that have suffered some loss or damage as a result of any breach of an enforcement undertaking made by the merging parties or an enforcement order imposed upon the merging parties to bring an action to recover that loss or damage (section 94 EA 2002). This also applies to the breach of any interim orders made concerning anticipated mergers or orders restricting further dealing or activities concerning completed mergers (section 95 EA 2002), whether such orders were imposed by statute (sections 77 and 78 EA 2002), or made by the CMA (under section 71 EA 2002). However, third-party claimants should it warned that there may be a defence available where the defendant can show that it took all reasonable steps and exercised all due diligence to avoid contravening the undertaking (section 94(5) EA 2002).

5.3.5 Judicial Review

According to section 120(1) EA 2002, any 'aggrieved person' (which includes third parties)[154] will have standing to make an application for judicial review of decisions taken by the CMA—including by the CMA Phase II Inquiry Group, *provided* that he or she has a 'sufficient interest' in challenging the decision.[155]

---

[154] See, eg, the *IBA Health* case (above n 101), discussed in section 5.3.2.1, and in the text that follows.
[155] Sch 4, para 12 EA 2002 empowered the CAT to adopt rules rejecting applications if an applicant lacked a 'sufficient interest' or 'any valid grounds' for bringing proceedings.

It should be noted that this judicial review does not amount to a full appeal to the CAT on the facts and/or the law. Rather, section 120(4) EA 2002 makes it clear that ordinary judicial review principles are to be applied by the CAT in these cases. Typically, this will mean that such applications for review will contain a strong focus upon procedural questions.

However, the *IBA Health* case illustrates the difficulties that the CAT experienced[156] in attempting to apply the principles of judicial review to the OFT's assessment of whether or not to refer the merger to the CC. The Court of Appeal in that case sought to provide guidance on how much the OFT (and, by analogy, now the CMA) had to explain in justifying its decision. The reasoning of Carnwath LJ is helpful in this respect. He held that:

> 105. In a case such as the present, where the subject-matter is complex and the supporting material voluminous, there is no statutory requirement for all the evidence to be set out in the decision letter. However, when a challenge is made, there is ... an obligation on a respondent public authority to put before the Court the material necessary to deal with the relevant issues ...

> 106. The question for the [CAT] was not whether the reasoning was adequately expressed in the decision, but whether the material ultimately before it, taken as a whole, disclosed grounds on which the [OFT] could reasonably have reached the decision it did.[157]

In the *IBA Health* case, it was the OFT's failure to explain properly how and why the numerous competition concerns it had raised in its 'issues letter' to iSoft and Torex had been dealt with in the very short time period (just eight days) between that letter and its Decision not to refer that led both the CAT and, on appeal, the Court of Appeal to quash the OFT's Decision not to refer the merger to the CC.[158] Similarly, in the subsequent judgment in *UniChem* v *OFT*,[159] the CAT quashed the OFT's decision not to refer the merger to the CC and remitted the matter to the OFT to adopt a new decision on the merger. The CAT's criticism of the OFT's approach in this case (which concerned the proposed acquisition by Phoenix Healthcare of East Anglian Pharmaceuticals (EAP))[160] centred upon the OFT's willing acceptance of information provided by the merging parties as the basis for its assessment of UniChem's position on the relevant market. It had done so without discussing or checking these matters with UniChem itself. In its appeal to the CAT, UniChem disputed many of the facts upon which the OFT based its Decision.[161] The OFT had taken the view that UniChem

---

[156] See *IBA Health Ltd v OFT* [2003] CAT 27, paras 217ff. See further the criticism by A Scott, 'The Cutting of Teeth: *IBA Health v Office of Fair Trading*' (2004) *Journal of Business Law* 672, at 682–83, of the Court of Appeal's approach to testing the 'credibility' of the arguments that convinced the OFT: he suggests that the only grounds of challenge available ought to be the issues of relevant/irrelevant considerations (as in *Padfield v Minister of Agriculture, Fisheries and Food* [1968] AC 997) and true 'irrationality' (as in *Council of Civil Service Union v Minister for the Civil Service* [1985] AC 374).

[157] *OFT v IBA Health Ltd* [2004] EWCA Civ 142, [2004] ICR 1364, [2004] 4 All ER 1103, [2005] ECC 1, paras 105 and 106 (with minor additions).

[158] See ibid, para 13 for the list of the OFT's 'hypotheses' that indicated the competition concerns that might be raised by the proposed merger.

[159] [2005] CAT 8.

[160] Thus creating the second largest wholesale full-line supplier of 'ethical pharmaceuticals' in East Anglia.

[161] OFT Decision, *Anticipated acquisition by Phoenix Healthcare Distribution Limited of East Anglian Pharmaceuticals Limited* (17 December 2004).

and another company (AAH) would provide sufficient competitive constraints upon the merged entity to overcome the OFT's *prima facie* competition concerns about the merger as expressed in its second issues letter.[162] The CAT found that these facts were essential to the OFT's decision not to refer the merger, so that the CAT was not convinced that all material and relevant matters had been taken into account by the OFT in the adoption of its Decision.[163] The CAT also held that the failure to consult UniChem about the various matters concerning its market position amounted to a procedural failure on the part of the OFT.[164]

The *UniChem* case raises a number of important points.

First, as in *IBA Health*, the CAT clearly placed significant weight upon the content of the issues letters and the need for the final decision to deal adequately with the competition concerns raised in such letters, showing clear reasoning based upon the relevant evidence gathered.[165]

Secondly, while the CAT was critical of the failure to consult UniChem on key factual matters relating to the assessment of competition concerns, it did not go so far as to require such consultation to be conducted extensively and in all cases.[166] Nevertheless, in the circumstances of this particular case the CAT took the view that the failure to ascertain UniChem's response was fatal to the decision in this case.

> 269. In our view such an approach is normally necessary as a matter of an adequate factual investigation, and as a matter of a balanced and fair procedure. In a case where facts about a third party are central to a decision, a balanced and fair procedure should not rely almost entirely on what the merging parties say about the third party without any cross-check of those facts with the third party concerned. That is particularly important where, as here, the decision is a final decision not to refer. A precaution of that kind should also greatly limit the likelihood of proceedings such as this before the Tribunal in future.

This amounts to some degree of strengthening for the role of third parties in the merger control process at the initial 'filter' stage.

Thirdly, in the *UniChem* judgment, the CAT in no way claims to prejudge the final findings on an SLC or a reference to the CC (now the Inquiry Group). Indeed, in a number of paragraphs in its judgment the CAT referred to a strongly arguable case that the decision not to refer the merger could be supported on the basis of the uncontested evidence it had gathered during its investigation.[167] At the same time, the CAT pointed out that:

> 271. In our judgment, it is not every error of assessment or procedural failure which will lead to the Tribunal remitting a matter to the OFT under section 120 of the Act. That said, given that these are review, rather than appellate proceedings, there is a limit to the extent to which we can go into the merits and say that a material point would have made no difference to the outcome, or that the same result could or should be reached by a different route.

---

[162] See [2005] CAT 8, paras 202–8 for these competition concerns.
[163] ibid, paras 194–263, esp paras 234, 241, 257 and 263 for the CAT's conclusions on the various assumptions and inferences drawn by the OFT without consulting UniChem.
[164] ibid, paras 264–270.
[165] ibid, paras 200–201.
[166] ibid, para 267.
[167] ibid, at (eg) paras 204, 206 and 278 (see also paras 232–233, 241 and 257).

At the very least, the *UniChem* case illustrates that the CAT will be diligent in its review of the CMA's decision-making powers under the EA 2002 with regard to merger references. It also shows that a full understanding of the possible procedural requirements that the CMA must fulfil in conducting merger investigations will require close and sensitive analysis of the facts of the case at hand, as well as a concern to ensure that 'a balanced and fair procedure' is followed. Both *IBA Health* and *UniChem* demonstrate that procedures followed by the CMA and the reasons given for a CMA decision not to refer a merger to the Inquiry Group will remain under close scrutiny by interested parties for the foreseeable future.

Finally, it should also be noted that aggrieved parties are not restricted to challenging the CMA's decision whether or not to make a reference to the Inquiry Group. Aggrieved parties can also challenge the correctness of the authority's substantive assessment. For example, in *Stagecoach v Competition Commission*[168] the CAT agreed with the applicant that the CC's choice of counterfactual was unreasonable and unsupported by the evidence.

5.3.6 Some Statistics

The following table summarises the UK Merger Inquiry Outcomes from 2004 until September 2015.

---

[168] Case No 1145/4/8/09 *Stagecoach Group plc Competition Commission* [2010] CAT 14. Other appeals on the substantive assessment include for example, the appeal brought by Ryanair against the final decision in Ryanair/Aer Lingus in Case No 1219/4/8/13 *Ryanair Holdings plc v CMA* [2014] CAT 3, upheld on appeal to the Court of Appeal [2015] EWCA Civ 83.

Table 5.2: UK Merger Inquiry Outcomes from 2004 until September 2015

Financial year	04/05	05/06	06/07	07/08	08/09	09/10	10/11	11/12	12/13	13/14	14/15	15/30 Sept
Phase 1 Decisions												
Referred	18	17	13	10	8	7	8	9	14	8	6	5
UIL accepted	5	6	7	5	6	5	4	5	10	0	3	3
Unconditional clearances	103	118	86	78	53	43	43	62	49	42	56	19
- 'de minimis' exception	0	0	0	3	4	7	4	3	4	3	7	1
Found not to qualify	45	69	22	15	9	10	14	21	23	12	10	1
Total decisions	171	210	128	111	80	72	73	100	100	65	82	29
Case review meetings at Phase 1												
Cases to CRM	35	36	30	22	29	22	21	30	32	19	24	8
Initial undertakings/Initial Enforcement Orders at Phase 1												
IU/IEOs accepted	6	10	10	10	11	10	9	25	24	27	30	9
Phase 2 Outcomes												
Cleared	8	7	4	5	1	6	1	7	4	6	2	5
Prohibited	2	1	0	0	2	0	0	1	1	2	0	0
Remedies (Behavioural)	2	0	0	2	1	0	0	0	0	1	0	1
Remedies (Divestiture)	1	2	5	5	0	2	0	3	3	3	1	0
Cancelled/abandoned	3	6	2	4	2	1	3	2	2	0	1	1
Total outcomes	16	16	11	16	6	9	4	10	10	12	4	7

6

The Application and Enforcement of Competition Law

6.1 Introduction

It is clear that without effective procedures the maintenance of any competition law will not amount to much in practical terms. In many parts of the law, the application of the rules is ensured by endowing the national civil courts with various legal obligations and powers. The means the enforcement of such rules are to be found in the national rules of civil procedure. In its *Courage v Crehan* judgment, the ECJ held that national law must take care to ensure that those undertakings or citizens that are disadvantaged by breaches of EU competition law can challenge those breaches. This led to the conclusion that an action for damages for such a breach must be available.[1] In the UK, these rules are to be found in the common law of obligations (whether in contract or the tort of breach of statutory duty). The application and enforcement of competition law, whether EU or UK, takes place by relying upon the same basic provisions of national (procedural) law (albeit with some provisions that are specific to competition law). Natural and legal persons can rely upon EU competition law because its most important provisions have direct effect within the national legal order and thus grant rights to individuals that national courts must protect. Because competition law is often connected with commercial agreements that contain arbitration clauses, arbitral proceedings are another forum in which the competition rules can be applied. The reader is referred to specialist works on the laws of civil procedure and arbitration for a fuller discussion of these elements and references to their role in the application and enforcement of competition law.[2]

EU competition law is seen by the ECJ as an important element of public policy. Thus, where national law includes a ground of 'failure to observe public policy' that allows the challenge of an arbitral award, then EU competition law would also fall under that heading.[3]

---

[1] Case C-453/99 *Courage Ltd v Crehan*.
[2] See, eg, N Andrews, *English Civil Procedure* (Oxford, Oxford University Press, 2003).
[3] Case C-126/97 *Eco-Swiss China Time Ltd v Bennetton International NV*, paras 36 and 37.

Alongside the national courts and arbitrators, the Commission is charged with the application and enforcement of EU competition law. To that end, the Commission has been granted a wide range of competences to seek out breaches of competition law and to fine those parties which can be shown to have committed such breaches. In UK competition law, the same basic role is performed by the CMA. One could say that the Commission and the CMA focus above all upon more serious breaches, leaving the national courts to deal with specific cases as and when those issues are raised in proceedings before them.

The competences of the Commission are not embedded in a general system of administrative law on the EU level. In practice, the field of EU administrative law has been developed gradually, inter alia through the legal developments in the application and enforcement of competition law. However, for a description of the procedural aspects of EU competition law we cannot simply fall back on a general system and in section 6.4 (below) we therefore provide a short analysis of the most important questions concerning EU competition procedure. For UK competition law, there is undoubtedly a clear administrative law background to the system, but at the same time it is clear that the competition law regime is becoming increasingly *sui generis* in many important respects of investigative powers, procedure and enforcement (both regulatory and private). The relevant procedures under UK competition law are treated in section 6.3 (below).

There is a certain degree of overlap between the competences of the Commission and the CMA in the competition field. It is thus useful to discuss separately (see section 6.7 below) the specific boundaries of the competences of both of these competition authorities and the extent of this overlap. This discussion will also examine the developing cooperation between the two authorities. The procedural rules concerning merger control have already been discussed in sections 5.2.2 and 5.3.2 while the procedural rules of EU law in the field of State aids will be discussed in section 7.5.3.

In the application of competition law, various institutions are of significance: the European Commission, the ECJ, the GC, the CMA, the national courts and arbitrators. Apart from the provisions of the European Convention for the Protection of Human Rights and Fundamental Freedoms (ECHR), The Charter of Fundamental Rights of the EU (Charter) and the International Covenant of Civil and Political Rights (ICCPR), these institutions are bound by various rules of procedural law.

6.2 The Application of Competition Law by the Courts[4]

On the face of the provisions of EU competition law, the national court has a very significant role to play in the application of the competition rules. The same applies to

---

[4] See in general GC Rodriguez Iglesias/L Ortiz Blanco, 'The judicial application of Competition Law', *Reports for the XXIV the FIDE Congress Madrid* (2010) 1–545. This book contains a general report, an institutional report and 20 national reports of EU Member States.

arbitrators in all cases in which the parties have agreed to submit any dispute between them to arbitration. The potential role of the courts has become even more important as a result of the fundamental changes in the rules for the application of competition law that were introduced by the entry into force of Regulation 1/2003/EC and the concomitant amendments to the UK rules in 2004 (discussed in section 6.3 below). National courts may now decide whether or not the exemption of Article 101(3) TFEU or section 9 CA 1998 is applicable in any case before them. The role of national courts is further stimulated by the adoption, in 2014 after years of debate, of Directive 2014/104/EU—the so-called 'damages directive'.[5] The purpose of this directive is to provide a harmonised basis across the EU facilitating private actions for damages caused by infringements of the competition rules.

In coming to its judgment, the national court has at its disposal the extensive case law of the ECJ and the GC and the extremely wide-ranging decisional practice of the Commission and the CMA. In consulting the decisions of the Commission and the national authorities, the national court must not forget that the last word on the legal interpretation of the EU competition rules lies with the ECJ. As a result, in cases where there are doubts as to the correct interpretation, the national court should make a reference to the ECJ for a preliminary ruling under Article 267 TFEU. As a result of section 60 CA 1998 and the ECJ's own case law on situations where national law has adopted the *exact* terms of EU law for application in national situations, it should also be possible for the national court to send such questions to the ECJ via Article 267 TFEU, even where those questions concern national competition law alone.[6]

6.2.1 The Substantive Provisions of EU and UK Competition Law

The ordinary civil courts at national level can be faced with various kinds of action in which one or other of the parties may rely upon Articles 101 and 102 TFEU and/or the prohibitions of Chapters I and II CA 1998. According to Article 3(1) of Regulation 1/2003 national courts must also apply Article 101 and Article 102 TFEU when applying national competition law. Article 3(2) of the Regulation states that the application of national competition law may not lead to results contrary to Article 101 TFEU. Member States are not precluded from adopting and applying on their territory stricter national laws which prohibit or sanction an abuse of a dominant position. This provision is not relevant for the UK because, as discussed in Chapters 3 and 4, the UK rules are essentially the same as the EU rules, therefore we treat here the application of the combined EU/UK system.

An action for damages might be involved, as could an action for the dissolution of a contract between the parties. Alongside this, one of the parties might rely upon these legal provisions as a defence against the enforcement of a contract against it.

---

[5] Directive 2014/104/EU of the European Parliament and the Council of 26 November 2014 on certain rules governing actions for damages under national law for infringements of the competition law provisions of the Member States and of the European Union [2014] OJ 2014, L 349 pp 1–19.

[6] See, eg, Cases C-297/88 and 197/89 *Dzodzi v Belgium* and Case C-28/95 *Leur-Bloem v Inspecteur der Belastingdienst/Onder-nemingen Amsterdam 2* [1997]. B Rodger (ed) *Article 234 and Competition Law. An Analysis* (Wolters Kluwer, 2008) 1–601.

6.2.1.1 Article 101 TFEU and/or the Chapter I Prohibition

Here, we provide a brief overview of the various steps that the national court (or arbitrator) must follow in such cases.

(a) First, it must be assessed whether or not an act falls within the scope of Article 101 TFEU/Chapter I of the CA 1998 or Article 102 TFEU/Chapter II of the CA 1998 and whether competition is restricted by the arrangement in question: such a restriction must be *appreciable* (see Chapter 3.2.4). It is here that UK competition law deals with the question of whether or not the effects of a particular practice are of *sufficient significance* to be caught by the UK legislation.

(b) If both of these requirements are satisfied, the national court must then decide whether or not the arrangement falls within the scope of a block exemption (either directly under EU law, as a parallel exemption under the UK regime or under any specific UK block exemption (see Chapter 3.4)).

(c) If no relevant block exemption is applicable, it then falls to the national court to rule upon whether or not the arrangement falls under the exemption of Article 101(3) TFEU or of section 9 CA 1998. In answering this question, the various Notices issued by the Commission (as discussed in Chapter 3.5.1) will be of importance, as will the decisional practice of the Commission and the CMA in cases where they have ruled on the question of the applicability of the exemptions under Article 101(3) TFEU or section 9 CA 1998.

(d) If the arrangement cannot be exempted from the application of the competition rules, then the national court must declare those clauses that breach competition law to be void and of no effect.

(e) After any such declaration, the national court must then check whether or not the arrangement can remain in force in the absence of those clauses.

(f) As will become clear in the following discussion, in a case where the relevant arrangement is also the subject of an investigation by the Commission, the national court must decide whether or not to suspend the case so as to wait for the Commission's decision on the matter. By contrast, it would seem that, while the CMA has the power to submit written and oral observations before any court hearing a case involving issues relating to Articles 101 TFEU and/or the Chapter I prohibition (or, for that matter, Article 102 TFEU and/or the Chapter II prohibition), there is no specific provision made under UK law or the CMA's various guidelines for the court to suspend proceedings before it where the subject matter is also under investigation by the CMA.

6.2.1.2 Article 102 TFEU and/or the Chapter II Prohibition

Where there is an allegation of an abuse of a dominant position then it is for the national judge to rule on whether or not this is the case. In this connection, the decisional practice of the Commission and the case law of the ECJ and the GC can be consulted (as discussed in Chapter 4). The only possible exemption from the application of Article 102 TFEU and the Chapter II prohibition is to be found in Article 106(2)

TFEU and section 3 *juncto* schedule 3, paragraph 4 of the CA 1998 (as discussed in Chapter 7.2), concerning the provision of services of general economic interest.

6.2.1.3 General Observation

A general point concerns the burden of proof in cases involving the application of Articles 101 and 102 TFEU. It is laid down in Article 2 of Regulation 1/2003/EC that the party or authority that alleges a breach of EU competition law shall bear the burden of proving the infringement. This accords with the approach under the general UK law of civil procedure.

6.2.2 Cooperation between the Commission, the CMA and the National Courts

Article 4(3) TEU imposes an obligation upon the Commission and the national courts (and the national competition authority) to cooperate in the application of EU competition law. The ECJ provided the first extended exposition of this obligation and its consequences in the *Delimitis* case,[7] explaining the interaction between the national court and the European Commission. The national courts have jurisdiction to apply Articles 101 and 102 TFEU as a result of the direct effect of both provisions and due to Article 6 of Regulation 1/2003/EC. As a result of this, Article 15 of Regulation 1/2003/EC provides for a more extensive form of cooperation between the national courts and the Commission than that developed by the ECJ in *Delimitis*. This cooperation is particularly important now that national courts also have jurisdiction to apply Article 101(3) TFEU.

In a case before a national court, it may be that the national court requires information held by the Commission concerning the case or that the court decides that it needs the Commission's opinion on the application of the EU competition rules in those circumstances. Article 15(1) of Regulation 1/2003/EC provides national courts with the power to ask for such information or advice from the Commission. On the basis of Article 15(3) of the same Regulation, the CMA and the Commission can on their own initiative submit written observations to the UK courts where the application of Articles 101 and/or 102 TFEU is of issue (and can make oral observations, with the permission of the national court). The CMA has similar powers with regard to cases before the High Court or the Court of Appeal in England and Wales where cases raise issues relating to the application of the prohibitions of Chapter I or Chapter II.[8] Where it is necessary to make those observations, the CMA and the Commission may request that

---

[7] Case C-234/89 *Delimitis v Henninger Bräu AG*.

[8] In its Guideline *Enforcement* (OFT 407) (paras 6.5 and 6.6), the CMA has explained the operation of this mechanism. The party raising the issue in the national court must notify the CMA. This is to enable the CMA to consider whether to exercise its right to submit observations. The CMA will notify the European Commission and/or relevant Regulators where it thinks it appropriate in order to enable them to consider whether to exercise their right to submit observations. When submitting written and oral observations to

the national court concerned ensure that any necessary documents are transmitted to the CMA/Commission (Article 15(3), second sentence, Regulation 1/2003/EC). More generally, Article 15(2) of Regulation 1/2003/EC requires Member States to ensure that a written copy of any judgment in which a national court has ruled upon the application of Articles 101 and/or 102 TFEU be forwarded to the Commission. The Commission has provided a more developed analysis of the operation of these rules on cooperation between the Commission and the national courts in a Notice published in 2004.[9]

Although the removal of the notification system means that situations where the Commission will be dealing with cases that are also pending before the national courts will be rare, the possibility remains (on the basis of Article 7 and to a much lesser extent Article 10 of Regulation 1/2003/EC) that this will occur in some cases in the future. As a result, the case law of the ECJ and the GC on this subject remains of importance. In its judgment in the *Masterfoods* case,[10] the ECJ provided an important clarification of how such cooperation works. The case concerned proceedings before the Irish Supreme Court, which had referred a series of questions to the ECJ for a preliminary ruling in a case in which a lower court had declared the agreement to be compatible with EU competition law. After these events, the Commission had taken a Decision[11] declaring the agreement to be in breach of Article 101(1) TFEU. Subsequently, the parties lodged an application for annulment of the Commission's Decision before the GC.[12] The ECJ held that:

> [W]here a national court is ruling on an agreement or practice the compatibility of which with Articles [101(1) and 102 TFEU] is already the subject of a Commission decision, it cannot take a decision running counter to that of the Commission, even if the latter's decision conflicts with a decision given by a national court of first instance. If the addressee of the Commission decision has, within the period prescribed in the fifth paragraph of Article [263] of the Treaty, brought an action for annulment of that decision, it is for the national court to decide whether to stay proceedings pending final judgment in that action for annulment or in order to refer a question to the Court for a preliminary ruling.[13]

the court, the CMA will seek to do so in a way that will best assist the courts and the development of competition law, rather than assisting any party to court proceedings and the CMA will not enter into discussions with parties regarding the detail of submissions it proposes making to the courts. While it is not the CMA's intention to submit observations frequently, it will do so whenever requested by the court. In its judgment in Case C-439/08, *Vlaamse federatie van verenigingen van Brood-en Banketbakkers, Ijsbereiders en Chocoladebewerkers (VEBIC) VZW*, the ECJ ruled that 'Article 35 of Regulation 1/2003 must be interpreted as precluding national rules which do not allow a national competition authority to participate, as a defendant or respondent, in judicial proceedings brought against a decision that the authority itself has taken. It is for the national competition authorities to gauge the extent to which their intervention is necessary and useful having regard to the effective application of European Union competition law. However, if the national competition authority consistently fails to enter an appearance in such judicial proceedings, the effectiveness of Articles 101 TFEU and 102 TFEU is jeopardised'.

[9] Commission Notice on the cooperation between the Commission and the courts of the EU Member States in the application of Arts 81 and 82 EC [2004] OJ C101/54.

[10] Case C-344/98 *Masterfoods Ltd v HB Ice Cream Ltd.*

[11] Decision 98/531/EC of 11 March 1998 (Case Nos IV/34.073, IV/34.395 and IV/35.436 *Van den Bergh Foods Limited*) [1998] OJ L246/1.

[12] Case T-65/98, *Van den Bergh Foods Ltd v Commission.* Appeal dismissed Case C-552/03 P-DEP.

[13] See n 10, above, para 60 of the judgment. See also Art 16(1) of Reg 1/2003/EC, which adopts much of this wording in clarifying the position to ensure maintenance of the uniform application of EC competition law.

To conclude this section, we should point out a few things that should be kept in mind when considering the division of work between the Commission, national competition authorities and the national courts. First, each organ has its own task in the overall job of ensuring that EU competition law is respected. The Commission provides a concrete forum for EU competition policy and conducts general supervision over its application and enforcement. The national competition authorities are responsible for the application and enforcement of those EU rules at national level, including assisting the Commission in its investigations. The national courts, by virtue of the direct effect of the prohibitions of EU competition law and Article 6 of Regulation 1/2003/EC, are called upon to apply and enforce those provisions in cases before them. Secondly, the procedures before the national court differ from those that are followed in cases before the Commission. Furthermore, the available remedies are also different: damages cannot be claimed from the party in breach of the competition rules in proceedings before the Commission, while the costs of proceedings before the Commission cannot be recovered.[14]

6.3 Competition Procedure and Enforcement under UK Law[15]

6.3.1 Introduction

The advent of the CA 1998 and the subsequent adoption of the Enterprise Act 2002 (EA 2002), marked a significant new stage in the development of UK competition law for a number of reasons. Perhaps one of the most significant of these was the introduction of extensive new powers of inquiry and investigation for the purpose of uncovering breaches of the competition rules. Prior to the 1998 Act, the fragmented nature of the substantive UK rules, the division of functions between the OFT and the Monopolies and Mergers Commission (MMC), and the absence of financial sanctions all served to hamper the ability of the authorities effectively to enforce the competition rules. The new provisions (as subsequently amended and enhanced), discussed below, mark an attempt to address this problem, particularly in the fields of investigations, obtaining information and sanctions. For example, as discussed in more detail below, the revised regime improved the investigative and enforcement tools available to the UK authorities, by: bringing UK law into alignment with the principles of

---

[14] The Commission details further differences between the two procedures in its Notice on the cooperation between the Commission and the courts of the EU Member States in the application of Arts 81 and 82 EC [2004] OJ C101/54.

[15] For reference, see E O'Neill and E Scaife, in A Howard and M Bloom (eds), *UK Competition Procedure* (Oxford, Oxford University Press, 2006).

Regulation 1/2003 and introducing a criminal 'cartel offence' which can result in the imprisonment of individuals for up to five years and provided for company directors to be disqualified if they knew, or ought to have known, of an infringement of EU or UK competition law. The amendments also simplified the procedure for third party appeals and made provision for monetary claims pursuant to findings of an infringement of UK or EU competition law by the competition authorities as well as providing for so-called 'super-complaints'.

Most recently, the entry into force of the Enterprise and Regulatory Reform Act 2013 (ERRA) further enhanced the UK competition authorities' powers of investigation by giving the CMA the power to require individuals to answer questions as part of an investigation under the CA 1998 and made it easier for the authorities to grant interim measures.[16]

6.3.2 Inquiries and Investigations

Two broad bases establish the core of the CMA's powers to investigate possible competition law infringements.[17]

First, the CMA has the power to conduct investigations on behalf of the European Commission or at the request of the national competition authority of another EU Member State, pursuant to Articles 20–22 of Regulation 1/2003. These powers are set out in sections 61–65 CA 1998.

Secondly, the CMA can carry out investigations and inquiries on its own behalf, the core provisions for which are set out in sections 25–29 CA 1998 (as subsequently modified).[18] It is the powers set out in these sections, that will form the principal focus of the below discussion.

Under section 25 CA 1998, the CMA may proceed to investigate if the case passes the threshold of 'reasonable grounds for suspecting' an infringement under Chapter I or Chapter II (whereas a final decision establishing an infringement must show 'strong and compelling evidence').

Section 25 CA 1998 gives the CMA discretion whether or not to conduct an investigation. Similarly to the European Commission, the CMA is not under an obligation to conduct an investigation. In April 2014, the CMA published its *Prioritisation Principles*,[19] which set out the principles that the CMA will apply when determining whether to open an investigation under section 25 CA 1998.

---

[16] In May 2016 the UK Government announced that it would be introducing the Better Markets Bill, by which it would seek to speed up the decision-making processes of the CMA. At the time of writing, however, details of the proposed changes are still to be announced, and the bill is expected to be introduced in Parliament in autumn 2016.

[17] In March 2014 the CMA published its Guidance on the CMA's investigation procedures in Competition Act 1998 cases (CMA 8), which sets out detailed information on the principal aspects of the legal framework and the CMA's practice when conducting investigations under the CA 1998.

[18] The CMA has also issued detailed explanatory notes on its investigative and enforcement powers in its Guideline Powers of investigation (OFT 404).

[19] CMA Prioritisation Principles (CMA 16).

If the CMA does choose to open an investigation, it can conduct that investigation in a number of ways, including by way of written inquiries and entering premises. We discuss these various options in turn.

6.3.2.1 *Written Inquiries*

If the section 25 threshold has been satisfied, the CMA may choose to send out formal information requests under section 26 CA 1998 by issuing a so-called 'section 26 notice' to any 'person', which includes undertakings (section 59(1) CA 1998). This is the power the CMA would expect to use most often to gather information during investigations.

A section 26 notice may require the production of documents or information considered relevant to the investigation, and it must specify the subject matter and purpose of investigation. The notice can also set the time, place and formal limits on supply of information, and it entitles the CMA to take copies or extracts of documents.

The CMA can fine any person who fails, without reasonable excuse, to comply with a formal information request. This may be either a fixed or daily penalty, or a combination of the two, depending on what is appropriate in the circumstances.[20] It is a criminal offence punishable by fine and/or imprisonment to provide false or misleading information,[21] or to destroy, falsify or conceal documents[22] (subject in each case to certain defences or conditions set out in the CA 1998).[23]

For the avoidance of doubt, the CMA has confirmed in its *Guideline on Powers of Investigation* that such a request for information may effectively require the creation of a document that contains the requested information, or the CMA can also ask for information that is not already written down, for example market share estimates based on knowledge or experience, and the CMA can also require past or present employees of the business providing the document to explain any document that is produced.[24]

6.3.2.2 *Interviews*

In certain circumstances the CMA may interview an individual under formal powers immediately after giving a formal notice to that person. This may include, for example, where the CMA considers that an individual may have information that would enable the CMA to take steps to prevent damage to a business or consumers, or where the effective conduct of the investigation means that the CMA considers it necessary to ask an individual questions about facts or documents immediately after having given

---

[20] Section 40A CA 1998.
[21] Section 44 CA 1998.
[22] Section 43 CA 1998.
[23] See further the OFT Guideline *Powers of Investigation* (OFT 404).
[24] OFT Guideline *Powers of Investigation* (OFT 404), para 3.7 and CMA Guidance on the CMA's investigation procedures in Competition Act 1998 cases (CMA 8), s 6.4.

a notice (which will generally be during the course of an inspection pursuant to the CMA's power to enter premises).

6.3.2.3 Powers to Enter Premises

The power to enter the premises of undertakings has proved a vital tool for the Commission in the enforcement of EU competition law, and the UK regime grants similar powers to the CMA. The term 'premises' includes (according to sections 27, 28 and 59(1) CA 1998) those of the party under investigation and those of a third party. This includes (see OFT 404, paragraphs 4.6 and 5.7) vehicles and 'business premises' (that is, any part of a building not used as a dwelling (such as domestic premises): section 27(6) CA 1998).[25]

The CMA's powers to enter premises are divided into two basic categories.

(i) Entry Without a Warrant

This is available to the CMA under section 27 CA 1998 and is basically a 'right of peaceable entry' for specified purposes. To use this power of entry, the officer in question must have been authorised in writing by the CMA and the entry must be in connection with a CMA investigation under section 25 CA 1998. The relevant procedural conditions attached to such entry depend upon the type of premises involved. In general, when acting without a warrant, the CMA must give the premises' occupier at least two working days' written notice of its intended entry. However, such prior notice is not required if the CMA has reasonable suspicion that the premises are, or have been, occupied by a party to an agreement that the CMA is investigating or a business whose conduct the CMA is investigating, or if a CMA authorised officer has been unable to give notice to the occupier, despite taking all reasonably practicable steps to give notice. Similarly, with respect to a party under investigation the CMA can exercise its powers of entry without a warrant under section 27 CA 1998 without having made prior use of section 26 CA 1998.

The occupier of the premises does not have to be suspected of having breached competition law. For example, the CMA could enter the premises of a supplier or a customer of the business suspected of breaching the law. In this case, however, the CMA has to take all reasonably practicable steps to notify the occupant at least two working days in advance of the CMA's intended entry, and provide the occupant with a notice indicating the details as required under section 26 CA 1998.

The powers the CMA officers may exercise in such circumstances are significant, but are also subject to restrictions. Thus, the officer may take any necessary equipment (laptop, tape recorder, etc) when entering the premises. The officers may also require any person to produce any documents the officers consider relevant, to say where a document is kept, to give an explanation of any document produced, to provide copies or extracts (but not originals) of documentation and to provide

---

[25] After the Competition Act 1998 and Other Enactments (Amendments) Regulations 2004 (SI 2004, No 1261) (see Regs 1, 4 and sch 1, para 12), domestic premises can no longer be entered without a warrant—see now s 28A CA 1998. This aligns the UK position with that obtaining under the EU Regulation 1/2003.

computer-held information in visible, legible and portable form (sections 27(5) and 59(3) CA 1998). However, no power of search is granted by section 27; this is only possible under the section 28 CA 1998 procedure (on which see the discussion in the subsequent paragraph). The use of any force is also not allowed, either to gain entry to the premises or once on the premises. Again, this is only possible under section 28 CA 1998.

(ii) Entry with a Warrant

Under sections 28 and 28A CA 1998, the CMA can apply to the court[26] for a warrant to enter and search business or domestic premises. The CMA would usually seek a warrant to search premises where the CMA suspects that the information relevant to the investigation may be destroyed or otherwise interfered with if the CMA requested the material via a written request.

A concomitant of the authority of the warrant is that the investigatory powers available to the CMA under these provisions are much greater. Indeed, this power of entry is often described as a 'right of forcible entry', again for specific purposes.

The warrant can only be issued where there are reasonable grounds for suspecting that there are documents on the premises that:

(a)   the CMA has required to be produced (pursuant to either section 26 or section 27) and which have not been produced;

(b)   the CMA has the power to require to be produced by written notice (pursuant to section 26), but if this notice were given then they would be concealed, removed, tampered with or destroyed;

(c)   the investigating officer could have required to be produced pursuant to section 27 but had been unable to enter the premises without a warrant.[27]

The warrant must authorise the investigator and any other CMA delegates by name, and it must also include the subject matter and purpose of the investigation and the offences that would be committed by non-compliance (section 29 CA 1998).

The powers available to the CMA when entering with a warrant are rather more extensive.

Thus, the CMA's officers and delegates can enter the specified premises using reasonable force, but only if otherwise prevented from entering, and they may never use force against any person. The investigators can require the production of documents of the 'relevant kind', which will be dependent upon the ground upon which the warrant was granted, as specified in the warrant.

With regard to the CMA's powers when conducting the inspection, in addition to the powers available to the CMA when entering premises without a warrant, in cases where it has obtained a warrant, the CMA has the authority to search the premises for documents that appear to be of the kind covered by the warrant and take copies of or extracts from them.[28] As such, the CMA officers can search offices, desks, filing cabinets, electronic devices such as computers and phones, as well as any documents.

---

[26] The High Court in England and Wales or Northern Ireland, the Court of Session in Scotland, or the Competition Appeal Tribunal.

[27] All from s 28(1) CA 1998.

[28] For business premises, s 28(2)(b) CA 1998. For domestic premises, s 28A(2)(b) CA 1998.

The CMA can also take away from the premises any document, or copies of it, to determine whether it is relevant to the investigation, when it is not practicable to do so at the premises—this includes original documents that appear to be covered by the warrant if the CMA thinks it is necessary to preserve the documents or prevent interference with them. The CMA's powers also extend to removing copies of computer hard drives, mobile phones, mobile email devices and other electronic devices.[29]

(iii) Surveillance

The CMA is included on the list of public authorities that can authorise the use of other methods of surveillance under the Regulation of Investigatory Powers Act 2000.[30] This means that the CMA can use directed surveillance (eg, watching an office) and covert human intelligence sources (eg, informants) as part of its investigation. The CMA has clarified, however, that it only intends to use such powers in relation to investigations into suspected cartels.[31]

6.3.2.4 Limits on Powers of Investigation[32]

Despite this wide-ranging set of investigative powers at the CMA's disposal, certain limits also exist to restrict the conduct of such investigations and the use of information obtained through them.

(i) Legal Professional Privilege

The CMA is not allowed to use its powers of investigation to require anyone to produce or disclose privileged communications. Section 30 CA 1998 defines privileged communications as including communications, or parts thereof, between a professional legal adviser and his client or a communication made in connection with, or in contemplation of, legal proceedings and for the purposes of those proceedings. For example, this would cover a letter from a company's lawyer to the company advising on whether a particular agreement infringed the law.

Such communications and documentation is not required to be produced by those under investigation. The protection offered under UK law is more extensive than that under EU law protection, since the class of privileged documents is wider. The CA 1998 covers in-house counsel and independent professional lawyers not qualified in an EU Member State, whereas the EU rules do not (see section 6.4.2 below).[33] The CMA intends the privilege under section 30 CA 1998 to be available under both EU and UK law infringements where it is the CMA that is investigating suspected infringements,

---

[29] For business premises, s 28(2)(c) CA 1998. For domestic premises, s 28A(2)(c) CA 1998. The CMA can only retain these documents for a maximum period of three months (for business premises, s 28(7) CA 1998. For domestic premises, s 28A(8) CA 1998).

[30] See the Regulation of Investigatory Powers (Directed Surveillance and Covert Human Intelligence Sources) Order 2003 (SI 2003, No 3171), r 2(7).

[31] CMA Guidance on the CMA's investigation procedures in Competition Act 1998 cases (CMA 8), s 4.10.

[32] See OFT 404, para 6.

[33] Case 155/79 *AM&S Europe Ltd v Commission*. Case C-550/07 P, *Akzo Nobel Chemicals and Akcros Chemicals v Commission*.

but only the EU range of privilege where the CMA is assisting the Commission in the latter's investigations.[34]

(ii) Self-incrimination

The question of how far undertakings have the right to refuse to answer certain questions posed by competition law investigators so as not to be forced to incriminate themselves is a very difficult one. This is especially true given the overlapping (and potentially conflicting) imperations of section 60 CA 1998 and the Human Rights Act 1998, requiring respectively that the EU case law[35] on the question be applied and that the requirements of the ECHR in this regard also be respected by national courts and public bodies (such as the CMA) when performing their functions.[36]

The CMA has confirmed that it intends to apply section 60 CA 1998 and the EU case law in its practice in this area.[37] In particular, the CMA intends to 'request documents or information relating to facts' but will not seek answers involving an admission of an infringement. When acting under a warrant, however, the CMA can ask for an explanation of 'any document appearing to be of the relevant kind'[38] and has the power to demand an 'explanation' (see section 6.3.2.2 above) of any document 'produced' (under section 26 or section 27 CA 1998) or found (under section 28 CA 1998).

(iii) Confidential Information

The treatment of confidential information in the hands of the CMA is dealt with by Part 9 of the EA 2002 (replacing sections 55 and 56 and schedule 11 CA 1998). The OFT's *Guideline on Powers of Investigation* includes a discussion of the position under the CA 1998 and sections 237–247 EA 2002.[39] The parties under investigation should identify any confidential information supplied to the CMA. However, there is no right for the parties to withhold information from a CMA investigation on grounds of confidentiality: this criterion assists only in preventing disclosure of such information by the CMA.

The CMA's guidance outlines the CMA's approach to and procedures for handling confidential information, including the setting up of confidentiality rings and data-rooms, and the CMA's rights and obligations concerning the publication of information.

(iv) Human Rights and Criminal Law Implications

The CAT has held that proceedings under Chapters I and II are 'criminal proceedings' for the purposes of the Human Rights Act 1998 (HRA 1998) (and Article 6 of the ECHR which the HRA 1998) implements into UK law).[40] However, this conclusion did not import a standard of proof of 'beyond reasonable doubt': the ordinary civil

---

[34] See OFT 404, paras 9.7–9.9.

[35] Such as Case 374/87 *Orkem v Commission*.

[36] See, eg, *Funke v France* (1993) 16 EHRR 297. Although *cf OFT v D* [2004] ICR 105, where Morison J seemed to take the view that consistency between the case law of the European Court of Human Rights and the ECJ has been reached: see [7]–[10], where he also held that the power to search under warrant was justifiable under Arts 6(2) and 8(2) ECHR and thus HRA-compatible.

[37] OFT 404, paras 6.5–6.7.

[38] Sections 28(2)(e) (business premises) and 28A(2)(b) (domestic premises) of the CA 1998.

[39] See OFT 404, paras 6.8–6.13 and CMA Guidance on the CMA's investigation procedures in Competition Act 1998 cases (CMA 8), ss 7.6–7.17.

[40] *Napp Pharmaceutical Holdings Ltd v DGFT* [2002] CAT 1.

standard of the balance of probabilities was to be applied, but allegations of a serious nature required 'strong and compelling evidence' to be provided. The CAT held that the defendant takes 'the presumption of innocence and any reasonable doubt that there may be'.[41]

The cartel offence (introduced by the EA 2002 and discussed below in section 6.3.5.2) is clearly a criminal offence, and in its Guidelines on the subject[42] the CMA makes clear and frequent reference to its duty to act in accordance with the Police and Criminal Evidence Act 1984 and its Codes of Conduct.[43]

6.3.2.5 Offences: Sanctions for Non-compliance

Sections 42–44 of the CA 1998 set out a series of offences that can be committed for failure to comply with an investigation by the CMA. These offences cover:

(a)   failing to comply with a requirement imposed under the powers of investigation in the Act;

(b)   intentionally obstructing an authorised officer carrying out an inspection either with or without a warrant;

(c)   intentionally or recklessly destroying or otherwise disposing of or falsifying or concealing a document that has been required to be produced or causing or permitting such destruction, disposal, falsification or concealment; or

(d)   providing to the CMA (either directly or indirectly) information that is false or misleading in a material way if the person knows, or is reckless as to whether, it is false or misleading.

Committing the above offences can be sanctioned either by way of fines or (if convicted on indictment) also by imprisonment. It is worth noting that the individual officers of companies are also punishable for committing these offences (see section 72 CA 1998).

6.3.3 Complaints

Although not specifically provided for in the CA 1998, one of the ways that can prompt the CMA to begin an investigation is if it receives a complaint from an individual or business about the behaviour of another business. From the CMA's perspective, it is important to get as much useful and relevant information from a complaint (and complainant) as possible. For most complaints, the CMA can be informed via its website, which informs complainants about the format and method for making the CMA aware of competition concerns.[44] In addition, given their sensitivity, the CMA has set up a specific 'hotline' for cartel-related complaints.

---

[41]   ibid, para 109.

[42]   *Powers for Investigating Criminal Cartels* (OFT 515): see, eg paras 3.10–3.17.

[43]   Note, however, the OFT's position in its decision of 19 February 2003, in Hasbro UK Ltd, Argos Ltd and Littlewoods Ltd, in which it considered that it was not obliged to comply with the Police and Criminal Evidence act in respect of interviews conducted under s 26A CA 1998.

[44]   See also the Annex to the Guideline *Involving third parties in Competition Act investigations* (OFT 451) which also provides guidance and further detail on the type of information that the CMA looks for in a written, reasoned complaint.

Many complainants want to retain their anonymity, causing difficulties in raising certain issues with an allegedly infringing undertaking. As set out above, Part 9 EA 2002 contains rules against the disclosure of certain information about individuals or undertakings, unless the situations foreseen in sections 239–242 EA 2002 arise. If the CMA intends to pursue a complaint it may require the complainant to submit a non-confidential version of the complaint that can be provided to the target undertaking.

For the sake of completeness, we should also note here that section 11 EA 2002 established the possibility for so-called 'super-complaints' to be made.[45] This innovation allows designated consumer bodies[46] to complain to the CMA if 'any feature, or combination of features, of a market in the UK for goods or services is or appears to be significantly harming the interests of consumers' (section 11(1) EA 2002).[47] The CMA is required to reply to the super-complainant, informing it of how the CMA intends to deal with the matter, within 90 days (section 11(2) EA 2002).

6.3.4 Opinions and Informal Advice

The removal of the notification system at the EU level precipitated a UK decision to remove its own notification regime as well. However, under certain conditions, the CMA will be willing to issue opinions or informal advice in relation to novel or unanswered questions.

The CMA will consider issuing an opinion if the following conditions are met:

(a)   sufficient precedent does not exist under EU or UK case law;
(b)   there is a need for a published Opinion, for example, because of the economic importance to consumers of the goods or services in questions, or because of the level of investment required in the agreement or conduct in question; and
(c)   it is possible to provide an Opinion without the need for substantial fact-finding.[48]

The CMA may provide confidential, informal advice on an ad hoc basis, however, it is not under any obligation to do so, and the advice given is not binding.[49]

6.3.5 Enforcement

The range of enforcement provisions available can usefully be divided into regulatory (section 6.3.5.1), criminal law (section 6.3.5.2) and private enforcement by means of litigation in the courts (section 6.3.5.3).

6.3.5.1 Regulatory Enforcement

The basic provisions relating to enforcement of UK competition law by the CMA are to be found in sections 31–40 CA 1998.

---

[45] See the OFT's Guideline, *Super-complaints* (OFT 514).
[46] As designated by the Secretary of State for Trade and Industry by order (s 11(5) EA 2002).
[47] The Annex to OFT 514 provides a schedule of the information required to be included in a super-complaint.
[48] *Modernisation* guidance (OFT 442), para 7.5.
[49] *Modernisation* guidance (OFT 442), para 7.20.

(i) Procedure

In its Guidance on the CMA's investigative procedures in CA 1998 cases (CMA 8, page 7) reproduced below, the CMA has provided a helpful diagram summarising the typical stages in the procedure of an investigation. The diagram serves to explain how the procedural provisions examined above lead to the stage of enforcement action being taken (in one form or another) by the CMA.

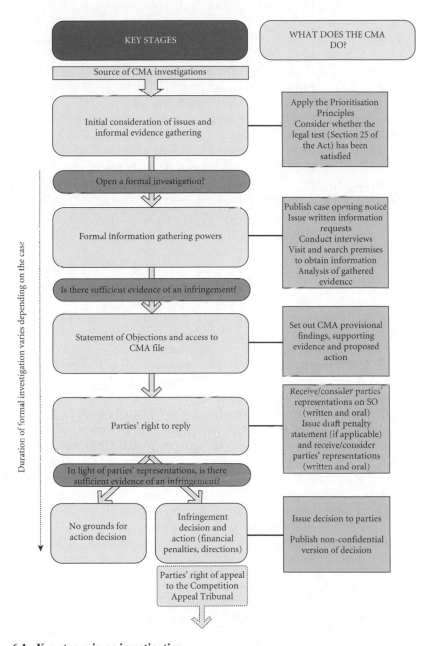

Figure 6.1: Key stages in an investigation

(ii) Accepting Commitments

In order to ensure alignment with the changes to the EU regime in 2004, the UK system introduced specific powers that enable the CMA to end a case by accepting binding commitments offered by the parties (sections 31A–31E CA 1998).

Section 31(2) of the CA 1998 enables the CMA to accept commitments from undertakings to take such action or refrain from such action as the CMA considers appropriate. It is also possible subsequently to vary, substitute or terminate commitments once they have been entered into.

The *Guideline on Enforcement* (OFT 407) provides a discussion of the commitments provisions and includes the CMA's Guidance on when it may be appropriate for it to accept commitments, and the relevant procedure (based on Schedule 6A CA 1998).[50] Once the CMA accepts commitments, it is precluded from finding an infringement under section 31 CA 1998 or issuing a direction under section 35 CA 1998.

The CMA is empowered to enforce such commitments by court order, while any person with a 'sufficient interest' may seek a judicial review of a CMA commitments decision before the CAT. It is also important to note that the CMA's acceptance of such binding commitments does not prevent a private party taking action in a national court under Article 101 or 102 TFEU or under the Chapter I or Chapter II prohibition. The OFT (as it was at the time) adopted its first Decision accepting commitments and closing the file in the *TV Eye* case of 24 May 2005.

(iii) Directions

The CA 1998 gives the CMA the power to issue directions to any person so as to bring to an end an infringement of UK competition law.[51] Any such infringement must be established by the CMA, but where this has been done then the CMA has the power to issue directions requiring any person to modify or terminate an agreement (concerning the Chapter I prohibition) or to change or end a particular practice or course of conduct (where the Chapter II prohibition is in issue). For an example of the CMA's practice in this field to date, see the DGFT's decision in *Napp Pharmaceutical*:[52] in it, the DGFT issued directions requiring Napp to amend its prices so as to bring to an end its infringement of the Chapter II prohibition.

A range of issues arises in this context and the CMA's *Guideline on Enforcement* (OFT 407) contains a helpful discussion on questions of procedure. One further question concerns whether or not it would be open to the CMA to classify requiring the selling off of assets or breaking up an undertaking as a 'direction'. Given the existence of the procedure for making Market Investigation References under the EA 2002 and the clear potential availability of structural remedies under that procedure, it is submitted that using directions to achieve such goals would not necessarily be an appropriate use of the power to issue directions.

Once such directions (including interim measures: section 6.3.5.1(iv) below) have been issued, they can be enforced by the CMA before a court under section 34 CA

---

[50] See OFT 407, paras 4.1ff and Annex A.

[51] See ss 32(1) (re Ch I) and 33 (re Ch II) CA 1998; for discussion, see OFT 407, paras 2.1–2.9.

[52] DGFT Decision CA98/2D/2001 (4 May 2001), following the DGFT's substantive decision (CA98/2/2001, 30 March 2001) that Napp's conduct had amounted to an infringement of the Ch II prohibition.

1998. This would involve the CMA seeking an order requiring compliance within a specified time, with failure to respect such an order possibly leading to contempt proceedings. The CMA has indicated[53] that it intends 'actively [to] seek to enforce directions in the courts'. Equally, undertakings can appeal to the CAT against such directions. If it considers it appropriate, the CAT may adopt interim measures, but the appeal itself will not (without more) have suspensory effect.[54]

(iv) Interim Measures

Under both the UK and EU regimes, it is possible for the CMA to adopt interim measures pending its final decision on whether or not there has been any infringement of Chapter I/Article 101 TFEU and/or Chapter II/Article 102 TFEU. The EU provisions do not provide for such a power for the CMA, however, so its basis must be sought in national law, whether or not the interim measures are adopted in the course of an EU or UK law competition investigation. The relevant provision is section 35 CA 1998 and it is discussed at some length by the CMA in its *Guideline on Enforcement*.[55]

For the CMA to issue an interim measures order, section 35 CA 1998 requires that it must be shown that:

(a) there is a 'reasonable suspicion' of infringement;
(b) any such interim measures have the purpose of preventing significant damage to a person or category of persons or the public interest (damage will be significant where the person is or may be restricted in their ability to compete effectively, but does not require that the person has or will leave the market);[56]
(c) it is necessary to act as a matter of urgency.

The CMA cannot adopt interim measures, however, if the undertakings are able to show that, on the balance of probabilities, the criteria of section 9 of the CA 1998 or Article 101(3) TFEU are satisfied (see sections 35(8) and (9) of the CA 1998).

From a procedural perspective, before giving directions implementing interim measures, the CMA must give the affected persons notice of its intention so as to enable them to put forward their view. Such notice must indicate the nature of the proposed direction and the CMA's reasons.

The possible content of interim measures could include requiring a party to continue supply of goods, services or other inputs (for example, access to essential infrastructure) where that supply is required to prevent significant damage to a person or persons in the market(s) or any associated market(s) in question, or to enable customers to obtain access to goods or services. Alternatively, the CMA might seek that the relevant undertaking reverse a price increase or decrease for any good or service where that price increase or decrease has or is likely to cause significant damage to any person's or category of persons' ability to compete effectively, or is likely to cause a detriment to the public.[57]

---

[53] OFT 407, para 2.9.

[54] Competition Appeal Tribunal Rules 2003 (SI 2003, No 1372), r 61. See, eg, *Genzyme Ltd v OFT* [2003] CAT 8.

[55] See OFT 407, paras 3.1–3.20.

[56] CMA Guidance on the CMA's investigation procedures in Competition Act 1998 cases (CMA 8), ss 8.14 and 8.15.

[57] CMA Guidance on the CMA's investigation procedures in Competition Act 1998 cases (CMA 8), s 8.17.

To date, the only time that the UK authorities have resorted to interim measures was in the London Metal Exchange case. The OFT (at the time) was concerned that the London Metal Exchange was about to commit an abuse of a dominant position by extending the hours of trading.[58] The OFT ultimately withdrew the decision following receipt of additional evidence.

(v) Penalties

As mentioned in section 6.3.1 (above), one of the key changes brought about by the CA 1998 was to provide real teeth for enforcing the UK competition rules, in the form of financial penalties for infringement. Where the CMA has established, on the basis of 'strong and compelling evidence',[59] that an infringement has occurred, section 36(1) and (2) CA 1998 empowers the CMA to require the undertaking(s) concerned to pay a penalty in respect of that infringement. However, section 36(3) CA 1998 makes clear that such penalties may only be imposed only if the infringement was negligent or intentional.[60]

Similar to the Commission, the CMA is empowered to impose penalties of up to 10 per cent of an undertaking's annual worldwide turnover.[61]

When fixing the level of the fine, section 36(7A) CA 1998 requires that the CMA must have regard to the seriousness of the infringement and the need to deter both the infringing undertaking and others from infringing either the UK or EU competition rules.

According to section 38(1) CA 1998, the CMA is required to prepare and publish (with the approval of the Secretary of State for Trade and Industry) guidance as to the appropriate amount of any penalty imposed, and it has done this in its publication *Guidance as to the Appropriate Amount of a Penalty* (OFT 423). The question of the appropriateness of the penalty imposed has become a regularly contested issue in proceedings before the CAT.[62] As a result, it is important to note that, following the entry into force of the ERRA 2013, the CAT is must have regard to the Guidance. Prior to the entry into force of the ERRA 2013, the CAT was not so bound. It had, however, nevertheless held that it would take the Guidance into account, adopting a 'broad-brush approach' and linking serious infringements with severe penalties (as well as considering mitigating factors),[63] thus focusing upon whether, overall, the penalties

---

[58]   OFT decision of 27 February 2006.

[59]   See the discussion in section 6.3.5.1.(v) above.

[60]   See *Napp Pharmaceutical Holdings Ltd v DGFT* [2002] CAT 1, paras 453, 456–57, showing that either suffices to establish a penalisable infringement. Note, however, that when the level of the penalty is assessed, it may well be very relevant to determine whether the infringement was negligent or intentional: see OFT 407, para 5.4.

[61]   See the amendments wrought to SI 2000, No 309 by the Competition Act 1998 (Determination of Turnover for Penalties) (Amendment) Order 2004 (SI 2004, No 1259), Art 2.

[62]   See, *Umbro Holdings Ltd, Manchester United plc, JJB Sports plc and Allsports Ltd v OFT* [2005] CAT 22, where the CAT made some marginal reductions (and one increase—concerning Allsports's activities) in the penalties originally imposed by the OFT for price-fixing of replica football shirts by the parties in various combinations.

[63]   See *Napp Pharmaceutical Holdings Ltd v DGFT* [2002] CAT 1, paras 502, 533, 537 and 538. See also *Argos Ltd and Littlewoods Ltd v OFT* [2005] CAT 13, esp paras 234–48, in which the CAT makes small reductions to the fines originally imposed by the OFT. It did so due to errors in the OFT's definition of the relevant product markets for the purposes of calculating the fines imposed, which led to the inclusion of turnover that was at best only peripherally related to the anti-competitive conduct being penalised.

imposed were appropriate and of sufficient deterrent effect given the infringements at issue. As such, the ERRA 2013 acts, in essence, to codify the already existing practice.

In the context of the possible imposition of penalties for infringements of UK competition law, it must be remembered that the impact of the CMA's policy on encouraging whistleblowing (by offering leniency to informants who report breaches of the competition rules in which they are involved) is significant. The UK approach to these matters is more generous than the EU regime: under UK competition law, leniency is available even for retail price maintenance, and whereas the Commission's approach operates a sliding scale of reductions to fines, the UK regime allows the CMA to exercise its discretion in determining the extent of any leniency to be allowed.[64] Total immunity from penalties is available under the UK regime on both an automatic and a discretionary basis: it is automatic for the first party to inform the CMA of the infringement before commencement of a CMA investigation,[65] while at the CMA's discretion reductions in penalties may extend to 100 per cent where information is provided after the CMA's investigation has commenced but prior to notification by the CMA of any proposed infringement decision. Partial immunity (up to 50 per cent) may also be available, again at the CMA's discretion, where evidence of a cartel is provided by an undertaking, but it is not the first to offer such information.[66] Finally, it should be noted that other information (including conduct in cooperating with any investigation) may count as a mitigating factor when the CMA comes to assess the appropriate amount of any penalty.[67]

(vi) Settlement

Similar to the Commission, the CMA also operates a system of settlement.[68] This is the process whereby a business under investigation:

(a)   clearly and unequivocally admits to the infringement;
(b)   terminates its involvement in the infringement;
(c)   confirms that it will pay a penalty set at a maximum amount; and
(d)   agrees to cooperate with the CMA during the administrative procedure.

In return, the CMA will impose a reduced penalty on the business. However, unlike the EU settlement system, which applies a fixed 10 per cent reduction on account of

---

[64] For a comprehensive view of the CMA's leniency regime, see the following guidance notes from the CMA: (i) Appropriate level of a penalty (OFT 423); and (ii) Leniency and no-action guidance (OFT 1495).

[65] Eg Hasbro UK, Argos and Littlewoods (OFT Decision CA98/8/2003, 2 December 2003), where Hasbro received 100% leniency for being the first to provide information of the infringement, prior to the OFT's investigation (the OFT also recorded that Hasbro subsequently cooperated fully in the investigation). One difficulty with the leniency regime concerns the interaction between UK and other (including EU) leniency regimes: a failure to report to all possible relevant competition authorities may lead the original whistleblower in (say) the UK to end up finding itself reported to another competition authority by another cartel member, and the original whistleblower may thus lose its position under the UK leniency regime if the Commission takes over the investigation and ultimately sanctions the case.

[66] OFT 1495.

[67] Note also that immunity from penalties is granted for 'small agreements' (ss 36(4) and 39 CA 1998) and 'conduct of minor significance' (ss 36(5) and 40 CA 1998) for agreements other than those fixing prices: see the Competition Act 1998 (Small Agreements and Conduct of Minor Significance) Regulations 2000 (SI 2000, No 262) for details on what is sufficiently insignificant to qualify for this immunity.

[68] For detailed guidance, see CMA Guidance on the CMA's investigation procedures in Competition Act 1998 cases (CMA 8), s 14.

settlement, under the UK rules, settlement discounts can be as high as 20 per cent. However, the actual discount awarded will take account of the resource savings achieved in settling that particular case at that particular stage in the investigation. The discount available for settlement pre-Statement of Objections will be up to 20 per cent and that available for settlement post-Statement of Objections will be up to 10 per cent.

The settlement process is distinct from the CMA's leniency policy and the CMA's power to accept commitments under section 31A CA 1998. The leniency policy and the use of settlements are not mutually exclusive—it is possible for a leniency applicant to settle a case under the CA 1998 and benefit from both leniency and settlement discounts.

The CMA retains broad discretion in determining which cases to settle and undertakings do not have a right to settlement. Similarly, businesses are not under any obligation to settle or enter into any settlement discussions where these are offered by the CMA. When determining whether a case is appropriate for settlement, the CMA will have regard to:

(a)   whether the CMA considers that the evidential standard for giving notice of its proposed infringement decision is met, and will proceed only if it considers this standard to be met;

(b)   the likely procedural efficiencies and resource savings that can be achieved, in particular in light of the stage in the case at which settlement is reached, whether it would result in a shortening of the case timetable and a reduction in case team resources,

(c)   the number of businesses involved in the investigation and the number potentially interested in settlement, and the number of alleged infringements in the case; and

(d)   the prospect of reaching settlement in a reasonable time frame.

(vii) Company Director Disqualification

For completeness, the reader should also note that section 204 EA 2002 inserts sections 9A–E into the Company Directors Disqualification Act 1986, adding the possibility for a court to issue a Competition Disqualification Order on an application from the CMA or the relevant sector regulator.[69] This serves to disqualify the director involved from acting in that capacity in the future for up to a maximum period of 15 years (section 9A(9) of the 1986 Act).

6.3.5.2   Criminal Law Enforcement: The Cartel Offence[70]

One of the key elements in the changes introduced by the EA 2002 was the provision of a criminal law enforcement mechanism for competition law in the form of the 'cartel

---

[69] See the OFT's Guidance *Competition Disqualification Orders* (OFT 510) for details on these provisions, factors to consider and the relevant procedural rules. In brief, there must have been both a breach of competition law by the company and conduct by the director concerned that the court considers makes him or her unfit to be involved in the management of a company: s 9A(1)–(3) of the Company Directors Disqualification Act 1986.

[70] See, generally, the CMA's Guidelines *Cartel Offence Prosecution Guidance (CMA 09)*.

offence'. This was intended to improve the deterrent effect of competition law in the UK still further (after the introduction of financial penalties by the CA 1998), by importing an important feature from US law.[71] The cartel offence under the EA 2002 is distinct from the Article 101 TFEU and Chapter I prohibition under the CA 1998. As such, where a cartel exists, the undertakings involved can be found liable under Article 101 TFEU or Chapter I CA 1998 while, at the same time, the individual people that participated in the cartel can also be prosecuted criminally under the cartel offence.

The entry into force of the ERRA 2013 brought important changes to the criminal cartel offence. First, it removed the requirement that, in order to be caught by the cartel offence, the person involved must have acted 'dishonestly'. Secondly, it reduced the scope of the cartel offence for certain situations. Thirdly, the ERRA 2013 introduced three new defences to the cartel defence. These aspects are treated in more detail below. It should be noted however, that references in the following paragraphs to the EA 2002 mean the EA 2002 as amended by the ERRA 2013.

The relevant provisions are sections 188–91 (the offence) and 192–202 (investigation, etc) EA 2002.

(i) Definition

Section 188 EA 2002 provides a very detailed definition of the cartel offence:

(1) An individual is guilty of an offence if he agrees with one or more other persons to make or implement, or to cause to be made or implemented, arrangements of the following kind relating to at least two undertakings (A and B).

(2) The arrangements must be ones which, if operating as the parties to the agreement intend, would
    (a) directly or indirectly fix a price for the supply by A in the United Kingdom (otherwise than to B) of a product or service,
    (b) limit or prevent supply by A in the United Kingdom of a product or service,
    (c) limit or prevent production by A in the United Kingdom of a product,
    (d) divide between A and B the supply in the United Kingdom of a product or service to a customer or customers,
    (e) divide between A and B customers for the supply in the United Kingdom of a product or service, or
    (f) be bid-rigging arrangements.

(3) Unless subsection (2)(d), (e) or (f) applies, the arrangements must also be ones which, if operating as the parties to the agreement intend, would
    (a) directly or indirectly fix a price for the supply by B in the United Kingdom (otherwise than to A) of a product or service,
    (b) limit or prevent supply by B in the United Kingdom of a product or service, or
    (c) limit or prevent production by B in the United Kingdom of a product.

Following the entry into force of the ERRA 2013, the above definition is subject to the provisions of section 188A, which provides that:

(1) An individual does not commit an offence under section 188(1) if, under the arrangements—
    (a) in a case where the arrangements would (operating as the parties intend) affect the supply in the United Kingdom of a product or service, customers would be given

---

[71] See the DTI's consultative White Paper, *A World Class Competition Regime* (Cm 5233, July 2001).

> relevant information about the arrangements before they enter into agreements for the supply to them of the product or service so affected,
> (b) in the case of bid-rigging arrangements, the person requesting bids would be given relevant information about them at or before the time when a bid is made, or
> (c) in any case, relevant information about the arrangements would be published, before the arrangements are implemented, in the manner specified at the time of the making of the agreement in an order made by the Secretary of State.

Section 188A(2) defines the term 'relevant information' referred to in section 188A(1) as meaning: (a) the names of the undertakings to which the arrangements relate; (b) a description of the nature of the arrangements which is sufficient to show why they are or might be arrangements of the kind to which section 188(1) applies; (c) the products or services to which they relate; and (d) such other information as may be specified in an order made by the Secretary of State.

In addition, section 188A(3) clarifies that an individual does not commit an offence under section 188(1) if the agreement is made in order to comply with a legal requirement (which has the same meaning as in paragraph 5 of Schedule 3 to the CA 1998).

The ERRA 2013 also introduced three new defences to the cartel offence. As such, in accordance with section 188B EA 2002, an individual will not be guilty of the cartel offence if he or she is able to demonstrate that:

(1) At the time of the making of the agreement, he or she did not intend that the nature of the arrangements would be concealed from customers at all times before they enter into agreements for the supply to them of the product or service.

(2) At the time of the making of the agreement, he or she did not intend that the nature of the arrangements would be concealed from the CMA.

(3) Before the making of the agreement, he or she took reasonable steps to ensure that the nature of the arrangements would be disclosed to professional legal advisers for the purposes of obtaining advice about them before their making or (as the case may be) their implementation.

In summary, the above makes clear that:

(a) individuals within a company can be prosecuted;

(b) the offence applies to price-fixing, limiting supply and/or production, market-sharing and bid-rigging. The purpose of section 188(3) EA 2002 is to make clear that price-fixing and supply or production limitations must be reciprocal in nature if they are to qualify for prosecution under the cartel offence (by their very nature, market-sharing and bid-rigging operate reciprocally). The offence applies only to horizontal agreements and does not cover vertical arrangements (sections 188(4) and 189 EA 2002). The offence can be made out even if the agreement is not implemented or if the individuals had no authority to act on behalf of their respective undertakings at the time of the agreement.

(c) an individual will not be guilty of the cartel offence if the potential customers were made aware (or in the case of section 188A(1)(c) EA 2002 ought reasonably to have been aware) that the relevant arrangement could constitute a cartel for the purposes of section 188 EA 2002.

An individual can escape liability under the cartel offence if he or she can demonstrate that, before entering into the arrangement he or she sought legal advice on the legality of the arrangement, or at the time of entering the arrangement did not intend that the nature of the arrangements would be concealed from customers or the CMA.

(ii) Powers of Investigation and Search

The CMA can open an investigation under the EA 2002 if it has reasonable grounds for suspecting that the cartel offence has been committed (section 193 EA 2002). Many of the powers of investigation and search available to the CMA in this field are very similar in scope and structure to those under CA 1998 (discussed in section 6.3.2 above), including requiring information via written inquiry and entry to premises with a warrant. One key difference concerns the so-called 'seize and sift' powers (section 194(5) EA 2002), which enables the CMA to remove documents from the premises for review when it is not practicable to determine, while on the premises, whether the documents can be seized or not. The CMA must give written notice of what is seized and is under an obligation to return any seized material that turns out to be subject to legal professional privilege (see the Criminal Justice and Police Act 2001, sections 52 and 55 respectively).

Failure to comply with the CMA's investigation, for example, by destroying documents, can result in the imposition of criminal sanctions, which could result in imprisonment for up to a maximum of five years (section 201 EA 2002).

(iii) Powers of 'Intrusive Surveillance' and 'Property Interference'

A key and potentially significant extension of investigatory powers under the cartel offence provisions (which does not apply to investigations under CA 1998) are the so-called 'intrusive surveillance' and 'property interference' powers (sections 199 and 200 EA 2002). These provisions allow for the installation of covert surveillance devices in residential premises (including hotels) and vehicles. Both the activity ('surveillance') and the installation ('property interference') are authorised by the EA 2002, although note that such surveillance requires the prior approval of the CMA's Chairman and the Surveillance Commissioner (unless used in an emergency situation, when the latter can grant ex post approval as the ultimate arbiter on the matter).

The CMA is also included on the list of public authorities that can authorise the use of other methods of surveillance under the Regulation of Investigatory Powers Act 2000 (RIPA 2000).[72] These powers permit the CMA to employ the techniques of directed surveillance (eg watching an office) and running covert human intelligence sources (eg informants). Finally, the reader should note that under the Regulation of Investigatory Powers (Communications Data) Order 2003,[73] the CMA is authorised to obtain access to communications (eg, the records of any telephone numbers called). This last set of powers can only be used to pursue investigations under EA 2002, but

---

[72] See the Regulation of Investigatory Powers (Directed Surveillance and Covert Human Intelligence Sources) Order 2003 (SI 2003, No 3171), r 2(7).

[73] SI 2003, No 3172 (as amended by the Regulation of Investigatory Powers (Communications Data) (Amendment) Order 2005 (SI 2005, No 1083)): see its Sch 2, Pt III.

the penultimate set under the RIPA 2000 can be used to pursue both EA 2002 and CA 1998 cartel investigations.

(iv) Prosecution and Penalty

As and when sufficient evidence has been gathered to make a serious allegation that a cartel offence has been committed, any prosecution will be brought either by the SFO or the CMA, and will generally be brought by the CMA.[74] The evidence to support a criminal prosecution will only be admissible if it has been obtained according to the proper UK criminal law standards. Thus, there can be no cross-use of statements previously obtained under a CA 1998 investigation unless there has been an interview in accordance with the provisions of the Police and Criminal Evidence Act and its Codes of Conduct.[75]

If the accused is found guilty of the cartel offence and the prosecution is brought on indictment in the Crown Court, the sentence is up to five years' imprisonment or an unlimited fine (section 190(1)(a) EA 2002). If the prosecution is brought in a magistrate's court, the relevant sentence is up to six months' imprisonment and a fine (section 190(1)(b) EA 2002). The prospect of significant custodial sentences is the lynchpin of the intended deterrent effect of the new cartel offence under UK competition law.

(v) 'No-action Letters'

One possible difficulty in squaring the new cartel offence with the goals of the new system of UK competition law concerned the likely disincentive effects that criminal sanctions would have for individuals who might otherwise have 'blown the whistle' on the cartel activities of undertakings (including their own). To deal with this potential problem, the CMA has published the *Leniency and no-action guidance* (OFT 1495). The 'no-action letter' is the device chosen by the CMA to communicate the position on any given individual's immunity from prosecution where that individual informs the competition authorities of cartel activity and cooperates fully with any subsequent investigation.[76] Such letters will be issued under section 190(4) EA 2002 and will specify the conditions that must be satisfied by the individual in question.[77] These letters are thus a key element in retaining a balance between the CMA's whistleblowing and leniency policy on the one hand, and the desire to pursue and deter cartel activity vigorously under the EA 2002 on the other.

6.3.5.3 Judicial Review and Private Enforcement

The role played by private parties in the enforcement of any system of competition law is one that has generated great interest over the years, particularly in comparing

---

[74] Section 190(1)(a) EA 2002. See also s 1.4 of the CMA Guidance on Cartel Offence Prosecution Guidance (CMA 09). A memorandum of understanding exists between the CMA and SFO which forms the basis on which the CMA and SFO will cooperate in investigations and the prosecution of individuals.

[75] See s 198 EA 2002.

[76] The detailed conditions for the issue of such a letter are laid down in OFT 1495.

[77] For a specimen 'no-action letter', see the annex to OFT 1495.

the nature of the different systems and the prevalence and desirability of private enforcement activity. Under the current UK system, a specific court exists for dealing with many competition law matters: the Competition Appeal Tribunal (CAT). The CAT exercises two principal functions: first, it operates as an appellate court hearing appeals against decisions taken by the CMA; secondly, it operates as a court of first instance to hear claims for compensation (ie, damages claims) brought by victims of anti-competitive conduct.

The existence of the CAT should not blind the reader, however, to the fact that the ordinary civil courts still have a potentially very significant role to play in this area (and not just in granting warrants for investigation, as discussed above (in section 6.3.2.2)), especially given that, prior to the entry into force of the Consumer Rights Act 2015, the CAT was not empowered to hear stand-alone claims for damages. Rather, with respect to damages claims, the CAT was only entitled to hear claims brought on the basis of a decision adopted either by the European Commission or the CMA (previously the OFT) finding the existence of an infringement of Articles 101/102 TFEU or the Chapter I/Chapter II prohibition (so-called 'follow-on' claims). In contrast, stand-alone claims (ie, actions for damages that were brought without a pre-existing decision of either the European Commission or the CMA) fell within the jurisdiction of the ordinary civil courts. This distinction has since been abandoned under the Consumer Rights Act 2015 and the CAT is now empowered to hear both stand-alone and follow-on damages claims.

There are a number of key points to be highlighted from the basic structure of the system of judicial enforcement. First, note the potential significance of the ECJ as recipient and dispenser of preliminary rulings under the Article 267 TFEU procedure. This is likely to hold for many questions of UK, as well as EU, competition law, by virtue of the ECJ's own case law[78] and thanks to the inclusion of section 60 CA 1998 (the so-called 'governing principles clause') and its requirement that UK law be developed consistently with those provisions of EU competition law that do not contain relevant differences from UK law.

Secondly, we should note the decision that was taken to provide for a full appeal to the CAT from decisions of the CMA under the CA 1998 on questions of fact and/ or law.[79] The idea was to focus the appellate function in a specialised tribunal that was well equipped to deal with such complex economic questions of characterisation and analysis,[80] as well as to provide for an independent tribunal to adjudicate on findings of infringement of the competition legislation, as required under Article 6 ECHR as a result of the HRA 1998. Standing is granted to any person in respect of whose conduct the CMA has adopted a decision (section 46(2) CA 1998), any party to an agreement where the CMA has adopted a decision concerning that agreement (section 46(1) CA 1998) and any third party (not within section 46(1) or (2) CA 1998)

---

[78] See n 6 above and, especially, Case C-7/97 *Oscar Bronner GmbH v Mediaprint Zeitungs-und Zeitschriftenverlag GmbH & Co KG.*
[79] See the Competition Appeal Tribunal Rules 2003 (SI 2003, No 1372), Pt II.
[80] This is underlined by the insertion of s 16 EA 2002, which allows the Lord Chancellor to adopt regulations providing for the transfer of cases to and from the CAT from the ordinary civil courts. However, no such regulations have been adopted as yet.

who has a 'sufficient interest' in the decision made (section 47 CA 1998).[81] One striking illustration[82] of this function of the CAT is provided by the case of *JJ Burgess &
Sons v OFT*,[83] an appeal from the OFT's Decision concerning the *Refusal to supply JJ
Burgess & Sons access to Harwood Park Crematorium*.[84] In this case, the CAT
overturned the OFT's assessment of the relevant market in the case, and went on to
substitute its own findings of dominance and abuse for those of the OFT, pursuant to
paragraph 3(2(e) of schedule 8 CA 1998.[85] The CAT was also strongly critical of the
OFT's conduct of the procedure in this case. The presentation of its views suggests
that it feared the OFT had not taken the case sufficiently seriously by virtue of the
fact that it involved a relatively small and local market. In its conclusions, the CAT
emphasised this point:

> 390. We observe, finally, in the procedural context that this case involved small or medium
> sized businesses operating in local markets. Competition issues arising in such markets can
> be important for the participants and for local consumers. Often the OFT represents the only
> viable route for enforcing the Act in such contexts, given the difficulty for smaller undertak-
> ings of obtaining the necessary market information or supporting the costs of legal proceed-
> ings. We hope the OFT may take the opportunity to review its procedures to ensure that such
> cases can be dealt with within an acceptable time frame.

In assessing this appellate function of the CAT, the question arises whether or not an
appealable decision has been taken by the CMA. The CA 1998 contains certain express
provisions as to what amounts to an 'appealable decision'.[86] These concern decisions
on infringements (of Chapter I, Chapter II, Article 101 or Article 102 TFEU), decisions cancelling a block or parallel exemption, decisions on whether or not to release
commitments, directions and any decision as to the imposition of a penalty. Where no
appeal is provided for by the CA 1998, judicial review of the CMA's actions may lie
with the Administrative Court.

---

[81]   Note that s 47 was inserted by s 17 EA 2002, to ease the position of third parties in making appeals.
[82]   See, even more recently, the CAT's judgment in *The Racecourse Association and the British Horseracing
Board v OFT* [2005] CAT 29, overturning the OFT's finding of an infringement of the Ch I prohibition by
the collective sale of various media rights from UK racecourses to Attheraces plc (see OFT Decision No
CA98/2/2004 *Attheraces* (5 April 2004)).
[83]   [2005] CAT 25.
[84]   This matter has had a relatively lengthy history before the OFT: the DGFT's Decision No
CA98/13/2002, *Harwood Park Crematorium Limited* (6 August 2002), in response to Burgess's complaints,
found no abuse of a dominant position by Harwood Park (itself owned by Austin's, a funeral services
business competing with Burgess) because no dominant position in the market for crematorium services.
Subsequently, by its Decision of 9 April 2003, *Harwood Park Crematorium Limited: decision of the OFT
pursuant to Section 47(5)* (Case CA98/0503), the OFT withdrew its Decision of 6 August 2002, to enable it
to investigate Burgess's continuing allegations further. Finally, in its Decision No CA98/06/2004, the OFT
reached the conclusion, once again, that there was no infringement of the Ch II prohibition. This was by
virtue of its market definition encompassing crematoria services within a 30 km radius of Stevenage and
Knebworth, near to which Harwood Park Crematorium was located.
[85]   *JJ Burgess & Sons v OFT* [2005] CAT 25, paras 128–139. The CAT justified substituting its judgment
(rather than remitting the matter to the OFT for decision) on the basis that there had already been a delay
of two years in the OFT reaching a final decision on the matter (which it considered to be incompatible with
the effective enforcement of the CA 1998, before the further delays that would be occasioned by remitting
the matter to the OFT) and because the parties had since reached agreement on access to the Harwood Park
Crematorium for Burgess (so that an expedited resolution of the litigation was in everyone's best interests,
to ensure that normal commercial relations could be restored as soon as possible).
[86]   See s 46(3) CA 1998, as amended by Art 10 of the Competition Act 1998 (Notification of Excluded
Agreements and Appealable Decisions) Order 2000 (SI 2000, No 263).

This leaves the question of whether or not the CMA's activities in considering and ultimately deciding not to pursue a complaint amount to an 'appealable decision' for these purposes. There has been a good range of case law before the CAT on this subject, which has emphasised that the matter is one of fact and substance: just because the CMA does not formally call its action a 'decision' is not decisive of the question. The cases confirm that a decision of 'non-infringement' is covered by the wording of the statute, so the question is how to draw the distinction between a situation where the Director has merely exercised an administrative discretion without proceeding to a decision on the question of infringement (for example, where the Director decides not to investigate a complaint pending the conclusion of a parallel investigation by the European Commission), and a situation where the Director has, in fact, reached a decision on the question of infringement.

In situations where the CMA explicitly decides that there has not been an infringement of the competition rules, there is little doubt that such a measure amounts to an appealable decision. In other cases, however, where the CMA closes the file without explicitly determining that there is no infringement, the situation is less clear-cut. In its ruling in *Claymore*,[87] the CAT listed a number of factors relevant to drawing this distinction, which include: the prioritising of other cases (while reaching no conclusion on the merits of the complaint at hand); taking the view that a market investigation reference would be more suitable based on the facts; the fact that another competition authority was pursuing an investigation into the matter; and that any further investigation might be detrimental to an ongoing criminal investigation into a possible commission of the cartel offence.[88] These distinctions require what is often a subtle analysis of the nature of the investigation undertaken and the wording of any document adopted by the CMA.[89]

When conducting its review of a no-infringement decision, the CAT's review will generally be limited to examining whether the authority's decision is adequately reasoned and correct in law. It will not, however, seek to positively establish that, contrary to the authority's decision, the undertaking under examination has infringed the competition rules.

The third point is the variety of avenues by which aggrieved parties may seek damages for breaches of the competition rules. From the outset, the ECJ clearly established in its ruling in *Courage and Crehan* that the Member States' legal systems must provide for a means by which actions may be brought by private parties to establish breaches of the UK competition rules and claim compensation for such breaches.[90]

The introduction of the EA 2002 facilitated the pursuit of damages claims by supplementing section 58 CA 1998 (which makes the CMA's findings of fact binding on the parties to any court action) with section 58A CA 1998[91] (which makes CMA's findings of infringements, whether of Chapter I or Chapter II or Articles 101 and/or

---

[87] *Claymore Dairies Ltd v DGFT* [2003] CAT 3, para 122(iii).

[88] See the summary in *Claymore Dairies* (ibid), para 151.

[89] Practice thus far would seem to indicate a preference for finding OFT actions to amount to appealable decisions, although the criteria for deciding otherwise are sufficiently broad to indicate that this is by no means a trend that will be continued unquestioningly by the CAT in future cases.

[90] Case C-453/99 Courage and Crehan, paras 24–27. See also *Hendry v WPBSA* [2001] Eu LR 770, [2002] ECC 8.

[91] As inserted by s 20 EA 2002.

102 TFEU, binding on the courts in any proceedings 'in which damages or any other sum of money is claimed in respect of' such an infringement.

Further, as a result of section 47B CA 1998,[92] a 'specified [consumer] body' may be empowered to bring actions before the CAT on behalf of two or more consumers. This is potentially relevant to damages claims as a result of section 47A CA 1998.[93] This provision allows '(a) any claim for damages, or (b) any other claim for a sum of money, which a person who has suffered loss or damage as a result of the infringement of a relevant prohibition may make in civil proceedings brought in any part of the United Kingdom' to be pursued before the CAT.[94] Note also that section 47A(10) makes clear that this possibility in no way prevents an individual from pursuing such claims in the ordinary courts.

In recent years, the UK Courts have become very active as a forum of choice for customers seeking to claim compensation from undertakings on the basis of infringement decisions by the European Commission, not least because of the disclosure requirements under the Civil Procedure Rules. Notable cases include the action brought by National Grid against members of the Gas Insulated Switchgear cartel;[95] or the claim brought by Emerald Suppliers, together with over 300 other claimants, against British Airways and other companies linked to the Air Cargo cartel.[96] The introduction of the Damages Directive (see further section 6.6 below) and the amendments brought into effect by the Consumer Rights Act 2015 are likely to encourage further private enforcement through damages actions.

6.4 Enforcement of EU Competition Law[97]

6.4.1 Introduction

At the level of the European Commission, it is the Directorate General (or DG) for Competition (often abbreviated to DG Comp) that is charged with implementing and enforcing EU competition law. The DG for Competition is subdivided into various

---

[92] As inserted by s 19 EA 2002. It is for the Secretary of State for Trade and Industry to specify such bodies: see s 47B(9) CA 1998.

[93] As inserted by s 18 EA 2002.

[94] Section 47A(1) CA 1998. The relevant prohibitions are, naturally, Chs I and II and Arts 81 and 82 EC (s 47A(2) CA 1998).

[95] Case No: HC08C03243.

[96] Case No: HC2008000002.

[97] See generally L Ortiz Blanco (ed), *EC Competition Procedure*, 3rd edn (Oxford, Oxford University Press, 2013). This edition includes a new part dedicated to the procedural aspects of arbitration. C Kerse and N Khan, *EU Antitrust Procedure*, 6th edn (Sweet & Maxwell, 2012). In March 2012 the Commission published *Antitrust Manual of Procedures Internal DG Competition working documents on procedures for application of Articles 101 and 102 TFEU*. This is a useful document providing a comprehensive overview of the Commission's procedures.

directorates, which are themselves divided into departments. These departments deal with special sectors or particular subjects.[98]

The Treaty on the Functioning of the EU itself does not lay down any procedural rules specific to competition law. These were established in 1962, five years after the entry into force of the (then) EEC Treaty, by Regulation 17/62/EEC[99] (usually known simply as Regulation 17). These rules were replaced as of 1 May 2004 by those of Regulation 1/2003/EC.[100] This Regulation effected radical changes to the procedural rules of EU competition law. The most important amendment is that the Commission's monopoly over the grant of individual exemptions has been removed. In its place, there is now a system under which Article 101(3) TFEU can also be applied by the national courts and the national competition authorities (in the UK, the CMA). As a consequence of this change, the system of prior notification to the Commission of agreements for which undertakings sought an exemption has also been abolished. Regulation 1/2003/EC also introduces a number of other important changes to the specifics of EU competition procedure. The Regulation codified the case law on procedural guarantees for the undertakings concerned and also declares respect for fundamental rights to be a key element in EU competition law. Although Regulation 1/2003 provides an extensive codification of the case law developed under Regulation 17, that case law remains of importance in cases in which the interpretation of Article 101 TFEU is in issue.

With respect to procedural rights, the new procedural regime thus aims to comply with the rights, freedoms and principles recognised by the EU in the Charter of Fundamental Rights of the European Union.[101] According to Article 6(1) TEU the Charter shall have the same legal value as the Treaties. An important role in safeguarding the procedural rights of the undertakings involved in anti-trust procedures is that of the Hearing officer.[102] The Hearing officer plays a role in all enforcement procedures. He or she has an independent position in the Commission separate from DG COMP.[103]

In 2011 the Commission published a notice on best practices for the conduct of proceedings concerning Articles 101 and 102 TFEU.[104] This notice gives a useful summary of the different procedures that may be launched by the Commission when it suspects infringements or when complaints are lodged. It provides practical guidance on the conduct of proceedings before the Commission on the basis of Regulation 1/2003 and the case law of the ECJ. The aim of the Commission in publishing this notice is to provide practical information thereby seeking to increase the understanding of the investigative process and enhance the efficiency of investigations. It also seeks to ensure a high degree of transparency and predictability in the process. Unfortunately, the Notice does not mention the settlements procedure described below in

---

[98] The DG Comp's website provides an organogramme and a chart illustrating its organisational structure.

[99] [1962] OJ 13/204, [1959–62] OJ English Special Edition 87.

[100] Council Reg (EC) No 1/2003 of 16 December 2002 on the implementation of the rules on competition laid down in Arts 81 and 82 of the Treaty [2003] OJ L1/1.

[101] [2000] OJ C364/1.

[102] [2011] OJ L 275, 29; Decision of the President of the European Commission of 13 October 2011 on the function and terms of reference of the hearing officer in certain competition proceedings.

[103] According to Art 2(2) of the decision: 'The hearing officer shall be attached, for administrative purposes, to the member of the Commission with special responsibility for competition'.

[104] [2011] OJ C 308, 6–32.

section 6.4.2. It should also be noted that the Notice does not create any new rights or obligations, nor alter, the rights or obligations under the TFEU, Regulation 1/2003, and the case law of the ECJ.

In 2012 the Commission has also published: 'DG Competition's manual of procedure for the application of Articles 101 and 102 TFEU' on its website.[105] This manual provides an extensive and useful insight into the Commission's working methods.

The application and enforcement of EU competition law involves the following procedures:

(a) the official procedure (where the Commission enforces the rules *ex officio*) (examined in section 6.4.2 below);
(b) complaints (section 6.4.3 below);
(c) determinations of the inapplicability of Article 101(1) or (3) TFEU, or of Article 102 TFEU (section 6.4.4 below).

We will discuss the provisions of Regulation 1/2003/EC in the context of these procedures. We will also examine certain other provisions of Regulation 1/2003/EC in what follows.

In section 6.5 below we treat the Commission's leniency policy. The enforcement of EU Competition law is subject to important procedural safeguards laid down in Regulation 1/2003/EC, the case law of the ECJ and the provisions of the ECHR, the Charter and the ICCPR. The law relating to the rights of the defence has evolved considerably over the past decades, therefore, we devote a separate section 6.7 to it. In order to put the procedures in EU competition law into the proper perspective, we then provide brief coverage in section 6.8 of the possible ways in which the actions of the Commission may be called into question by undertakings before the GC and/ or the ECJ (whether in direct actions or in a reference from a national court for a preliminary ruling). Finally, in section 6.9 we examine the division of competence and cooperation between the European Commission and the UK authorities (principally the CMA) in the field of competition law.

6.4.2 The Official Procedure—*Ex Officio* Enforcement by the Commission

6.4.2.1 General

In the course of performing its various duties, the Commission often acquires information that raises doubts as to the compatibility with EU competition law of certain agreements or behaviour of undertakings. A great deal of this information comes from the press, whether from specialised trade publications or from ordinary newspapers. In such cases, it is extremely important that the Commission has competence to carry out

---

[105] According to the Commission: 'The manual is an internal working tool intended to give practical guidance to staff on how to conduct an antitrust investigation. Read the notice at the beginning of the document for more information on the purpose and use of this manual.' Notwithstanding this caveat, the manual provides a useful insight into the Commission's internal procedure.

its own investigations into such matters. Article 18 of Regulation 1/2003/EC empowers the Commission to request information from undertakings. This can be done by way of a simple request, without any threat of fines for non-compliance with the request, or by way of a formal decision obliging the addressee to provide complete responses within a prescribed deadline. In cases where there is a suspicion of a grave breach of the competition rules (whether of collusion or abuse of dominance), the Commission can take more drastic measures. Article 19 of Regulation 1/2003/EC provides that the Commission is competent to interview any natural or legal person in order to gather information relating to its investigation, so long as the person in question consents. The Commission carries out such interviews in cooperation with the CMA where they take place on the premises of any undertaking in the UK. Article 20 of Regulation 1/2003/EC offers the Commission the option of conducting an inspection of any undertaking. This involves visiting facilities and offices, where books, records and computing equipment can be examined. Copies of such records (or extracts therefrom) may be taken and business premises or books may be sealed for as long as necessary to facilitate the inspection. This all happens with the assistance of the national competition authority and (where necessary) with the presence and assistance of the police.

Article 21 of Regulation 1/2003/EC provides the Commission with the power to inspect other premises (including vehicles) 'if a reasonable suspicion exists that books or other records related to the business and to the subject-matter of the inspection' are being kept there. This includes the private residences of directors, managers and other staff members. Article 21(3) contains a precise description of the matters that the Commission must take into account in using this power. Any decision to use the power to investigate other premises must be authorised in advance by the national courts. Article 21(3) also specifies the extent to which the national court can review the Commission's decision to use such measures.[106]

Any information acquired on the basis of these various provisions of Regulation 1/2003/EC will then be studied carefully by the Commission. If it is of the opinion that there may have been a breach of the competition rules, it will have to decide which procedure to follow. At this stage there are two principal options:

1. The adoption of a Statement of Objections with a view to adopting a prohibition decision: the formal procedure.[107]

---

[106] 'The national judicial authority shall verify that the Commission decision is authentic and that the coercive measures envisaged are neither arbitrary nor excessive having regard in particular to the seriousness of the suspected infringement, to the importance of the evidence sought, to the involvement of the undertaking concerned and to the reasonable likelihood that business books and records relating to the subject matter of the inspection are kept in the premises for which the authorisation is requested. The national judicial authority may ask the Commission, directly or through the Member State competition authority, for detailed explanations on those elements which are necessary to allow its control of the proportionality of the coercive measures envisaged. However, the national judicial authority may not call into question the necessity for the inspection nor demand that it be provided with information in the Commission's file. The lawfulness of the Commission decision shall be subject to review only by the Court of Justice.' These rules are taken from the judgment of the ECJ in Case C-94/00 *Roquette Frères v Directeur general de la concurrence, de la consommation et de la répression des frauds, and Commission*. This judgment provided a very extensive treatment of the question of judicial review of such Commission decisions and is of great importance for this subject.

[107] As will be discussed below for cartel cases the settlement procedure may be available.

2.   The parties subject to the investigation may consider offering commitments to end the conduct in question.

6.4.2.2   The Formal Procedure

The formal procedure involves the publication and notification to the undertakings concerned of a Statement of Objections (often referred to as a SO). This is a kind of competition law summons, in which the most important conclusions of the Commission on the case are set out. The undertakings concerned then have the opportunity to respond to the allegations made by the Commission. After a written procedure there follows an oral hearing, and a report of that hearing is drawn up by the Hearing Officer who was not involved during the earlier stages of that particular procedure. The Hearing Officer then compiles an independent report on the case and presents this to the Director-General of Competition. If, after the hearing and the independent report of the Hearing Officer, the Commission is still of the opinion that the case should be pursued, it will prepare a draft decision. This draft will then be submitted to the Advisory Committee on Restrictive Practices and Dominant Positions (as provided for by Article 14 of Regulation 1/2003/EC), which is made up of representatives (usually from the competition authorities) of the EU Member States.[108] After the Advisory Committee has delivered its opinion, the definitive Commission decision finding that there has been an infringement of EU competition law will be adopted. A non-confidential version of this decision will either be published in the 'L' series of the *Official Journal of the European Union* or (increasingly) on DG Competition's website. Article 7 of Regulation 1/2003/EC offers the Commission a range of measures that it can impose once a finding of an infringement has been made: it may act to correct the infringing behaviour of the undertaking(s) concerned or, where no effective behavioural remedy exists, it may impose structural remedies.[109] Any remedy imposed must satisfy the general EU law principle of proportionality, and this is also true for any fine or periodic penalty payment imposed by the Commission in its decision.[110] The power to impose fines is laid down in Article 23 of Regulation 1/2003/EC, while periodic penalty payments are covered by Article 24 of the same Regulation. The Commission may impose a fine of up to a maximum of 10 per cent of the worldwide turnover of the undertakings concerned. The Commission has published Guidelines on the

---

[108]   The Commission 'shall take the utmost account of the opinion delivered by the Advisory Committee' in coming to its final decision (Art 14(5) of Reg 1/2003/EC). Art 14 also provides more detailed rules on time limits and the possible publication of the Committee's opinion, as well as the opportunity to use the Committee for more general discussion of EU competition law issues. For further discussion of this Committee, see section 6.4.4 below.

[109]   The availability of such structural remedies is a change from the position under Reg 17/62/EEC and has generated some controversy. Recital 12 to Reg 1/2003/EC states that 'Structural remedies should only be imposed either where there is no equally effective behavioural remedy or where any equally effective behavioural remedy would be more burdensome for the undertaking concerned than the structural remedy. Changes to the structure of an undertaking as it existed before the infringement was committed would only be proportionate where there is a substantial risk of a lasting or repeated infringement that derives from the very structure of the undertaking.'

[110]   Case C-441/07 *Alrosa v Commission*, para 39.

method of setting fines.[111] Nevertheless the ECJ has held that: 'the proper application of the EU competition rules requires that the Commission may at any time adjust the level of fines to the needs of that policy'.[112] The highest fine imposed on a single undertaking to date has been €1.06 billion imposed upon Intel in a decision of 13 May 2009.[113] Previously the highest fine was € 497,196,304 for Microsoft.[114]

In the course of cartel proceedings the Commission may decide that the case is suitable for settlement.[115] This procedure has been used by the Commission since 2008.[116] It allows for a shorter and faster administrative process. The parties involved may benefit from a shorter procedure and a reduction in the fine of 10 per cent. The final decision is usually considerably shorter than decisions adopted under the normal procedure, which can potentially be advantageous for the parties to the cartel seeking to avoid follow-on damages claims from victims seeking to use the decision as a basis for seeking compensation before national courts. Settlement does, however, come at a price: the settling parties are required, as part of their settlement submission to the Commission to admit liability for the cartel conduct. As of the end of 2014 there were 17 settlements.[117] The detergents decisions provide a good example of the application of the settlement procedure.[118] It should be noted that settlement may be total, ie, including all participants, or partial, ie, not including all participants, in which case, the normal procedure will continue with respect to the non-settling parties.

6.4.2.3 Commitments

On the basis of Article 9 of Regulation 1/2003/EC, the Commission may also bring an infringement procedure to a close by adopting a decision in which it accepts commitments offered by the undertaking(s) concerned. Such commitments must address the concerns raised by the Commission such that it can decide that there are no longer grounds for action in the case. Any decision adopted under Article 9 may be adopted for a specified period and, once adopted, is binding upon the undertakings concerned.

---

[111] Guidelines on the method of setting fines imposed pursuant to Art 23(2)(a) of Reg 1/2003, OJ [2006] C 210/2.

[112] Case C-397/03 P *Archer Daniels Midland Co v Commission*, para 21. In para 91 the Court held: 'It should be noted ... that, whilst rules of conduct designed to produce external effects, as is the case of the Guidelines, which are aimed at traders, may not be regarded as rules of law which the administration is always bound to observe, they nevertheless form rules of practice from which the administration may not depart in an individual case without giving reasons that are compatible with the principle of equal treatment.'

[113] C (2009) 3726 final. In Case T-286/09 the GC dismissed the action with the following words: 'it must be held that the fine is appropriate to the circumstances of the case.' Intel has appealed to the ECJ C-413/14 P. On 19 July 2016 the Commission fined truck producers €2.93 billion for participating in a cartel, IP/ 16/2582.

[114] [2007] OJ L 32, 23.

[115] See for an extensive discussion of settlements: CD Ehlermann and M Marquis (eds), *European Competition Law Annual 2008—Antitrust Settlements under EC Competition Law* (Oxford, Hart Publishing, 2010).

[116] Art 10(a) of Commission Reg 773/2004 as amended by Commission Reg 622/2008, OJ 2008, L 171/3. As well as the Commission Notice on the conduct of settlement procedures in view of the adoption of Decisions pursuant to Art 7 and 23 Reg No 1/2003, cartel cases. [2008] OJ C 167/1.

[117] Commission Staff working paper, Brussels, 30.5.2012 SWD 2012, 141 final p 15.

[118] Commission decision C (2011) 2528 final 97 Brussels 13.4.2011. A summary is published in [2011] OJ C 193, 14–16.

Any such decision to accept commitments, however, does not involve a decision as to whether there has been or still is any infringement of EU competition law. It also leaves intact the competence of the national court and national competition authority to act to enforce the competition rules on the facts of the case in question.[119] In the *Alrosa* judgment[120] the ECJ held that: 'the application of the principle of proportionality by the Commission in the context of Article 9 of Regulation No 1/2003 is confined to verifying that the commitments in question address the concerns it expressed to the undertakings concerned and that they have not offered less onerous commitments that also address those concerns adequately. When carrying out that assessment, the Commission must, however, take into consideration the interests of third parties.'[121]

The Commission has adopted a significant number of Article 9 decisions. Several decisions were adopted in the energy sector after an investigation under Article 17 of Regulation 1/2003/EC revealed a lack of competition in that sector. Article 17 allows the Commission to conduct an inquiry where the trend of trade, the rigidity of prices or other circumstances suggest that competition may be restricted. The Commission has launched such investigations in the financial services, the energy and the pharmaceutical sectors.[122]

According to the Commission's website there have been 21 commitment decisions until 12 May 2015. In July 2016 the European Commission adopted a decision that renders legally binding the commitments offered by 14 container liner shipping companies. The commitments aim to increase price transparency for customers and to reduce the likelihood of coordinating prices.[123] The commitments address the Commission's concerns that the companies' practice of publishing their intentions on future price increases may have harmed competition and customers. This practice may have raised prices on the market for container liner shipping services on routes to and from Europe, in breach of EU antitrust rules.

It may be useful to compare settlements to commitments decisions: The website of DG COMP provides the following overview:

A settlement is different from a commitments decision in that:

— a settlement decision does establish an infringement and requires an admission of guilt from the parties, whereas a commitment decision does not establish an infringement and does not require any admission by the parties;
— a settlement decision simply requires a "cease and desist" of past behaviour, whereas commitments decision requires commitment to future behaviour;
— a settlement procedure is only available for cartels whereas commitment decisions are appropriate in all antitrust cases except for cartels.

---

[119] See Recitals 13 and 22 of Reg 1/2003/EC).

[120] Case C-441/07, *Alrosa v Commission*.

[121] Para 41. In para 48 the ECJ also explained that: 'Undertakings which offer commitments on the basis of Article 9 of Regulation No 1/2003 consciously accept that the concessions they make may go beyond what the Commission could itself impose on them in a decision adopted under Article 7 of the Regulation after a thorough examination. On the other hand, the closure of the infringement proceedings brought against those undertakings allows them to avoid a finding of an infringement of competition law and a possible fine.'

[122] The reports are available on the website of DG COMP.

[123] IP/16/2446.

6.4.2.4 Interim Measures

Under Article 8 of Regulation 1/2003/EC the Commission also has the power to adopt interim measures 'in cases of urgency due to the risk of serious and irreparable damage to competition'. Such interim measures will apply while the Commission's investigation is continuing.[124]

6.4.3 Complaints

The opportunity for private individuals to make a complaint to the Commission about the conduct of undertakings on the market is an important aspect of the application and enforcement of EU competition law. Every year, the Commission receives many complaints alleging breaches of competition law. According to Article 7(2) of Regulation 1/2003/EC, natural or legal persons who can show a 'legitimate interest', and Member States, are entitled to lodge complaints with the Commission. The procedure for dealing with such complaints is laid down in Chapter IV of Commission Regulation 773/2004/EC.[125] The Commission has also issued a 'Notice on the Handling of Complaints by the Commission under Articles 101 and 102 TFEU.'[126] The Annex to that Notice contains 'Form C', which explains the details and information required to be included when submitting a complaint to the Commission.[127]

The Commission must investigate the complaint seriously. In so doing, it can make use of the various investigative powers provided by Regulation 1/2003/EC, as discussed above. After completing a preliminary investigation, the Commission must inform the complainant (by way of a letter) about the state of play and whether or not the Commission intends to take the complaint further.[128] The Commission issues a preliminary rejection by way of letter. In this letter the complainant is informed that it has the right to submit observations within a certain time period. If the complainant does not submit written observations within the time limit, then the Commission will deem the complaint to have been withdrawn and will take no further action. In this case, there is no challengeable act (and therefore, no means to seek annulment under Article 263 TFEU). If, however, the complainant does submit observations, then the Commission is under an obligation to adopt a formal rejection decision. It is this decision which can be challenged before the Union Courts. Where such an application is upheld, the GC will annul the Commission's decision and require it to re-examine the complaint and adopt a new decision thereon.

---

[124] For the conditions that must be satisfied for the Commission to adopt such interim measures, see Case T-44/90 *La Cinq SA v Commission*. The Commission has not, however, made extensive use of this power, and there are very few examples of cases in which the Commission has awarded interim measures. Some notable examples (all of which pre-date the adoption of Reg 1/2003/EC) include, Case IV/30.696 *Ford Werke*, Case IV/34.072 Mars, Case IV/34.174 *B&I—Sealink* and Case D3/38.044 *IMS Health*.
[125] [2004] OJ L123/20. Amended by Commission Reg 1792/2006 and Commission Reg 622/2008.
[126] [2004] OJ C101/65.
[127] Form C is also included as an Annex to Reg 773/2004/EC.
[128] Article 7 of Reg 773/2004/EC.

On the other hand, the Commission has the right to set its own priorities and thus to reject a complaint because it does not sufficiently affect the 'Union interest'.[129] It also has the right to rely on a similar decision by an NCA.[130] Article 13 of Regulation 1/2003/EC allows the Commission to reject a complaint whenever it concerns an agreement or practice that is being (Article 13(1)) or has already been (Article 13(2)) dealt with by a competition authority of an EU Member State.[131]

It is vital for the Commission not to be placed in a position where it is required to take on all complaints, for the simple reason that its available resources for the enforcement of competition law are limited. The Commission's Notice on handling complaints provides an extensive discussion of the division of work between the Commission and the NCAs. It is possible that the Commission may not itself take on the investigation of an allegation made by a complainant, but may ask a particular NCA to pursue the matter further in view of the importance of the case. This approach is an obvious one to take in cases where the complaint is particularly concerned with national markets or sub-markets, even where they also satisfy the criterion of having an effect upon inter-Member State trade (this example is specifically mentioned by the Commission in its Notice).

In all cases where it is clearly possible for the natural or legal person to bring the matter to be heard before a national court, it is not necessary to take up the already scarce resources of the Commission to deal with the case and thus save the day for the complainant. This point is also made strongly by the Commission in its 'Notice on the Cooperation between the Commission and the Courts of the EU Member States in the Application of Articles 101 and 102 TFEU'.[132]

Potential complainants are also reminded of the possibility of applying for interim measures while the complaint is dealt with or of complaining anonymously so as to protect their position. If the Commission fails to reply, or only replies extremely tardily, to a complaint, the complainant can initiate proceedings for failure to act on the basis of Article 265 TFEU. The GC will then rule on the basis of the concrete circumstances of the particular case as to whether or not the Commission has dealt with the matter in a sufficiently timely manner and whether or not the Commission has come to a considered view on the case.[133] If the GC finds that the Commission has unjustifiably taken no action at all, or has yet to act where it should have done so, then it will order the Commission to take a decision on the complaint. It remains possible for the

---

[129] Case T-24/90 *Automec Srl v Commission* (*Automec II*) and Case C-119/97 P *UFEX v Commission*.

[130] See Case T-355/13 *EasyJet* 'Accordingly, the circumstance—even on the assumption that it is proved—that, in the present dispute, the NMa did not close the complaint which had been brought before it by taking a decision within the meaning of Article 5 of that Regulation and that it relied on priority grounds did not preclude the Commission from finding, pursuant to Article 13(2) of that Regulation, that that complaint had been dealt with by a competition authority of a Member State and from rejecting it on that ground.' Para 40.

[131] Presumably, the exact wording of Art 13(2) ('another competition authority') would allow the Commission to reject a complaint even if that other authority were not one of an EU Member State; by contrast, Art 13(1) explicitly only allows the Commission to reject a complaint where that authority is of an EU Member State.

[132] [2004] OJ C101/54.

[133] Case T-127/98 *UPS Europe SA v Commission*.

Commission's subsequent decision in such a case still to come to the conclusion that there is insufficient Union interest involved in the matter for it to take the complaint any further itself. Such a decision must of course be thoroughly reasoned. If the Commission takes the view that the case does indeed involve a sufficient Union interest (ie, that it is important from a theoretical or practical point of view), then it will move to deal with the matter under the procedures described in section 6.4.2 (above).

6.4.4   Determinations of the Inapplicability of Article 101(1) or (3) TFEU, or of Article 102 TFEU

As we have already noted in section 6.4.1 (above), the system of notification of agreements for an individual exemption has been abandoned at EU level. Prior administrative control has been replaced by supervision and oversight after the fact. Undertakings can no longer apply for clearance from the Commission before putting their agreements into operation. Instead, they must assess for themselves whether or not their agreements are compatible with EU competition law. Obviously, this places a great responsibility upon the shoulders of those who advise companies on matters of competition law. They must keep the executives and management well informed about the acceptability of proposed agreements. In doing this they have the advantage of the many previous Commission Decisions in which various types of agreements have been analysed in many different economic sectors. Further, the Guidelines on horizontal and vertical agreements[134] (and possible future guidelines) can provide additional assistance.

Since the adoption of Regulation 1/2003/EC, there remains only a very limited possibility for undertakings to request that the Commission issue a decision on the basis of Article 10 of Regulation 1/2003/EC.[135] The text of that provision makes clear that the Commission will very rarely be prepared to adopt such decisions. The corresponding Recital (no 14) in the preamble to this Regulation refers to 'new types of agreements or practices that have not been settled in the existing case law and administrative practice'. This Recital indicates that a Commission decision adopted under Article 10 of Regulation 1/2003/EC will be of 'a declaratory nature'. The provision thus establishes that the agreement in question will, from the moment that it entered into force, have been in conformity with the requirements of Article 101(3) TFEU, or will not have amounted to an infringement of Article 101(1) or Article 102 TFEU.

When taking decisions under Article 10 of Regulation 1/2003/EC the Commission is obliged to seek the advice of the Advisory Committee on Restrictive Practices and

---

[134] On which see Chapter 3.6.2 and 3.6.3 (above).

[135] 'Where the Community public interest relating to the application of Articles 81 and 82 of the Treaty so requires, the Commission, acting on its own initiative, may by decision find that Article 81 of the Treaty is not applicable to an agreement, a decision by an association of undertakings or a concerted practice, either because the conditions of Article 81(1) of the Treaty are not fulfilled, or because the conditions of Article 81(3) of the Treaty are satisfied. The Commission may likewise make such a finding with reference to Article 82 of the Treaty.'

Dominant Positions, which is made up of representatives from the NCAs. Article 14 of Regulation 1/2003/EC lays down the procedural rules that apply to this advisory function. Decisions issued by the Commission under Article 10 are binding upon the national courts and NCAs, as laid down by Article 16 of Regulation 1/2003/EC. Article 16 also requires that national courts and NCAs refrain from adopting decisions that run counter to decisions already adopted by the Commission or to 'a decision contemplated by the Commission in proceedings it has initiated'.[136]

As discussed above in section 6.4.2 the Commission can also give indications about the compatibility of certain behaviour with Articles 101 and/or 102 TFEU in the context of the procedure under Article 9 of Regulation 1/2003/EC. This provision gives the Commission the power to accept commitments made by undertakings to adjust their behaviour, where the Commission is planning to adopt a decision ruling that there has been a breach of Article 101 or 102 TFEU. This can be seen as a kind of settlement of the case. By examining the content of the commitments made and accepted, one can establish which amendments had to be made to the agreements or practices to ensure that the conditions of (say) Article 101(3) TFEU were satisfied. Recital 22 of the preamble to Regulation 1/2003/EC states that such:

> Commitment decisions adopted by the Commission do not affect the power of the courts and the competition authorities of the Member States to apply Articles 101 and 102 TFEU.

> The national court remains competent to deliver judgments concerning breaches of Article 101 and/or 102 TFEU and the applicability of Article 101(3) TFEU.

Nevertheless, it is clearly possible (and perhaps even probable) that the Commission's practice in accepting commitments may lead to the development of a particular line in its competition policy. A previous incarnation of a similar development under the old regime can be seen in the Commission's use of comfort letters, albeit that such letters usually resulted in the publication of less information than the commitments-based system seems likely to generate.[137]

6.5 Leniency Policy

Since 1996, the Commission has pursued a policy that aims to encourage undertakings involved in cartels to report these illegal practices to the Commission, in return for being granted immunity from, or a reduction in the level of, fines.[138] The Commission's

---

[136] On this point, see further ss 6.2 (above) and 6.7 (below).

[137] See, eg, CS Kerse and N Khan, *EC Competition Procedure*, 5th edn (London, Sweet & Maxwell, 2005), paras 2-001 and 6-052.

[138] Commission Notice of 8 December 2006 [2006] OJ C 298/17.

Notice is careful to relate the extent of any reduction in fines to the speed and extent of the cooperation provided by the undertaking concerned. As discussed above in section 6.3.5.1(v), the UK system has also adopted rules on whistleblowing and leniency. Leniency has become a very important instrument for the Competition Authorities in their fight against hardcore cartels. The website of DG COMP gives the following summary of the Commission's leniency policy:

> In order to obtain total immunity under the leniency policy, a company which participated in a cartel must be the first one to inform the Commission of an undetected cartel by providing sufficient information to allow the Commission to launch an inspection at the premises of the companies allegedly involved in the cartel. If the Commission is already in possession of enough information to launch an inspection or has already undertaken one, the company must provide evidence that enables the Commission to prove the cartel infringement. In all cases, the company must also fully cooperate with the Commission throughout its procedure, provide it with all evidence in its possession and put an end to the infringement immediately. The cooperation with the Commission implies that the existence and the content of the application cannot be disclosed to any other company. The company may not benefit from immunity if it took steps to coerce other undertakings to participate in the cartel.

> Companies which do not qualify for immunity may benefit from a reduction of fines if they provide evidence that represents 'significant added value' to that already in the Commission's possession and have terminated their participation in the cartel. Evidence is considered to be of a 'significant added value' for the Commission when it reinforces its ability to prove the infringement. The first company to meet these conditions is granted 30 to 50% reduction, the second 20 to 30% and subsequent companies up to 20%.[139]

In the *Pfleiderer* judgment[140] the ECJ had to decide whether or not to protect information supplied to the Commission or a NCA under a leniency application. The ECJ noted that access to information in the possession of the Commission or a NCA is important for successful claims for damages against the perpetrators of cartel infringements. On the other hand, it noted that such access may reduce the effectiveness of leniency applications. Accordingly, the ECJ held that it was for the national court to weigh on a case-by-case basis, according to national law, and taking into account all the relevant factors in the case whether such access should be given. In January 2012 the court in Bonn which handles all cases against the German NCA (the Bundeskartellamt) denied access on the ground that such access would jeopardise the effectiveness of the leniency policy.[141] In its judgment in the *DHL* case, the ECJ has already held that the leniency programme established by the Commission, through its Leniency Notice, is not binding on Member States. That conclusion also applies to the ECN Model Leniency Programme.[142]

---

[139] http://ec.europa.eu/competition/cartels/leniency/leniency.html.
[140] Case C-360/09, *Pfleiderer v Bundeskartellamt*. The UK High Court (Mr Justice Roth) has also had to undertake such a balancing exercise in *National Grid v ABB and others*.
[141] ECN brief 1/2012. See also the Resolution of the Meeting of Heads of European Competition Authorities of May 2012.
[142] Case C-428/14, *DHL Express (Italy) Srl v Autorità Garante della Concorrenza e del Mercato*, para 42.

6.6 Private Actions for Damages[143]

After a decade of discussions within the Commission and in the literature a directive on damages was adopted on 26 November 2014.[144] The directive is designed to make it easier for victims of antitrust violations to claim compensation. To that end the directive, notably, obliges Member States to facilitate access to evidence of infringements of the competition rules. While certain national jurisdictions, such as the UK, contain an equivalent requirement already exists under the rules governing civil procedure, for other Member States such an obligation represents a dramatic departure from the standard rules of civil litigation. The deadline for Member States to implement the directive is 27 December 2016.

The following paragraphs highlight the most prominent provisions of the directive. The key provision of the directive is Article 3(1): persons suffering harm caused by an infringement of competition law should be able to claim and obtain full compensation for that harm. Article 3(2) states that full compensation means that the victim shall be placed in the position that it would have been in if the infringement had not been committed. However, in accordance with Article 3(3) full compensation must not lead to overcompensation. Article 4 embodies the well-known principles of effectiveness and equivalence developed by the ECJ in order to ensure that the EU claims are placed on an equal footing with claims under national law.[145] This is followed in Articles 5 and 6 with specific obligations to provide disclosure of evidence. According to Article 6(6) national courts cannot, for the purposes of damages actions, order disclosure of leniency statements and settlement submissions. Article 7(1) provides a further safeguard for such evidence, by which such evidence shall either be deemed to be inadmissible in actions for damages or is otherwise protected under the applicable national rules under Article 6.

Article 9 obliges Member States to allow final decisions of national competition authorities and courts to be used as irrefutable proof. Article 10 requires Member States to provide for limitation periods within which claims for damages must be brought. Article 11 provides for joint and several liability in case undertakings have infringed the competition rules through joint behaviour. Article 12 provides rules for the passing on defence. This defence allows the defendant reduce the amount of damages payable if it is able to prove that the claimant passed the overcharges resulting from an infringement on to its customers. According to Article 14 Member States

---

[143] Directive 2014/104 of the European Parliament and of the Council on certain rules governing actions for damages under national law for infringements of the competition law provisions of the Member States and of the European Union. OJ 2014 L 349/1. For a summary see Competition policy brief January 2015 Issue 2015-1/January 2015 'The Damages Directive—Towards More Effective Enforcement of the EU Competition Rules.'

[144] See the Commission White Paper: *Damages actions for breach of the EC Antitrust Rules* COM (2008) 154 final, 2 April 2008. See also the Staff Working paper SEC (2008) 404 and the Impact Assessment SEC (2008) 405. See a brief discussion of the directive in Competition policy brief, Issue 2015-1/January 2015.

[145] Case C-158/80 *Rewe v Hauptzollamt Kiel* para 44.

should ensure that indirect purchasers have the burden of proof that the higher prices have been passed on to them. Indirect purchasers are those that have procured their products or services from the original purchaser.

The provision of Article 6(6) denying claimants access to leniency evidence and settlement evidence has been criticised as being unnecessary for the protection of the leniency program and a major stumbling block for claims for damages.[146] Critics argue that such access is often the only way for claimants to obtain evidence.

6.7 Rights of the Defence

An important element running through all aspects of the procedure described in the preceding paragraphs is the requirement that the Commission must respect the rights of the defence in all of its actions taken to enforce EU competition law. In short, this comes down to respecting the provisions of the ECHR, the Charter of Fundamental Rights of the EU, the ICCPR and the case law of the ECJ.

In 2011 several important judgments clarified issues of due process in competition law cases; one by the ECtHR in *Menarini*,[147] and two by the ECJ in its *Copper Industrial Tubes*[148] and *Copper Plumbing Tubes* judgments.[149] According to these judgments the fact that the Commission competition decisions are subject to full judicial review, ensures an adequate protection of the fundamental rights of the persons concerned by those decisions. According to the ECtHR the EU system respects the guarantees flowing from the right to a fair trial laid down in Article 6 ECHR in particular because: (i) decisions of the competition authority are subject to judicial review on questions of fact and law; and (ii) the courts can verify the proportionality of the sanction imposed and have the power to change that sanction. The ECJ reached a similar conclusion in its *Copper Industrial Tubes* and *Copper Plumbing Tubes* judgments. It ruled that the review by the GC of Commission decisions imposing fines, fulfills the guarantees of the principle of effective judicial protection as laid down in Article 47 of the Charter of Fundamental Rights.

Here, we provide a brief coverage of the most important points that have come to light in the case law of the ECJ, the GC and the ECtHR.

(a) First, throughout the whole procedure the Commission must guarantee the confidentiality of business secrets. This duty arises from the moment that undertakings

---

[146] See Lazar Radic Boskovic: 'The blanket prohibition of disclosure of corporate statements contained in Article 6(1) of the proposed Directive for actions for antitrust damages: Proportional safeguard of public enforcement or insurmountable burden for claimants', Masters Thesis, University of Amsterdam 2014.

[147] Judgment of the ECtHR of 27 September 2011, *A Menarini Diagnostics SRL v Italy*, Application No 43509/08, paras 57–67.

[148] Case C-272/09 P *KME Germany AG v Commission*.

[149] Cases C-386/10 P *Chalkor AE Epexergasias Metallon v Commission* and C-389/10 P *KME Germany AG and Others v Commission*.

provide information to the Commission, whether the information is supplied at the Commission's request or not.[150]

(b)   Secondly, the Commission must allow the undertakings concerned to have access to the file.[151] Companies and their representatives and lawyers must be put in a position to be able to examine the Commission's dossier on the case and the documents on the basis of which the Commission has formed the view that a breach of the competition rules has occurred.

(c)   Thirdly, the Commission must respect legal professional privilege as between a lawyer and his or her client. On the basis of this privilege, the undertaking concerned may refuse to supply the Commission with its correspondence with its external legal advisers[152] when the Commission sets up an investigation. The privilege does not extend to internal legal advisers.[153] Regulation 1/2003/EC makes no mention of questions of legal professional privilege, so the applicable rules continue to be drawn from the relevant case law of the EU courts.

(d)   A fourth issue concerns the rules that must be respected during the investigation, ie, searching company buildings and offices, and (where appropriate) other premises. As mentioned above,[154] Article 21(3) of Regulation 1/2003/EC lays down detailed rules in this regard based upon the ECJ's *Roquette Frères* judgment and the ruling of the European Court of Human Rights at Strasbourg in *Société Colas Est*.[155]

(e)   A fifth element is the reasonableness of the period for delivering judgment. In the *Baustahlgewebe* judgment the ECJ reduced the fine because the GC took too long to conclude the procedure.[156] In its judgment *Der Grüne Punkt v Commission*[157] the ECJ held that a period of five years and 10 months was excessive.[158] Nevertheless, the ECJ held that the failure to adjudicate within a reasonable time had no effect on the outcome of the dispute, therefore the setting aside of the judgment would not remedy the infringement.[159] However, the failure of the GC can give rise to a claim for damages against the Union under Article 268 TFEU and the second paragraph of Article 340 TFEU.[160]

It should be noted that there is also the need to ensure that the parties have had the right to be heard on all of the objections raised against them. This is the *raison d'etre* of the SO.

---

[150]   See Art 28 of Reg 1/2003/EC and Art 16 of Reg 773/2004/EC [2004] OJ L123/20. See also para 81 of the Best Practices Notice.

[151]   Article 15 of Reg 773/2004/EC [2004] OJ L123/20.

[152]   Case 155/79 *AM&S Europe Ltd v Commission*. Note that the UK rules (discussed in s 6.3.2.3(i) above) explicitly envisage granting wider scope to the category of legal professional privilege under UK competition law: this would include in-house legal advice as well as advice given by external lawyers. (*cf*, however, Case T-30/89 *Hilti v Commission*, where a mere report by an internal legal adviser of what an external legal adviser had said was held by the GC to be covered by such privilege.)

[153]   Case C-550/07P, *Akzo Nobel v Commission*.

[154]   See above, n 106 and the accompanying text.

[155]   *Société Colas Est v France* (2004) 39 EHRR 17.

[156]   Case C-185/95P *Baustahlgewebe v Commission*.

[157]   Case C-385/07 P, *Der Grüne Punkt v. Commission*.

[158]   Para 183.

[159]   In this case there was no fine involved so the remedy of a reduction of the fine was not an option.

[160]   Para 195.

6.8 Judicial Protection in EU Competition Law

Judicial protection of individuals' rights in EU competition law follows the same basic lines as are to be found in general EU law on the subject. For those not initiated in this area of EU law, it is perhaps useful at this stage to provide an abbreviated overview of the most important elements of this legal regime.

The starting point is that decisions taken by the Commission must be clearly and sufficiently reasoned so as to ensure that judicial control over the legality of such decisions is possible (Article 296 TFEU). An appeal against any Commission decision is possible for those to whom the decision is addressed as well as for any party that is 'directly and individually concerned' by the decision (in the wording of Article 263 TFEU on applications for the annulment of EU acts). In our context, this means the following types of decision are challengeable in this way:

(a) decisions taken after a complaint, where the Commission decides not to take on the case due to the absence of a Union interest in pursuing the matter; decisions in which the Commission accepts commitments offered by the undertaking(s) concerned, making them binding on the undertaking(s) and addressing the competition concerns raised by the Commission's investigations (Article 9 of Regulation 1/2003/EC);

(b) decisions in which a request for a decision on the basis of Article 10 of Regulation 1/2003/EC is rejected or granted;

(c) decisions which establish a breach of the competition rules (including its procedural rules); and

(d) decisions in which fines or penalty payments are imposed for failure to respond to requests for information or in which interim measures are adopted.[161]

Since 1989, all private individuals (including companies) must make their application for annulment to the GC. They can then appeal against a judgment of the GC to the ECJ, but only on points of law.

It is possible for the applicant to apply for interim measures to be adopted by the President of the GC (who takes this decision under an accelerated procedure), to protect its position while the main action is pending. This is to be contrasted with the possibility for the party under investigation to seek interim measures from the Commission while the Commission's investigation is ongoing.[162] Here, it is the party making the application to the GC who would apply for such interim measures, and this will not necessarily be the party that has been under investigation by the Commission. For example, if the Commission decides to accept commitments under Article 9 of Regulation 1/2003/EC instead of adopting an infringement decision, another party

---

[161] This also applies to merger decisions (whether clearance or prohibition; and other administrative penalty decisions—eg, penalty imposed for failing to respect the standstill provisions of the Merger Regulation.

[162] See section 6.4.2.4 above.

affected by those commitments may feel that competition concerns remain and thus may appeal against the Commission's decision accordingly.[163]

Parties challenging a Commission decision may, under Article 151 of the rules of Procedure of the GC, apply for an expedited procedure. This is what parties did in the *ING* case[164] because the Commission had imposed very onerous obligations for the approval of the aid. Since ING asked for annulment of these obligations it was important to have the Court's decision before the obligations had to be implemented. The GC rejected the request. But, the President of the Court decided, on the request of the Third Chamber, to order that the cases be given priority, pursuant to the first sentence of Article 67(2) of the Rules of Procedure. Nevertheless, the procedure before the GC took two years and ING had to implement the first tranche of the obligations.[165] In many cases, the EU courts have emphasised that they attach great importance to securing effective judicial protection in EU law. A number of developments illustrate this, including the approach taken to the standing (or *locus standi*) of applicants to challenge Commission decisions in the competition field[166] and the question of when a statement by the Commission may be said to be a reviewable act under Article 263 TFEU. On this latter point, the *IBM* case made clear that Commission statements may be the subject of an application for annulment where they have binding legal effects. In that case, the ECJ held that 'procedural measures adopted preparatory to the decision which represents their culmination' did not have such effects and were thus not reviewable.[167] By contrast, an action that provides confidential details to third parties does amount to a measure with binding legal effects, against which the undertaking concerned can lodge an appeal.[168] In the *Schlüsselverlag* judgment, the ECJ ruled that the Commission was obliged to take a formal position on a request that the Commission should investigate a concentration that had been approved by the Austrian competition authority. If the Commission failed to do so, then the applicant was entitled to bring an action for failure to act on the basis of Article 265 TFEU (see above for a brief discussion).[169]

The number of challenges against Commission decisions in competition cases has declined over the years. According to Prek and Lefèvre this is the result of the introduction of the settlement and the commitment procedures as well as the success of the leniency program.[170]

---

[163] One further example is where a national court has requested under Art 15 of Reg 1/2003 that the Commission provide it with documents for use in national damages proceedings. In such a case, interim measures could be awarded to prevent the Commission from sending the requested documents pending the outcome of the main action. Otherwise, if the documents were disclosed prior to the handing down of the final judgment, this would render the main proceedings meaningless (see Case T-164/12 *Alstom v Commission*).

[164] Case T-29/10, *Netherlands and ING Groep v Commission*.

[165] The GC annulled the Commission decision because it had failed to apply the market economy investor test. The ECJ dismissed the Commission's appeal Case C-224/12 P.

[166] See the discussion of these cases (such as Case 26/76 *Metro v Commission* (*Metro I*), establishing the standing of complainants) in eg PP Craig and G de Búrca, *EU Law: Text, Cases, and Materials*, 5th edn (Oxford, Oxford University Press, 2011), Ch 14.

[167] Case 60/81 *IBM v Commission*, para 21.

[168] Case 53/86 *Akzo v Commission* ('*Akzo II*'), para 29.

[169] Case C-170/02 *Schlüsselverlag JS Moser v Commission*. On actions for failure to act, see, eg, Craig and de Búrca, above n 166, 512–15 and the references cited therein.

[170] M Prek and S Lefèvre, 'Competition Litigation before the General Court: Quality if not quantity?' (2016) *CMLRev* 53: 65–90. Miro Prek is judge at the GC and Silvère Lefèvre, legal secretary.

The extent of the review by the courts in competition cases is a subject of lively debate.[171] The traditional view is that Community courts exercise a limited review. 'They will verify whether the relevant rules on procedure and on the statement of reasons have been complied with, whether the facts have been accurately stated and finally, whether there has been any manifest error of assessment or misuse of power.'[172] Under this standard the Commission is allowed a margin of appraisal. There is evidence that this standard is increasingly substituted for a more intensive review particularly following the ECJ's rulings in the Copper Industrial Tubes and Copper Plumbing Tubes cases.[173]

The EU judicature (in this case, the ECJ) can also be faced with competition law questions via another route. Where a national court is dealing with a case concerning EU competition law and comes to the conclusion that an interpretation of EU competition law by the ECJ is needed to enable the case to be decided, then the national court can refer questions to the ECJ for a preliminary ruling under Article 267 TFEU.[174] Given the direct effect of the main provisions of EU competition law, which, after the entry into force of Regulation 1/2003/EC, extends to the grant of exemptions under Article 101(3) TFEU, it is to be expected that this already significant source of case law for the ECJ will increase in volume.

6.9 Division of Competence and Cooperation Between the Commission and the National Competition Authorities

For a clear understanding of this subject, it is of great importance to appreciate that both the EU and the UK authorities (or the National Competition Authorities of the other Member States)[175] are authorised to take action only on the basis of their compe-

---

[171] See, eg, I Forrester, 'A bush in the need of pruning: The luxuriant growth of "light judicial review"' in: Ehlermann and Marquis (eds), *European Competition Law Annual 2009, Evaluation of Evidence and its Judicial Review in Competition cases* (Oxford, Hart Publishing, 2011) 407–453. See also Chapter 5.2.7.

[172] Prek and Lefèvre, *op.cit* p 68.

[173] Prek and Lefèvre, *op.cit* p 89.

[174] Note that the Treaty on the Functioning of the European Union now provides for the possibility of transferring such references to the GC, as a result of the amendments introduced by the Treaty of Nice: see Art 256(3) TFEU. Note also that such questions of EU competition law could arise indirectly where national law is precisely modelled on the EU competition law provisions and the national court seeks an interpretation of EU competition law so as to secure close coordination of the EU and national rules (even where the facts concern only national law): see, eg Case C-7/97 *Oscar Bronner v Mediaprint Zeitungs- und Zeitschriftenverlag*.

[175] In its judgment in Case T-355/13 *EasyJet v Commission* the GC held in para 37: 'By contrast, the interpretation put forward by the applicant, the effect of which would be to require the Commission to review a complaint systematically each time a competition authority of a Member State has investigated a complaint but has not taken one of the decisions provided for in Art 5 of Reg No 1/2003 or taken a decision

tences as laid down by the relevant legislative instruments.[176] As illustrated by Figs 2.1 and 2.2 above, the Commission is competent to act against breaches of the competition rules only insofar as they affect trade between the Member States. On the basis of Article 5 of Regulation 1/2003/EC and section 25(3), (5) and (7) and section 31(2)(c) and (d) CA 1998, the CMA is also competent to act in such circumstances. The CMA loses this competence, however, if and when the Commission decides to take control of the investigation of a particular case. This is laid down by Article 11(6) of Regulation 1/2003/EC, concerning the situation where the Commission opens proceedings for the adoption of a decision under Chapter II of that Regulation.

Articles 11, 12 and 13 of Regulation 1/2003/EC provide detailed rules on cooperation between the Commission and national competition authorities, while the Commission's subsequent Notice develops these rules still further.[177] Article 11 of Regulation 1/2003/EC obliges the national competition authorities and the Commission to exchange information with each other concerning their ongoing cases. If a national competition authority intends to take a formal decision[178] in a particular case, it must inform the Commission (at least 30 days prior to the adoption of that decision). One of the consequences of this procedure is that it provides the Commission with the opportunity to take over that case if it considers it appropriate to do so. This will be the case where the case has effects upon competition in more than three different Member States.[179] Article 12 of the Regulation makes it possible for the Commission and the national competition authorities to exchange information with each other, including confidential information. As laid down in Article 12(2), such information must only be used as evidence in the application of Articles 101 and 102 TFEU (unless national competition law is being applied in parallel in the same case and does not lead to a different outcome). In this connection, it is important to recall that Article 28 of Regulation 1/2003/EC imposes a clear obligation upon the Commission and national competition authorities and their personnel to respect the confidentiality of such information.

A decision by the Commission to accept commitments from the parties on the basis of Article 9 of Regulation 1/2003/EC does not bind the national court or the national competition authority, as is clear from Recital 13 in the preamble of Regulation 1/2003/EC. Thus the UK courts and/or the CMA remain competent to rule upon whether or not there has been a breach of the EU competition rules. It is questionable, however, whether the UK courts or the CMA would exercise this opportunity in light of section 60 CA 1998.

---

to reject the complaint on priority grounds, would not be compatible with the objective of Art 13(2) of that Regulation, which is to establish, with a view to ensuring effectiveness, an optimal allocation of resources within the European competition network. The cooperation for leniency applications is explained in Case C-248/14, *DHL Express (Italy) Srl, v Autorità Garante della Concorrenza e del Mercato*'.

[176] According Art 35 of Reg 1/2003, the Member States are under an obligation to provide the necessary legislation ensuring the effectiveness of the provisions of the Regulation. See Case C-439/08, *Vlaamse federatie van verenigingen van Brood- en Banketbakkers, Ijsbereiders en Chocoladebewerkers (VEBIC) VZW*.

[177] Notice on cooperation within the Network of Competition Authorities [2004] OJ C101/43.

[178] Where that decision is one 'requiring that an infringement be brought to an end, accepting commitments or withdrawing the benefit of a block exemption Regulation' (Art 11(4) of Reg 1/2003/EC).

[179] See para 14 of the Notice on cooperation within the Network of Competition Authorities [2004] OJ C101/43.

The division of competence between the Commission and the UK authorities in the field of merger control has already been discussed briefly in Chapters 2.2.2.3 and 5.3.1 (above). Little needs to be added to that outline here. It should be noted, however, that there are two specific sets of provisions of EU law that concern the respective competences of the Commission and the national competition authorities in this field. First, on the basis of Article 4(4) or Article 9 of Regulation 139/2004/EC (the EUMR), the Commission can decide, on the application of the notifying parties or the relevant Member State, to refer the notified concentration to the national competition authority to be assessed. In recent years, the referral of mergers to national competition authorities has become a more frequent occurrence. A good example is provided by the takeover by Heineken of the Spanish company Cruzcampo. This merger was referred to the Spanish competition authority, at the request of the Spanish government.[180] One example of a reference to the UK authorities by the Commission was the proposed acquisition by the Blackstone Group of NHP plc. This case concerned the UK care homes market, which the Commission found to be local in scope within the UK and to have the potential to affect competition in certain local UK markets.[181]

A second possibility of cooperation between the Commission and the national competition authorities in the merger field is offered by Article 22 ECMR. On the basis of this provision, a Member State can request that the Commission assess a merger, even though the concentration fails to meet the thresholds of the Union dimension (on which see Chapter 5.2.4 above). At the request of the Netherlands, the Commission investigated the proposed mergers between Endemol and HMG and between Blokker and Toys 'R' Us. In both cases, the Commission came to the conclusion that the merger could not be allowed to proceed.[182]

---

[180] IP/99/632.

[181] Case No COMP/M.3669 *Blackstone (TBG CareCo)/NHP* (1 February 2005).

[182] *RTL/Veronica* [1996] OJ L294/10; *Blokker/Toys 'R' Us* [1998] OJ L316/1. At the request of the Finnish government, the merger between the supermarkets Kesko and Tuko was prohibited by the Commission: [1997] OJ L110/53.

Competition Law and the State

7.1 Introduction

Competition law is aimed at securing the healthy functioning of the market. The rules of Articles 101 and 102 TFEU are thus addressed to undertakings. Nevertheless, there are various situations in which the activities of the State can have an important influence upon the market and competitive relations thereon.[1] These situations are the subject of this chapter.

First of all, the State can develop a role in certain activities that are not 'typically' seen as tasks of the State. Whether such activities are a typical State task or not is decided by the application of the rules on whether or not the activity falls within the concept of an 'undertaking' (this question has been discussed in Chapter 2.1.1 above). Where such activities cannot be classified as those of an undertaking engaging sufficiently in economic activity, such as police supervision or the supply of passports, then as a rule they fall outside competition law scrutiny.

Where the relevant State activities are those of an undertaking, then in principle the normal rules of competition law must be applied to them. However, it is possible that such activities will be carried out by public undertakings, or by undertakings that have been charged with the performance of special tasks or which operate under an exclusive or a special right in the field. In such cases, special rules may apply to these activities, which may (to some extent) result in a derogation from the application of the competition rules. Under the regime of UK competition law, these rules are to be found in section 3 read together with schedule 3, paragraph 4 CA 1998. In the EU, the corresponding provision is Article 106 TFEU. The application of these rules is discussed in section 7.2 below.

At the other end of the spectrum, it is possible that the behaviour of the undertaking, which would normally run contrary to competition law, is positively required by

---

[1] For a wide-ranging discussion, see the OECD's Report on its Best Practice Roundtable on *Regulating Market Activities by Public Sector* (DAF/COMP (2004) 36, 1 February 2005) (available on the internet at http://www.oecd.org/dataoecd/61/5/34305974.pdf).

national law.[2] If the rules of national law leave no room for the undertakings concerned to compete, then according to the case law of the ECJ the prohibition on collusive anti-competitive practices will not apply.[3] If those national rules only restrict the range within which competition is possible but do not exclude it altogether, then the undertakings must compete within those margins.[4]

Secondly, the activities of the State (*qua* State and not *qua* undertaking) can exercise an important influence upon competition on the market. Under EU law, such State activities can be tested against the norm of Article 4(3) TEU and Articles 101 or 102 TFEU. This line of case law is considered in section 7.3 below, and is followed by a summary of how this system of rules is to be applied in situations where there is a combination of activities by government and undertakings (section 7.4). This is a difficult area and it is important to gain a clear grasp of the overall analytical structure that must be applied in such circumstances.

Thirdly, by means of support measures, it is possible for the State to intrude upon the operation of the forces of competition in the market.[5] In EU law, the giving of such 'State aid' is in principle forbidden. The rules laid down by the TFEU on state aids are treated in section 7.5 below.

7.2 The Rules for Public Undertakings and Undertakings with Exclusive or Special Rights

7.2.1 The EU Rules for Public Undertakings—Article 106 TFEU

At the time when the EEC Treaty was being put together, in 1955–56, there were many public companies in France and Italy. Large sectors of the economy were controlled by the State. This State control covered not only traditional sectors, such as the public sector, but also other sectors, such as the oil and gas industries, the banking and insurance sectors, the tobacco industry, the alcohol industry and the production of matches. As a result, a compromise had to be found concerning the application of the competition rules and the organisation of these industrial sectors. For the southern Member States, it was not acceptable that competition law should simply apply, without further specification, to all public companies. At the same time, it was unacceptable to those

---

[2] This point was made most clearly in Joined Cases C-359 and 379/95 P *Commission and France v Ladbroke Racing*.

[3] Although note that such national rules may well conflict with the norms laid down by the combination of Arts 4(3) TEU and 101 or 102 TFEU: see s 7.3 for discussion of these norms.

[4] Cases 240–42, 261, 262, 268 and 269/82 *Stichting SSI v Commission*.

[5] More generally, see the OECD's Report on its Best Practice Roundtable on *Competition Policy in Subsidies and State Aid* (DAFFE/CLP (2001) 24, 12 November 2001), available at http://www.oecd.org/dataoecd/31/1/2731940.pdf.

Member States that were striving to develop and achieve a market-oriented political approach that large parts of the economy in France and Italy should remain beyond the reach of the competition rules. If that had been permitted it clearly could have allowed serious incursions upon competitive behaviour on the market. The resulting compromise is to be found in Article 106 TFEU.

Article 106 TFEU provides:

1. In the case of public undertakings and undertakings to which Member States grant special or exclusive rights, Member States shall neither enact nor maintain in force any measure contrary to the rules contained in the Treaties, in particular to those rules provided for in Article 18 and Articles 101 to 109.
2. Undertakings entrusted with the operation of services of general economic interest or having the character of a revenue-producing monopoly shall be subject to the rules contained in the Treaties, in particular to the rules on competition, in so far as the application of such rules does not obstruct the performance, in law or in fact, of the particular tasks assigned to them. The development of trade must not be affected to such an extent as would be contrary to the interests of the Union.
3. The Commission shall ensure the application of the provisions of this Article and shall, where necessary, address appropriate directives or decisions to Member States.

7.2.1.1 Services of General Economic Interest

The notion of public services or services of general economic interest (SGEI) has become a key concept in EU law and politics.[6] It is a notion that is particularly important in all sectors that have been liberalised, including transport, energy, telecoms and post, as well as in other sectors such as broadcasting. The Treaty of Amsterdam in 1997 added a new article to the Treaty (now Article 14 TFEU), in which

> the Union and the Member States, each within their respective powers and within the scope of application of the Treaties, shall take care that such services operate on the basis of principles and conditions, particularly economic and financial conditions, which enable them to fulfill their missions.[7]

The Lisbon Treaty has expanded this Article by providing legislative power for enacting regulations to establish the principles and conditions for such services.[8]

---

[6] Its political importance was highlighted during the French campaign for the referendum on the Constitutional Treaty in the spring of 2005. One of the arguments of the 'No' camp was that the Community was gradually undermining the public services. Note also that the concepts of public service obligations and services of general economic interest are of significance in the field of EU free movement law as well as under the competition rules: see, eg, the discussion of the free movement of goods in the *Energy* cases (n 30, below) and of the free movement of capital in the various *Golden shares* cases (see, eg Case C-58/99 *Commission v Italy*; Case C-367/98 *Commission v Portugal*; Case C-483/99 *Commission v France*; Case C-503/99 *Commission v Belgium*; for discussion, see H Fleischer (2003) 40 *Common Market Law Review* 493).

[7] See M Ross, 'Article 16 EC and Services of General Interest: From Derogation to Obligation' (2000) 25 *European Law Review* 22.

[8] See in general on this topic and the revisions of the Lisbon Treaty: U Neergaard, E Szyszczak, JW van de Gronden and M Krajewski (eds), *Services of General Interest in the EU* (Springer, 2013).

Article 36 of the EU's Charter of Fundamental Rights[9] recognises and respects services of general economic interest. There has been a lively discussion on the proper function of public services and the extent to which such services are exempted from the competition rules and the State aid rules.[10] The latter question is largely dealt with under Article 106(2) TFEU. An important element has been developed by the Court's judgment in the *Altmark* case[11] which provided important guidelines for the compatibility of financial compensation for such services with the State aid rules.

To understand the importance of the *Altmark* judgment, it should first be noted that the State aid rules (discussed in detail in section 7.5 below), generally prohibit Member States granting selective advantages to undertakings. The *Altmark* judgment provided that compensation by governments for the provision of SGEIs will not constitute State aid, provided that there is no over-compensation and as long as the specific conditions enumerated by the Court in *Altmark* are fulfilled. In this respect, the Court ruled that:

> public subsidies intended to enable the operation of urban, suburban or regional scheduled transport services are not caught by [the State aid rules] where such subsidies are to be regarded as compensation for the services provided by the recipient undertakings in order to discharge public service obligations. For the purpose of applying that criterion, it is for the national court to ascertain that the following conditions are satisfied:
>
> — first, the recipient undertaking is actually required to discharge public service obligations and those obligations have been clearly defined;
> — second, the parameters on the basis of which the compensation is calculated have been established beforehand in an objective and transparent manner;
> — third, the compensation does not exceed what is necessary to cover all or part of the costs incurred in discharging the public service obligations, taking into account the relevant receipts and a reasonable profit for discharging those obligations;
> — fourth, where the undertaking which is to discharge public service obligations is not chosen in a public procurement procedure, the level of compensation needed has been determined on the basis of an analysis of the costs which a typical undertaking, well run and adequately provided with means of transport so as to be able to meet the necessary public service requirements, would have incurred in discharging those obligations, taking into account the relevant receipts and a reasonable profit for discharging the obligations.[12][13]

The *Altmark* judgment has raised questions about the interpretation of the four conditions that it laid down, as well as about the relationship between those conditions and Article 106(2) TFEU.

---

[9] According to Art 6(1) the Charter shall have the same legal value as the Treaties. it forms Part III of the Treaties.

[10] See the Communication from the Commission on this subject (COM (2000) 580 final, of 20 September 2000), as well as its 'Non-Paper' on 'Services of General Economic Interest and State Aid' (COMP-2002–01759) of 12 November 2002. On 12 May 2003, the Commission published a Green Paper on services of general economic interest (COM (2003) 270 final). In this publication, the Commission examines a variety of public service obligations and the Community instruments in force in the field of services of general interest. The Commission issued a White Paper on the same topic in 2004 (COM (2004) 374 final). The Commission has published further documents in the run up to the revision of its rules in 2011.

[11] Case C-280/00 *Altmark Trans GmbH and Regierungspräsidium Magdeburg v Nahverkehrs- gesellschaft Altmark GmbH and Oberbundesanwalt beim Bundesverwaltungsgericht*.

[12] ibid, para 95.

[13] The Commission takes the view that measures establishing SGEIs should be not discriminate between undertakings as well as technologies. See, eg, the Art 108(2) decision call for tenders for additional capacity in Brittany. OJ [2016] C 46/69.

In 2012 the Commission published a communication on the application of the EU State aid rules to compensation granted for the provision of services of general economic interest.[14] This communication clarifies the application of Article 107 TFEU (which establishes the substantive rules on State aid) and the criteria set by the *Altmark* ruling for such compensation. This document provides an overview of the relevant principles. It is complemented by three more specific measures.[15]

First, there is the Commission Decision based upon Article 106(3) TFEU that deals with cases where the *Altmark* conditions are not met.[16] This Decision sets out the conditions under which State aid for public service compensation is compatible with the internal market and exempt from notification. Article 2(1)(a) of the Decision exempts services of less than EUR 15 million per annum. It also exempts compensation granted to hospitals and other healthcare services as well as social housing.

Secondly, the Commission has also published a Community framework for State aid in the form of public service compensation.[17] The framework addresses situations that do not fall within the scope of application of the Decision.[18] Such measures have to be notified.

Thirdly, the Commission adopted a regulation applying Articles 107 and 108 TFEU to *de minimis* aid for the provision of SGEIs.[19] This regulation lays down certain conditions under which public service compensation shall be deemed not to meet all the criteria of Article 107(1) TFEU (and therefore will not be prohibited as State aid). According to Article 2(2) *de minimis* aid granted to any one undertaking providing services of general economic interest not exceeding EUR 500 000 over any period of three fiscal years shall be deemed not to meet all the criteria of Article 107(1) and be exempt from notification.

The Commission's measures are explained in a communication[20] and a staff working paper.[21]

---

[14] OJ C8, 11.01.2012, pp 4–14. Unlike the Commission decision and the framework, of which earlier versions were adopted in 2005, this document is new.

[15] The Communication notes, in point 5, that it is without prejudice to the application of the public procurement rules and other Treaty requirements for the establishment of public service obligations discussed below. The Commission also announces that it will answer individual questions about the application of the State aid rules to SGEIs.

[16] Commission Decision of 20 December 2011 on the application of Art 106(2) of the Treaty on the Functioning of the European Union to State aid in the form of public service compensation granted to certain undertakings entrusted with the operation of services of general economic interest. OJ L7, 11.01.2012, pp 3–10. The decision is an update of the 2005 decision. Art 2(d) also exempts public service compensation to maritime and air transport links to islands which do not exceed 300,000 passengers. Art 2(e) exempts compensation for airports with fewer than 200,000 passengers and ports with fewer than 300,000 passengers.

[17] European Union framework for State aid in the form of public service compensation (2011). OJ C8, 11.01.2012, pp 15–22. Like the decision, the framework is also an update of its 2005 framework.

[18] Para 21 of the preamble to the Decision (n 16, above).

[19] Reg 360/2012 on the application of Arts 107 and 108 of the Treaty on the Functioning of the European Union to *de minimis* aid granted to undertakings providing services of general economic interest, (2012) OJ L 114/8.

[20] Communication from the Commission to the European Parliament, the Council, the European Economic and Social Committee and the Committee of the Regions. Reform of the EU State Aid Rules on Services of General Economic Interest, COM (2011) 146 final Brussels 23.3.2011.

[21] Commission Staff working paper, 'The application of EU State Aid rules on Services of General Economic Interest since 2005 and the Outcome of the Public Consultation', SEC (2011) 397 Brussels 23.3.2011.

Earlier, the Commission enacted a Directive amending the Transparency Directive.[22] The Commission's view on the appropriate scope of the *Altmark* judgment is explained in several individual decisions. As can also implicitly be gleaned from these cases, as well as its decision based upon Article 106(3) TFEU, the Commission holds the view that, in those instances where the *Altmark* conditions are not fulfilled, an exemption from Article 107(1) TFEU may be possible on the basis of Article 106(2) TFEU, provided that the compensation is commensurate with the extra cost of providing the public service.

The foregoing discussion presupposes that the relevant public service obligations have been established in accordance with the requirements of EU law. This was the subject of the *Analir* and *Coname* cases. In the *Analir* judgment,[23] although the Court granted the Member States a fairly wide discretion in establishing public service obligations, it also imposed clear conditions upon the exercise of that discretion.

The Court held that Public Service obligations must be based on objective, non-discriminatory criteria which are known in advance to the undertakings concerned, in such a way as to circumscribe the exercise of the national authorities' discretion.

Although this case involved an interpretation of specific provisions in the Regulation on cabotage in maritime transport, the conditions formulated in *Analir* can be taken to be of more general significance across the whole transport sector and, indeed, for other sectors in which such public service obligations arise. In the *Coname* judgment, the ECJ provided further guidance in this matter in cases where no compensation is involved.[24] The direct award of a concession must, on the basis of Articles 49 and 56 TFEU, comply with transparency requirements such as to enable an undertaking from another Member State to have access to appropriate information so that it would have been in a position to apply for the concession. The Court stressed that the transparency requirements do not necessarily imply an obligation to hold a tender. It should be observed that the fourth condition of the *Altmark* judgment suggests a preference for a tendering procedure when the authorities provide for compensation for the services. Even though the *Coname* and the *Altmark* judgments do not *require* a tender, the *Brixen* judgment *does*.[25] Both the Commission Decision under Article 106(3) TFEU and the framework are silent on this question. The Commission's decisions in individual cases suggest a preference for tendering, to the extent that the presence of a tender establishes a rebuttable presumption that the conditions of transparency are satisfied.

Having dealt with the notion of Services of General Economic Interest and specific instances of compensation for such services in the context of Article 106 TFEU, we now consider that Treaty provision in more detail.

---

[22] Commission Directive 2005/81/EC of 28 November 2005 amending Directive 80/723/EEC on the transparency of financial relations between Member States and public undertakings as well as on financial transparency within certain undertakings [2005] OJ L312/47.

[23] Case C-205/99 *Asociación Profesional de Empresas Navieras de Líneas Regulares (Analir) and Others v Administración General del Estado.*

[24] Case C-231/03 *Consorzio Aziende Metano (Coname) v Comune di Cingia de' Botti.*

[25] Case C-458/03 *Parking Brixen GmbH v Gemeinde Brixen.* The judgment also provides a useful clarification of the question when the accord of public service concessions cannot be regarded as a transaction to which the EU public procurement rules apply.

7.2.1.2 Article 106(1) TFEU

The first paragraph of Article 106 TFEU is addressed to the Member States. They must ensure that they comply with the rules of the Treaty when they establish public undertakings and prescribe their relevant tasks and duties. Thus, Member States must not provide (for example) that public undertakings shall give preference in hiring personnel to citizens from their own country: such a requirement would breach the general prohibition on discrimination on grounds of nationality laid down in Article 45 TFEU. Equally, Member States must not adopt rules or give directions that would require such undertakings to act contrary to the principle of equal pay for equal work by men and women (as laid down in Article 157 TFEU).

For our subject, the key question is the scope that is left to Member States when establishing public undertakings and when laying down regulations. The case law of the ECJ starts from the premise that, in principle, Member States are free to set up public undertakings. The limiting factor is that they must not do so in such a way that the public undertaking must necessarily end up breaching competition law as soon as it starts to pursue the relevant activities. To do so would be a breach of Article 106(1) TFEU. Setting up a public undertaking will always bring with it a certain restriction of competition. The matter turns on whether or not the undertaking is left sufficient room to be able to act in such a way as to remain within the rules of competition law. If this is not the case, then the State has acted in breach of Article 106(1) TFEU. Two examples from the case law will explain this idea.

In the *Höfner* case, the matter concerned a state body—the *Bundesanstalt für Arbeit*—that had been granted a statutory monopoly over running employment agencies.[26] Furthermore, the German Civil Code provided that any contract concluded in contravention of that monopoly right was void. In spite of these provisions, there were various private employment agencies active on the German market against which the German government had taken no action. A further relevant factor was that the government had failed to provide the *Bundesanstalt* with sufficient means to be able to fulfill its tasks properly and to their full extent. The ECJ first pointed out that the creation of a dominant position, by granting a monopoly, was not in itself contrary to Article 102 TFEU in combination with Article 106(1) TFEU. It went on, however, to hold that where a Member State brought a situation into being that led to a breach of Article 102 TFEU then that Member State had acted contrary to Articles 102 and 106 TFEU. The *Bundesanstalt* did not satisfy the demand for employment services on the market and this abused its dominant position. This abuse, set out in Article 102(b) TFEU, consisted of the limiting of production to the detriment of users of such services.

The *Crespelle* case concerned a situation in which the French government had restricted competition by setting up regional monopolies but had nevertheless left sufficient scope for the undertakings concerned to continue to compete in the market.[27] The regional monopolies were for the artificial insemination of cows. The complaint

---

[26] Case C-41/90 *Höfner v Macrotron*.
[27] Case C-323/93 *Société Civile Agricole du Centre d'Insémination de la Crespelle v Coopérative d'Elevage et d'Insémination Artificielle du Département de la Mayenne*.

was that the creation of these monopolies had the effect of driving up prices, so that the government had been guilty of acting contrary to EU law. The ECJ held that the creation of the monopolies had not been the direct cause of any disproportionately high costs being charged by the undertakings. In other words, insofar as abuses of a dominant position could be established in *Crespelle*, this was down to the behaviour of the undertakings in question and could not be attributed to the government. Where this is the case, the undertakings concerned remain responsible for any abuse of their dominant position and cannot hide behind the monopoly that they have been granted (subject to the application of Article 106(2) TFEU, discussed in section 7.2.1.3 below).

In the *AG2R* judgment the ECJ confirmed its position that the mere creation of a dominant position is not in itself incompatible with the Treaty.[28]

Article 106(1) TFEU has direct effect when used in connection with the other relevant directly effective provisions of the TFEU to which the paragraph itself refers. In competition law, the relevant provisions are naturally Articles 101 and 102 TFEU. This explains why, in the two examples used above, a private party can rely upon Article 106(1) TFEU in conjunction with Article 102 TFEU and can do so before the national courts as well as in arbitral proceedings.[29]

7.2.1.3 Article 106(2) TFEU

The possible exception from the Treaty rules provided by Article 106(2) TFEU can be relied upon by both the Member States and individual undertakings. The State can call upon the exception to justify legislative or administrative measures concerning public undertakings (or those granted exclusive or special rights) that would normally amount to an infringement of the rules of the TFEU. This was in issue in the series of *Energy* cases decided by the ECJ in 1997.[30] To take the case brought by the Commission against the Netherlands[31] as an example, Article 34 of the Dutch Electricity Act 1989 prohibited the importation of electricity into the Netherlands except where this was carried out by the SEP, which was the association of cooperating electricity producers. This prohibition was clearly at odds with Article 37 TFEU, which forbids all discrimination concerning the conditions of sale and supply. The Dutch government relied upon Article 106(2) TFEU to justify this statutory prohibition on imports, arguing that without such a prohibition the planning of electricity supply within the Netherlands would be rendered excessively difficult. The ECJ upheld this argument and found the Dutch rules to be justified under Article 106(2) TFEU.

---

[28] Case C-437/09 *AG2R*. See PJ Slot, 'Public distortions of Competition: The importance of Article 106 TFEU and the State Action Doctrine' and C Heide-Joergensen, 'Private Distortions of Competition and SSGIs' in U Neergaard, E Szyszczak, JW van de Gronden and M Krajewski (eds), *Social Services of General Interest in the EU* (Springer, 2013) chs 10 and 11.

[29] *cf* PJ Slot in G Blanke and P Landolt (eds), *EU and US Antitrust Arbitration* (Wolters Kluwer, 2011) ch. 29, paras 29-045 and 29-068 (at 1030 and 1036).

[30] These concerned various national import and export monopolies in electricity and (in one case) in natural gas: Cases C-157/94 *Commission v Netherlands*, C-158/94 *Commission v Italy*, C-159/94 *Commission v France* and C-160/94 *Commission v Spain*, on which see PJ Slot (1998) 35 *Common Market Law Review* 1183.

[31] Case C-157/94 *Commission v Netherlands*.

In the *Almelo* case, the energy company IJsselmij relied upon Article 106(2) TFEU to justify contracts that would normally have infringed Articles 101 and 102 TFEU.[32] Here, the competition law issue concerned exclusive contracts under which the customers of the IJsselmij energy company were required to source all of their electricity requirements from IJsselmij. Such contracts are prohibited under normal competition rules. Although the ECJ accepted that in this case Article 106(2) TFEU could give some scope for an exception from competition rules, on the case's return to the national court this exception was not upheld on the facts.[33]

An important question for the application of this exception is which interests can qualify as a justification for otherwise anti-competitive conduct: what counts as a 'service of general economic interest'? From the case law of the ECJ, we can deduce that such interests must be compelling demands of general importance, such as the national electricity supply system, postal systems, a national alcohol monopoly (eg in Sweden)[34] and lotteries.

A further condition for the application of Article 106(2) TFEU is that the task of general economic interest must clearly have been bestowed upon the relevant undertaking by the State, by either some legislative or other public law measure.[35] The Commission's *GVL* Decision[36] provides a good illustration of this point.[37]

> 65. Pursuant to Article [106](2), undertakings entrusted with the operation of services of general economic interest shall be subject to the rules contained in the Treaty, and in particular to the rules on competition, only in so far as the application of such rules does not obstruct the performance, in law or in fact, of the particular tasks assigned to them. Private undertakings may also come under that provision where they are entrusted with the operation of services of general economic interest by an act of the public authority (*cf* judgment of the Court of Justice in *BRT II*). Since Article [106](2) permits, in certain circumstances, an arrangement which derogates from the Treaty, the concept of an undertaking which may rely on this provision must, however, be interpreted strictly.

> 66. GVL is not entrusted, either by an official Act or otherwise, by the public authority with the operation of services. Admittedly, it carries on its activities subject to official authorization, but no specific task is assigned as a result of this 'precondition of authorization'. Official authorization is granted subject merely to a check as to whether the company requesting the authorization satisfies the preconditions relating to associations for the exploitation of performers' rights laid down in the Wahrnehmungsgesetz.

> Such granting of authorization is, therefore, by its very nature not an assignment of particular tasks, but only a permission to carry on certain activities. Authorization, which merely

---

[32] Case C-393/92 *Gemeente Almelo v Energiebedrijf IJsselmij*.

[33] The Arnhem court held (judgment of 22 October 1996, rolnr 87/280) that the parties had not adduced any evidence on which it could be concluded that the statutory task (electricity distribution) would have been impossible to carry out in the absence of the conclusion of the exclusive contracts.

[34] See Case C-189/95 *Criminal proceedings against Franzén*, also discussed by PJ Slot in (1998) 35 *Common Market Law Review* 1183.

[35] Which may include 'the grant of a concession governed by public law': see the *Almelo* case (n 32, above), para 47. Note that this is also required under the first Altmark condition.

[36] Decision 81/1030/EEC [1981] OJ L370/49.

[37] See also Case C-159/94 *Commission v France*, paras 60ff: EDF and GDF (the French electricity and gas undertakings respectively) had been granted their status by concession, *but* their tasks could not be said to include environmental and regional policy goals as France had failed to show that any obligations in these spheres went beyond straightforward compliance with the general national law on these matters (paras 69–70 and subsequent discussion).

overrides a statutory prohibition, has a completely different legal content from the entrusting of a task, whereby specific responsibilities and hence specific obligations are officially conferred upon an undertaking. The necessarily strict interpretation of the concept 'undertaking' contained in Article [106](2), therefore, shows that GVL does not fall under that provision.

67. Even if it were accepted, however, that GVL had been 'entrusted' with the operation of services, such services must be 'of general economic interest'.

68. GVL protects only the private interests of artists. The Court of Justice of the European Communities held in its judgment in *BRT II* that such a general interest is not protected where an undertaking manages private interests, including property rights protected by law. This also applies to GVL.

Even when all of this has been established, another important question remains: who bears the burden of proof in Article 106(2) TFEU cases and how heavy is that burden? In the series of *Energy* cases discussed above, it was held that it fell to the party (whether government or undertaking) seeking to rely upon the ground of justification to satisfy the burden of proof. And what must be shown? It is clear after the *Energy* cases that the exception does not require evidence that there is no alternative way of fulfilling the general economic interest task in question. Rather, the ECJ has accepted that it is sufficient for the claimant to establish that the restrictions allow the relevant task(s) to be performed under 'economically acceptable conditions'.[38] It is not necessary to show that the economic survival of the undertaking would be threatened in the absence of the granting of the exception from the competition rules. The ECJ affirmed this view in its *AG2R* judgment.[39]

The final condition for the application of this exception is that the development of trade must not be affected to an extent that is contrary to the interests of the Union (Article 106(2) TFEU, last sentence). As a matter of the jurisdictional scope of the competition rules, a mere effect upon inter-Member State trade will suffice to allow the EU competition rules to apply (see Chapter 3.2.5 above). Thus, this criterion must require that something more be shown: the effect on trade must be an adverse one when examined in the light of the Union interest. This element was also discussed by the ECJ in the *Energy* cases, where it was held that the Commission had failed to define the Union interest in relation to which the development of trade must be assessed. Further, the ECJ emphasised that the Commission had to take care to establish how trade might have taken place. This was a particularly important element in the *Energy* cases due to the nature of the industry and the fact that most cross-border exchanges up to that time had been for the purposes of ensuring a balance between national systems, rather than for normal trading reasons.[40]

---

[38] See the various *Energy* cases (n 30, above) and Joined Cases C-147 and 148/97 *Deutsche Post AG v Gesellschaft für Zahlungssysteme mbH GZS)*.

[39] Case C-437/09, *AG2R*, para 80.

[40] Although note that the first Directive on the internal electricity market (Directive 96/92/EC [1997] OJ 27/20) had been adopted the year before the judgments in the *Energy* cases (n 30, above) were handed down, making it surprising that the ECJ did not see fit to refer to the Directive's provisions requiring significant market opening and the concomitant increase in the scope for trade in electricity to develop (see the case note by PJ Slot (1998) 35 *Common Market Law Review* 1183 for discussion). The sector is now covered by a more far-reaching Directive, which mandates greater and more rapid market opening than originally foreseen in the 1996 and the 2003 rules: see Directive 2009/72/EC [2009] OJ L2116/55.

It is clear that the questions of whether or not an undertaking has been entrusted with a service of general economic interest[41] and whether or not the application of the Treaty provisions would obstruct the performance of those assigned tasks[42] are provisions of Article 106(2) TFEU that have direct effect and can therefore be relied upon by undertakings before national courts. It is less clear that the same applies to the criterion that the effect on trade must not be contrary to the interests of the Union: some argue that this provision should only lead to such an assessment by the Commission and that national courts are not best placed to evaluate this criterion.[43] Others have suggested that the last sentence of Article 106(2) TFEU is in fact a clarification of the proportionality of the restrictive effects of any measure otherwise contrary to the Treaty rules, thus meaning that the provision as a whole has direct effect.[44]

Undertakings that have been granted a special or an exclusive right by the State on the basis of Article 106(1) TFEU, or which fulfil a task of general economic interest on the basis of Article 106(2) TFEU, must conduct their activities according to special accounting requirements laid down by the so-called 'Financial Transparency Directive'.[45] The goal of these requirements is to avoid such undertakings from obtaining a competitive advantage by means of subsidies (on which see our discussion of State aid in section 7.5 below) or by cross-subsidisation. Cross-subsidisation refers to operating in the unregulated sector by using profits made from the sector in which the undertaking holds special or exclusive rights to operate.[46]

7.2.1.4 Article 106(3) TFEU

Article 106(3) TFEU makes the Commission responsible for the enforcement of Articles 106(1) and (2) TFEU and provides a legal basis for the Commission to adopt directives and decisions. This is one of very few Treaty provisions that grant the Commission primary legislative power. The Commission can therefore adopt directives and decisions itself in this area.[47] The 2012 Decision mentioned above in section 7.2.1.1 is an example of the exercise of the Commission's legislative powers. The Commission can also adopt individual decisions addressed to Member States dealing with specific infringements. This can occur on the Commission's own initiative (perhaps in response to information provided or a complaint made by another undertaking) or as a result of (what the Commission considers to be) an incorrect application of the

---

[41] Case 127/73 *BRT v SABAM*.

[42] Case C-260/89 *ERT v Dimotiki*, para 34 and Case 393/92 *Almelo*, para 50.

[43] See, eg, R Whish and D Bailey, *Competition Law*, 8th edn (Oxford, Oxford University Press, 2015), 253.

[44] For discussion and references, see J-L Buendia Sierra, *State Intervention and EU Competition Law* (Oxford, Oxford University Press, 2013), paras 8.262–8.299.

[45] Directive 2013/50 [2013] OJ L294/13.

[46] See further L Hancher and J-L Buendia Sierra, 'Cross-subsidisation and EC Law' (1998) 35 *Common Market Law Review* 901 and GB Abbamonte, 'Cross-subsidisation and Community Competition Rules: Efficient Pricing v Equity?' (1998) 23 *European Law Review* 414. See further Zhijun Chen and Patrick Rey: 'CompetitiveCross-Subsidization' http://fbe.unimelb.edu.au/__data/assets/pdf_file/0010/1049644/Zhijun_Chen.pdf.

[47] See the Decision adopted by the Commission mentioned in section 7.2.1.1.

exemption by a national court. Where the reliance upon the exception is made by a Member State, the Commission must direct itself to that Member State (for which no specific procedural framework exists, other than the need for the Commission to give reasons for its approach, as per Article 296 TFEU). Where an undertaking relies upon the exemption, the Commission must direct its action toward that undertaking, on the basis of its normal competences as laid down by Regulation 1/2003/EC (discussed in Chapter 6).

The Commission has adopted several decisions under this provision,[48] such as, for example, its essential facilities-based Decision in *Port of Rødby*.[49] The Commission has also adopted Directives under Article 106(3) TFEU, such as those on telecommunications equipment[50] and on telecommunication services.[51] However, note that Article 106(3) TFEU is not intended to be used for the adoption of pure harmonisation measures—these require a basis under Article 114 TFEU and joint adoption by the Council and the European Parliament under the ordinary legislative procedure of Article 294 TFEU.

Can disgruntled parties seek a judicial review of the Commission's actions under Article 106(3) TFEU? The addressee of any formal decision will clearly have standing under Article 263 TFEU to bring such an action for annulment.[52] The ECJ has also held that:

> exceptional situations might exist where an individual or, possibly, an association constituted for the defence of the collective interests of a class of individuals has standing to bring proceedings against a refusal by the Commission to adopt a decision pursuant to its supervisory functions under Article [106](1) and (3) [TFEU].[53]

This is because the Commission's action could be shown to have been of direct and individual concern to the applicant under the Article 263 TFEU criteria.[54] However, these actions are unlikely to succeed, due both to the ECJ's unwillingness to characterise the Commission's refusal to take action under Article 106(3) TFEU as a measure producing binding legal effects[55] and to the wide discretion afforded to the Commission in making its assessments in this area.[56]

---

[48] See the Website of DG Comp.

[49] [1994] OJ L55/52, [1994] 5 CMLR 457.

[50] Directive 88/301/EEC [1988] OJ L131/73.

[51] Directive 90/388 [1990] OJ L131/73.

[52] Case T-54/99 *Max.mobil Telekommunikation Service v Commission*, paras 64–72. While the CFI's characterisation of the measure in the case itself was overturned on appeal by the ECJ (Case C-141/02 P *Commission v T-Mobile Austria*, the validity of this general point on standing still holds.

[53] Case C-107/95 P *Bundesverband der Bilanzbuchhalter v Commission*, para 25.

[54] On standing to make such applications under Art 263 TFEU, see generally PP Craig and G de Búrca, *EU Law: Text, Cases, and Materials*, 5th edn (Oxford, Oxford University Press, 2011), ch 14.5; A Albors-Llorens, 'The Standing of Private Parties to Challenge Community Measures: Has the European Court Missed the Boat?' (2003) *Cambridge Law Journal* 72; and JA Usher, 'Direct and Individual Concern—an Effective Remedy or a Conventional Solution?' (2003) 28 *European Law Review* 575.

[55] Thus meaning that it did not amount to a reviewable act under Art 230 EC, now Art 263 TFEU: Case C-141/02 P *Commission v T-Mobile Austria*, para 70.

[56] See the comments of the ECJ in the *Bilanzbuchhalter* case (n 53, above, para 27) and the CFI in its *Max.mobil* judgment (n 52, above, paras 58–59).

7.2.2 The Rules for Public Undertakings Under UK Law

The UK provision laying down the exclusion from the operation of the competition rules for services of general economic interest is to be found in found in section 3 read together with schedule 3, paragraph 4 of the CA 1998. The substance of the exclusion is in paragraph 4 of schedule 3, which provides:

> Neither the Chapter I prohibition nor the Chapter II prohibition applies to an undertaking entrusted with the operation of services of general economic interest or having the character of a revenue-producing monopoly in so far as the prohibition would obstruct the performance, in law or in fact, of the particular tasks assigned to that undertaking.

This provision effectively replicates that found in Article 106 TFEU, albeit that the UK provision is more simply phrased and omits the requirement that the development of trade must not be affected contrary to the interests of the Union.

The OFT has published a *Guideline on the Services of General Economic Interest Exclusion*,[57] while the guidelines adopted by the various sectoral regulators have also considered the application of the exclusion.[58] To date, however, there has been little practice in the UK specific to this exclusion: in the decisions that have been taken by the OFT, ORR, Ofgem and Ofcom where the exclusion might have been relevant, the relevant agency has either found no breach of the CA 1998[59] or has concluded that any restriction of competition could be objectively justified.[60]

One key issue raised in the practice thus far has been whether or not a given entity counts as an 'undertaking' for the purposes of the CA 1998 (on which see Chapter 2.1.1 above). The mixture of public and private operators in some fields raises questions of competition law, necessitating an answer to the question whether or not an entity amounts to an 'undertaking'. This is illustrated well by the *BetterCare* case, where, in certain respects, the position adopted by the Competition Commission Appeal Tribunal (as the Competition Appeal Tribunal was then known) diverged from that taken by the GC (at the time the CFI) in FENIN. BetterCare provided residential care and nursing home services in Northern Ireland. While the North & West Belfast Health & Social Services Trust bought those services from BetterCare in some areas, it managed its own facilities for residential care in others (where it recouped some of the costs from the residents of its care facilities). BetterCare alleged that the Trust was abusing its dominant position by extracting unfairly low prices and unfair terms in its contracts with BetterCare. This raised the important preliminary question of whether or not the Trust was an 'undertaking' under the CA 1998, and the CCAT rejected

---

[57] OFT 421.

[58] See, eg, Ofgem, *Application in the Energy Sector* (OFT 428), paras 3.34–3.38.

[59] eg OFT Decision CA98/09/2003, *BetterCare Group Ltd/North & West Belfast Health & Social Services Trust* (18 December 2003); Director General of Telecommunications Decision, *BT Broadband* (11 July 2003); Ofgem Decision, *United Utilities plc* (17 December 2004); and Director General of Water Services Decision CA98/01/2003 *Thames Water Utilities/Bath House and Albion Yard* (31 March 2003).

[60] eg Rail Regulator's Decision, *Suretrack Rail Services Ltd and P Way Services Ltd complaint against London Underground Group concerning the supply of safety critical personnel* (23 June 2004): objective justification of alleged restrictions on grounds of safety. For a recent court case in which the issue has been raised but not ruled upon (due to the case concerning an application to strike out an amendment of claim, rather than being a full trial of the action), see *Attheraces Ltd v BHB Ltd* [2005] EWHC 1553 (Ch), esp [58]–[60].

the DGFT's view[61] (the forerunner of the OFT) and held instead that the Trust did carry out economic activities such as to render it an undertaking for the purposes of the CA 1998.[62] As a result, the case was remitted to the DGFT to reach a decision on the substance of the allegation. Upon remission, it was finally decided that no abuse of a dominant position had been perpetrated by the Trust, while not reaching a firm position on whether or not the Trust was an undertaking.

In the light of this case, the OFT has since issued a number of Policy Notes[63] and Guidelines on public bodies and competition law.[64] In its latest guidance, the CMA (which has adopted the OFT's guidance on Public Bodies and competition law) recalls that as a matter of both EU and UK law, the focus of the assessment of whether a body is an undertaking is on the nature of the particular activity undertaken, not the nature of the body that undertakes it. As such:

(a) The term 'undertaking' can apply equally to public sector bodies and not-for-profit bodies, as well as to private sector bodies. Public authorities, State-controlled enterprises, charities, etc all fall within the definition of an undertaking, if they are carrying on an economic activity.

(b) The legal form of the body in question is also irrelevant to the question of whether it acts as an undertaking. A body need not, for example, be an incorporated company in order to be an undertaking.

(c) The fact that a body is intended to be non-profit making will not, of itself, be sufficient to deprive it of its status as an undertaking.

Furthermore, and taking account of the ECJ's ruling on appeal in *FENIN*,[65] the 'functional' approach towards the definition of 'undertaking' means that a public body may act as an undertaking—and therefore be subject to competition law—in respect of some of its activities, but not in respect of others. In this respect, the CMA comments that a public body should ask itself the following questions for each of its activities separately:

(a) Am I offering or supplying a good or service, as opposed to, for example, exercising a public power?

(b) If so, is that offer or supply of a 'commercial'—rather than an exclusively 'social'—nature?

If the answer to both these questions is yes, then—for the purposes of that activity (and any related upstream purchasing)—the CMA considers that the public body is likely to be regarded as an undertaking subject to UK and EU competition law. In this

[61] DGFT Decision CA/98/11/2002, *North & West Belfast Health & Social Services Trust* (30 April 2002).

[62] *BetterCare Group Ltd v DGFT* [2002] CAT 7, paras 163–277. See the discussion of the *BetterCare* saga by B Rodger, CLaSF Working Paper No 01 (September 2003).

[63] OFT, Policy note 1/2004 (OFT 443, January 2004).

[64] *Public Bodies and Competition Law: A Guide to the Application of the Competition Act 1998* (OFT 1389, December 2011).

[65] See in particular fn 34 of the OFT's Guidance *Public Bodies and Competition Law* (OFT 1389, December 2011).

way, the CMA's practice has been brought into line with the ECJ's ruling in both *AOK Bundesverband* and *FENIN*.[66]

Beyond this issue, the remainder of the UK provisions in this area follow closely the model of Article 106(2) TFEU and the case law that has developed thereunder. Thus, it must be shown that the undertaking was entrusted with the service in question and that this was done by a public authority in a sufficiently formal manner (legislation, regulation, licence governed by public law) (OFT 421, paragraphs 2.9–15). Equally, the existence of such an obligation in one limited area of the undertaking's activities does not imply that the exclusion from the prohibitions of the CA 1998 extends to other activities (OFT 421, paragraphs 2.13–14).

Assuming that the obligation in question can be categorised as one for the provision of services of general economic interest (OFT 421, paragraphs 2.16–22), there remains the question of how far the exclusion can permit restrictions upon competition (OFT 421, paragraphs 3.1–3.8). On this point, it seems clear that the CMA intends strictly to scrutinise any claim in reliance of the exclusion: it intends to apply what appears to be a strong proportionality test to assess whether the obligations could be discharged in ways less restrictive of competition (OFT 421, paragraphs 3.2 and 3.8). The CMA is clear in its guidance that it will interpret the exclusions strictly, and that they will generally be applicable in only a limited number of circumstances, particularly in light of the significant privatisation and liberalisation in the UK, which has significantly reduced the number of services where a single body has been entrusted with the exclusive right to provide the relevant service (OFT 1389, paragraph 3.3). This will include an exacting burden and standard of proof being placed upon the undertaking seeking to rely upon the exclusion, with an expectation that the result of applying the competition law prohibition(s) would 'necessarily result in economically unacceptable conditions', not merely that there is a 'mere possibility' of such an outcome (OFT 421, paragraph 3.7).

7.3 The Norm of Article 4(3) TEU and Articles 101 or 102 TFEU[67]

The policy of the governments of EU Member States always has a big influence upon the economy. This also holds for policies that are not specifically directed at market

---

[66] OFT's guidance Public Bodies and competition law (OFT 1389, December 2011), ss 2.1–2.8. The CMA's guidance continues by providing more detailed guidance on each of the above elements at ss 2.9–2.27, in which it recalls and relies on the principal case law of the Union courts in this area.

[67] The norm is sometimes referred to as the State Action Doctrine (SAD) the term which is common in US Antitrust law. In its judgment in *Parker v Brown* 317 US 341 (1943) the Supreme Court held that a scheme adopted by the State for regulating the handling, disposition, and prices of raisins produced in

behaviour, such as environmental policy. The actions of government can thus operate as a clear influence upon competitive relations. In this connection, it is also important to appreciate that the establishment of a 'system ensuring that competition in the internal market is not distorted' is one of the key goals and activities of the EU. This principle was enshrined in Article 3(1)(g) EC. After the entry into force of the Lisbon Treaty it is laid down in Protocol 27 to this Treaty. Although competition law is directed at undertakings, the behaviour of the State cannot simply be dismissed from any picture of a system of healthy competition. From these starting points, the ECJ has sought to find a solution that will allow the behaviour of Member State governments to be tested against the principles of undistorted competition, while acknowledging that Member States are entitled to pursue domestic economic and social policy goals. In the case of *van Eyke v Aspa*, the relevant EU law norm was formulated as follows:

> The Court has consistently held, however, that Articles 101 and 102 TFEU, in conjunction with Article 4(3) TEU, require the Member States not to introduce or maintain in force measures, even of a legislative nature, which may render ineffective the competition rules applicable to undertakings. Such would be the case, the Court has held, if a Member State were to require or favour the adoption of agreements, decisions or concerted practices contrary to Article 101 TFEU or to reinforce their effects, or to deprive its own legislation of its official character by delegating to private traders responsibility for taking decisions affecting the economic sphere.[68]

Although the second sentence of this quotation seems to be indicative only (in its reference to collusion under Article 101 TFEU), it should be noted that the case law has not extended the relevant category of behaviour any further. On the contrary, in a series of judgments the ECJ has expressly refused to extend the category of Member State activity to include measures that create the same effects as cartels.[69]

The first form of State activity listed by the ECJ in *van Eycke* is the imposition of cartels. It would seem that the ECJ has yet to find a Member State measure to have fallen foul of this limb of the norm, although some of the cases could have been analysed in this manner.[70] One possible scenario might be where a State requires undertakings to conclude some form of covenant as a condition for the adoption of legislation or of making subsidies available.

California, was not within the intended scope of, and not a violation of, the Sherman Act. According to the US case law Governmental action pursuing the public interest does not violate the antitrust laws if it is clearly articulated and actively supervised. The Government action should have been clearly articulated. See the judgment of US Supreme Court in *FTC v Phoebe Putney* 568 US 2013. Whenever applicable, the doctrine exonerates actions by undertakings.

[68] Case 267/86 *Van Eycke v ASPA NV*, para 16.

[69] Cases C-245/91 *Criminal proceedings against OHRA Schadeverzekeringen NV*, C-185/91 *Bundesanstalt für der Güterfernverkehr v Gebruder Reiff GmbH & Co KG* and C-2/91 *Criminal proceedings against Wolf W. Meng* respectively. The Report for the Hearing in Case C-2/91 *Meng et seq* contains an extensive overview of the discussion between the ECJ and the Member States on extending the scope of this norm. See further N Reich, 'The "November Revolution" of the European Court of Justice: *Keck, Meng* and *Audi* revisited' (1994) 31 *Common Market Law Review* 459.

[70] eg Joined Cases 209 to 213/84 *Ministère Public v Asjes* and Case 136/86 *Bureau national interprofessionnel du cognac (BNIC) v Aubert*: in both cases there was significant evidence that could have been treated in this way. In *Asjes*, the Member State had showed a strong preference that tariffs should be fixed by agreement among the airlines, while in *BNIC v Aubert* it was French legislation that had set up BNIC as a forum for the exchange of ideas and information on cognac production, including quotas, prices and quality. See L

The second form of State activity concerns the encouragement of collusive practices or the reinforcement of their effects. This was at issue in the *Asjes* case.[71] Prior to the liberalisation of air transport in the EU, it was common for the airlines to set tariffs collectively in the context of IATA, the air transport association. After the general meeting of IATA, the agreement reached on tariffs would then be presented to the government. In many Member States the minister of transport then ensured that the tariffs and other terms and conditions were adopted in the form of legislation. The ECJ ruled in *Asjes* that such behaviour on the part of the Member State ran contrary to its duties under the norm of Articles 4(3) TEU and Article 101 TFEU.

The third form of impermissible State behaviour under this heading concerns the delegation of rule-making competences by the State to private entities. An example of this can be found in the situation that led to the *Reiff* judgment.[72] In Germany the tariffs for the carriage of goods by road are set by a tariff commission and are subsequently approved by a published order by the Minister of Transport, at which point they become binding upon the relevant undertakings. In the judgment itself, the issue was whether or not this tariff commission had a sufficient governmental element that its activities could be characterised as the State exercising its own authority. If the tariff commission was nothing more than a group of representatives from private commercial interests, the representatives of which then set the relevant tariffs, then the Member State would have delegated its rule-making powers, which would have breached EU law. The ECJ held that in this case the government had provided sufficient guarantees to ensure that the tariff commission acted in the public interest. These guarantees consisted in the fact that the members of the commission who were drawn from the commercial sphere were not treated as representatives of the various trade organisations. Further, there was a representative of the Minister present at all meetings of the tariff commission. Also, the Minister had the power under the relevant legislation to reject the tariffs proposed by the commission and instead to set the tariffs himself. Finally, when making their proposals the members of the tariff commission were required expressly to take into account other important interests (including the agricultural sector, medium-sized undertakings and those regions which were economically weak or which had inadequate transport facilities).[73] In parallel, the Minister had been charged by the legislation with the duty of harmonising tariffs to avoid unfair competition between different modes of transport. This system ensured the compatibility of the tariff-setting process with EU law.

In the case concerning *Italian customs agents*,[74] both the Commission and the ECJ took the view that the members of the National Council of Customs Agents could not be viewed as independent experts but rather acted as representatives of professional customs agents. As a result, the mandatory tariffs set for the services of customs

---

Gyselen, 'Anti-Competitive State Measures under the EC Treaty: Towards a Substantive Legalist Standard' (1993) *European Law Review Supplement* (Competition Law Checklist) CC55, esp at CC58.

[71] Joined Cases 209 to 213/84 *Ministère Public v Asjes* (also known as the '*Nouvelle Frontières*' case).
[72] Case C-185/91 *Bundesanstalt für der Güterfernverkehr v Gebruder Reiff GmbH & Co KG* (see esp paras 16–24).
[73] See the extensive discussion of these factors in the Opinion of AG Darmon (ibid). His opinion provides a very useful overview of the important elements to take into account when developing national regulation in which commercial parties are to be given a significant role in the rule-making process.
[74] Case C-35/96 *Commission v Italy*.

agents by that National Council amounted to prices set by a cartel. Thus, the Italian legislation that gave these tariffs the force of law was held to run contrary to the norm of Articles 4(3) TEU and 101 and 102 TFEU. As the *Wouters* judgment demonstrates such rules are not prohibited if the purpose is to promote an important public policy objective. This case concerned a prohibition of multi-disciplinary partnerships of members of the Bar and accountants. The Court held that the ethical rules (rules to ensure the proper practice of the legal profession) set by the Bar of the Netherlands are not decisions of undertakings contrary to Article 101 TFEU.[75] Consequently, the Court declined to answer the question whether the Dutch government had infringed the rule of Articles 4(3) TEU and 101 and 102 TFEU.

The ECJ has in several other judgments held that agreements entered into within the framework of collective bargaining between employers and employees and intended to improve employment and working conditions must, by virtue of their nature and purpose, be regarded as not falling within the scope of Article 101(1) TFEU.[76]

From a national law perspective, the question is whether or not this norm is applicable in the UK legal order. The ECJ's judgment in the *CIF* case[77] has clarified that this norm must be applied by the national courts and by the CMA as well as the NCAs of the other Member States. It is more difficult to state with certainty whether or not the norm is applicable where there is no effect on trade between Member States (ie, where neither Articles 101 nor 102 TFEU are applicable): will section 60 CA 1998 lead to the parallel adoption of a similar approach under UK competition law? The first point to note is that it *will* often be possible to show an effect upon inter-Member State trade: in the *Italian customs agents* case the ECJ relied upon the case law relating to the compartmentalisation of national markets as 'by its very nature' having an effect upon trade. Where EU law per se is genuinely not at issue and national law is the only determining factor, it would seem that it is unlikely that UK law would develop a similar norm that constrained government activity in the absence of any reference to this point by the legislation. Further, there is no mention of the norm in any of the CMA's Guidelines on the UK legislation. Finally, early practice in other Member States would seem to suggest similar hostility to such incorporation by extension from the EU case law.[78] Thus, it is submitted that such a development is highly unlikely in UK competition law.

---

[75] C-309/99 *Wouters*, para 109. See also Chapter 3.2.4.1.

[76] Joined Cases C-115 to 117/97 *Brentjens' Handelsonderneming v Stichting Bedrijfspensioenfonds*, para 57; Case C-219/97 *Maatschappij Drijvende Bokken v Stichting Pensioenfonds*, para 47; Joined Cases C-180/98 to C-184/98 *Pavlov and Others*, para 67; and Case C-222/98 *van der Woude*, para 22). In its judgment in Case C-413/13 *FNV Kunsten Informatie en Media* the ECJ concluded that a provision of a collective labour agreement, in so far as it sets minimum fees for service providers who are 'false self-employed', cannot, by reason of its nature and purpose, be subject to the application of Art 101 TFEU.

[77] Case C-198/01 *Consorzio Industrie Fiammiferi v Garante della Concorrenza e del Mercato* (discussed by J Temple Lang, 'National Measures Restricting Competition and National Authorities under Article 10 EC' (2004) 29 *European Law Review* 397).

[78] See the decision of the Commercial Court of Appeal in the Dutch case of *Nederland FM en Arrow v Staatssecretaris* (27 February 2002, AWB 99/1039 and 99/1053), where the Court summarily dismissed the argument made by analogy with the norm of Arts 3(1)(g), 10 and 81 EC.

7.4 How to Assess Mixed Situations?

7.4.1 The Joint Operation of the Rules

In the previous paragraphs we have looked at the conduct of governments and undertakings in so-called 'mixed situations', that is to say: situations where either undertakings acted in the context of government influence or where governments acted in concert with business. This can be contrasted with the situation where it is clear that *either* the actions of the government *or* those of the undertakings are the subject of scrutiny. It may be useful to summarise the joint operation of these different rules.

This is illustrated by an example from the health care industry, which was the subject of the *AOK-Bundesverband* case.[79] The case deals with the specific but often recurring question about the power of the Member States to prescribe prices. More specifically, it analyses the questions of whether and to what extent the fixing of maximum prices for which reimbursement will be made for drugs by health care organisations is contrary to Articles 101, 102 and 106 TFEU.[80] The relevant national law provided that the Federal Association of health care organisations and physicians were to decide the categories of drugs for which maximum prices will be fixed.[81] These prices represent the maximum that will be reimbursed to members of the health care organisations for drugs they buy after seeing their physician. This necessarily involves an analysis of the health insurance system in Germany as laid down in the relevant legislation, as well as of the conduct of the health care organisations and of the German government.

There are basically six steps that are relevant.

(1) EU competition law is only applicable where undertakings are involved. This concept is discussed in Chapter 2.1.1 above.

(2) It is necessary to examine whether the nature and purpose of an agreement fall within the scope of Article 101(1) TFEU, and if so, whether Article 101(3) TFEU applies.[82] As discussed in section 7.3, agreements entered into within the framework of collective bargaining between employers and employees and intended to improve employment and working conditions must, by virtue of their nature and purpose, be regarded as not falling within the scope of Article 101(1) TFEU.

(3) When the prohibition of Article 101(1) TFEU is applicable (and the Article 101(3) TFEU criteria are not met) it has to be assessed whether the national legislation precludes the undertakings from engaging in autonomous conduct. If so they will

---

[79] Joined Cases C-264, 306, 354, 355/01, See PJ Slot, 'Applying the competition Rules in the Healthcare sector' (2003) 24(11) *European Competition Law Review* 580–593. The *BUPA judgment* provides another interesting example; Case T-289/03 *British United Provident Association Ltd (BUPA) and BUPA Ireland v Commission.*

[80] Referred to hereinafter as 'maximum prices'.

[81] Sozialgesetzbuch, Fünftes Buch (Social Code, pt V).

[82] Case C-437/09, *AG2R Prévoyance v Beaudout Père et Fils SARL*, para 30.

be exonerated from the prohibition of Article 101(1) TFEU. This is the effect of the *Ladbroke* judgment.[83]

(4) If the relevant legislation does not leave scope for autonomous conduct the legislation itself could be contrary to Article 106(1) TEU or to the rule laid down in the ECJ's case law on Articles 4(3) TEU and 101 or 102 TFEU. If that is the case, the government could be liable for its infringements of EU law. If the legislation were to be considered incompatible with the rule of Articles 106(1) TFEU or Articles 4(3) TEU and 101 and/or 102 TFEU, the liability of the undertakings would be activated from the moment that it was clear to them that they are no longer shielded by the *Ladbroke* rule. This was clarified in the *CIF* judgment.[84]

(5) If conditions 1 and 2 are satisfied and the *Ladbroke* condition does not apply, it has to be assessed whether or not the acts of the undertakings may nevertheless benefit from the exception of Article 106(2) TFEU.

(6) It could be asked whether, assuming that the legislation is incompatible with the rule of Articles 4(3) TEU with 101 and/or 102 TFEU, it would be possible to save the otherwise illegal conduct of the legislator under Article 106(2) TFEU. The reason for this is that the norm of Article 106(1) TFEU is addressed at similar types of anticompetitive behaviour as the norm of Articles 4(3) TEU with 101 and/or 102 TFEU. Whereas Article 106(1) TFEU addresses the granting of special or exclusive rights, the rule of Article 4(3) TEU with 101 and/or 102 TFEU addresses all types of interference with competition by governments.

The ECJ has never ruled that Article 106(2) TFEU can exempt government rules that infringe Articles 4(3) TEU with 101 and/or 102 TFEU.[85] It would also seem that even if such an argument were—in principle—to be accepted, the specific facts of the *AOK Bundesverband* would strongly argue against the application of such an exemption. The glaring absence of proper procedural safeguards against the fixing of maximum prices would exclude its application because the principle of proportionality was manifestly not observed by the German legislator.

---

[83] C-359 and 379/95P *Commission and France v Ladbroke Racing Ltd*, para 34.

[84] Case C-198/01 *Consorzio Industrie Fiammiferi (CIF) v Garante della Concorrenza e del Mercato*.

[85] There has been a reference to such a justification in the questions that the ECJ addressed to the governments during proceedings in the *Meng* case (n 69, above). The questions and the answers by the Member States are reported in the Report for the hearing: Case C-2/91. Advocate General Jacobs argued, in para 85 of his Opinion in Joined Cases C-264, 306, 354 and 355/01 *AOK-Bundesverband*, that Art [106(2) TFEU] can exonerate the conduct of governments under the norm of Articles [4(3) TEU and Article 101 TFEU]. It should be noted that the ECJ in Case C-379/98 *PreussenElektra*, rejected the application of that norm in the field of state aid. The ECJ held, in paras 64 and 65, that: 'In that respect, it is sufficient to point out that, unlike Art [101] of the Treaty, which concerns only the conduct of undertakings, Art [107] of the Treaty refers directly to measures emanating from the Member States. In those circumstances, Art [107] of the Treaty is in itself sufficient to prohibit the conduct by States referred to therein and Art [4(3)] of the [TEU], the second paragraph of which provides that Member States are to abstain from any measure which could jeopardise the attainment of the objectives of the Treaty, cannot be used to extend the scope of Art 107 conduct by States that does not fall within it'. It could well be argued that similar reasons would lead to the rejection of the application of Art [106(2) TFEU] for exonerating governmental conduct falling foul of the norm of Arts [4(3) TEU and Article 101 TFEU]. Advocate General Jacobs seems to include an analysis of the norm of Arts [4(3) TEU and Article 101 TFEU] in his analysis of Art [106(2) TFEU]: see, in particular, para 97 et seq.

7.4.2 Evaluation: Are Governments Limited in Their Pursuit of General Interests?

The discussion of the rules of competition law and the State may leave the reader with the impression that governments are seriously restricted in their economic policy choices when operating on the market involving undertakings. Such an impression would be wrong.[86]

Governments have ample discretion to conduct their economic policies and whether or not to involve undertakings. First, as follows from the discussion of the concept of undertaking in Chapter 2.1.1, governments decide which activities they will control themselves and which they will leave to the market. Secondly, they are also, under the free movement rules of the Treaty, free to assume full ownership or control of undertakings. The main constraint is that they cannot have their cake and eat it too. Article 345 TFEU[87] does not shield them from the application of the free movement rules nor does it provide a justificatory ground in addition to the well-known category of free movement exceptions.

Thirdly, even when activities are established as market operations, Article 106 TFEU as interpreted by the ECJ allows Member States a considerable margin to establish SGEIs and to grant them exclusive or special rights for operating such services. The case law under Article 106(2) TFEU also allows governments a considerable margin for laying down the relevant parameters. Moreover, Article 106(2) TFEU grants the undertakings entrusted with SGEIs ample room to fulfill their special tasks. Fourthly, the norm of Articles 4(3) TEU, and 101 and 102 TFEU has not evolved into a general rule limiting governmental actions whenever they have an effect on competition. This is partly the result of the case law of the ECJ which refused to extend the norm to national rules restricting competition when such rules are adopted without having been preceded by an agreement.[88] The norm of Articles 4(3) TEU, and 101 and 102 TFEU has not led to many cases where governments are censured for their behaviour.[89] The law as it stands on this norm only prohibits egregious cases of governmental interference by means of actions of undertakings.

Reviewing the case law on Article 106 TFEU and the combination of Article 4(3) TEU, and Articles 101 and 102 TFEU, one could say that the evolution of this part of EU law has greatly increased the possibilities for governments to run SGEIs. This is also the result of the clearer delineation of competences following the Lisbon Treaty.[90]

---

[86] See PJ Slot, 'Public Distortions of Competition: The Importance of Article 106 TFEU and the State Action Doctrine' in U Neergaard, E Szyszczak, JW Van de Gronden and M Krajewski (eds), *Social Services of General Interest in the EU* (Springer 2013) 245–262.

[87] Art 345 reads: 'The provisions of the Treaties shall in no way prejudice the rules in Member States governing the system of property ownership.' This provision allows Member States to decide whether or not they want to keep or establish ownership of the means of production.

[88] Case C-2/91, *Meng*; Case C-245/91, *Ohra*; Case C-185/91, *Reiff*. See N Reich, '"The November Revolution" of the European Court of Justice: *Keck, Meng and Audi* Revisited' 31 *Common Market Law Review*, 1994 459.

[89] See R Wainwright and A Boucquet, 'State Intervention and Action in EC Competition Law' in Barry Hawk (ed, 2004) *Annual Proceedings of the Fordham Corporate Law Institute: International Antitrust Law & Policy* (2003) 539–579, at p 551.

[90] PJ Slot in Neergaard, *Public Distortions of Competition—The Importance of Article 106 TFEU and the State Action Doctrine* (see n 86).

7.5 EU State Aid Law: A General Introduction

7.5.1 Introduction

For a long time, EU State aid law was the poor relation of EU competition law. Whereas competition law was widely practised and the subject of many books and articles, State aid law was largely neglected. How times have changed. State aid law has become a major subject in its own right.[91] Massive amounts of state aids are granted by Member States eager to protect the world wide competiveness of their industries. State aid is also an important element in furthering social and regional objectives. The apogee of this development is now reflected in the recent spectacular Commission decisions in the banking sector. Huge amounts of State aid have been authorised by the Commission sometimes in less than a week.[92] The Commission provides an annual overview of the State aid granted by Member States.[93]

Article 107 TFEU, which lays down the substantive rules on State aid, and Article 108 TFEU, which provides for the procedural rules, form part of the chapter on competition in the TFEU. The guiding concept of the rules on State aids is found in Protocol (No 27) to the Lisbon Treaty on the internal market and competition. The text of this Protocol is identical to Article 4(3) TEU—a system ensuring that competition in the internal market is not distorted. This is reflected in the case law of the ECJ and in numerous Commission decisions. Unlike Articles 101 and 102 TFEU, the rules on State aid have taken shape only slowly. Until the end of the 1990s, the major developments took place in the decisional practice of the Commission and in the case law of the ECJ (and latterly the CFI), rather than in the form of legislation: indeed, there was very little legislation in the State aid field.[94]

However, there are now several important pieces of legislation. The first is Council Regulation 2015/1588, which applies Articles 107 and 108 TFEU.[95] The effect of the Regulation is that the Commission is authorised to adopt block exemptions for certain categories of aid. On this basis the Commission has adopted a number of regulations, which will be discussed in section 7.5.2.6 below.

---

[91] *cf* W Mederer, N Paresi and M van Hoof, *EU Competition Law, Volume IV State Aid* (Leuven, Claeys & Casteels, 2008); *EC State Aid Law: Liber Amicorum Francisco Santaolalla Gadea* (Wolters Kluwer, 2008); L Hancher, T Ottervanger and PJ Slot, *EU State Aids*, 5th edn (2016); C Quigley, *European State Aid Law and Policy*, 3rd edn (Oxford, Hart Publishing, 2015).

[92] A very useful overview is provided in the Commission Staff Working paper: 'The effects of temporary State aid rules adopted in the context of the financial and economic crisis', SEC (2011) 1126 final Brussels 5 October 2011.

[93] See the State Aid score board published on the website of DG COMP. The latest score is on 2015; see also Commission Staff working document: 'Facts and figures on state aid in the EU Member States', SEC (2011) 1487, 01.12.2011.

[94] The only legislation was in field of shipbuilding where there have been several directives succeeded by Reg 1540/98/EC [1998] OJ L202/1.

[95] [2015] OJ L248/1.

The most important Council regulation is Regulation 2015/1589[96] repealing Regulation 659/1999,[97] which lays down detailed rules for the application of Article 108 TFEU, ie, the procedural rules which will be discussed in section 7.5.3. Regulation 659/1999 was largely a codification of the case law of the ECJ and the GC.

The substantive rules have been developed in the case law of the ECJ and the GC. These rules have contributed greatly to the clarification of the main concepts of Article 107(1) TFEU. In addition, the Commission enacted regulations and published other instruments called guidelines, frameworks, notifications or communications.[98] These rules have been further developed in the many decisions given by the Commission in individual cases.

7.5.2 Material Principles

The structure of Article 107 TFEU is not unlike that of Article 101 TFEU. Therefore, a systematic analysis of the different elements contained in this Article will be useful, as it is for Article 101 TFEU. The following four criteria must be satisfied if the prohibition of Article 107 TFEU is to bite: the existence of 'State aid' must be shown, it must operate in a 'selective' manner, and there must be an effect upon both competition and trade between the Member States. We will now examine each of these criteria in turn.

7.5.2.1 The Concept of 'State Aid'[99]

The Treaty is silent on the matter of definition, but the case law of the ECJ has made it clear that the concept of 'aid' is wider than that of a subsidy.[100] The definition is in fact very wide. The outer limit was defined in *Sloman Neptune*:[101] only benefits granted directly or indirectly out of state resources are to be regarded as state aid. In its *PreussenElektra* judgment, the Court held that the charges levied by the state on private companies in order to finance environmental objectives were not to

---

[96] [2015] OJ L 248/9.

[97] [1999] OJ L 83/1.

[98] *cf* Commission, *Competition Law in the European Communities, I: Rules Applicable to State Aids, Situation at 1 February*, 2014. Available at: http://ec.europa.eu/competition/state_aid/legislation/compilation/state_aid_01_02_14_en.pdf. The terminology is not very consistent: the central feature of all of these rules is that they are not adopted on the basis of an article in the Treaty or secondary legislation.

[99] An extensive analysis of this concept is provided by L Rubini, *The Definition of Subsidy and State aid. WTO en EC Law in Comparative Perspective* (Oxford, Oxford University Press, 2009, reprint 2011). Juan Jorge Piernas Lopez, *The Concept of State Aid under EU Law. From internal market to competition and beyond* (Oxford, Oxford University Press, 2015). In May 2016 the Commission published a draft communication: 'Commission Notice on the notion of State aid as referred to in Article 107(1) TFEU.' The Notice provides an extensive (68 pages) and useful summary of the case law.

[100] Case 30/59 *De Gezamenlijke Steenkolenmijnen in Limburg v High Authority of the ECSC*, at 19, recently confirmed in Case C-387/92 *Banco de Crédito Industrial SA, now Banco Exterior de España SA v Ayuntamiento de Valencia*.

[101] Cases C-72/91 and C-73/91 *Sloman Neptune*.

be treated as State aid measures.[102] In the *Association Vent De Colère* judgment, which involved similar charges, the ECJ found that since they were managed by a body under public control they constituted state resources.[103] Nevertheless, this still leaves a broad range of benefits covered by the scope of Article 107 TFEU: direct subsidies, interest subsidies, low interest, interest-free loans, capital injections, grants, asset revaluation, compensation for government-imposed financial burdens, the foregoing of recovery of sums due, preferential terms, price reductions, public supply contracts, reduction in social security charges, state guarantees,[104] state participation in capital tax concessions, and the foregoing of state revenue.

The Court's case law in this area has undergone a further development as a result of the *Altmark* judgment, as discussed above in section 7.2.1.1.

The aid must be effected by a Member State or through state resources. An example of the latter is the preferential tariff accorded to the fertiliser industry by the Dutch gas company, Gasunie.[105] In the *Stardust Marine* case the ECJ held that although the French government owned 80 per cent of the shares of the company, the Commission should in addition establish that the actions of the company could be imputed to the government. Since this was not the case the transfers from the company could not be assessed under the State aid rules.[106] The *Stardust Marine* rule is particularly important now that governments have often acquired control of undertakings as a result of rescue operations during the credit crisis. Without this rule many actions such as the provision of credit by banks would have to be screened under the State aid rules.[107]

7.5.2.2 Selectivity

The prohibition under Article 107 TFEU does not apply if all undertakings within a Member State benefit from assistance without any distinction being made between them. General measures of economic policy, such as the lowering of the tax rate applicable to corporate profits, fall outside the scope of Article 107 TFEU.

The distinction between general and specific measures is not always easy to apply. Thus, the Italian reduction in the rate of social security contributions was deemed to constitute a State aid because it specifically benefited the Italian textile industry.[108] The Italian government claimed that the reduction was only restoring the competitive position of the textile industry because the industry employed a very high percentage of female workers which created a situation whereby the contributions for the social security system exceeded the benefits.[109] The concept of selectivity is particularly

---

[102] Case C-379/98 *PreussenElektra AG v Schleswag AG*. This judgment is interesting because the Court's decision would probably have been different had the undertakings concerned been owned by the State.

[103] Case C-262/12 *Association Vent De Colère*, paras 33–34.

[104] See, eg, Case C-559/12 P *France v Commission*. The Court held that the implied unlimited guarantee granted by the French State in favour of La Poste constitutes unlawful State aid.

[105] Case 67/85 *Kwekerij Gebroeders van der Kooy BV and others v Commission*.

[106] Case C-482/99 *Commission v France*.

[107] I am grateful to JL Buendia Sierra who pointed this out to me.

[108] Case 173/73 *Italy v Commission*.

[109] The benefits of the Italian social security were based on the needs of the family of the worker and the contributions were levied on the basis of the wage costs of each company. The Italian textile sector had a disproportionately low percentage of male workers who could claim such benefits as head of a family. As

difficult to apply to tax measures.[110] This is highlighted by the fierce criticism of the Commission decision of 30 August 2016 ordering Ireland to recover € 13 billion tax benefits from Apple.[111] According to the case law there is no selective advantage when tax measures differentiate between undertakings if such differentiation arises from the nature and general scheme of the system of which they form part. In the reform of the Gibraltar corporate tax case the governments of Gibraltar and the UK argued that the new payroll tax based on the number of employees employed in Gibraltar was not selective because every employer was liable to pay the tax. The choice of the tax base consisting of the number of persons employed in Gibraltar was, according to the governments, a natural consequence of their fiscal sovereignty.[112] The ECJ held that the UK government had not adduced any justification for the selective advantage.[113] In the *Azores* case the Portuguese government claimed that there was no selectivity because the Azores autonomous region was, also in tax matters, independent from the central government and thus could set its own tax rates at levels different to those of Portugal. The Commission claimed that the selectivity should be assessed according to the national tax system. The ECJ accepted Portugal's argument in principle, but ruled that the degree of autonomy of the Autonomous Region of the Azores is in fact limited. Therefore, it upheld the Commission's decision.[114]

7.5.2.3 Effect upon Competition and Trade between Member States

The granting of benefits must result in a distortion of competition in order to be caught by Article 107(1) TFEU. For this purpose it is necessary to consider whether the aid strengthens the position of the beneficiary enterprise compared with other enterprises operating in the same line of trade.[115] It is not, however, necessary for the Commission to produce a fully-fledged analysis of the relevant product and geographical market along the lines of the analysis required by Article 101 and especially Article 102 TFEU.[116] Nevertheless, the Commission must produce something more than a statement that competition has been or may be distorted.[117] In practice this

a result, the textile industry was paying substantially more to the system than the benefits its male workers received.

[110] See for a very good overview Wolfgang Schön in Hancher, Ottervanger and Slot (eds), *EU State Aids*, 5th edn (2016), ch. 13; D Triantafylloou, 'La Fiscalité faconnée par la discipline des aides d'Etat' in *EC State Aid Law Liber Amicorum Francisco Santaolalla Gadea* (Wolters Kluwer, 2008), ch 19, pp 409–424. See also the older Commission notice on the application of the State aid rules to measures relating to direct business taxation OJ, 1998, C 384, 3–9.

[111] IP 16/2923

[112] Joined Cases C-106 and 107/09P, *Commission v Gibraltar and the United Kingdom*, para 145 with further citations of this principle.

[113] Para 149 of the judgment.

[114] Case C-88/03 *Portugal v Commission*.

[115] Case 730/79 *Philip Morris Holland BV v Commission*.

[116] See Cases C-72/91 and C-73/91 *Sloman Neptune*.

[117] Cases 296 and 318/82 *The Netherlands and Leeuwarder Papierwarenfabriek BV v Commission*. For the OFT's suggestions on how to use an economic approach to address the question of the distortion of competition caused by State aid, see its recent proposals in *European State Aid Control* (OFT 821) (23 November 2005).

requirement is easily met.[118] The ECJ has so far not endorsed a '*de minimis* rule'. Nevertheless, the Commission will have to show that the aid will have an impact on trade between the Member States.[119]

In its guidelines on State aids for small and medium-sized enterprises, the Commission has taken the view that while all financial assistance affects competitive conditions to some extent: not all aid has a perceptible impact on trade and competition between Member States. This is so especially for aid provided in very small amounts, mainly though not exclusively, to SMEs, and often under schemes run by local or regional authorities.

The '*de minimis* rule' has its legal basis in Article 2 of Regulation 994/98/EC and in the block exemption Regulation on *de minimis* aid.[120]

It should further be noted that in practice the effects on competition and those on trade between the Member States will almost always coincide. It is therefore common practice to employ these two concepts interchangeably even though there is a theoretical difference between them (although this should not lead one to assume that there will never be differences between the two concepts in practice).

7.5.2.4   The 'Market Economy Investor Principle'[121]

An important concept to enable the Commission to distinguish between benefits granted by governments that are prohibited by Article 107(1) TFEU and those that are not, is the market economy investor principle. The concept was especially developed in the context of government participation in the capital of enterprises.[122] According to this principle, government actions which take place under market conditions and terms do not give rise to the application of Article 107(1) TFEU. If the provision of funds by the state has been made subject to certain conditions which would also have been required by a private investor, such action will not be considered to amount to a grant of aid. The *Corsica Ferries* judgment shows that the test may involve a sectoral and geographic analysis.[123]

In the *Land Burgenland* judgment the ECJ pointed out that the Commission had correctly applied the private vendor test.[124]

---

[118]   See, eg, Case T-274/01, *Valmont v Commission*. This case concerned the purchase of a plot of land of three hectares for approximately € 400.000. The Commission took the view that provincial government enabled Valmont to buy the land too cheaply and took a decision prohibiting the alleged aid. The striking feature of this case is that none of the parties raised the question whether this transaction could have an effect on trade between the Member States. See Case C-494/06 P *Italy and Wam Spa v Commission* and the note by M Farley in EStAL (2010) 'The Role of Economics-based Approaches when Analysing Effects on Trade and Distortions of Competition after Wam'.

[119]   Case 248/84 *Germany v Commission*.

[120]   Commission Reg 1407/2013 on the application of Arts 107 and 108 TFEU to *de minimis* aid OJ 2013, L 352/1 see section 7.5.2.5.

[121]   The draft Commission Notice on the notion of State aid pursuant to Art 107(1) TFEU (2016) provides in s 4.2 a useful summary of this principle. For trenchant criticism of this principle and its application, see M Parish, '*On the Private Investor Principle*' (2003) 28 European Law Review 70. See further: N Khan and KD Borchart, 'The Private Market Investor Principle: Reality Check or Distorting Mirror?' in *EC State Aid Law: Liber Amicorum Francisco Santaolalla Gadea* (Wolters Kluwer, 2008), 109–125.

[122]   Cases 296 and 318/82 *Leeuwarder Papierwarenfabriek*.

[123]   Cases C-533 and 536/12 P *Corsica Ferries*.

[124]   Cases C-214, 215 and 223/12 P *Land Burgenland*.

The Commission has also consistently applied this principle in the context of the review of tariffs of public enterprises. In a decision of 7 December 1993 concerning the price for gas use by industry as a raw material[125] the Commission stated:

> If Gasunie has agreed temporarily to grant the abovementioned discounts, it is clearly in its commercial interests to do so. Given the prospects for the relevant industry, Gasunie would not wish to lose an important group of customers which in the Netherlands buys approximately one third of its supplies to industry. It is also in Gasunie's interest that the relevant industry should survive in the countries to which it exports gas. The Commission notes that the export prices fixed by Gasunie enable distribution companies in the importing countries, namely Belgium, France and Germany, to apply pricing policies similar to its own policy in the Netherlands ... In its examination of the decision by Gasunie to grant the discounts in question, the Commission has been unable to detect any behaviour on the part of the Dutch authorities that went beyond that of a private shareholder. In view of the situation on the ammonia and nitrogenous fertiliser market, the Commission considers that, in providing support for an important group of customers whose survival is manifestly in jeopardy, Gasunie has acted out of purely commercial considerations.

> The Commission has accordingly decided that the temporary and limited price concessions that Gasunie plans to grant to Dutch ammonia producers do not constitute State aid within the meaning of [Article 107 (1) TFEU].

The market economy investor principle has become an important instrument to differentiate between lawful and unlawful government assistance. The Commission has provided useful guidance in the Transparency Directive.[126] It is not the intention of the Commission to replace the investor's judgement. It recognises that the investor has a wide margin of judgement. Only when there are no objective justifications for the investment will the Commission consider Article 107(1) TFEU to be applicable. In the *Chronopost* judgement, the Court held that where the principle is applied to a company that performs services of public importance, the relevant comparison that must be made is with the cost price of the performance of those services by *that* company, not with that of a company in the market sector.[127]

The Commission applies a similar test, the private creditor test, when a government provides loans on terms that are more favourable than those given by banks.[128]

In the *ING* judgment the GC applied the principle to answer the question whether an amendment to the repayment terms of an aid measure constitutes State aid. The ECJ dismissed the appeal lodged by the Commission confirming that the Commission should have applied the private investor test.[129] This will be further discussed in section 7.5.4.

In the *Bank Burgenland* case the question was whether the Austrian government had acted in accordance with the private vendor test when privatising Bank Burgenland.

---

[125] [1994] OJ C35/6.

[126] Directive 2006/111, [2006] OJ L 318/17 of November 2006 on the transparency of financial relations between Member State and public undertakings as well as on financial transparency within certain undertakings.

[127] Cases C-83, 93 and 94/01 P *Chronopost SA v Ufex*.

[128] Joined Cases T-267/08 and 279/08, *Région Nord-Pas-de-Calais and Communauté d'agglomération du Douaisis v Commission*. The appeal against the judgment has been denied, C-389/11 P.

[129] Case C-224/12P *Commission v Netherlands and ING*.

The Commission as well as the ECJ ruled that Austria, by attaching unlawful conditions to the tender, failed this test.[130]

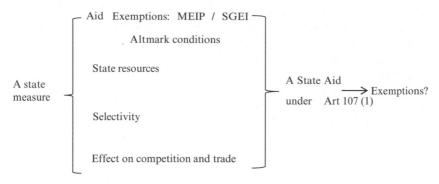

Figure 7.1: Summary Article 107(1)

7.5.2.5 *Exceptions*

Once a government measure granting certain benefits meets the conditions of Article 107(1) TFEU it is incompatible with the common market. It can then only be exempted by the provisions of Article 107(2) or 107(3) TFEU or the provisions of Articles 93 or 106(2) TFEU.

As we discussed in section 7.2.1.1 above, the *Altmark* case[131] and the Commission decision[132] have made it clear that in some cases the provision of financial compensation for the performance of public services is not to be regarded as State aid.

The Court ruled in *Altmark* that, where the criteria laid down in that judgment are satisfied, such compensation for the provision of public services did not fall within the scope of the prohibition of Article 107(1) TFEU. In such a case, Article 106(2) TFEU is also inapplicable, and there is also no obligation to notify such a regime. Thus, this reasoning process incorporates the 'exception'-style analysis within the notion of what counts as a 'State aid' in the first place. Functionally, however, the analysis is one that exempts such payments from the standstill obligation and is thus properly treated here.

Assuming that the financial benefit in question does qualify as a State aid, there are still means to exempt such aid from the prohibition of the EC Treaty, which we discuss in the following text.

The exemptions from the prohibition of Article 107(1):

---

[130] Case C-214/12P, C-215/12P and C-223/12P *Bank Burgenland*.

[131] Case C-280/00 *Altmark-Trans*. For helpful discussion of this case, see A Bartosch CLaSF Working Paper No. 02 (October 2003) and F Louis and A Vallery, '*Ferring* Revisited: the *Altmark* Case and State Financing of Public Services Obligations' (2004) 57 *World Competition* 53.

[132] Commission Decision of 20 December 2011 on the application of Art 106(2) of the Treaty on the Functioning of the European Union to State aid in the form of public service compensation granted to certain undertakings entrusted with the operation of services of general economic interest. OJ L7, 11.01.2012, pp 3–10. See further section 7.2.1.1.

(a) Aid That Is Compatible with the Common Market, Article 107(2) TFEU

This provision provides for three categories of aid which *shall* be compatible with Common Market.

(a)   aid having a social character, granted to individual consumers, provided that such aid is granted without discrimination related to the origin of the products concerned;

(b)   aid to make good the damage caused by natural disasters or exceptional occurrences;

(c)   aid granted to the economy of certain areas of the Federal Republic of Germany affected by the division of Germany, in so far as such aid is required in order to compensate for the economic disadvantages caused by that division. Five years after the entry into force of the Treaty of Lisbon, the Council, acting on a proposal from the Commission, may adopt a decision repealing this point.

The word 'shall' is taken to imply that the Commission does not enjoy any discretion to decide whether or not the exemption applies. Similar wording is used in Article 93 TFEU. Of the three categories, category (c) is by far the most important. This provision allows for aid granted to the economy of the Federal Republic of Germany affected by the division of Germany. The interpretation of this provision has been hotly debated ever since the reunification of Germany. The Commission has adopted a restrictive interpretation of this provision that has been endorsed by the EU courts.[133] According to this interpretation, if general disadvantages in East Germany cannot be cured through the application of this exemption, they should be dealt with as exceptions under Article 107(3)(a) and (c) TFEU. There are only few exemption decisions based on this provision.

(b) Aid That May Be Compatible with the Common Market, Article 107(3) TFEU

According to this provision the following categories of aid that *may* be exempted:

(a)   aid to promote the economic development of areas where the standard of living is abnormally low or where there is serious underemployment, and of the regions referred to in Article 349, in view of their structural, economic and social situation;

(b)   aid to promote the execution of an important project of common European interest or to remedy a serious disturbance in the economy of a Member State;

---

[133] In Case C-156/98 *Germany v Commission*, the ECJ held, in paras 52–55, that: 'the phrase "division of Germany" refers historically to the establishment of the dividing line between the two occupied zones in 1948. Therefore, the economic disadvantages caused by that division can only mean the economic disadvantages caused in certain areas of Germany by the isolation which the establishment of that physical frontier entailed, such as the breaking of communication links or the loss of markets as a result of the breaking off of commercial relations between the two parts of German territory.

By contrast, the conception advanced by the German Government, according to which Art 92(2)(c) of the Treaty permits full compensation for the undeniable economic backwardness suffered by the new Länder, disregards both the nature of that provision as a derogation and its context and aims.

The economic disadvantages suffered by the new Länder as a whole have not been directly caused by the geographical division of Germany within the meaning of Art 92(2)(c) of the Treaty.

It follows that the differences in development between the original and the new Länder are explained by causes other than the geographical rift caused by the division of Germany and in particular by the different politico-economic systems set up in each part of Germany.' See further M Heidenhain, *Handbuch des Europäischen Beihilfenrechts* (Munich, CH Beck Verlag, 2003) 188 et seq.

(c)   aid to facilitate the development of certain economic activities or of certain economic areas, where such aid does not adversely affect trading conditions to an extent contrary to the common interest;

(d)   aid to promote culture and heritage conservation where such aid does not affect trading conditions and competition in the Union to an extent that is contrary to the common interest;

(e)   such other categories of aid as may be specified by decision of the Council on a proposal from the Commission.

It is important to note that the application of this provision is subject to the Commission's discretion. Furthermore, as an exemption from the general principles of the Treaty, it has been interpreted in a restrictive manner. Thus, in its judgment in *Philip Morris*,[134] the ECJ supported the Commission's interpretation according to which State aids can only be allowed to the extent that they are necessary for the achievement of objectives accepted under Article 107(3) TFEU.

In summary, the requirements are as follows:

(a)   the aid must promote or further a project that is in the Union interest as a whole;

(b)   the aid must be necessary for the achievement of this result, and the objective could not have been obtained in the absence of this measure; and

(c)   the duration, intensity and scope of the aid must be proportionate to the importance of the intended result.[135]

The second element has been specified by the Commission as follows:

> State aids are in principle incompatible with the common market. The discretionary power of the Commission should only be exercised when the aids proposed by Member-States contribute to the achievement of the Community objectives and interest set out in Article 107(3) TFEU. The national interest of a Member State or the benefits obtained by the recipient of the aid in contributing to the national interest do not by themselves justify the positive exercise of the Commission's discretionary powers.[136]

The ECJ accepted the validity of the compensatory justification principle in its *Philip Morris* judgment.[137] These principles of interpretation have strengthened the Commission's hand considerably.

The Union courts have stressed that the Commission has a broad discretion in applying the provisions of Article 107(3), the exercise of which involves economic assessments which must be made in an EU context.[138]

Article 107(3)(a) is the basis for Commission decisions on regional aid in areas where there is serious unemployment or a very low standard of living, where the per capita income does not exceed 75 per cent of the average in the EU. Thus according to the accession Treaties for the new Member States the whole territory is eligible for

---

[134] Case 730/79 *Philip Morris Holland BV v Commission*.
[135] See the Commission's 12th Report on Competition Policy (1983), para 160.
[136] ibid, para 160.
[137] Case 730/79 *Philip Morris Holland BV v Commission*, para 16.
[138] Case C-290/07 P *Commission v Scott*, para 64.

State aid under this provision. A similar provision was included in the accession Treaty for Greece.

Article 107(3)(b) was for practical purposes a dead letter until the Commission started applying it to assess aid to the financial sector. This is discussed in section 7.5.4.

Article 107(3)(c) is applied for State aid to less disadvantaged regions. The disadvantage relates to disparities between regions at the national level. As a result, poor regions in wealthy Member States, eg, the former DDR regions in Germany, qualify for State aid. The Commission's regional policy was developed in the 1980s through guidelines.

Article 107(3)(c) is also the legal basis for rescue and restructuring aid. This type of aid played a major role in the restructuring of the East Bundesländer (the former DDR) industry. The policy in the area has been defined since the 1970s. The Commission published its first guidelines in 1994.

7.5.2.6 Block Exemptions and Guidelines

As the EU State aid policy developed and matured, block exemptions have been enacted and guidelines published to clarify the above outlined Treaty exemptions. As the term indicates, block exemptions exempt certain categories of aid from the prohibition of Article 107(1) TFEU. The foundation for this policy is found in Regulation 2015/1588, applying Articles 107 and 108 TFEU, which authorises the Commission to adopt block exemptions for certain categories of aid. Until the 2014 reform some 65 per cent of the State aid cases were block exempted. Furthermore, aid is exempted on the basis of previously approved aid schemes.[139] The major 2014 reform of the General Block exemption regulation has increased this percentage further. Combined with the *de minimis* regulation, it has increased this percentage to about 90 per cent. This reform *de facto* creates a system of *ex post* State aid control whereas until now it was largely an *ex ante* system. The important consequences of this revision of the system will be discussed in this section. The extension of the scope of the block exemption allows the Commission to devote even more time and resources for the novel and hard cases, such as the massive aid to the financial sector. These will be discussed in section 7.5.4. On the other hand, as will be discussed, the *ex post* system will require resources to supervise the Member States.

The following block exemptions are presently in force:[140]

(a)   Commission Regulation (EC) No 1407/2013 on the application of Articles 107 and 108 of the Treaty to *de minimis* aid.[141]

(b)   Regulation 1370/2007 of 23 October 2007 on public passenger transport services by rail and by road and repealing Council Regulations 1191/69 and 1107/70.[142]

---

[139] The 2014 Staff Working Paper, published on the website of DG COMP, puts this percentage at 88%.
[140] Readers should consult the website of DG Comp for the actual rules in force.
[141] [2013] OJ L 352, 1.
[142] [2007] OJ L 315, pp 1–13 Commission reg 1191/69 was the subject of Case C-280/00 *Altmark*.

(c)   Commission Regulation 651/2014 declaring certain categories of aid compatible with the common market in application of Article 107 and 108 of the Treaty (General block exemption Regulation GBER).[143]

Regulation 1407/2013 exempts aid of no more than €200,000 over a three-year period from the prohibition. Such aid need not be notified. Article 1 excludes aid to certain sectors such as agriculture, fisheries, road transport and aid for exports to third countries. According to Article 3(2) of the Regulation Member States shall record and compile all the information regarding the application of this Regulation. Such records shall contain all information necessary to demonstrate that the conditions of this Regulation have been complied with. Regulation 1370/2007 of 23 October 2007 provides special rules for public passenger transport services by rail and by road. Such rules are necessary because

> many Member States have enacted legislation providing for the award of exclusive rights and public service contracts in at least part of their public transport market, on the basis of transparent and fair competitive award procedures. As a result, trade between Member States has developed significantly and several public service operators are now providing public passenger transport services in more than one Member State. However, developments in national legislation have led to disparities in the procedures applied and have created legal uncertainty as to the rights of public service operators and the duties of the competent authorities. The Community legal framework ought therefore to be updated.[144]

The General Block exemption (GBER) applies to the majority of State aid measures.[145] It will expire on 31 December 2020. Article 1 excludes, in a very unintelligible manner, several types of aid. Therefore, it should be read carefully. The GBER does not apply to agriculture, fisheries and aquaculture, as well as regional aid schemes which are targeted at specific sectors. The GBER further excludes *ad hoc* aid to large enterprises. According to Article 3, aid schemes that satisfy the conditions mentioned therein are exempted and do not have to be notified. Chapter II exempts a large number of aid schemes and individual aid measures.

In order to provide guidance as to how it will apply Article 107(1) and the exemptions of Article 107(3) TFEU and the block exemptions, the Commission has published guidelines, codes, frameworks, communications and notices. Although the designations are not consistent, these instruments all serve the same purpose. The ECJ has held that although such rules cannot be regarded as rules of law, they nevertheless form rules of practice from which the Commission may not depart in an individual case without giving reasons which are compatible with the principle of equal treatment.[146] These rules do not bind Member States. They remain free to request an exemption from the Commission under Article 107(3) in specific exceptional circumstances.[147]

---

[143] [2014] OJ L 187, 1–87.
[144] Parh 6 of the preamble.
[145] Art 43 of the Reg. See K van de Casteele in Hancher, Ottervanger & Slot (eds), *EC State Aids*, 4th edn (2012), ch 11.03. See also point 68 of the preamble.
[146] Joined Cases C-106/09 P and C-107/09 P, *Commission v Gibraltar and the United Kingdom*, 128.
[147] Case C-526/14, *Tadej Kotnik and Others*.

Important guidelines, presently in force, are:[148]

(a) Communication from the Commission—Criteria for the compatibility analysis of state aid to disadvantaged and disabled workers subject to individual notification.[149]

(b) Communication from the Commission—Criteria for the compatibility analysis of training state aid cases subject to individual notification.[150]

(c) Guidelines on national regional aid for 2014–2020.[151]

(d) Guidelines on regional State aid for 2014–2020: Acceptance of the proposed appropriate measures pursuant to Article 108(1) of the Treaty on the Functioning of the European Union by all Member States.[152]

(e) Communication from the Commission concerning the criteria for an in-depth assessment of Regional aid to large investment projects.[153]

(f) Community Framework for State aid for Research and Development and Innovation.[154]

(g) Guidelines on State aid for environmental protection and energy.[155]

(h) Guidelines on State aid for rescuing and restructuring non-financial Undertakings in difficulty.[156]

(i) Guidelines on risk finance 2014–2020.[157]

7.5.3 Procedural Rules, Article 108 TFEU and Regulation 2015/1589/EU

7.5.3.1 Introduction

The basic procedural rules are found in Article 108 TFEU. This Article provides for a system of *ex ante* control of new State aid. This system is not unlike the system as it was applied in Regulation 17 for agreements prohibited under Article 85 EEC (now 101 TFEU).[158] It should be noted however, that the recent changes in the legislation have fundamentally altered the previously existing *ex ante* system for the control of State aid. The 2014 General Block Exemption Regulation (GBER) now covers a major part of all State aids. It is estimated that together with the *de minimis* rule, now some 90 per cent of the cases are block exempted. This means that the present system

---

[148] This list excludes the guidelines in the financial sector that will be dealt with in s 7.5.4. A complete overview can be found on the website of DG Competition.

[149] [2009] OJ C 188/6.

[150] [2009] OJ C 188/1.

[151] [2013] OJ C 209.

[152] [2014] OJ C 101.

[153] [2009] OJ C 223/3.

[154] [2014] OJ C 198/1.

[155] [2014] OJ C 200/1.

[156] [2014] OJ C 249/1.

[157] [2010] OJ C19/4-34.

[158] See Chapter 6.4.1. Reg 17 provided prior notification of agreements in order to obtain an exemption from the Commission on the basis of Art 101(3). In the course of time this prior notification requirement was relaxed for some categories. Subsequently, block exemptions were introduced.

can be characterised as an *ex post* control system. Under this system, which is outlined in the GBER, it is the responsibility of the Member States to supervise the granting of State aid. This is done largely through obligations on the Member States to play by the rules of the GBER and to keep records of the State aid that they have been granting under the block exemptions. Furthermore, Member States have an obligation to report to the Commission. The Commission in turn will supervise the Member States. All aid measures not exempted under the block exemption remain subject to notification. The rules described below are therefore meant to control the non-exempted aid measures.

An important role in the new system is for the national courts which have to apply the directly effective rules of the block exemptions in addition to the control they exercise on the basis of Article 108 TFEU and the procedural regulations.

As has been observed above, the procedural rules are embodied in Regulation 2015/1589, which are further detailed in Regulation 794/2004/EC, amended by Regulation 2015/2282.[159] Regulation 794/2004 includes a notification form for new aid. First of all, Regulation 2015/1589 provides a set of definitions. Chapter II provides the procedure for notified aid. Chapter III deals with unlawful aid, that is, aid that has been put into effect without respecting the obligation to notify. Chapter IV lays down rules for the misuse of aid, that is, the aid has not been implemented in accordance with conditions set out by the Commission or specified by the Member State. Chapter V provides the procedure for existing aid. Chapter VI defines the rights of interested parties, including (among others) the intended beneficiaries and complainants, which will usually be competitors of each other. Chapter VII gives the Commission powers to conduct on-site monitoring and obliges Member States to submit annual reports on all existing aid schemes. Chapter VIII deals with the publication of decisions, professional secrecy and other matters.

Article 108 TFEU reads as follows:

1. The Commission shall, in cooperation with Member States, keep under constant review all systems of aid existing in those States. It shall propose to the latter any appropriate measures required by the progressive development or by the functioning of the common market.

2. If, after giving notice to the parties concerned to submit their comments, the Commission finds that aid granted by a State or through State resources is not compatible with the common market having regard to Article 107, or that such aid is being misused, it shall decide that the State concerned shall abolish or alter such aid within a period of time to be determined by the Commission. If the State concerned does not comply with this decision within the prescribed time, the Commission or any other interested State may, in derogation from the provisions of Articles 258 and 259, refer the matter to the Court of Justice direct.

On application by a Member State, the Council may, acting unanimously, decide that aid which that State is granting or intends to grant shall be considered to be compatible with the common market, in derogation from the provisions of Article 107 or from the regulations provided for in Article 109, if such a decision is justified by exceptional circumstances. If, as regards the aid in question, the Commission has already initiated the procedure provided for in the first subparagraph of this paragraph, the fact that the State concerned has made its application to the Council shall have the effect of suspending that procedure until the Council has made its attitude known.

---

[159] [2015] OJ L 325/1-180.

If, however, the Council has not made its attitude known within three months of the said application being made, the Commission shall give its decision on the case.

3. The Commission shall be informed, in sufficient time to enable it to submit its comments, of any plans to grant or alter aid. If it considers that any such plan is not compatible with the common market having regard to Article 107, it shall without delay initiate the procedure provided for in paragraph 2.

The Member State concerned shall not put its proposed measures into effect until this procedure has resulted in a final decision.

4. The Commission may adopt regulations relating to the categories of State aid that the Council has, pursuant to Article 109, determined may be exempted from the procedure provided for in paragraph 3 of this Article.

It is of the greatest importance for an understanding of this area of law to draw a distinction between *existing aid* (section 7.5.3.2) and *new aid* (section 7.5.3.3). Control of existing aid takes place *ex post*, while new aid, not exempted under the block exemptions, is controlled *ex ante*.

7.5.3.2 Existing Aid

Existing aid is defined in Article 1 of Regulation 2015/1589. The most important categories are aid which has been authorised by the Commission and aid applied in a Member State before the entry into force of the EEC Treaty[160] or before accession of a new Member State. Only existing aid schemes can be challenged. According to Article 108(1) TFEU as well as Article 21 of Regulation 2015/1589, existing aid schemes[161] in Member States must be kept under constant review by the Commission. According to Article 21 of the Regulation the Commission proposes measures to the Member States if the aid is not or is no longer compatible with the internal market. Member States shall be bound by the Commission's proposals if they accept them. If the Member State does not accept the proposals, the Commission is entitled to proceed with the formal examination procedure of Article 108(2) TFEU. Article 1 of the Regulation defines aid schemes as 'any act on the basis of which, without further implementing measures being required, individual aid awards may be made to undertakings defined within the act in a general and abstract manner and any act on the basis of which aid which is not linked to a specific project may be awarded to one or several undertakings for an indefinite period of time and/or for an indefinite amount'.

Existing aid, whether it is an existing aid scheme or an individual aid, cannot be challenged in national courts. However, existing aid schemes can be challenged by bringing a complaint to the Commission. The Commission may take action on the basis of Articles 22 and 23 of Regulation 2015/1589. If the Commission finds that such aid is incompatible with the common market it may propose appropriate measures.

---

[160] An example can be found in Case C-44/93 *Namur-Les Assurances du Crédit SA v Office National du Ducroire and Belgium*. This case also demonstrates how difficult it can be to draw the distinction between the two categories.

[161] Art 108(1) TFEU uses the term 'aid system' whereas the Reg in Arts 1, 21 and 22, uses the term 'aid schemes'.

If Member States accept these, they shall be bound by them. Otherwise the Commission shall initiate the formal procedure which may lead to the adoption of a decision prohibiting the aid. The acceptance by the Member State as well as the decision pursuant to Article 23(2) of Regulation 2015/1589 shall be binding upon them. Their binding force can be enforced by national courts because of their direct effect.

The distinction between the two types of aid (existing aid and new aid) is not always straightforward. In the *AEM* case[162] the applicant, relying on the *Namur-Les Assurances*[163] judgment, sought to argue that measures introduced in Italy before the entry into force of the EEC Treaty would qualify as measures under this provision. The ECJ dismissed the argument noting that the measures were substantially different to the original ones and concluded that the measures constituted new aid.

7.5.3.3 New Aid

7.5.3.3.1 Introduction

New aid—ie any plans to grant or alter aid—must, under Article 108(3) TFEU, be notified to the Commission in sufficient time to enable the Commission to communicate its comments. Regulation 794/2004[164] (referred to as 'the implementing Regulation' in what follows) includes in its Annex I the necessary notification form.[165] Its Article 4 also provides that:

> An alteration to existing aid shall mean any change, other than modifications of a purely formal or administrative nature which cannot affect the evaluation of the compatibility of the aid measure with the common market. However an increase in the original budget of an existing aid scheme by up to 20% shall not be considered an alteration to existing aid.

As a result, such small changes need no longer be notified as 'new' aid. Article 4 goes on to subject alterations to existing aid outside this definition to a simplified notification procedure (using the form in included in Annex II of the Regulation). These aids concern budget increases over 20%, the prolongation of an existing aid scheme by up to six years and any tightening of the criteria for application of an authorised aid scheme.

7.5.3.3.2 The Preliminary Examination Procedure

On the basis of Article 108(3) TFEU and Article 4 of Regulation 2015/1589, the Commission may, after summary examination, either conclude that the aid is compatible with the Internal Market or open the procedure provided for in Article 108(2) TFEU and Article 6 of Regulation 2015/1589. This is called the preliminary examination procedure and is specified in Article 4 of the Regulation. New aid which has been notified may not, according to the last sentence of Article 108(3) TFEU, be put

---

[162] Case T-301/02 *AEM v Commission* para 126. The appeal was denied, Case C-320/09. In the same vein see Case T-292/02 *ACEA v Commission* para 123 and Case T-222/04 *Italy v Commission* para 99.
[163] Case C-44/93 *Namur-Les Assurances*.
[164] As amended by Reg 2015/2282.
[165] The Reg was amended by Commission Reg 1125/2009 of 23 November 2009 as regards Part III.2, Part III.3 and Part III.7 of its Annex I.

into effect until this procedure, ie, the procedure of Article 108(3) TFEU and Article 4 of Regulation 2015/1589 and/or Article 108(2) TFEU and Article 6 of Regulation 2015/1589, has resulted in a final Decision. This is called the standstill clause.

The last sentence of Article 108(3) TFEU and the similarly worded Article 3 of Regulation 2015/1589 have direct effect. New aid within the scope of the block exemptions referred to above does not have to be notified and is not subject to the standstill clause.[166]

Under the preliminary procedure the Commission has a period of two months to make up its mind. If it finds that the aid is compatible with the Internal Market, it will inform the Member States concerned accordingly. Such a decision may be reviewed in the General Court.[167] Judgments of the General Court may be appealed to the Court of Justice on points of law only.

If the Commission is of the opinion that it needs more time to complete the review of the state aid, it must open the procedure of Article 108(2) TFEU. The decision to open the Article 108(2) TFEU procedure is a contestable act within the meaning of Article 263 TFEU.[168]

If the Commission fails to act, the Member State concerned may, according to Article 4(6) of the Regulation, implement the aid, after giving notice to the Commission. The aid then becomes an existing aid.[169]

7.5.3.3.3 The Formal Investigation Procedure

The Article 108(2) TFEU procedure is laid down in Articles 6 and 7 of the Regulation. It is called the formal investigation procedure. It is a contentious procedure, which means that the parties concerned may submit comments. The Commission will publish a notice in the C-series of the Official Journal of the EU, describing the aid plans and inviting comments. In practice, it is quite common for Member States, beneficiaries and interested parties, competitors as well as trade associations, to provide comments. Such comments strengthen the hand of the Commission considerably. The comments will be submitted to the Member State concerned for comments.

According to Article 9(6) of the Regulation 2015/1589, the Commission has 18 months to adopt a decision. If that period has lapsed the Member State concerned can request the Commission to take a decision within two months. This brings the total time for the Commission under this procedure to 20 months. The combination of the two procedures, Article 108(3) and 108(2) TFEU, leads to a maximum of 22 months.

After completing the Article 108(2) TFEU procedure, the Commission may either:

(a)   declare the aid compatible with the Internal Market, with or without conditions; or

(b)   declare it incompatible with the Internal Market.

---

[166] The block exemption Regulations oblige the Member States to forward a summary of the aid they provided under these Regulations.

[167] Apart from the Member State the intended beneficiary of the aid or a competitor which manifested itself clearly also have standing, Case C-198/91 *William Cook plc v Commission*. Until April 2004, appeals by Member States were reviewed by the ECJ.

[168] Cases C-312/90 *Spain v Commission* and C-47/91 *Italy v Commission*.

[169] Case 120/73 *Gebrüder Lorenz GmbH v Germany*.

Either decision may be subject to review by the General Court with a possibility of appeal to the ECJ on points of law.

A final positive decision ends the operation of the standstill clause of Article 108(3) TFEU and Article 3 of the Regulation. A positive decision may be accompanied by conditions which should alleviate the effect on competition.[170] The Commission's decision in the *Air France* case provides a good example of this practice.[171] In this case, the Commission imposed a series of conditions which included the requirement that Air France was not to use any of the aid received for the purpose of increasing its aircraft fleet. A positive decision may also approve the aid in successive tranches whereby the approval of the next tranche is subject to the satisfactory implementation of a restructuring program.[172]

In the case of a negative final decision, the standstill clause (contained in the last paragraph of Article 108(3) TFEU) does *not* lapse after the Commission concludes the Article 108(2) TFEU procedure; instead, the standstill obligation is henceforth based on the negative decision.

7.5.3.3.4 The Simplified Procedure

In 2009 the Commission introduced a simplified procedure in an effort to streamline the notification process.[173] This procedure is intended 'for measures which only require the Commission to verify that the measure is in accordance with existing rules and practices without exercising any discretionary powers.' 'Other aid measures will be subject to the appropriate procedures and normally to the Code of Best Practice (see below).' According to Section 2 of the Notice the procedure can be used for three categories of aid: 1: Aid measures falling under the 'standard assessment' sections of existing frameworks or guidelines; 2: Aid measures corresponding to well-established Commission decision-making practice and; 3: Prolongation or extension of existing schemes.

Section 3 outlines the elements of the procedure. According to the Commission, pre-notification contacts with the notifying Member State are beneficial. Such contacts allow identification at an early stage of the relevant Commission instruments or precedent decisions, the degree of complexity which the Commission's assessment is likely to involve and the scope and depth of the information required for the Commission to make a full assessment of the case.

The Member State is invited to submit a draft notification form with the necessary supplementary information sheets. In simple cases a draft notification is not necessary.

In addition, the Commission has published a Best Practices Code in order to explain and further facilitate the procedure.[174] The Code also stresses the importance of pre-notification meetings.

---

[170] According to Art 107(3)(c) and (d) TFEU, 'such aid should not affect trading conditions and competition in the Community to an extent that it is contrary to the common interest'.

[171] [1994] OJ L254/73.

[172] This was the case in *Air France* as well as in *Aer Lingus*: Decision 94/118, [1994] OJ L54/30. This decision was challenged in Case T-140/95 *Ryanair Ltd v Commission*.

[173] Commission Notice on a Simplified procedure for the treatment of certain types of State aid [2009] OJ C136/3-12.

[174] Commission Notice on a Best Practices Code on the conduct of State aid control proceedings, [2009] OJ C 136/13-20.

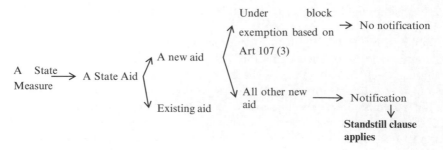

Figure 7.2: Summary of procedures

7.5.3.3.5 The Position of Complainants

Complainants have, according to Article 24 of the Regulation 2015/1589, a right to inform the Commission of any alleged unlawful aid or the misuse of aid. Complainants can bring an action under Article 232 EC if the Commission fails to act.[175] Furthermore, as the Court of Justice observed in the *Sytraval* judgment, complainants, as third parties which are 'directly and individually concerned', will have a right to challenge state aid decisions addressed to governments of Member States[176] The Court also pointed out that, although the Commission is not obliged to hear complainants, it must nevertheless respond to facts and points of law raised by the complainant. Article 24(2), second paragraph, states that the Commission shall inform the interested party it has not provided sufficient grounds to show on the basis on a *prima facie* examination the existence of unlawful aid or misuse of aid. The complaint shall be deemed to be withdrawn if the interested party fails to make known its views within the prescribed period. This provision was embodied in the 2013 changes of the previous Regulation 659/99, improving the handling of complaints.[177]

7.5.3.3.6 Unlawful Aid

Unlawful State aid, ie, aid that has not been notified, is not automatically incompatible with the internal market. The Commission is under a duty to review such aids.[178] According to Article 15(2) of the Regulation, the Commission shall not be bound by the normal time limits in this case. It also has powers to issues injunctions to suspend or provisionally recover the unlawful aid (Article 13 of the Regulation). As explained in the next section national courts have an important role in preventing unlawful aid from being implemented before the Commission has reached a decision on the compatibility of the aid.

---

[175] Case T-95/96 *Gestevision Telecinco SA v Commission.*
[176] Case C-367/95 P *Commission v Chambre Syndicale (Sytraval).*
[177] This provision is now embodied in Art 24 of Reg 2015/1589.
[178] Case C-301/87 *France v Commission (Boussac).*

7.5.3.3.7 The Role of National Courts

Because of the direct effect of the last sentence of Article 108(3) TFEU and Article 3 of the Regulation 2015/1589, national courts have an important role in enforcing the procedural requirements of the EU State aid regime. Increasingly, national courts also have an important role in applying the block exemptions. The application of the substantive requirements, other than the rules of the block exemptions, remains the exclusive power of the Commission. National courts enforce the standstill clause. National courts can also award damages in cases of unlawful aid,[179] and grant injunctions. Such remedies may be of vital importance in aid cases where the timing is often a crucial element in rescue operations. The role of national courts has been stressed in a Commission Communication on the cooperation between national courts and the Commission in the field of State aids.[180] This is a useful document explaining the respective roles and the methods of cooperation. This role was originally highlighted in the judgment of the ECJ in the *SFEI* case.[181] The ECJ held in this judgment that national courts seized of a request relating to an infringement of Article 93(3) EEC (now 108(3) TFEU), in case of an aid which is also under review by the Commission, are not required to declare that they lack jurisdiction or stay the proceedings until such time as the Commission has adopted a position. The *CELF* judgments as well as the *Residex* judgment now provide detailed rules.[182] Therefore, the rules explained in the Commission notice on the enforcement of State aid law by national courts will need updating.

National courts may provide several remedies. First, national courts have to order the aid recipient to pay interest in respect of the period of unlawfulness of the aid.[183] Secondly, national courts have an obligation to adopt safeguard measures where three conditions are satisfied. These conditions are set out in paragraph 36 of the CELF 2 judgment.[184] Such remedies may be of vital importance in aid cases where the timing is often a crucial element in rescue operations. If these conditions have not been met, the national court must dismiss the application for such remedies. According to the *Residex* judgment national courts have jurisdiction to cancel a guarantee in a situation in which unlawful aid was implemented by means of a guarantee provided by a public

---

[179] Case C-354/90 *Fédération Nationale du Commerce Extérieur des Produits Alimentaires and Syndicat National des Négociants et Transformateurs de Saumon v France.*

[180] Commission notice on the enforcement of State aid law by national courts [2009] OJ C 85/1.

[181] Case C-39/94 *Syndicat Français de L'Express International (SFEI) and others v La Poste and others.*

[182] Case C-199/06 *Centre d'exportation du livre Français (CELF) and Ministre de la Culture et de la Communication v Société internationale de diffusion et d'Edition (SIDE)* (CELF 1); Case C-1/09 *Centre d'exportation du livre Français (CELF) and Ministre de la Culture et de la Communication v Société internationale de diffusion et d'Edition (SIDE),* (CELF 2). See also Case C-284/12 *Deutsche Lufthansa.* See Christopher Vajda and Paul Stuart, 'Effects of the Standstill Obligation in National Courts—all said after *CELF*? An English Perspective' (2010) 3 *EStAL* 629; Case C-275/10 *Residex Capital IV v Gemeente Rotterdam.*

[183] The German Supreme Court (Bundesgerichtshof) has applied this rule in an interesting judgment concerning a dispute between Deutsche Lufthansa and Ryanair. I ZR 136/09, of 10 February 2011.

[184] 'There is an obligation to adopt safeguard measures only if the conditions justifying such measures are satisfied, namely, that there is no doubt regarding the classification as State aid, that the aid is about to be, or has been, implemented, and that no exceptional circumstances have been found which would make recovery inappropriate. If those conditions are not satisfied, the national court must dismiss the application.'

authority.[185] The guarantee was provided in order to cover a loan granted by a finance company to an undertaking which would not have been able to secure such financing under normal market conditions. National courts are required to ensure that the aid is recovered and, to that end, they can cancel the guarantee, in particular where, in the absence of less onerous procedural measures, that cancellation is such as to lead to or facilitate the restoration of the competitive situation which existed before that guarantee was provided. Thirdly, national courts may also award damages in cases of unlawful aid.[186]

In case of doubt about the question whether a measure constitutes an aid in the sense of Article 107(1) TFEU national courts may refer a question to the ECJ or consult the Commission. The Commission may also be consulted on matters of procedure.

7.5.3.3.8 Other Procedural Issues

The second paragraph of Article 108(2) TFEU states that the Commission or an interested Member State may bring an action before the ECJ in derogation of the provisions of Articles 258 and 259 TFEU[187] if the Member State concerned does not comply with the Commission's decision.[188]

According to the third paragraph of Article 108(2) TFEU, the Council, acting unanimously, may on an application by a Member State decide that an aid shall be considered compatible with the internal market if such a decision is justified by exceptional circumstances.[189] This derogates from the usual rules that empower the Commission. However, the Council can only take such a decision as long as the Commission has not adopted a decision and only by unanimity.[190]

The ECJ has ruled that the Council can no longer take such decisions once the three-month period is over or whenever the Commission has declared the aid incompatible with the Internal Market. It rejected the view of the Council that it was entitled to adopt a decision authorising new aid distinct from that declared incompatible by the Commission. In a series of 2013 judgments, *Commission v Council*,[191] the ECJ

---

[185] Case C-275/10 *Residex Capital IV* v *Gemeente Rotterdam* para 49 states: 'in order to cover a loan granted by a finance company to an undertaking which would not have been able to secure such financing under normal market conditions. National courts are required to ensure that the aid is recovered and, to that end, they can cancel the guarantee, in particular where, in the absence of less onerous procedural measures, that cancellation is such as to lead to or facilitate the restoration of the competitive situation which existed before that guarantee was provided.'

[186] CELF 1 para 53; Case C-354/90 *Fédération Nationale du Commerce Extérieur des Produits Alimentaires and Syndicat National des Négociants et Transformateurs de Saumon v France*.

[187] This means that the Commission does not have to give a reasoned opinion, as is required by Arts 258 and 259 TFEU. Therefore, the procedure of Art 108(2) TFEU is much more expedient.

[188] The Commission followed this procedure in Case 70/72 *Commission v Germany* (*Kohlegesetz*); Cases 31/77R and 53/77 R *Commission v United Kingdom*; Case 203/82 *Commission v Italy*; Case 52/83 *Commission v France*; Case 93/84 *Commission v France*; Case 52/84 *Commission v Belgium*; Case 213/85 *Commission v Netherlands*; Case C-5/89 *Commission v Germany*.

[189] For an example of such a Council decision see Case C-122/94 *Commission v Council*. Advocate General Cosmas reports that there had been no such decision from 1960 till 1967 and only 14 between 1967 and 1983. However, there were 23 such decisions between 1984 and 1994.

[190] Case C-110/02 *Commission v Council*. See also cases C-111, 117 and 118/10, *Commission v Council of the European Union*; Case C-272/12 P *Commission v Ireland cs*.

[191] Case C-399/03 *Commission v Council*; Case C-110/10 *Commission v Council (Lithuania)*; Case C-117/10 *Commission v Council (Poland)*; Case C-118/10 *Commission v Council (Latvia)*; Case C-121/10 *Commission v Council (Hungary)*, paras 50–70.

clarified the competence of the Council further. It recognised the right of Member States, in well-defined cases, to notify an aid not to the Commission but to the Council when seeking authorisation for aid schemes. It clarified the circumstances under which a measure constitutes aid on which the Commission has definitely ruled meaning that the Council is no longer competent to take decisions. The judgments also confirm the discretionary margin of appreciation of the Council.

7.5.3.4 Recovery[192]

According to Article 14 of the Regulation 2015/1589 the Commission has the power to order recovery of illegally implemented aid.[193] The Commission may also order recovery of interest advantages where unlawful aid has been implemented prior to Commission approval.[194]

When ordered to recover aid, a Member State cannot invoke a rule of domestic law to oppose recovery orders.[195] According to the case law the beneficiary cannot rely on the principle of protection of legitimate expectations if the State aid measure was not notified.[196] In this context, it is important to note that the Commission has, for many years, when publishing notices under the Article 108(2) TFEU procedure, warned the enterprises concerned that illegally implemented aid can be recovered.

Commission decisions ordering recovery of illegally implemented aid normally require the Member States concerned to report to the Commission the measures that have been taken to implement the decision. Commission decisions ordering recovery do not normally indicate the exact amount to be recovered.[197] Thus in the case of the electricity power purchase agreements the Hungarian government had to calculate the exact amount to be recovered.[198] This practice often gives rise to lengthy discussions between the Commission and the Member State about how to calculate the exact amount. As was noted above, national courts may, in such a situation, use their discretion to determine the amounts to be repaid.[199]

Sometimes it is difficult to identify the company that should pay back the aid. This is particularly the case when a company has sold subsidiaries that benefitted from the aid.

---

[192] Recovery notice: Commission Notice Towards an effective implementation of Commission decisions ordering Member States to recover unlawful and incompatible State aid OJ 2007 C 272/ 4-17. See E Rigihini, 'Godot is here: Recovery as an effective State Aid Remedy' in *EC State Aid Law*: Liber Amicorum *Francisco Santaolalla Gadea* (Wolters Kluwer, 2008). The handbooks listed above in n 91 all provide extensive treatment of the subject.

[193] Case 70/72 *Commission v Germany*.

[194] Case 310/85 *Deufil GmbH & Co KG v Commission*.

[195] Case 94/87 *Commission v Germany*; and, in particular, Case C-24/95 *Land Rheinland-Pfalz v Alcan Deutschland GmbH*. See also the pending case C-527/12. According to the AG the question in this case is: 'May the recovery of aid found incompatible with the internal market be rendered absolutely impossible because of the obligation to respect the right to effective judicial protection enjoyed by the recipient of that aid and, if so, in what circumstances and for how long?'

[196] Case C-217/06 *Commission v Italy*, para 23. An interesting case in point is the Commission decision on the Arbitral Award *Micula v Romania*, SA.38517, OJ 2015, L 232/43; Appeal Case T-646/14.

[197] See Case C-69/13, *Mediaset SpA*.

[198] Art 4 of Commission Decision 2009/609, [2008] OJ L 225, p 53. See also Joined Cases T- 80/06 and T-182/09, *Budapesti Eromu Zrt v Commission*, para 21.

[199] Note 182 above. See also Case C-69/13, *Mediaset*.

7.5.4 State Aid to the Financial Sector[200]

7.5.4.1 Introduction

The collapse of Lehman Brother's bank in the USA in September 2008 led to a major crisis in the banking sector worldwide.[201] The EU economy was faced with a steep downturn of a level not seen since the 1930s. As a result, many Member States in the EU resorted to massive State aid to prevent their banks from going under. The Commission approved some €4 506 billion in State aid.[202] The EU Commission was flooded with notifications, which, as a result of the extreme urgency of the crisis, had to be dealt with at the greatest possible speed. Often decisions were taken during the weekend in order to avoid a run on the particular bank. Only by approving very substantial aid packages before the opening of the stock exchanges worldwide on Monday could confidence be restored.

The European Council of 15 October 2008 endorsed the Commission's application of the State aid rules and asked for speedy and flexible action. Initially the Commission followed the rules for rescue and restructuring aid as laid down in the 2004 Guidelines.[203]

7.5.4.2 The Commission Communications

As from October 2008, the Commission issued guidance to Member States and financial institutions on the conditions that would need to be met for the State aid granted in response to the financial crisis to be considered compatible with the Treaty.[204] Between October 2008 and July 2009 it published four Communications setting out the principles that it would apply to State guarantees for bank liabilities, recapitalisations, impaired asset relief and restructuring aid. In January 2009 it issued a Communication providing for further possibilities for Member States to support companies in the real economy during the crisis and the conditions such support should satisfy. The latest measure is the Communication from the Commission on the application, from 1 August 2013, of State aid rules to support measures in favour of banks in the context of the financial crisis ('Banking Communication').[205] This Communication withdraws the 2008 Banking Communication and amends the Impaired Assests and Restructuring Communication.

---

[200] For an overview see Francois-Charles Laprévote, 'Selected issues raised by Banking restructuring plans under EU State Aid rules' (2012) 1 *EStAL* 93. This section contains direct quotes and other data from the useful and comprehensive Commission Staff Working Paper, 'The effects of temporary State aid rules adopted in the context of the financial and economic crisis', SEC (2011) 1126 final, Brussels 5.10.2011, henceforth referred to as the 'Staff Working Paper', pp 1–112.

[201] Victoria Ivashinaa and David Scharfstein, 'Bank lending during the financial crisis of 2008' 97(3) *Journal of Financial Economics* 319.

[202] EU Commission, 'State Aid score board' 2013 http://ec.europa.eu/competition/state_aid/scoreboard/financial_economic_crisis_aid_en.html.

[203] [2004] OJ C 244/2.

[204] Commission Staff Working Paper, p 10.

[205] [2013] OJ C 216/1.

The Banking Communication[206] was the first instrument to set out the general principles to be applied, namely: non-discrimination,[207] the need for the aid to be clearly defined and limited in time and scope; adequately paid for by the beneficiaries that should bring an appropriate contribution; and subject to behavioural constraints so as to prevent any abuse of the State support, such as aggressive expansion on the back of a State guarantee.[208] That first Communication already emphasised the need for structural adjustment measures for the financial sector as a whole and for restructuring individual financial institutions that benefited from State intervention. In this Communication the Commission explained that it was confronted with a systemic crisis and therefore the application of Article 107(3)(b) was called for. According to paragraph 94 of the 2013 Banking Communication, the 2008 Communication was withdrawn with effect from 31 July 2013.

Building on these principles, the *Recapitalisation Communication*[209] provided additional detailed guidance on how the Commission would assess recapitalisation measures specifically. In particular, it established detailed principles for the remuneration of the injections of capital made by States into banks, which should reflect the price that a normally functioning market would require for the relevant capital.

The Impaired Asset Communication[210] in turn provided guidance for aid linked to 'relieving' banks from assets which were broadly considered as 'toxic' or 'impaired'.[211] Many banks had a substantial portfolio of such assets

The Restructuring Communication[212] set out in more detail the Commission's approach to the conditions as to when banks needed to submit a restructuring plan and what measures such a plan should include in order to meet the Commission's approval. In particular, it stipulated that banks in need of substantial amounts of aid must, in return for the aid, demonstrate strategies to remedy unsustainable business models and achieve long-term viability without State support under adverse economic conditions. The 2013 Banking Communication amends the Restructuring Communication on several points.

---

[206] Communication from the Commission, 'The application of State aid rules to measures taken in relation to financial institutions in the context of the current global financial crisis' [2008] OJ C 270/8.

[207] Initially Ireland provided only aid to Irish banks and not to banks from other Member States.

[208] In Case C-526/14 *Tadej Kotnik and Others*, the ECJ upheld the validity of the Communication.

[209] Communication from the Commission, 'Recapitalisation of financial institutions in the current financial crisis: limitation of the aid to the minimum necessary and safeguards against undue distortions of competition' [2009] OJ C 10/2.

[210] Communication from the Commission on the Treatment of Impaired Assets in the Community Banking sector ([2009] OJ C 72/1).

[211] According to the Commission Staff Working Paper the notion of 'impaired asset' has broadened over time. Initially, impaired assets were understood as: (i) assets whose intrinsic value is perceived to lie significantly above their market value, possibly due to failing or missing markets (due to massive asymmetric information and valuation uncertainty). However, over time, impaired assets are also understood as including: (ii) assets that incorporate relatively high expected losses; and even (iii) long-term assets without high expected losses ('good safe assets'), but that still need to be hived off the balance sheet, because the banks that carried them faced sharply higher funding costs that led them to record continuing losses over the life-time of the assets.

[212] Communication from the Commission on 'The return to viability and the assessment of restructuring measures in the financial sector in the current crisis under the State aid rules' ([2009] OJ C 195/9).

Finally, a *Communication on a Temporary Framework of aid to the real economy*[213] was adopted to promote companies' access to finance and to support the production of green products. Under these rules Member States could grant a maximum of €500,000 in aid, provided that the aid is granted in the form of a scheme. This is €300,000 more than under the *de minimis* guidelines. The aid has been applied to small and medium size enterprises. According to the Commission's own evaluation the latter instrument 'has allowed a coordinated response to tackle companies' difficulties in accessing finance during the crisis.'[214]

The above instruments have been extended and amended by fresh Commission Communications.[215]

The Communications have extended the scope for rescue aid for large firms and they have allowed rescue aid for more than six months. They have also extended the requirements for restructuring aid to a period up to five years. The Commission's approach, based on the above communications, consists of a first stage approval of rescue aid and a second stage approval of restructuring aid. The first stage approval is subject to the condition that the Member State will submit a restructuring plan within six months from the approval. The second stage approval is often subject to extensive conditions, which can be quite onerous for the financial institution involved. The 2013 Banking Communication embodies the latest round of amendments. According paragraph 23 of the Communication: 'This Communication establishes the principle that recapitalisation and impaired asset measures will be authorised only once the bank's restructuring plan is approved. This approach ensures that the amount of aid is more accurately calibrated, that the sources of the bank's problems are already identified and addressed at an early stage and that financial stability is assured. Guarantee schemes will continue to be available in order to provide liquidity to banks. Such schemes can, however, only serve as a means to provide liquidity to banks without a capital shortfall as defined by the competent supervisory authority.' As can be seen, this is a new approach. Under the old rules aid could only be authorised subject to the condition that a restructuring plan was submitted within six months.

During the period between October 2008 and December 2010 the Commission adopted more than 200 decisions. During 2010 the number of decisions decreased substantially. However, most of the measures approved in the past are still operational. The majority of the decisions were adopted within a very short time frame, in particular in the few weeks following the bankruptcy of Lehman Brothers. The first schemes notified by Member States in the course of October 2008 were for instance approved by the Commission in less than 10 days.

---

[213] Communication from the Commission, 'Temporary Community framework for State aid measures to support access to finance in the current financial and economic crisis' ([2009] OJ C 16/1). The Commission adopted this Communication formally on 19 January 2009.

[214] Commission Staff Working Paper, 'The effects of temporary State aid rules adopted in the context of the financial and economic crisis', SEC (2011) 1126 final (Brussels 5.10.2011), at 6.

[215] Communication from the Commission on the application, from 1 January 2011, of State aid rules to support measures in favour of banks in the context of the financial crisis [2010] OJ C 329/07. Communication from the Commission on the application, from 1 January 2012, of State aid rules to support measures in favour of banks in the context of the financial crisis [2011] OJ, C 356/7.

The vast majority of the decisions adopted by the Commission were decisions not to raise objections, because the proposed State aid could be approved on the basis of Article 107(3)(b) TFEU in light of the principles set out in the Communications. Exchanges between the Commission and Member States after the notification of State aid were essential in ensuring that the proposed aid measure would be approved by the Commission. The Commission only adopted one negative decision,[216] with recovery of the aid, concerning aid to the financial sector throughout the crisis. So far three decisions have been appealed by parties.[217] A final judgment was given by the ECJ in the ING case. The Court dismissed the appeal confirming the partial annulment by the GC.[218]

The enforcement of the state aid rules by the Commission has been essential in containing the crisis. The Commission's efforts have been supplemented by the policies of the ECB which provided 'enhanced credit support'.

---

[216] Restructuring of BPP [2011] OJ L 159, pp 95–106. The Commission ordered the recovery by Portugal of the State aid granted to BPP.

[217] In the cases *ING*, *WestLB* and *ABN AMRO*; the decisions under appeal are: Commission Decision of 18 November 2009 on State aid C 10/09 (ex N 138/09) implemented by the Netherlands for ING's Illiquid Assets Back Facility and Restructuring Plan (OJ L 274, 19.10.2010, p 139), Commission Decision of 12 May 2009 on State aid which Germany proposes to grant towards the restructuring of WestLB AG (C 43/08 (ex N 390/08)) (OJ L 345, 23.12.2009, p 1) and C 11/2009 (not yet published). In Case T-319/11, *ABN-AMRO*, the GC rejected claims that the Commissions had wrongly applied the Rescue and Restructuring Communication, ie, by imposing a ban on new acquisitions.

[218] Case C-224/12 P. In its judgment the General Court annulled in part, the contested decision, holding, inter alia, that the Commission was required to assess the economic rationality of the amendment to the repayment terms in the light of the private investor test. In order to determine the advantage conferred in the case of a capital injection, that test requires the difference in the terms under which the State has granted the injection and the terms under which a private investor would have done so to be taken into account. The Commission did not have to re-examine the amendment to repayment terms following the judgment of the ECJ because it had already taken a fresh decision following the view of the GC. Commission decision of 12 May 2012, Decision C (2012)3150 final. The Netherlands Central Bank intervened in support of the Netherlands and ING.

The International Dimensions of Competition Law

8.1 Introduction

The ever-increasing globalisation of the commercial world has led to a situation in which, today, only very few goods and services are produced and traded in an exclusively national context. Within Europe, this trend of globalisation is further stimulated by the process of European integration, in the form of the EU and, more particularly, the development of the internal market. UK and EU businesses have multiple points of contact with companies outside the EU. Each year, more and more international goods and services transactions are carried out and international mergers are the order of the day. All of these developments have an unavoidable impact upon competition law and policy, a point well illustrated by the fact that the widely publicised investigations of the practices of Microsoft by both US and EU competition authorities were mainly initiated in response to a complaint by Sun Microsystems—both Microsoft and Sun are US-based companies, yet Sun submitted a complaint to the EU Commission, which investigated the matter with alacrity. Competition law and policy have, in their turn, developed a number of devices for dealing with these international phenomena. From a purely UK perspective, EU competition law is naturally one answer to the questions posed by the strongly internationally oriented economic interrelationships that have developed in the UK. Since this book deals with the combined system of EU and UK competition law, we have explained in Chapter 6.9 the cooperation between the Commission and the CMA.

From the perspective of the EU, these international economic interconnections raise, first, the question of the geographic scope of application of EU competition law. This is discussed in section 8.2 below. In the recent past, the EU has adopted and developed various instruments to allow it to face up to the internationalisation of competitive relations and behaviour. In this context, it is first important to see the form that such internationalisation takes *within* the EU, with the rules provided in Regulation 1/2003 for cooperation between the Commission and the NCAs. The EU has established the European Competition Network (ECN) as a form of cooperation between the NCAs and the Commission. The ECN has evolved into a permanent forum for consultation and the exchange of information. The main means used by the EU beyond the inner circle of the ECN has been the conclusion of treaties. The Treaty establishing a European Economic Area perhaps provides the example which comes closest to a multilateral instrument that addresses competition issues. Alongside this, many bilateral agreements have been concluded which have encompassed competition rules. On the basis of these agreements, regular consultations take place, with some occurring on a frequent basis. These instruments and their implementation are looked at below, in section 8.4. Finally, section 8.5 provides brief coverage of some key concepts that have come to the fore in the development of international cooperation and enforcement of competition law, as experienced in the context of EU–US relations in the field.

8.2 The Geographic Scope of Application of EU and UK Competition Law

As discussed in Chapter 2.3.1 above, EU competition law applies not only to activities that take place within the territory of the EU,[1] but also to arrangements that have been entered into outside the EU but which have been implemented within it,[2] or which will have an immediate and substantial effect within the EU.[3] The scope of application of the prohibition on the abuse of a dominant position will necessarily be limited to those cases where the undertaking concerned holds a dominant position within the EU, or at least one which falls in part within the EU. Of course, it is also possible that an undertaking may hold a dominant position on a worldwide market, a good illustration of this phenomenon being the *Microsoft* case, discussed in Chapter 4.2.4.10 above. In such a case, an abuse may be made of a dominant position by arrangements concluded outside the EU, but which are implemented, or have a substantial effect, within the EU. The *Lysine cartel* cases provide a good example of a (secret) price cartel that was put into operation on a worldwide basis. We will discuss these cases in section 8.5 below.

For UK competition law to apply to collusive arrangements or abuses of a dominant position, trade and competition within the UK must be affected (sections 2(1) and 18(1) CA 1998). However, section 2(1) CA 1998 'applies only if the agreement, decision or practice is, or is intended to be, implemented in the UK' (section 2(3) CA 1998). This provision aims to ensure that the EU law position on 'implementation' of such

---

[1] According to Art 52 TEU, the Treaties apply to the 28 Member States of the EU. In addition, Art 355(1) TFEU provides that the Treaty applies to the European territory of the Member States, as well as to the French overseas *départements* (known as '*départements d'outre-mer*'), the Azores, Madeira and the Canary Islands.

[2] Joined Cases 89, 104, 114, 116, 117 and 125 to 129/85 *Åhlström Osakeyhtiö and others v Commission* ('*Woodpulp I*').

[3] Case T-102/96 *Gencor v Commission*; Case T-286/09 *Intel v Commission*.

arrangements is reflected in UK law, while at the same time excluding any possible extension of UK law to cover situations where a mere 'effect' is felt within the UK.[4] The Chapter II prohibition contains no such specific reference to jurisdictional questions, but it seems tolerably clear that the relevant dominant position must be held within the UK (section 18(3) CA 1998). This could include a dominant position on a market wider than the UK alone, provided that some part of UK territory was covered.

So far as the EU Merger Control Regulation 139/2004/EC (the EUMR) is concerned, the geographic scope of its application is determined by the turnover rules of its Article 1. These rules have been discussed above in Chapter 2.3.1 and 5.2.4. The basic idea of these rules is that if the undertakings involved in the merger in question have developed extensive economic activities within the EU, then this justifies EU intervention. Anyone who operates on EU markets must also abide by the rules of the game that apply in that stadium (so to speak). The turnover thresholds in the EUMR lay down what is meant in this context by 'extensive economic activities'. As such, these thresholds can be seen as an exception to the *Woodpulp I* judgment of the ECJ.[5] It is important to point out here that when the EUMR was adopted, third countries (ie, non-EC Member States) made no protests against its provisions. In the *Gencor/Lonrho* judgment the GC ruled that the jurisdictional rules of the merger control regulation are in conformity with international public law.[6] From time to time, however, there are protests where the EUMR is applied in particular cases, such as the Commission's Decision in the *Boeing/McDonnell Douglas* case.[7] Such protests are understandable, given that this sort of merger affects the interests of many different countries. In the case of the merger between Boeing and McDonnell Douglas, both undertakings had large interests in the defence industry. The thresholds of Article 1 EUMR were easily satisfied due to the extensive sales of the relevant products within the EU, even though neither Boeing nor McDonnell Douglas had a sales office or property within the EU. In this case, extensive discussions and negotiations took place between the Commission, the US government and the undertakings concerned.

In July 2001, the European Commission blocked the merger between General Electric and Honeywell.[8] Both companies had their headquarters in the USA, where the Federal Trade Commission had already cleared the merger to be implemented.[9] This case whipped up much comment (a great deal of it adverse from the US side) and strengthened the hand of those calling for further coordination between the Commission and the US antitrust authorities. The GC upheld the Commission's Decision, although it also ruled that the Commission had made manifest errors in three areas.[10] Interestingly, the GC was highly critical of the Commission's treatment of the so-called 'portfolio' or

---

[4] Were the EU case law to move in the direction of an 'effects'-based jurisdictional test, in the rubric of the s 60 CA 1998 'governing principles' clause (on which see Chapter 2.2.1 above), this would be a 'relevant difference' that would justify the UK authorities and courts taking a different approach to questions of jurisdiction under UK competition law (although none of the CMA's Guideline documents discusses this issue).

[5] As was explained by the GC in Case T-102/96 *Gencor Ltd v Commission.*

[6] ibid; see also the annotation by PJ Slot (2001) 38 *Common Market Law Review* 1573.

[7] Commission Decision 97/816/EC of 30 July 1997, [1997] OJ L336/16.

[8] Case COMP/M.2220 *GE/Honeywell* (3 July 2001).

[9] Commission Press Release IP/01/939, 3 July 2001.

[10] Case T-209/01 *Honeywell v Commission*; Case T-210/01, *General Electric v Commission.*

'bundling' effect. It was precisely this element in the Commission's Decision that had drawn heavy criticism from US antitrust lawyers, because the US authorities had considered that the bundling effects would benefit consumers. The GC upheld the Commission's prohibition of the merger, approving the Commission's finding that in three markets the merger would create or strengthen a dominant position. This finding was a sufficient basis upon which the Commission could legitimately conclude that the merger was incompatible with the internal market. It is noteworthy that the parties in the case did not challenge the jurisdiction of the EU to rule upon the acceptability of the merger.

Under UK merger law,[11] the establishment of jurisdiction requires that the relevant 'merger situation' would result in 'a substantial lessening of competition within any market or markets in the United Kingdom' (sections 22(1) and 33(1) EA 2002). Such markets may clearly include both markets operating solely within a part of the UK and those of which the UK itself is only a part (ie, extending into other countries) (section 22(6)(b) and (a) EA 2002 respectively). Similarly, the additional threshold tests concerning either the level of turnover or 25 per cent share of supply (laid down in section 23 EA 2002) both require that the turnover be made, or market of supply share held, in the UK or a substantial part thereof.

A further important issue in this context is whether or not EU competition law is also applicable to export cartels, concerning exports from within the EU to third countries. The ECJ has held that export cartels that involve exports to third countries cannot be said to restrict competition in the internal market.[12]

For judges in the USA, meanwhile, dealing with damages claims brought against American companies for their activities outside the USA has been a difficult development. Such so-called 'treble damages actions' (due to the availability of three times the normal quantum of damages under US antitrust law) had been declared admissible by a number of lower courts,[13] but in the *Empagran* case the US Supreme Court held that such claims are not admissible in US courts.[14] This judgment raised the difficult question of how to reconcile various competing precedents with *Empagran*, in particular the Supreme Court's earlier judgment in *Pfizer*.[15] For Ryngaert:

> What actually distinguishes *Pfizer* from the *Vitamins* case is the nature of the plaintiffs and the location of the defendants. The plaintiffs in *Pfizer* were states, in the *Vitamins* case private

---

[11] For discussion of the UK merger regime, see Chapter 5.3 above.

[12] Case 174/84 *Bulk Oil (Zug) AG v Sun International Limited and Sun Oil Trading Company*.

[13] See, eg, *Pfizer Inc v Government of India* 434 US 308 (1978) (an earlier judgment of the Supreme Court), and *Kruman v Christie's International plc* 284 F 3d 384 (2nd Cir 2002) and *Empagran SA v Hoffman-La Roche Ltd* 315 F 3d 338 (DC Cir 2003) (the last of which was the subject of the appeal to the Supreme Court, see n 14 below). *cf*, for a case where jurisdiction for the US courts was not found, *Den Norske Stats Oljeselskap AS ('Statoil') v HeereMac VOF* 241 F 3d 420 (5th Cir 2001), cert denied, 534 US 1127 (2002).

[14] *Hoffmann-La Roche Ltd v Empagran SA* 315 F.3d 338, vacated and remanded by 542 US 155; 134 S Ct 2359; 159 L Ed 2d 226 (2004) (Sup Ct, 14 June 2004). A further point of interest in the case was the focus of the Supreme Court upon the issue of interpreting the relevant statute (the Foreign Trade Antitrust Improvements Act) in the light of international law, to ensure compliance of the former with the latter where possible. The Court relied upon the principle of comity and the danger that an expansive interpretation of the extraterritorial reach of US antitrust law would lead to an unacceptable interference in the domestic regulations of other countries. On this issue prior to the Supreme Court's decision in *Empagran*, see, eg, A Johnston and E Powles, '"The Kings of the World and their Dukes" Dilemma: Globalisation, Jurisdiction and the Rule of Law' in PJ Slot and M Bulterman (eds), *Globalisation and Jurisdiction* (The Hague, Kluwer Law International, 2004) 45–52, and the references cited therein.

[15] See n 13 above.

claimants. The defendants in *Pfizer* were US companies, the defendants in the *Vitamins* case were foreign companies. Furthermore, the plaintiffs in *Pfizer* made purchases in the United States, whereas the transactions in the *Vitamins* case took place abroad. All these differences point to a greater nexus between the *Pfizer* conspiracy and US commerce. The last difference is probably decisive: if a foreign company (or state) purchases goods at an inflated price in the United States, this company (or state) can sue the members of the price-fixing cartel in the United States, whatever their nationality, as the higher price paid in the United States constitutes the domestic effect required for jurisdiction under the Sherman Act. If the foreign company purchases goods outside the United States, it can only sue the cartelists, whatever their nationality, in the United States provided that the harm caused to it by the price-fixing agreement is dependent on harm caused by this agreement in the United States.[16]

This kind of issue has also been faced by the UK courts in the UK instalment of the *Vitamins cartel* cases, *Provimi*,[17] in which the claimants sought to recover the amount that they had overpaid for vitamin supplies as a result of the existence of the cartel. In this case, the claimants included (alongside English subsidiaries that had purchased vitamins from the subsidiaries of the members of the cartel in England) German subsidiaries, which had purchased vitamins from the German subsidiaries of the parent companies involved in the cartel (the parent companies were Swiss: Roche and Aventis). This makes it clear that one of the claims related to activities that had taken place wholly outside the UK. Nevertheless, this could still be the basis for an action against the English subsidiaries in an English court, provided that the court accepted that the behaviour of the English subsidiaries was vital to the successful functioning of the cartel across Europe. If this were accepted, then the Swiss parent company could be joined to the action in the UK court, provided that a sufficiently close connection between the relevant claims could be found to justify proceeding against the parent company in a country other than that of its domicile (Article 2 of Regulation 44/2001/EC).[18]

The claim was contested by the parent companies, on a number of grounds.[19] First, it was argued that there was an insufficiently close connection between the sales in Germany and those in the UK, so that Article 6(1) of Regulation 44/2001/EC[20] would

---

[16] C Ryngaert, 'Foreign-to-foreign Claims: the US Supreme Court's Decision (2004) v the English High Court's Decision (2003) in the *Vitamins* Case' [2004] *ECLR* 611, at 613.

[17] *Provimi Ltd v Aventis Animal Nutrition SA* [2003] EWHC 961, [2003] ECC 29, [2003] Eu LR 517, [2003] 2 All ER (Comm) 683, [2003] UKCLR 493, discussed by FW Bulst, 'The *Provimi* Decision of the High Court: Beginnings of Private Antitrust Litigation in Europe' (2003) 4 *European Business Organization Review* 623 and Ryngaert, ibid, the latter of which also discusses the *Empagran* case in the USA (n 13 above).

[18] [2001] OJ L12/1: in tort cases, an action must ordinarily be brought in the court of the domicile of the defendant.

[19] Points were also taken on the Swiss, German and French jurisdiction clauses contained in some of the relevant contracts: see [50]ff, [67]ff and [103]ff, respectively, for discussion. Aikens J heard extensive expert evidence on the relevant foreign law, and held that none of these jurisdiction clauses was sufficiently wide to include the claims brought in *Provimi*, as all would have been tort claims and thus not covered by these clauses.

[20] Art 6(1) of Reg 44/2001/EC enables entities to be joined to proceedings when the claims against them are 'so closely connected that it is expedient to hear and determine them together to avoid the risk of irreconcilable judgments resulting from separate proceedings'. Art 6(1) of Reg 44/2001/EC has now been replaced by Art 8 of Reg 1215/2012, which applies to proceedings issued on or after 10 January 2015. The substantive elements of Art 8 of Reg 1215/2012 remain unchanged as compared to Art 6(1) of Reg 44/2001/EC.

not justify joining the parent companies to the proceedings. Secondly, it was claimed that mere implementation by a subsidiary of a cartel could not amount to an infringement of Article 101(1) TFEU by that subsidiary. This was because the subsidiary and the parent formed a single economic unit, so that any implementation by the subsidiary was simply an internal practice within an undertaking, rather than an infringing agreement.[21] Thirdly, even if the subsidiary could in principle commit such an infringement, it would also require knowledge of the existence of the cartel for its implementation thereof to amount to an infringement; in the absence of such knowledge, there could be no concurrence of wills between the subsidiary and the other undertakings in the cartel, hence no agreement and thus no liability. Fourthly, the argument was made that the cartel could not be shown to have caused the loss suffered by the German claimant. This was because each group set its prices centrally and thus the German claimant would never have been able to purchase vitamins from the English selling subsidiary at a price different from that available in Germany.

Rejecting the application by the parent companies to strike out the claims, Aikens J held that:

> It seems to me to be arguable that where two corporate entities are part of an 'undertaking' (call it 'Undertaking A') and one of those entities has entered into an infringing agreement with other, independent, 'undertakings', then if another corporate entity which is part of Undertaking A then implements that infringing agreement, it is also infringing Article 101. In my view it is arguable that it is not necessary to plead or prove any particular 'concurrence of wills' between the two legal entities within Undertaking A. The E[U] competition law concept of an 'undertaking' is that it is one economic unit. The legal entities that are a part of the one undertaking, by definition of the concept, have no independence of mind or action or will. They are to be regarded as all one. Therefore, so it seems to me, the mind and will of one legal entity is, for the purposes of Article 101 TFEU, to be treated as the mind and will of the other entity. There is no question of having to 'impute' the knowledge or will of one entity to another, because they are one and the same.[22]

As a result of this reasoning, both the 'single economic unit' and the 'knowledge' points fell away and Aikens J found that the claimants had an arguable case against the parent companies. On the causation issue,[23] meanwhile, Aikens J held that the key question was:

> 37. …what would the situation have been if there had been no cartels? There may still have been centralised pricing within the groups of companies … But it must be arguable that, without the cartels, there would have been competition between, say, the Roche group and the Aventis group. As a consequence, the various claimants, including Trouw Germany, may have been able to buy vitamins from another group at a lower price than the price fixed by the cartels.

> 38. If, as I have held, it is arguable that all companies within an 'undertaking' who 'implemented' the cartel are infringers of Art.101, then their action in 'implementing' the

---

[21] See, eg, Case C-73/95 *Viho Europe Ltd v Commission* and our discussion in Chapter 2.1.1 above.
[22] *Provimi Ltd v Aventis Animal Nutrition SA* [2003] EWHC 961, [2003] ECC 29, [2003] Eu LR 517, [2003] 2 All ER (Comm) 683, [2003] UKCLR 493, at [31].
[23] See the comments of Ryngaert, n 16 above, 614–16.

cartel could cause the loss that the claimants allege. On this analysis, each infringing entity is a tortfeasor. I do not think it matters whether they are to be regarded as joint or several tortfeasors for the purpose of the causation argument. Each entity would have contributed to a situation where it took part in the cartel, upheld the cartel prices and so (arguably) caused loss.

Thus, the parent companies' arguments were rejected and the judge held that the claimants did indeed have an arguable case against the parent companies.

The practical consequence of the court's finding in *Provimi* that the English court did indeed have jurisdiction to hear the claim is that, in future, claimants will be able to bring an action against the English subsidiary of a member of a cartel to recover losses suffered across Europe, rather than being forced to proceed either in the cartelist parent's own Member State of domicile or in each individual Member State where a loss was incurred. This approach, which has subsequently been followed by the Court of Appeal in the *Toshiba Carrier* case,[24] and has also been adopted by the CCAT,[25] is likely to encourage private actions to recover such losses incurred as a result of cartels (or other anti-competitive activities) in the EU to be pursued in the UK.

The scope of the Provimi doctrine is not however, without its limits. In its ruling in *Deutsche Bahn v Morgan Advanced Materials plc*,[26] the Supreme Court held that the English courts can only take jurisdiction for claims against parent companies domiciled outside of the UK on the basis of the *Provimi* doctrine provided that the claim against the anchor defendant (ie, the UK subsidiary company) is admissible. In the case at hand, Deutsche Bahn's claim against the UK subsidiary Morgan was brought out of time (ie, after the expiry of the relevant limitation period) and was therefore inadmissible. As a result, the Supreme Court ruled that the claim against the non-UK parent companies was also inadmissible.

Finally, there have also been instances where claimants have sought to establish jurisdiction by reference to contractual jurisdiction clauses in contracts with the defendant. Following the Court of Appeal decision in *Ryanair Limited v Esso Italiana SRL*,[27] however, a contractual jurisdiction clause cannot be relied upon if it does not specifically envisage the bringing of a claim on the basis of a breach of competition law.

---

[24] See, eg, *Toshiba Carrier UK Ltd and others v KME Yorkshire Ltd and others* [2012] EWCA Civ 169. It is interesting to note, however, that the *Provimi* approach has not received universal approval from the Court of Appeal. In the *Cooper Tire* case, Longmore LJ (delivering the judgment of the court) noted that the point was 'also arguable the other way'. He emphasised that the Commission's fining practice was to single out those who are primarily responsible or their parent companies and questioned whether a subsidiary could be held liable where it did not deal in the relevant product or service at all. Had the point been necessary for the decision in that case, the court would have been inclined to seek the views of the Court of Justice by making an Art 267 TFEU reference for a preliminary ruling (*Cooper Tire & Rubber Company Europe v Dow Deutschland* [2010] EWCA Civ 864, [2010] UKCLR 1277, [45]–[47]).

[25] *DSG Retail Limited and Dixons Retail Limited v MasterCard Incorporated and others* [2015] CAT 7.

[26] *Deutsche Bahn AG and others (Respondents) v Morgan Advanced Materials Plc (Appellant)* [2014] UKSC 24.

[27] *Ryanair Limited v Esso Italiana SRL* [2013] EWCA Civ 1450.

8.3 International Cooperation

8.3.1 The European Competition Network (ECN)

From the perspective of a third country observer, the ECN may well be viewed as international cooperation. From the perspective of an intra EU observer it is EU cooperation. The website of the Directorate General for Competition of the Commission (DG COMP) describes the ECN as follows:

[t]he European Commission and the national competition authorities in all EU Member States cooperate with each other through the European Competition Network (ECN). This creates an effective mechanism to counter companies which engage in cross-border practices restricting competition. As European competition rules are applied by all members of the ECN, the ECN provides means to ensure their effective and consistent application. Through the ECN, the competition authorities inform each other of proposed decisions and take on board comments from the other competition authorities. In this way, the ECN allows the competition authorities to pool their experience and identify best practices.

The ECN operates a closed internet network for the exchange of information, as required by Articles 11 and 12 of Regulation 1/2003. The website of the ECN is a valuable source of information about its activities and reports.[28]

The ECN regularly publishes issues of its briefs which provide summaries of cases handled by the NCAs as well as reports of national court decisions.[29] In November 2011, the ECN published its 'Best Practices on cooperation between EU National Competition Authorities in Merger Review'. The Commission's *Annual Report on Competition Policy 2010* contains the following summary:

[i]n 2010, the European Competition Network (ECN) continued to be a very active forum for discussion and exchange of good practices on the enforcement of EU antitrust rules across the 27 Member States. The Commission was informed under Article 11(3) of Regulation 1/2003164 of 158 new case investigations launched by NCAs in 2010, inter alia in the transport, energy, manufacturing, media and telecom sectors. Moreover, the number of enforcement decisions reported by NCAs and reviewed by the Commission increased by 36% compared to 2009. As in previous years, the Commission did not initiate in 2010 any proceedings with the view to ensuring coherency in decision-making.

---

[28] See http://ec.europa.eu/competition/ecn/index_en.html.

[29] Thus, eg, in the eleventh brief of 12 February 2012 there was a report from the Court of Bonn in Germany with its final decision on the *Pfleiderer* case (C-360/09). The Court of Bonn decided that the threat to the effective detection and prosecution of competition law infringements justified the refusal of access to the leniency applications. The comment in the brief is: 'Leniency Programme strengthened by Final Decision regarding Access to File.' On the *Pfleiderer* judgment, see Chapter 6.5.

8.3.2 The EEA Treaty and the Europe Agreements

The Treaty establishing the European Economic Area (the EEA Treaty) was established to allow the European Free Trade Association (EFTA) to connect itself to the internal market of the EU without the complications of the full institutional structure of the EU. After the rejection of the Treaty by Switzerland (which failed to ratify it) and the accession of Finland, Austria and Sweden to the EU, only Norway, Iceland and Liechtenstein remain as EFTA members and thus partners with the EU in the EEA. The EEA Treaty contains provisions on competition law that are practically identical to those found in the TFEU. There are separate institutions—the EFTA Surveillance Authority—which is responsible for ensuring that competition law is observed and the EFTA court. Both the Authority as well as the Court will interpret the competition rules in the same way as the ECJ and CG.[30] Alongside this Authority, the national courts also have jurisdiction to enforce these competition rules. Just as with the EU rules, the competition rules in the EEA Treaty have direct effect. There is a far-reaching system of cooperation on competition matters between the EU Commission and the EFTA Authority. In the application of their competition laws, both authorities are obliged to take into account the effect upon trade between EU Member States and the EEA Member States.[31] In many of its antitrust and merger decisions the Commission applies both EU and EEA provisions.

Rather rapidly after the implosion of the communist regimes in the countries of Central and Eastern Europe, an intensive programme of cooperation was established between those countries and the EU. The ultimate goal of this cooperation was the accession of these countries to the EU. Since the realisation of this goal required a considerable investment of time and effort before it would be practicable, an interim solution was formulated. The Europe Agreements were created to provide a clear and intensive context for this cooperation during the somewhat lengthy period before these countries were ready to accede to the EU. These were agreements between the EU and the countries of Central and Eastern Europe, which provided for the creation of a free trade zone for industrial goods within a period of 10 years.[32] All of these Agreements contain rules on competition law that are largely identical to those contained in the TFEU.[33] Under the Agreements, the competition rules are to be interpreted and applied in accordance with the principles developed by the ECJ, the GC and the European Commission.

---

[30]   This follows from Art 3 of the Surveillance and Court Agreement.

[31]   For general discussion of the EEA Treaty and its legal elements, see A Evans, *The Integration of the European Community and Third States in Europe: A Legal Analysis* (Oxford, Oxford University Press, 1996).

[32]   The very sensitive agricultural sector was left outside the scope of these agreements.

[33]   See, eg, Arts 63–65 of the Agreement between the EC and Poland [1993] OJ L348/1.

8.4 International Agreements

8.4.1 International Agreements and Their Implementation

8.4.1.1 Introduction

In recent years, there has been a general realisation that the international aspects of competition and competition law will play an ever greater role in the future. This has made the time and climate ripe for the development of international cooperation in this field.

This, however, has not always been the case. During a lengthy period, between 1945 and the mid-1960s, the governments of the Western European countries, Japan and China joined together in their opposition to the extraterritorial application of the American antitrust legislation. This began the moment that the American judge Justice Learned Hand, in the famous *Alcoa* judgment, ruled that the Sherman Act (the US antitrust legislation) applied to activities conducted outside the USA, provided that these activities had an effect upon competition in the USA.[34] Thus was the 'effects doctrine' born. The application of this doctrine created a lot of bad blood among the Member States of the EU, because at that time a much more liberal competition policy was applied in Europe. Even the UK took strong exception to the application of American antitrust law in this way, making strong representations to the US government and presenting a number of *amicus curiae* briefs in cases brought in American courts against UK companies under this doctrine.[35]

The attitude of the EU changed in the 1980s when EU competition law began to develop a clearer and more coherent form, which brought with it a much-sharpened set of national competition laws. A greater degree of understanding began to emerge concerning the American position. This appreciation was definitively encapsulated at the end of the 1980s by the judgment of the ECJ in *Woodpulp I*[36] and the setting of the rules on the geographic scope of the EUMR.[37] It was in this, more favourable, climate

---

[34] *United States v Aluminium Co of America (Alcoa)* 148 F 2d 416 (2nd Cir 1945).

[35] For a helpful account of this process up to the early 1980s, see AV Lowe, *Extraterritorial Jurisdiction* (Cambridge, Grotius Publications, 1983), 156–93 (where documentation on the UK approach is extracted) and DE Rosenthal and WM Knighton, *National Laws and International Commerce: The Problem of Extraterritoriality* (London, RIIA/Routledge & Kegan Paul, 1982). In this context, it would seem (in spite of s 60 CA 1998 and the possible argument that at least an 'implementation' doctrine, *à la Woodpulp I*, should be applied to ensure consistency with EC law) highly unlikely that the UK authorities or courts would seek to apply the UK's competition rules in an extraterritorial manner. For a summary account of the US case law and some reactions thereto, see Johnston and Powles, above n 14.

[36] See n 2 above.

[37] It should be noted, however, that this understanding does not extend to the extraterritorial application of US legislation in the field of foreign trade. Thus, the application of the so-called Helms–Burton and D'Amato Acts (properly entitled the Cuban Liberty and Democratic Solidarity (Libertad) Act 1996 and the Iran and Libya Sanctions Act 1996 respectively), under which dealings by European undertakings

that negotiations led to the conclusion of two agreements between the US and the EU concerning the application of their respective competition rules.

Since then the EU has pursued a twofold strategy to address the increasing globalisation: it developed and strengthened direct bilateral relations with main trading partners and it invested substantially in multilateral bodies such as the OECD or the International Competition Network (ICN).[38]

8.4.1.2 General Notes on Bilateral Competition Relations

According to the website of the Directorate General of Competition, the Commission has an active cooperation policy with competition authorities of many countries outside the EU.[39] For the main trading partners of the EU this cooperation is based on bilateral competition agreements dedicated entirely to competition (the so-called 'dedicated agreements'). The EU has such agreements with seven countries.[40] In the relations with other countries, competition provisions are included as part of wider general agreements such as free Trade Agreements, Partnership and Cooperation Agreements, and Association Agreements.[41]

The USA Department of Justice Antitrust Division also pursues an active policy on bilateral relationships.[42] It is committed to establishing new agreements as was evidenced by the conclusion of Memorandum of Understanding on Antitrust Cooperation with the three Chinese antimonopoly agencies on 27 July 2011.[43] The website of the Department of Justice lists 12 bilateral agreements.[44] All of these agreements have been concluded with both US antitrust agencies: the Department of Justice and the Federal Trade Commission.

In 1994 the US Congress passed the International Antitrust Enforcement Assistance Act (IAEAA).[45] The Act was designed to address the statutory limitations on the ability of the US antitrust authorities to obtain confidential information. Under

with Cuba, Iran and Libya were made punishable offences, led to fierce protests and countermeasures being taken by the EC (Reg 2271/96/EC [1996] OJ L307/1 and Joint Action 96/668/CFSP 1996] OJ l309/7). On this topic, see M Hillyard and V Miller, 'Cuba and the Helms–Burton Act' (House of Commons Research Paper 98/114, 14 December 1998) and MA Groombridge, 'Missing the Target: the Failure of the Helms–Burton Act' (Cato Institute, Trade Briefing Paper No. 12, 5 June 2001).

[38] An overview of the international activities of the EU can be found in the Commission's annual *Report on Competition Policy*.

[39] http://ec.europa.eu/competition/international/bilateral/index.html.

[40] The website of DG COMP http://ec.europa.eu/competition/international/bilateral/index.html lists the following countries: Brazil, Canada, China, Japan, Korea, Russia and the USA.

[41] There are 29 of such agreements. Some are of a very general nature, others, in particular the agreement with Switzerland, are very comprehensive.

[42] The Antitrust Division's International Program. US Department of Justice November 2011. http://www.justice.gov/atr/public/international/program.pdf.

[43] The agencies are: the Ministry of Commerce in charge of merger control, the State administration of industry and commerce in charge of non-price related anti-competitive behaviour and the National Development and Reform Commission in charge of price related anti-competitive behaviour.

[44] Australia, Brazil, Canada, Chili, China, Germany, India, Israel, Japan, Mexico, Russia and the EU.

[45] See Annex I-C 'U.S.Experience with international antitrust enforcement cooperation.' Website DOJ http://www.justice.gov/atr/icpac/1c.htm. M Chowdhury, 'From Paper Promises to Concrete Commitments: Dismantling The Obstacles to Transatlantic Cooperation in Cartel Enforcement', AAI Working Paper No 11-09.

the IAEAA bilateral treaties can be concluded that allow for more extensive cooperation, provided that the counterpart has legislation that allows entry into agreements under which information may be exchanged in antitrust matters. Furthermore, such countries must have a strong regime of confidentiality laws that will protect non-public information obtained from US companies.

The only agreement concluded under this act so far is with Australia.[46] This will be discussed in section 8.4.1.3.4 below.

It would, at the present stage of the development of EU law, seem difficult for the EU to assume obligations as specified in this treaty.

In the US the agreements under the IAEAA have provisions on the protection of confidential and privileged information commensurate with US law. In addition to the IAEAA the USA also has a whole network of bilateral mutual legal assistance treaties. Such treaties allow for close cooperation in criminal matters.[47] They may also be used for the purpose of cooperation in the field of antitrust law, provided that the antitrust laws of the partner country also qualify infringements of competition law as a criminal matter. For practical purposes this excludes cooperation with the EU on the basis of such treaties. It would, however, allow cooperation with the UK given the nature of UK national law. However, the exclusive nature of the EU competence excludes a 'UK going it alone' action.[48]

8.4.1.3   Comprehensive Bilateral Treaties

8.4.1.3.1   The Bilateral Treaties Between the EU and the USA of 1991 and 1998

The first agreement was concluded by the Commission in 1991, three years after the *Woodpulp I* judgment. It was finally brought into force by a Decision of the Council of Ministers in 1995.[49] The most important principles of the agreement are that the parties are to inform each other in detail of competition cases that are imminent or pending. Further provision is made for the exchange of information between the EU and US competition authorities, insofar as the rules concerning the protection of confidential information in both systems allow such exchanges to be made. Article IV of the agreement establishes a system of cooperation and coordination in the enforcement activities of both parties' competition authorities, while Article V lays down further important principles concerning anticompetitive activities in the territory of one party that adversely affect the interests of the other party. The latter focuses in particular upon the possibility that anticompetitive activities in (say) the USA may have an impact upon EU interests and the EU may request the US authorities to commence 'appropriate enforcement activities', providing information which is as specific as possible to the US authorities and offering further information and cooperation where possible. Article VI obliges each party to consider the important interests of

---

[46] http://www.justice.gov/atr/public/international/docs/usaus7.htm.

[47] See US experience with International Antitrust Enforcement Cooperation, Annex I-C http://www.justice.gov/atr/icpac/finalreport.html, Chowdhury, ibid, p 8.

[48] Please note that this sentence was written before Britain's exit from the European Union.

[49] OJ, 1995, L95/45.

the other party throughout its enforcement activities and to take various measures to avoid conflicts arising from the enforcement of their respective competition laws. Specifically, the Article provides that:

> On the basis of this agreement, the Commission's Competition Directorate General regularly cooperates with the antitrust authorities in the US, the Department of Justice and the Federal Trade Commission. This cooperation usually occurs during particular cases concerning multinational companies that have both US and EU connections; on a practical working level, the contacts are usually between the relevant officials handling the case in question.

The second agreement was concluded in 1998.[50] This agreement went a step further and provides for so-called 'positive comity'. The comity principle means that States must respect the justifiable interests of other States as much as possible. In most cases, the comity principle is formulated in a negative way: a State should refrain from actions that could damage the interests of other States. This formulation of the principle was, to a certain extent, reflected in the terms of the first EU–US agreement. In the second agreement, however, the comity principle is given a positive formulation: States should actively assist each other where that is possible and necessary to look after each other's important interests. To this end, Article III of the 1998 agreement offers each party the possibility to request the competition authorities of the other party 'to investigate and, if warranted, to remedy anti-competitive activities in accordance with the Requested Party's competition laws'. Under Article IV, it is possible that one of the parties may defer or suspend their own investigative or enforcement activities and procedures 'during the pendency of enforcement activities of the Requested Party'. In practice, these principles make it possible for the most appropriate competition authority to address breaches of competition law, rather than simply the party that coincidentally happens to become aware of the case first. Cooperation on the basis of these agreements has been intense in recent years. A number of important antitrust and merger cases investigated affected both markets.[51]

These provisions allow for far reaching coordination of the enforcement activities of the three agencies.[52] Taken together the rules on comity have created a very fruitful cooperation.

Both agreements provide for rules on the exchange of information. Article III of the 1991 Agreement reads:

Confidentiality and Use of Information

1. The Parties agree that it is in their common interest to share information that will (a) facilitate effective application of their respective competition laws, or (b) promote better understanding by them of economic conditions and theories relevant to their competition authorities' enforcement activities and interventions or participation of the kind described in Article II, paragraph 5. [...]

---

[50] OJ, 1998, L 173/28, The Agreement was approved by a Decision of the Council and of the Commission of 29 May 1998, OJ, 1998, L 173/26.

[51] This can be inferred from the Annual Reports on Competition available at the website http://ec.europa. eu/competition/publications/annual_report/index.html.

[52] On the US side both the Department of Justice (DOJ) and the Federal Trade Commission may be involved.

3. Each Party will provide the other Party with any significant information that comes to the attention of its competition authorities about anticompetitive activities that its competition authorities believe is relevant to, or may warrant, enforcement activity by the other Party's competition authorities.

4. Upon receiving a request from the other Party, and within the limits of Articles VIII and IX, a Party will provide to the requesting Party such information within its possession as the requesting Party may describe that is relevant to an enforcement activity being considered or conducted by the requesting Party's competition authorities.

8.4.1.3.2 EU and USA Best Practices on Cooperation in Merger Investigations

On 14 October 2011, 20 years after the first bilateral treaty, the cooperation between the two partners was extended to establishing 'Best Practices on cooperation in reviewing mergers'.[53] The cooperation in the merger area had been under some pressure after the EU prohibited the *General Electric/Honeywell* merger after it had been approved by the US authorities.[54] A key paragraph of the memorandum reads as follows:

6. For example, at the start of any investigation in which it appears that substantial cooperation between the US agencies and DG Competition may be beneficial, the relevant DOJ Section Chief or FTC Assistant Director and DG Competition Unit Head (or their designees) should seek to agree on a tentative timetable for regular inter-agency consultations, which takes into account the nature and timing of the merger. While it will normally be beneficial to keep each other informed on a continuous basis and discussions may take place at any time between the reviewing agencies, consultations are likely to be particularly useful at key stages of the investigation, including: (a) before the relevant US agency either closes an investigation without taking action or issues a second request; (b) no later than three weeks after the European Commission initiates a Phase I investigation; (c) before the European Commission opens a Phase II investigation or clears the merger without initiating a Phase II investigation; (d) before the European Commission closes a Phase II investigation without issuing a Statement of Objections or before DG Competition anticipates issuing a Statement of Objections; (e) before the relevant DOJ section/FTC division makes its case recommendation to senior leadership; (f) at the commencement of remedies negotiations with the merging parties; and (g) prior to a reviewing agency's final decision to seek to prohibit a merger.[55] Consultations between the senior leadership of DG Competition and their counterparts in the US agencies may also be appropriate at any time. The senior leadership of the reviewing agencies should be kept informed of key milestones throughout the investigation. Consultations also may take place between the reviewing agencies' economic counterparts at appropriate points in the investigation.

---

[53] This document revises the best practices agreed between DG Competition and the US agencies in 2002 and builds on the experience gained in a significant number of cases since 2002. US-EU Merger Working Group, Best Practices on Cooperation in Merger Investigations, *available at* http://ec.europa.eu/competition/international/bilateral/eu_us.pdf; http://www.justice.gov/atr/public/international/docs/200405.htm.

[54] See Case T-209/01 *Honeywell v Commission* and Case T-210/01 *General Electric v Commission*.

[55] Pursuant to the terms of the Administrative Arrangements on Attendance of 1999, officials of the relevant US agency and DG Competition, as appropriate, may attend certain key events in the other's investigative process.

This paragraph shows clearly how intensive the cooperation may be in actual cases. The instrument proved to be a useful framework in, for example, the Cisco/Tandberg[56] and Novartis/Alcon cases.[57] Nevertheless, intensive cooperation will not always result in full alignment of the positions of the agencies on both sides of the Atlantic.[58] Similar cooperation in trans-Atlantic relations took place in the GE/ALSTOM case.[59]

8.4.1.3.3 Canada

There are two agreements between the USA and Canada. One concluded in October 2004 and one earlier from August 1995.[60] As the 2004 agreement notes, the close economic relations between the two countries in the framework of NAFTA (North American Free Trade Agreement) call for close coordination. The August 1995 US-Canada Cooperation Agreement contains similar provisions to the 1991 EU–USA agreement. Article V contains a similar provision on positive comity. The 2004 Agreement on the Application of Positive Comity Principles takes matters further. Article III reads 'Positive Comity' and provides as follows:

> The competition authorities of a Requesting Party may request the competition authorities of a Requested Party to investigate and, if warranted, to remedy anticompetitive activities in accordance with the Requested Party's competition laws. Such a request may be made regardless of whether the activities also violate the Requesting Party's competition laws, and regardless of whether the competition authorities of the Requesting Party have commenced or contemplate taking enforcement activities under their own competition laws.

It may be noted that this provision is basically identical to the positive comity provision in the EU–USA 1998 agreement. In addition, the agreement provides for the usual notification and exchange of information. Another form of advanced cooperation is the 1999 Agreement between the European Communities and the Government of Canada regarding the application of their competition laws.[61] The agreement largely resembles the first US–Canada agreement. It contains the usual provisions on notification, consultation and coordination of enforcement activities. It also provides for positive comity in similar terms.

8.4.1.3.4 Australia

The 1999 agreement between the USA and Australia[62] is, so far, the only bilateral agreement concluded on the basis of the 1994 International Antitrust Enforcement

---

[56] Case No COMP/M.5669—CISCO/Tandberg.

[57] Case No COMP/M.5778—NOVARTIS/Alcon.

[58] An example in the area of antitrust is the investigations of Google where notwithstanding the fact that the FTC did not pursue the allegations of abuse of dominance whereas the EC Commission continued its action. Vice-President Almunia stated: 'After meeting Eric Schmidt, executive chairman of Google, today in Brussels, I have decided to continue with the process towards reaching an agreement based on Article 9 of the EU Antitrust regulation. Since our preliminary talks with Google started in July, we have substantially reduced our differences regarding possible ways to address each of the four competition concerns expressed by the Commission'. Speech 12/967 of 18/12/2012, http://europa.eu/rapid/press-release_SPEECH-12-967_en.htm.

[59] IP 15/5606.

[60] http://www.justice.gov/atr/public/international/int-arrangements.html.

[61] OJ, 1999, L 175, p 149.

[62] http://www.justice.gov/atr/public/international/int-arrangements.html.

Assistance Act (IAEAA). The agreement provides for a very far reaching form of cooperation. This is evidenced by Article II that spells out the object and scope of the agreement:

A. The Parties intend to assist one another and to cooperate on a reciprocal basis in providing or obtaining antitrust evidence that may assist in determining whether a person has violated, or is about to violate, their respective antitrust laws, or in facilitating the administration or enforcement of such antitrust laws.

B. Each Party's Antitrust Authorities shall, to the extent compatible with that Party's laws, enforcement policies, and other important interests, inform the other Party's Antitrust Authorities about activities that appear to be anticompetitive and that may be relevant to, or may warrant, enforcement activity by the other Party's Antitrust Authorities.

C. Each Party's Antitrust Authorities shall, to the extent compatible with that Party's laws, enforcement policies, and other important interests, inform the other Party's Antitrust Authorities about investigative or enforcement activities taken pursuant to assistance provided under this Agreement that may affect the important interests of the other Party. ...

D. Assistance contemplated by this Agreement includes but is not limited to:

a. disclosing, providing, exchanging, or discussing antitrust evidence in the possession of an Antitrust Authority;
b. obtaining antitrust evidence at the request of an Antitrust Authority of the other Party, including
    i. taking the testimony or statements of persons or otherwise obtaining information from persons,
    ii. obtaining documents, records, or other forms of documentary evidence, [...]

8.4.1.3.5 Switzerland

A special form of cooperation is embodied in the EU agreement with Switzerland.[63] When assessing this agreement, it should be remembered that Switzerland took part in the negotiations leading to the conclusion of the European Economic Area. Following a referendum in which the EEA treaty was rejected, Switzerland aimed at concluding a series of bilateral agreements that de facto secured the benefits of the EEA. The bilateral treaties between Switzerland and the EU can be characterised as establishing a far-reaching form of cooperation. This is particularly true in the area of air transport as reflected in the Agreement between the European Community and the Swiss Confederation on Air Transport.[64] This agreement establishes an internal market for air transport. For this purpose, a far reaching form of cooperation needed to be created. This cooperation includes antitrust matters. This is reflected in Article 19 which reads as follows:

1. Each Contracting Party shall give the other Contracting Party all necessary information and assistance in the case of investigations on possible infringements which that other Contracting Party carries out under its respective competences as provided in this Agreement.

[63] http://ec.europa.eu/competition/international/bilateral/#s.
[64] OJ, 2002, L 114, pp 72–90.

2. Whenever the Community institutions act under the powers granted to them by this Agreement on matters which are of interest to Switzerland and which concern the Swiss authorities or Swiss undertakings, the Swiss authorities shall be fully informed and given the opportunity to comment before a final decision is taken.

8.4.1.4 Less Comprehensive Bilateral Agreements

The spectacular growth of the market economy in China and its desire to be included in the world trading system led to the adoption of competition law and rules on merger control in China. The introduction of competition laws in turn has stimulated international cooperation. The appetite for cooperation was further wetted when China blocked the acquisition by Coca Cola of Hui Yuan.[65] These developments have resulted in Memoranda of Understanding both with the USA and the EU.[66] As the title—Memorandum of Understanding on Cooperation in the area of anti-monopoly Law—shows they embody only a first and rather timid form of cooperation. Put in simple terms the parties have agreed to talk and exchange non-confidential information. In the terms of Hans-Christian Andersen, one could say that the present cooperation barely wears any cloths. Moreover, the Memoranda are not 'full dress' agreements but only executive agreements between the competition enforcement agencies.

8.4.1.4.1 The 2011 USA–China Memorandum[67]

As regards the structure of the cooperation, the Memorandum states:

> The framework for cooperation between the U.S. antitrust agencies and the PRC antimonopoly agencies is composed of two parts: the first is the joint dialogue among all parties to this Memorandum on competition policy at the senior official level (the "joint dialogue") and the second is communication and cooperation on competition law enforcement and policy between individual U.S. antitrust agencies and PRC antimonopoly agencies.

As regards the content of the cooperation, the Memorandum states:

> The U.S. antitrust agencies and the PRC antimonopoly agencies recognize that it is in their common interest to work together, including in the following areas, subject to reasonably available resources: (a) keeping each other informed of significant competition policy and enforcement developments in their respective jurisdictions; (b) enhancing each agency's capabilities with appropriate activities related to competition policy and law such as training programs, workshops, study missions and internships; (c) exchanging experiences on competition law enforcement, when appropriate; (d) seeking information or advice from one another regarding matters of competition law enforcement and policy; (e) providing comments on proposed changes to competition laws, regulations, rules and guidelines; (f) exchanging views with respect to multilateral competition law and policy; and (g) exchanging experiences in

---

[65] http://fldj.mofcom.gov.cn/article/ztxx/200903/20090306108494.shtml (Chinese only). In April 2013 MOFCOM approved the Glencore-Xstrata merger with the condition that parties would divest one of their Peruvian Copper Mines.

[66] http://ec.europa.eu/competition/international/bilateral/index.html and http://www.justice.gov/atr/public/international/int-arrangements.html.

[67] http://www.justice.gov/atr/public/international/int-arrangements.html.

raising companies', other government agencies' and the public's awareness of competition policy and law.

8.4.1.4.2 The EU–China Memorandum of 2012[68]

The EU–China Memorandum of 2012 covers largely the same ground as the Memorandum between China and the US, although it is phrased in even more restrictive terms.[69] It provides for technical assistance in the area of competition law. Importantly, the Memorandum does not include cooperation in the field of merger control.[70] It is interesting to note that the United Kingdom has also concluded a bilateral agreement with China.[71]

8.4.1.5 OECD, ICN, WTO and UNCTAD

The UN Conference on Trade and Development (UNCTAD)[72] has published several documents about the experiences on international cooperation on competition policy issues.[73] However, due to the discussions pursued by industrialised nations in other fora (such as the OECD and WTO) and the relatively politicised nature of the document,[74] the impact of the UNCTAD Code, first adopted in 1980 and reaffirmed in 2000, has been relatively limited substantively: however, it has been suggested that its significance lies in the establishment of a network within which competition law and policy could be discussed and developed, leading to a more competition-law-receptive climate in such countries in more recent times.[75]

Under the auspices of the Organization for Economic Cooperation and Development (OECD), recommendations on cooperation in the field of competition law were adopted as early as 1978.[76] The goal of these OECD recommendations is that the relevant (usually national) competition authorities should inform and advise each other about intended actions within the sphere of competition policy where undertakings

---

[68] http://ec.europa.cu/competition/international/bilateral/index.html.

[69] See on EU-China relations: Qianlan WU: 'EU-China Competition Dialogue: A New Step in the Internationalisation of EU Competition Law?' (2012) 18 *European Law Journal* 3, 461–477.

[70] See n 1 of the Memorandum.

[71] https://www.oecd.org/.../competition/competition-inventory-list-of-MOUs-interagency.

[72] See BJ Sweeney, *The Internationalisation of the Competition Rules* (Abingdon, Routledge, 2010), 319–321.

[73] Experiences gained so far on international cooperation on competition policy issues and the mechanisms used, Revised report by the UNCTAD secretariat, TD?B?COM.2?CLP/21/Rev.3, 14 September 2005; A presentation of types of common provisions to be found in international, particularly bilateral and regional, cooperation agreements on competition policy and their application, report by the UNCTAD secretariat, TD/RBP?CONF.6/3, 6 September 2005; A synthesis of recent cartel cases which are publicly available, report by the UNCTAD secretariat, TD/RBP/CONF.6/4, 5 September 2005.

[74] Focusing as it does upon how the activities of multinational corporations in developing countries might be constrained, and lacking any commitment on the part of such countries to establishing and developing their own national competition law, policy and institutions.

[75] I Maher, 'Competition Law in the International Domain: Networks as a New Form of Governance' (2002) 29 *Journal of Law and Society* 111 and Sweeney (n 72, above).

[76] See the OECD's Recommendation concerning Action against Restrictive Business Practices Affecting International Trade Including those Involving Multinational Enterprises 1), (20 July 1978—C(78)133/Final).

of other States may be concerned. The OECD has developed a number of further recommendations on various competition law topics, including cooperation between competition authorities on various matters[77] and substantive issues such as hardcore cartels (1998) and merger review (2005). Much of the OECD's contribution in this field has been 'soft law' encouraging cooperation between and convergence among various systems of competition law. However, its technical assistance and support have also often proved invaluable to countries introducing competition law into their national legal and administrative systems.[78] The Commission participates actively in OECD discussions.[79]

A further initiative on an international level, was taken when the various competition authorities joined together to form the International Competition Network (ICN)[80]

> The ICN is a specialized yet informal network of established and newer agencies, enriched by the participation of non-governmental advisors (representatives from business, consumer groups, academics, and the legal and economic professions), with the common aim of addressing practical antitrust enforcement and policy issues. By enhancing convergence and cooperation, the ICN promotes more efficient and effective antitrust enforcement worldwide to the benefit of consumers and businesses.[81]

In September 2002, after significant comparative efforts by the ICN's Mergers Working Group, a set of general principles on mergers was agreed at the ICN's inaugural conference.[82] While it is acknowledged that the 'Principles are non-binding and it is left to governments and agencies to implement them as appropriate' and even in the absence of detailed agreement upon international, legally binding and harmonised substantive rules, such initiatives are a key means of coordinating international competition law enforcement and alleviating the difficulties which can be created by the non-collaborative exercise of potentially extraterritorial jurisdictional claims.[83]

As the principles of the market economy have gained acceptance around the globe, more and more countries have adopted competition laws.[84] Nevertheless, because of

---

[77] See, most recently, its Recommendation concerning cooperation between member countries on anti-competitive practices affecting international trade (27 July 1995—C(95)130/FINAL), available at http://webdomino1.oecd.org/horizontal/oecdacts.nsf/Display/ BCC35C142D75D40DC1256FE800600F45?Open Document (last accessed 31 December 2005).

[78] See further PJ Lloyd and KA Vautier, *Promoting Competition in Global Markets: a Multi-National Approach* (Cheltenham, Edward Elgar, 1999), 131–38 and MM Dabbah, *The Internationalisation of Antitrust Policy* (Cambridge, Cambridge University Press, 2003), 252–54, and the references cited therein.

[79] *Report on Competition Policy 2010*, para 150.

[80] See http://www.internationalcompetitionnetwork.org, where the ICN is described as 'a competition authority forum supported by the competition authorities themselves'. See the speech by Vice President Almunia of 24 April 2013 'The evolutionary pressure of globalisation on competition control' Speech 13/360.

[81] ICN Factsheet and key messages (April 2009).

[82] See generally G Tesauro, 'International Competition Network: First Annual Conference, Naples—Opening Speech' (2003) 26 *World Competition* 277 and M Todino, 'International Competition Network: The State of Play after Naples' (2003) 26 *World Competition* 283.

[83] For further reading, see P Lugard (ed), *The International Competition Network: Origins, Accomplishments and Aspirations* (Antwerp: Intersentia, 2011).

[84] eg China and Russia. See: J Emch, J Regazzini and V Rudomino (eds), *Competition Law in the Bric countries* (Wolters Kluwer, 2012), providing a brief overview of the laws of Brazil, China, India, Russia and South Africa.

economic globalisation, activities that result in the restriction of competition may take place outside those countries that have clear and regularly enforced competition laws. Furthermore, an ever-growing number of jurisdictional conflicts occur between those countries that possess and enforce competition laws. There is, therefore, a clear need for international rules in some form to cover this area. To date, it has not proved possible to adopt such international rules under the auspices of the World Trade Organization (WTO). This failure can principally be explained by differences of opinion between the USA and the EU. Discussions on this issue seemed to have been gaining increasing momentum a few years ago,[85] but at the time of writing it seems highly unlikely that such rules may yet be introduced by the WTO in the near future, if at all.

8.5 Relevant Concepts

In the context of the international dimensions present in the application and enforcement of competition law in the modern world, it is useful briefly to consider certain key concepts, the application of which has proved interesting or controversial in the practice to date. What follows is only a brief summary, but in it we hope to provide the reader with a feel for some of the issues that have arisen in practice.

8.5.1 Ne Bis in Idem[86]

Not a single word in the EU–US agreements of 1991 and 1998 is devoted to the application of general principles of law such as *ne bis in idem*.[87] The role of the principle of *ne bis in idem* (among other things) in the bilateral cooperation between the EU and US competition authorities was an issue in the treatment of the *Lysine cartel* cases.[88] In these cases, the European Commission imposed substantial fines upon the

---

[85] The literature on this topic is substantial and constantly increasing. For a selection of the mass of recent contributions, see P Marsden, *A Competition Policy for the WTO* (2003) (reviewed by A Scott (2005) 68 *Modern Law Review* 135); Dabbah, ibid; F Jenny, 'Competition Law and Policy: Global Governance Issues' (2003) 26 *World Competition* 609; and J Drexl, 'International Competition Policy after Cancún: Placing a Singapore Issue on the WTO Development Agenda' (2004) 27 *World Competition* 419.

[86] For a general treatment of this topic, see: B van Bockel, *The Ne Bis in Idem Principle in EU law* (Kluwer Law International, 2010).

[87] Or *ne bis in idem*. This is the general principle against what is known as 'double jeopardy' in the USA, which restricts one defendant from being prosecuted or penalised more than once for the same offence. On the application of the principle in EC competition law, see W Wils, 'The Principle of *Ne Bis in Idem* in EC Antitrust Enforcement: a Legal and Economic Analysis' (2003) 26 *World Competition* 131.

[88] Cases T-220/00 *Cheil Jedang Corporation v Commission*, T-223/00 *Kyowa Hakka Kogyon Co v Commission*, T-224/00 *Archer Daniels Midland Company and Archer Daniels Midland Ingredients Ltd v Commission* and T-230/00 *Daesang Corporation Sewon Europe GmbH v Commission*. Case C-397/03 P *Archer Daniels Midland*.

parties to a worldwide cartel of producers of ingredients for animal fodder. The Commission based its decision almost entirely upon details received by it from the American competition authorities, which themselves had already imposed substantial fines upon the parties on the basis of the same facts.

The GC came to the conclusion that the Commission was allowed to impose those penalties on the undertakings concerned because the principle of *ne bis in idem* did not apply in the context of the bilateral cooperation on competition matters between the EU and the USA. The GC stated that:

89. … the Community judicature has held that an undertaking may be made the defendant to two parallel sets of proceedings concerning the same infringement and, thus, incur concurrent sanctions, one imposed by the competent authority of the Member State in question, the other a Community sanction. That possibility is justified where the two sets of proceedings pursue different ends …

90. That being so, the principle *non bis in idem* cannot, a fortiori, apply in the present case because the procedures conducted and penalties imposed by the Commission on the one hand and the American and Canadian authorities on the other clearly pursued different ends. The aim of the first was to preserve undistorted competition within the European Union and the EEA, whereas the aim of the second was to protect the American and Canadian markets.[89]

According to the GC, however, it was open to the Commission to take into account the level of any fines and the severity of any sanctions already imposed upon the parties as a matter of reasonableness; but no obligation in the nature of the *ne bis in idem* principle could be derived from EU law or the EU–US agreements. However, the *ne bis in idem* principle provides no grounds for questioning the validity of any decision to investigate particular practices, nor any decision finding that those practices infringe the competition rules. In circumstances such as these, the lack of any international regulation on such matters is keenly felt, not least by the parties in question. The ECJ upheld the GC's judgments, thereby also confirming the Commission's Decisions.[90]

The principle also arose in a somewhat different factual context in the *Toshiba* judgment.[91] This case concerned an international cartel on the market for gas insulated switchgear in which a number of well-known European and Japanese undertakings in the electrical engineering sector participated for different periods between 1988 and 2004. Both the Commission and the Czech competition authority dealt with certain aspects of this case in 2006 and 2007, and each imposed fines on the undertakings concerned, although the Czech competition authority did so only under national antitrust law and only in relation to a period prior to the Czech Republic's accession to the European Union on 1 May 2004. The Czech competition authority initiated its own proceedings on 2 August 2006 against the same participants for infringement of the Czech Law on the Protection of Competition. On 26 April 2007 it issued a decision, against which the claimants lodged an administrative appeal.[92] The national court referred the case to the ECJ for a preliminary ruling.

---

[89]   These paras are taken from Case T-224/00 *Archer Daniels Midland v Commission*.
[90]   Case C-397/03 P *Archer Daniels Midland v Commission*, Case C-289/04 P *Showa Denko v Commission*.
[91]   Case C-17/10 *Toshiba Corporation v Úřad pro ochranu hospodářské soutěže*.
[92]   The facts are taken from the Opinion of Advocate General Kokott in Case C-17/10.

The ECJ summarised its case law as follows:

93. The second part of the second question concerns the issue whether, in a situation such as that at issue in the main proceedings, the *ne bis in idem* principle precludes the application of national competition law by the national competition authority.

94. The *ne bis in idem* principle must be complied with in proceedings for the imposition of fines under competition law ... That principle precludes, in competition matters, an undertaking from being found guilty or proceedings from being brought against it a second time on the grounds of anti-competitive conduct in respect of which it has been penalised or declared not liable by a previous unappealable decision (*Limburgse Vinyl Maatschappij v Commission*, paragraph 59).

95. It is of little importance that the decision whereby the said authority imposed fines relates to a period prior to the accession of the Czech Republic to the Union. The temporal applicability of the *ne bis in idem* principle in the context of EU law depends not on the date on which the facts being prosecuted were committed, but, in a situation such as that at issue in the main proceedings, falling under competition law, on that on which the proceeding for the imposition of a penalty was opened. On 2 August 2006, when the Úřad pro ochranu hospodářské soutěže opened the proceeding at issue in the main proceedings, the Czech Republic was already a Member State of the Union, with the result that that authority was required to comply with that principle.

96. It must be held that, in a situation such as that at issue in the main proceedings, the *ne bis in idem* principle does not preclude the application of national competition law by the national competition authority.

97. The Court has held, in competition law cases, that the application of that principle is subject to the threefold condition of identity of the facts, unity of offender and unity of the legal interest protected (*Aalborg Portland and Others v Commission*, paragraph 338).

98. In the case at issue in the main proceedings, it must be noted that, in any event, one of the conditions thus laid down, namely identity of the facts, is lacking.

99. Whether undertakings have adopted conduct having as its object or effect the prevention, restriction or distortion of competition cannot be assessed in the abstract, but must be examined with reference to the territory, within the Union or outside it, in which the conduct in question had such an object or effect, and to the period during which the conduct in question had such an object or effect.

100. In this case, the referring court and the applicants in the main proceedings consider that the territory of the Czech Republic is covered by the Commission's decision in relation to both the period before and the period after 1 May 2004. They cite as evidence for this the fact that the Commission speaks of a worldwide cartel and did not expressly exclude the Czech Republic from the scope of its decision.

101. In that regard, it should be noted, first, that the Commission's decision refers specifically, in many of its passages, to the consequences of the cartel at issue in the main proceedings within the European Community and the EEA, referring expressly to the 'Member States of the time' and the States 'which were contracting parties' to the EEA Agreement. Next, ... that decision does not penalise the possible anti-competitive effects produced by that cartel in the territory of the Czech Republic during the period prior to the accession of that State to the Union. Finally, it is apparent from the methods of calculation of the fines that, in its decision, the Commission did not take account of the States which acceded to the Union on 1 May 2004. According to point 478 of the grounds of the Commission's decision, the latter used as

the basis for calculation of the fines the turnover figures achieved by the members of the said cartel in the EEA during 2003.

102. It must therefore be concluded that the Commission's decision does not cover any anti-competitive consequences of the said cartel in the territory of the Czech Republic in the period prior to 1 May 2004, whereas, according to the information supplied by the national court, the decision of the Úřad pro ochranu hospodářské soutěže imposed fines only in relation to that territory and that period.

103. Having regard to the above, the answer to the second part of the second question is that the *ne bis in idem* principle does not preclude penalties which the national competition authority of the Member State concerned imposes on undertakings participating in a cartel on account of the anticompetitive effects to which the cartel gave rise in the territory of that Member State prior to its accession to the European Union, where the fines imposed on the same cartel members by a Commission decision taken before the decision of the said national competition authority was adopted were not designed to penalise the said effects.

It is important to note that the *Lysine* cases raised the question of whether undertakings could be penalised (and proceedings instituted against them) for the same infringement in the EU and the USA, while the *Toshiba* judgment concerned proceedings against undertakings for infringements committed in the Czech Republic in the period before 1 May 2004 and the infringements in the EU before 1 May 2004.

8.5.2 Convergence

Although there are many differences between the American and the European systems of competition law, the intensive cooperation between the US and EU authorities has contributed to an increasing degree of convergence between EU and US competition law: this might be termed an 'organic growth' of both systems in a common direction. This development benefits both the authorities involved and the undertakings in question, because it reduces the risk that the two competition authorities on each side of the Atlantic will reach conflicting decisions in any given case. Nevertheless, this development does not offer any guarantees as to a consistent outcome, as (for example) was illustrated by the *GE/Honeywell* case, where the US authorities and the Commission came to different conclusions (the former cleared the merger, while the later refused to do so).[93] Shortcomings have also been identified in other areas: the companies concerned have little influence over the information exchanged between the US and EU authorities, while the procedural guarantees for both sides in various jurisdictions can

---

[93] See n 6 above. Appeals against the Commission's decision to block the merger were ruled upon by the CFI: Cases T-209/01 *Honeywell International Inc v Commission* and T-210/01 *General Electric Co v Commission*. One key difficulty was caused by the disparities in the procedural constraints that applied. The *GE/Honeywell* merger and its treatment on both sides of the Atlantic provided a vivid illustration of the consequences of adherence to the time limits under which investigations must be conducted. As a result, not only did the final substantive results of the US and EU investigations differ, but the former delivered a decision long before the latter, resulting in severe commercial uncertainty for those involved in the deal. For discussion, criticism and suggestions for some procedural alignment see the case note by PJ Slot (2001) 38 *Common Market Law Review* 1573.

often be significantly divergent and (as we discussed in the preceding text) undertakings run the risk of facing condemnation for breach of competition rules in a number of cases, based upon information that has come to light in one investigation.

One further potentially significant driver for convergence is the ICN (mentioned above in section 8.4.1.5).

8.5.3 Problems in the Application of the Leniency Rules

As we discussed in Chapter 6.5 above, both EU and UK competition law have recently begun to make (greater) use of leniency rules. Companies that voluntarily report to the authorities on cartels to which they are connected may receive a full or partial remission of any fines that would otherwise have been imposed. However, a new wrinkle in the application of these rules has become apparent as a result of experience gained in the operation of the transatlantic cooperation in competition matters. This problem occurs where cartels are involved that have an impact in both the EU and the USA, and it is caused by the rules of civil procedure in the USA. The rules on 'discovery' permit the parties under suspicion of a breach of the competition rules to be required to provide details of any relevant material at their disposal. This discovery procedure is mostly used in civil cases where a claim for damages has been brought. On the basis of section 4(a) of the Clayton Act, a civil party that has suffered loss as a result of a breach of US antitrust law may claim treble damages, along with the recovery of its costs of bringing the proceedings, including its legal costs.[94] The rules of discovery thus require the parties to supply documents and details that have been provided in connection with the competition law leniency rules in the EU or the UK. These rules can thus come to hang like the sword of Damocles over the heads of undertakings that have made use of the leniency rules. The European Commission has thus declared itself prepared to accept the oral provision of information in its application of the leniency rules.[95] There is reason to believe that the impact of the US discovery rules on the EU leniency programme may not be as drastic as it is often made out to be. In a 2007 judgment the US Supreme Court in the *Bell Atlantic Corp v Twombly*[96] held that plaintiffs have to meet the pleading standard in order to be able to bring a case in the first place. According to this standard, 'fishing expeditions' will not be allowed. According to Supreme Court, there must be allegations plausibly suggesting that there was an agreement restricting competition. Nevertheless, the pleading standard rule will not entirely eliminate the risks of discovery orders. There will always be cases where this standard can be met. It is difficult to imagine that Commission decisions fining cartelists would not be sufficient to meet the standard.

---

[94] Whereas the normal rule in the USA is that such process costs cannot be recovered.

[95] See (2003) 2 *Competition Policy Newsletter* 18, at 20 and I Van Bael and J-F Bellis, *Competition Law of the European Community*, 5th edn (The Hague, Kluwer Law International, 2010), 1128 (and generally 1125–48). See also the guidelines laid down on information acquired from undertakings claiming the benefit of a leniency programme in the context of the European Competition Network and cooperation between national competition authorities *inter se* and with the Commission: these are available in the Commission's Notice on cooperation within the Network of Competition Authorities [2004] OJ C101/43, paras 37–42.

[96] 550 US 544 (2007).

In 2004 the US Supreme Court delivered a judgment in this area in the *Intel v AMD* case, holding that the European Commission qualifies as a 'tribunal' for the purposes of a request for discovery in the USA.[97] The case involved AMD's complaint to the European Commission alleging that Intel had abused its dominant position on the market for computer microprocessors. AMD wanted the Commission to take into consideration certain documentation that had come to light in another action in the USA concerning Intel's trade secrets, but the Commission declined to review such documents. AMD then brought proceedings in the USA seeking access to those documents so that it could use them to support its complaint to the Commission. The Supreme Court upheld the Appeals Court's ruling that discovery should be granted, holding that just because the Commission had not been willing to demand the documents did not mean that it would not willingly accept them were they to be provided by other means. Further, the Supreme Court held that since the tribunal 'proper' (the GC) would typically rely upon the evidence presented to the Commission in any review of a Commission decision, it would be impractical to wait until the case came before the GC before discovery could be ordered. On the basis of this judgment, a party that has previously submitted a complaint to the European Commission can make an application before a US court, seeking discovery of further documentation and information. Such information could then be used in the application of EU competition law.

In the EU the questions of access to confidential information were raised in the *Pfleiderer* case,[98] the ECJ was asked whether private parties claiming damages in cartel cases should be given access to information given for the purposes of a leniency application. The ECJ answered as follows:

> In the light of the foregoing, the answer to the question referred is that the provisions of European Union law on cartels, and in particular Regulation No 1/2003, must be interpreted as not precluding a person who has been adversely affected by an infringement of European Union competition law and is seeking to obtain damages from being granted access to documents relating to a leniency procedure involving the perpetrator of that infringement. It is, however, for the courts and tribunals of the Member States, on the basis of their national law, to determine the conditions under which such access must be permitted or refused by weighing the interests protected by European Union law.

The referring court was the district court in Bonn in Germany, which is the competent court for appeals against decisions of the German NCA, the *Bundeskartellamt*. Subsequently, the Bonn court ruled that the interest in the proper leniency procedures takes precedence over the interest of private parties claiming damages for cartel offences.[99] In the *National Grid* case[100] the English High Court (Roth J) was required to consider the *Pfleiderer* judgment in the context of an application for disclosure of certain documents. The request was made in a follow-on claim for damages. The judge considered that the application of the *Pfleiderer* judgment is not limited to leniency material

---

[97] *Intel Corp v Advanced Micro Devices Inc* 292 F.3d 664 (2004), affd 542 US 241 (2004) (Sup Ct, 21 June 2004). Note that the Commission had filed a brief before the Supreme Court supporting Intel's argument that the Commission did not amount to a 'tribunal' for discovery purposes.

[98] Case C-360/09 *Pfleiderer v Bundeskartellamt*.

[99] The eleventh ICN brief of 12 February 2012: 'Leniency Programme strengthened by Final Decision regarding Access to File.' On the *Pfleiderer* judgment, see Chapter 6.5.

[100] *National Grid Electricity Transmission v ABB and Others* [2012] EWHC 869.

provided in national procedures. The judge had no doubt that he did have jurisdiction to rule on the disclosure application. The judge recognised the difficulty of conducting the balancing test referred to in *Pfleiderer*. Furthermore, the Court ruled that the defendant could not rely upon the legitimate expectations that leniency material would not be disclosed. Roth J did order disclosure of certain leniency material into a confidentiality ring, but not all.[101]

The relevance of all this is that if, according to the *Pfleiderer* judgment, information is released, it could potentially also be used in the context of discovery procedures or in *Intel*-like procedures in the US.

8.5.4 State Owned Enterprises (SOEs)

Across the world, State Capitalism is on the rise.[102] At the same time, globalisation continues to expand. The combination of these two trends will lead to an increasing presence of State Owned Enterprises (SOEs) in international trade relations. This poses considerable challenges for Competition Authorities, Regulatory Authorities and private parties. The concept as applied to SOEs from third countries has not been very well developed in the decisional practice of the Commission, nor has it been the subject of judgments of the EU courts. The Commission's Jurisdictional Notice has two sections which deal with SOEs:[103] section 1.7, concerning 'Concentrations involving State-owned undertakings'; and section 5.4, which addresses the 'Allocation of turnover for State-owned undertakings'. Section 1.7 provides some general guidance in paragraphs 52 and 53. Section 5 starts (in paragraph 192) with the basic assumption that discrimination between the public and private sector should be avoided, and it continues by stating that the key criterion is whether there is: 'an economic unit with an independent power of decision, irrespective of the way in which their capital is held or of the rules of administrative supervision applicable to them'. These sections raise interesting issues that have not, or at least not extensively, been tested in the Commission's practice and in the EU courts.

SOEs also play a role in EU law, notably in the field of State aid, where cases like *Van der Kooij (Gasunie)*,[104] *Stardust Marine*[105] and *PreussenElektra*[106] have raised interesting issues about the concept/definition of SOEs and their role in the economy. We have discussed the concept of a public undertaking in Chapter 7.2. The position of SOEs also plays an important role in the liberalisation and regulation of the network-bound and oil sectors. A very telling example is the Commission's probe of Russia's

---

[101] See judgment of 4 April 2012 by Roth J in [2012] EWHC 869 (Ch).

[102] *The Economist* (21–27 January 2012) featured a leader, supported by a 'Special Report', on the rise of State Capitalism: according to its report, State Capitalism increasingly looks like the coming trend. See also: Max Büge, Matias Egeland, Przemyslaw Kowalski, Monika Sztajerowska 'State-owned enterprises in the global economy: Reason for concern?' VOX at http://www.voxeu.org/article/state-owned-enterprises-global-economy-reason-concern.

[103] Commission Consolidated Jurisdictional Notice under Council Regulation (EC) No 139/2004 on the control of concentrations between undertakings [2008] OJ C95/01.

[104] Case 67/85 *Kwekerij Gebroeders Van der Kooy and others v Commission*.

[105] Case C-482/99 *France v Commission*.

[106] Case C-379/98 *PreussenElektra v Schleswag*.

Gazprom.[107] On 22 April 2015 the Commission sent a Statement of Objections to Gazprom.[108]

While the application of the concept of SOE is relatively easy to apply within the EU legal order, it raises far more complications when dealing with SOE's from third countries.

8.5.4.1 Commission Decisions to Date Dealing with SOEs from Third Countries

A preliminary analysis of recent decisions in the area of merger control reveals that the Commission has been confronted with some Chinese companies with ties to their national government. Thus far, it has been able to avoid "cracking the nut"—that is to say, expressing a view on the question of what degree of control or what form of control would be relevant for the application of the EU rules. The Commission has been able to do so because: (a) there was no real doubt that the transaction had a 'Community Dimension'; and (b) there were no competition concerns even if all of the Chinese SOEs in the relevant market were taken together. Nevertheless, it is very likely that in the future, in other factual situations, the Commission and eventually the EU courts will have to clarify the concept of SOE and the related concepts in the Commission's Jurisdictional Notice. In the EDF-CGN case the Commission aggregated the market shares of Chinese SOEs in a relevant market for the first time. It observed that:

> In view of the fact that Central SASAC can interfere with strategic investment decisions and can impose or facilitate coordination between SOEs at least with regard to SOEs active in the energy industry, the Commission concludes in the case at hand that CGN and other Chinese SOEs in that industry should not be deemed to have an independent power of decision from Central SASAC. The turnover of all companies controlled by Central SASAC that are active in the energy industry should therefore be aggregated.[109]

An extensive discussion of the SOE concept can be found in Case *DSM/Sinochem/ JV*, a summary of which is provided below. A substantial discussion of the position of an SOE and its possible effects on the structure of competition can also be found in various merger cases—including *China National Blue Star/Elkem* and *China National Agrochemical Corporation/Koor Industries*—while several other merger decisions have involved third country SOEs (eg Case No COMP/M.6151 *Petrochina/Ineos*).

---

[107] Gazprom was included in the Commission's action against natural gas companies in 2012. Antitrust: Commission opens proceedings against Gazprom European Commission—IP/12/937 04/09/2012.

[108] Memo/15/4829 of 22 April 2015.

[109] Case M.7850—EDF/CGN/NNB GROUP OF COMPANIES para 49. In para 69 the Commission noted that the precise market definition concerning those markets do not need to be analysed in further details as they are not affected markets and the proposed transaction does not raise serious doubts as to its compatibility with the internal market under any possible approach. In the end the Commission did not oppose the creation of the joint venture.

8.5.4.2 An Instructive Example

A good illustration of the issues involved in SOEs is found in the Commission decision in *DSM/Sinochem/JV*.[110]

This case concerned a joint venture agreement whereby Sinochem was to acquire joint control of the anti-infectives business of DSM (DAI) by way of a purchase of shares. Sinochem is a Chinese State-owned enterprise (SOE) under the supervision of the Central State-owned Assets Supervision and Administration Commission of the State Council (Central SASAC). Sinochem is indirectly owned by the Chinese State, as 100 per cent of its shares are held by SASAC, an entity established directly under the supervision of the State Council of the People's Republic of China; SASAC is responsible for the oversight and management of SOEs.

The undertakings concerned have a combined aggregate world-wide turnover of more than €5 000 million. The question arises as to which turnover is attributable to Sinochem. Calculation of the turnover of an undertaking concerned in a concentration needs to take account of undertakings making up an economic unit with an independent power of decision, irrespective of the way in which their capital is held or of the rules of administrative supervision applicable to them.

The Commission has in the past considered several concentrations involving undertakings owned by Member States. In those cases, the Commission assessed the extent to which the companies concerned held decision-making power independently of the State, inter alia by looking into the possibility for the State to influence the companies' commercial strategy and the likelihood that the State would in practice coordinate the companies' commercial conduct, either by imposing or facilitating such coordination.

In order to assess whether the State has the power to coordinate the commercial conduct of companies, the Commission has previously taken into account factors such as: the degree of interlocking directorships between entities owned by the same entity; or the existence of adequate safeguards ensuring that commercially sensitive information is not shared between such undertakings. When assessing the chain of control of State-owned companies, the approach is: first, to establish whether the company has an independent power of decision; and, secondly, if this is not the case, to determine the identity of the ultimate State entity and which other undertakings owned by this entity need to be considered as a single economic entity.

In the present case, the ownership of Chinese SOEs lies either with the central government, with regional/municipal governments, or occasionally with other public entities. Sinochem is one of the 129, mostly large, SOEs financed and owned by the central government. As an undertaking under central government ownership, Sinochem reports to Central SASAC.

The Parties submitted that Sinochem was an economic unit that has decision-making power which is independent from the Chinese state. They argued that SASAC's limited statutory powers—such as various provisions of the Law of the People's Republic of China on State-Owned Assets of Enterprises or Interim

---

[110] Case No COMP/M.6113—*DSM/Sinochem/JV* of 19 May 2011. The following text is a summary of the Commission Decision.

Regulations on Supervision and Management of State-owned Assets of Enterprises—prevented it from exercising a decisive influence over Sinochem and that SASAC does not intervene in the strategic decision-making process (eg, by approving business plans or budget). They emphasised provisions regarding a separation of ownership from management, the operational autonomy of SOEs, and the purely supportive role of SASAC, which does not interfere in SOEs' production and operation activities, apart from performing the responsibilities of an investor. Sinochem submitted that SASAC's rights are limited to approving the scope of Sinochem's business activities. Furthermore, Sinochem stated that there are no interlocking directorships between Sinochem and other Central or local SASAC-owned companies.

Nonetheless, the core legislation itself and the associated information outlined on SASAC's website contain a number of provisions which can be read as suggesting that SASAC does in practice have certain powers to involve itself in Sinochem's commercial behaviour in a strategic manner, among others the right to approve mergers and/or strategic investment decisions. At the same time, a number of external sources suggested that commercial decisions of SOEs could be influenced by the Chinese State. It appeared from such sources that influence could be exercised through formal channels such as SASAC, but also in less formal ways. Sinochem's and SASAC's own official statements provided certain indications in this regard. For example, Sinochem's Annual Report shows that there is at least a very close cooperation between Sinochem and the Chinese Government.

Epilogue: A Brief Overview of the Development of EU Competition Law

9.1 Introduction

As the foregoing chapters demonstrate, competition law in the EU today has come a long way from what it was some 60 years ago when the Rome Treaty entered into force on 1 January 1958. In the formative stages of the EEC the Court of Justice (ECJ) interpreted the main provisions of competition law with a view to market access and integration. While these themes are still inspiring many important competition law decisions, other objectives closer to the heart of the Member States' interests are being recognised. This is taking place in the area of the case law on free movement, but also in the case law on Article 106 TFEU and Article 4(3) TEU and Article 101 TFEU.

The aim of this final chapter is to provide readers with a brief overview of the principal developments in EU competition law over the past half century. The chapter starts with a summary of the early and formative years, the period that ended in 1989 when the Merger Control Regulation entered into force. The second period lasted from 1989 until 1 May 2004 and the entry into force of Regulation 1/2003. The third period is characterised by the entry into force of the new procedural regime of Regulation 1/2003 and the accession of the new Member States, the former republics of Central and Eastern Europe.

9.2 The Early and Formative Years 1958–1989

9.2.1 Introduction

Initially the development of EEC competition policy followed very much a top-down approach with an administrative organ, the Commission, designing and enforcing it. Gradually other actors entered the field, first the national courts, and in their slipstream, arbitral panels. This happened because the ECJ ruled that Articles 85 and 86 EEC had direct effect.[1] The direct effect of Articles 85 and 86 EEC also made it possible for national courts to ask the ECJ to give preliminary rulings.[2] This led to important judgments in cases such as *Delimitis* and *Pronuptia*.[3] The result was a new balance between the enforcer/legislator; the ECJ; and the national courts. Subsequently, with a considerable time lag, national competition authorities also assumed a role as enforcers and to some extent even as policy-makers. This resulted in a rather complex system, whereby it could no longer be said that the Commission was the apex of the system. This phenomenon was later reflected in the area of merger control where Article 9 of Regulation 4064/89 provided for the possibility of referral from the Commission to the national competition authorities as well as, in Article 22(3), the referral from the national competition authorities to the Commission. These mechanisms have been expanded with the revision of the Regulation in 2004. Article 4(5) of Regulation 139/2004 (the 'Merger Regulation') gives the undertakings concerned the right to request that the Commission examine the merger. The cooperative nature of the combined system of Community competition law and national competition law is also a distinct feature of Regulation 1/2003. The Commission has, since the entry into force of this Regulation, focussed on the main elements of competition policy such as the fight against major cartels and mergers, leaving the competition authorities of the Member States with the geographically narrower infringements and the local finetuning. This has accentuated the cooperative nature of the system. The creation of the network of competition authorities led to intensive cooperation between the Commission and the national competition authorities.

   In order to understand how this system evolved it is necessary to give a brief sketch of its development since the entry into force of the Rome Treaty.

---

[1] See Commission Notice on the cooperation between the Commission and the courts of the EU Member States in the application of Articles 81 and 82 EC, [2004] OJ C 101/54.
[2] An overview of all references until 2004 can be found in: B Rodger (ed), *Article 234 and Competition Law. An Analysis* (Wolters Kluwer, 2008).
[3] For an analysis of the interaction between national courts, the ECJ and the legislator, see Piet Jan Slot, *Le rôle du juge et du législateur dans le développement du droit communutaire et du droit dans les états membres* (Paris, Éditions A Pedone, 1998).

9.2.2 Regulation nr 17/62

In the first years after the entry into force of the Rome Treaty the general principles of Articles 85 and 86 EEC (now Articles 101 and 102 TFEU) were implemented and subsequently applied. The Commission, pursuant to its mandate provided for in Article 87 EEC, drafted what became known as Regulation 17 to give effect to the principles of Articles 85 and 86 EEC. The Commission had gained some experience with enforcing the competition provisions of the ECSC Treaty (Article 65 on anticompetitive agreements and Article 66 requiring prior approval of mergers). After protracted negotiations, Regulation 17 was finally adopted by the Council on 6 February 1962.[4] This key Regulation embodied a system of administrative *a priori* control of agreements having anticompetitive effects. The Regulation required the notification of both existing agreements and those that entered into force after 13 March 1962, the date of the entry into force of the Regulation. Without notification, agreements would fall foul of Article 85(1) EEC and could not be exempted under Article 85(3).[5] The system had the virtue of being simple both for the industry as well as for national courts. This system also allowed the Commission to develop a cartel policy and that is precisely what the Commission did. During this period the entire edifice of block exemptions and notices was built. These rules were rather detailed and tailored to fit specific sectors, the block exemption for the automobile industry being the clearest example. The notice on the effect on trade between the Member States and the *de minimis* notice were designed to manage the Commission's workload.

9.2.3 Developing the Policy

As was to be expected, the enactment of Regulation 17 led to a flood of notifications. The Commission had to devise a plan to deal with the enormous amount of notifications. The first part of its strategy was to select from the notifications, individual cases that represented the key elements of the provisions of the cartel prohibition in an effort to clarify and establish the main principles for a future policy. The major part of the notifications concerned vertical agreements and in particular exclusive distribution and purchasing agreements. It was therefore no surprise that the Commission picked the *Consten-Grundig* case as a clear example of such agreements and territorial restrictions. It adopted a decision declaring such agreements to be contrary to Article 85(1) EEC. The parties appealed to the ECJ which clarified many key principles and in doing so confirmed the Commission's view.[6] The second prong of the Commission's approach to deal with the flood of notifications was the development of the system of notices and block exemptions.

---

[4] OJ 21 February 1962, pp 204–211. See, for a fuller account of this period: DG Goyder, *EC Competition Law*, 2nd edn (Oxford, Oxford University Press, 1992) 33–38.
[5] Art 4 of Reg 17 exempted some agreements from the obligation to notify. They were not exempted from the prohibition of Art 81(1) EEC.
[6] Cases 56 and 58/64 *Consten and Grundig v Commission*.

From the point of view of substance, the emphasis in this period was on achieving market integration. The classical objectives of antitrust—the protection of the consumer and the small trader—were still largely absent. A first reference to the protection and promotion of small business appeared in the *Metro* judgment.[7]

Once the main challenges posed by the application of Article 85 EEC had been addressed, the Commission turned to the application of Article 86 EEC. Like its approach under Article 85 EEC, it started with some landmark cases defining the key concepts of the prohibition of abuse of a dominant position. In the absence of a notification mechanism the Commission had to rely on complaints and its powers to bring infringement procedures. By its very nature therefore the Commission had fewer means to develop a policy on Article 86. It had to wait until suitable cases presented themselves. Consequently, it took quite some time before cases such as *United Brands,*[8] *Hoffmann-LaRoche,*[9] *Commercial Solvents*[10] and *Continental Can*[11] presented themselves. As was to be expected, these cases reached the ECJ which did not fail to give them proper attention. The Court duly endorsed the Commission's interpretation of the key concepts.

During this period the Commission did not address the politically sensitive subject matter of public undertakings and exclusive and special rights that is addressed in Article 90 EEC.[12]

9.2.4   Extraterritorial Jurisdiction

Conflicts of jurisdiction, resulting from the US extraterritorial application of its antitrust laws were, as a result of the application of the Alcoa/effects doctrine,[13] quite common in those days.[14] These conflicts gave rise to the enactment of blocking statutes in several Member States enjoining their companies to hand over documents to foreign authorities. The most far-reaching statutory provision was embodied in the UK protection of trading interests statute, which provided for a claw-back provision in case UK nationals suffered from treble damages awards under US antitrust law. In the mid-1970s the Department of Justice (DOJ) Grand Jury conducted an investigation of the shipping sector which led to diplomatic protests from several EEC Member States. The problems were, for practical purposes, solved by the *Woodpulp I* 1988 judgment in which the ECJ held that: 'The decisive factor is therefore the place where

---

[7] Case 26/76 *Metro v Commission*.

[8] Case 27/76 *United Brands v Commission*.

[9] Case 85/76 *Hoffmann-La Roche v Commission*.

[10] Joined Cases 6 and 7/73 *Instituto Chemioterapico Italiano and Commercial Solvents v Commission*.

[11] Case 6/72 *Continental Can v Commission*.

[12] The only judgment which briefly discusses Art 90(2) EEC is Case 10/71 *Muller v Porte de Mertet*, which was a preliminary ruling.

[13] 148 F.2d 416(2nd Circuit 1945).

[14] For a brief summary see Bellamy & Child, *European Community Law of Competition*, 6th edn (Oxford, Oxford University Press, 2008) 66–70; DG Goyder, *EC Competition Law*, 2nd edn (Oxford, Oxford University Press, 1993) 460–467.

[the agreement] is implemented'.[15] This amounted to a cleverly designed formula which on the face of it is different from the US effects doctrine but which in practice allows enforcement in the EU whenever its interests are at stake. This also opened the door for international agreements on mutual cooperation, the so-called negative and positive comity agreements. On the basis of these agreements the antitrust authorities of the EU and the US nowadays cooperate actively and frequently.

9.2.5 Excluded Sectors

Towards the end of this period the ECJ confirmed in the *Nouvelles Frontières* and *Ahmed Saeed* judgments[16] that the competition rules also applied in the air transport sectors. Earlier the ECJ had ruled that the competition rules apply to the banking sector.[17]

9.3 1989–2004: A Period of Consolidation

9.3.1 Merger Control

After a discussion lasting more than 20 years, the merger control system was finally enacted in 1989. It resulted in a large number of notifications. Although the great majority of the mergers were approved without much ado during the first phase, several mergers were only approved conditionally in the second phase.[18] The number of outright prohibitions was small. A landmark case was the prohibition of the *GE-Honeywell* merger. The Commission's decision was upheld by the ECJ. The merger had been approved by the US authorities. This led to a renewed debate about the necessity for closer cooperation between the authorities on both sides of the Atlantic as well as the need for similar substantive rules. In this period many other countries enacted their own merger control system. This has led to the creation of networks of competition authorities—European Competition Network (ECN) and the International Competition Network (ICN).

---

[15] Joined Cases 89, 104, 114, 116, 117 and 125–129/85 *Ahlström Osakeyhtiö and Others v Commission*.

[16] Joined Cases 209–213/84 *Ministère Public v Lucas Asjes and Others (Nouvelle Frontières)*; Case 66/86 *Ahmed Saeed Flugreisen and Silver Line Reisebüro GmbH v Zentrale zur Bekämpfung unlauteren Wettbewerbs*.

[17] Case 172/80 *Zürchner v Bayerische Vereinsbank*.

[18] Under Reg 4064/89 conditions could only be imposed after the opening of the second phase. This inflated the number of second phase decisions. The revised merger Reg 139/2004 allows conditional approvals.

A side-effect of the merger control system was that the numerous notifications all, of course, providing extensive data about the relevant markets, gave the Commission a valuable insight into many markets. In this period several senior Commission officials joined the private sector. Thus, major law firms also became well informed as well.

For about ten years the negative Commission decisions and the conditional decisions went unchallenged. Even if the decisions were annulled, the merger could not automatically be implemented subsequently.[19] This changed around the turn of the century with some landmark judgments such as *Airtours*[20] and *Schneider Electric*.[21] In both judgments the Court of First Instance (CFI) annulled the Commission decision. The latter judgment led the wronged parties to bring a claim for damages. The CFI accepted the claim and ordered the Community to make good two-thirds of the loss represented by the reduction in the transfer price of Legrand. Moreover, the CFI ordered that the amount of that loss be assessed by an expert and awarded interest on the compensation relating to that loss.[22] Upon appeal the ECJ set aside this part of the CFI judgment.[23] The ECJ did, however, accept the CFI's reasoning awarding damages for making good the loss represented by the expenses incurred by Schneider as a result of its participation in the resumed merger control procedure, which followed delivery of the *Schneider I* and *Schneider II* judgments.

9.3.2 Simplification of the Block Exemptions

An important development in this period is the gradual simplification of the block exemptions, in particular the Block Exemption Regulation for vertical restraints (Regulation 2790/99). By embodying the principle that what is not prohibited is allowed, this block exemption represented a major simplification. It should be remembered that the system introduced by Regulation 2790/99 consisted of a black list of clauses that were prohibited outright. The previous Regulation had a white list with clauses there were allowed and a third category of grey clauses which had to be assessed by the Commission who would decide whether or not they were acceptable.

9.3.3 Liberalisation

This period is also characterised by the drive towards the completion of the internal market.[24] The internal market was to be completed by a major harmonisation

---

[19] The CFI judgment could of course be appealed to the ECJ and the end result would be a fresh Commission decision approving the merger.

[20] Case T-342/99 *Airtours v Commission*.

[21] Case T-310/01 *Schneider Electric v Commission*.

[22] Case T-351/03 *Schneider v Commission*.

[23] Case C-440/07 *Commission v Schneider*, at para 218.

[24] Completing the internal market (COM (85) 310 final) (the 'White Paper').

programme. At the same time the Commission started its action towards liberalisation of the closed sectors. It started actively to apply Article 90 EEC, subsequently Article 86 EC, notably in the telecoms sector. In the important telecoms judgment of *France v Commission*,[25] the ECJ confirmed the Commission's legislative power under Article 90(3) EEC. Other judgments defined the key concepts of this Article. The definition of the concept of an undertaking delineated the scope of application of the competition rules in the public and private sector.[26] According to this case law, Member States are free to set up a public undertaking and to grant it exclusive or special rights. However, Member States must not do so in such a way that a public undertaking must necessarily end up breaching the competition rules in carrying out its activities.[27]

Due to pressure from the Member States and the European Parliament, the Commission soon had to give up its use of Article 86(3) EC as the basis for legislation. Such legislation was henceforth based on Article 95 EC.[28] The results of this policy in the air transport and telecoms sectors are now clearly visible for every citizen. In the first sector, Easy Jet, Ryan Air and Air Berlin have become household names for all but the business class traveller. The telecoms sector has also developed beyond recognition, with the mobile phone sector being the most obvious example. The liberalisation in the energy sector has been less spectacular, mainly as a result of fierce opposition by the Member States and the incumbents. Directive 96/92 on the internal market for electricity and Directive 98/30 on the internal market for natural gas, mark the first steps towards liberalisation. They embody the principles of third-party access, unbundling of production, transmission and distribution, as well as, initially limited, freedom to choose the supplier.[29] Both Directives were amended in 2003 and in 2009 to implement further liberalisation.[30]

It should be noted that the liberalisation policy was made possible because of the application of the free movement rules but also because gradually the Member States had all warmed up to the idea of the need for a national competition policy. During this period most Member States adopted national competition policies. The Euro agreements that were concluded with the former socialist countries all included copies of the EC competition rules.

---

[25] Case C-202/88 *France v Commission*.

[26] Case C-41/90 *Höfner v Macrotron*.

[27] Case C-41/90 *Höfner v Macrotron*; Case C-323/93 *Crespelle v Coopérative d'Elevage et d'Insémination Artificielle*.

[28] For the air and maritime transport sector this was Art 84(2) EEC.

[29] Directive 96/92 concerning common rules for the internal market in electricity, OJ 1997, L 27/20 (also referred to as the Electricity Directive); and Directive 98/30, concerning common rules for the internal market in natural gas, OJ 1998, L 204/1 (also referred to as the Natural Gas Directive).

[30] Directive 2003/54 concerning common rules for the internal market in electricity, repealing Directive 96/92, OJ 2003, L 176/37. Directive 2003/55 concerning common rules for the internal market in natural gas, repealing Directive 98/30 OJ 2003, L 176/57; Directive 2009/72 concerning common rules for the internal market in electricity, OJ 2009, L 211/55; Directive 2009/73 concerning common rules for the internal market in natural gas, OJ 2009, L 211/94.

9.4 Accession of the New Member States and the Enactment of Regulation 1/2003 on 1 May 2004

9.4.1 Accession

This period is first and foremost characterised by the accession of ten new Member States. The significance of the accession for the development of Europe can hardly be exaggerated. The competition law regime in the EU was extended to the former planned economies of Central and Eastern Europe. The new Member States had gradually been preparing for the application and enforcement of the competition rules. The preparation had started in the early 1990s with the Euro-agreements which all contained provisions modelled after Articles 81–90 EC. Many training sessions and meetings were organised to create a competition law culture in the new Member States. Notwithstanding this extensive preparation, many disputes have arisen about the implementation and enforcement of the competition rules, some of them leading to claims often brought in arbitral proceedings.

9.4.2 Regulation 1/2003

A long and intensive negotiation process finally led to the enactment of Regulation 1/2003 to replace Regulation 17 at the same time as the new Member States' accession, thus avoiding what would have been a very complex transitional regime. A look at the transitional regime for the application of the State aid Articles 87 and 88 EC shows how complex such a regime would have been.[31] The Regulation represents a major shift in the enforcement of competition law to the level of the Member States. All Member States now have national competition authorities. It should be remembered that it was a requirement for accession of the new Member States to have the necessary authorities for the enforcement of the competition rules. At the same time, the Commission issued a Notice on cooperation within the Network of Competition Authorities.[32] The judgments of the ECJ in *Courage*[33] and *Manfredi*[34] have stimulated national courts to apply the competition rules. In 2004 the Commission also published a Notice on cooperation between the Commission and the courts of the EU Member States in the application of Articles 81 and 82 EC.[35] In 2008 it published a

---

[31] This made it possible to avoid the complexities of the provisional validity regime of the *Bosch* case law in the sixties and seventies after the enactment of Reg 17.

[32] OJ C 101, 27.04.2004, pp 43–53.

[33] Case C-453/99 *Courage v Crehan*.

[34] Joined Cases C-295-298/04 *Manfredi v Lloyd Adriatico Assicurazion SpA*.

[35] OJ C 101, 27.04.2004, pp 54–64.

White paper on actions for damages.[36] In 2014 a directive was adopted the objective of which is to facilitate actions for damages under national law for infringements of the competition law provisions.[37]

In the meantime, as arbitral tribunals were increasingly applying the competition rules, this has led to new questions. It should be noted that, according to the *Nordsee* case law,[38] arbitral tribunals cannot ask preliminary questions. This has also led to Commission action whereby it submits comments in arbitral proceedings. The *Benetton* case[39] raised the issue of applying the competition rules *ex officio* at the final stage of the enforcement of the arbitral award.

The entry into force of Regulation 1/2003 had far reaching implications and meant that the Commission had to redefine its enforcement tasks. Whereas previously the Commission had been the principal enforcer of Articles 81 and 82 EC, the entry into force of Regulation 1/2003 resulted in the application of Articles 81 and 82 being mainly dependent on national authorities, courts and, in their slipstream, arbitral tribunals. This not only has procedural consequences, but, in time, will inevitably lead to changes in the substance of the law. The Commission has, of course, retained its legislative powers which it largely uses to adopt block exemptions and publish notices. It is no longer obliged to spend time on individual exemptions. A negative consequence is that the Commission no longer acquires valuable knowledge resulting from notifications. The notifications of mergers and the application of its power to investigate sectors of the economy, however, have largely compensated for this.

9.4.3 Pursuing High-profile Infringements

In this period we see the Commission pursuing a very active enforcement policy of imposing very high fines on hard core cartels. In the calendar year 2007 the Commission imposed some €3,338 million in fines. In 2008, the fines amounted to €2,271 million.[40] In several of these cases applications for leniency have been the impetus for instituting the proceedings.

In 2009 there were six cartel decisions with fines totalling €1.62 billion. In the *Marine Hoses*, *Power Transformers* and *Heat Stabilizers* cases there was intensive cooperation with the US and Japanese authorities.[41] In 2016 the Commission fined five truck producers a total of €2.93 billion for participating in a cartel.[42]

Note that these are all horizontal agreements of the hardcore type.

In less 'hardcore' cases, the Commission began taking decisions on the basis of Article 9 of Regulation 1/2003 and accepting commitments.

---

[36] White paper on damages actions for breach of the EC antitrust rules {SEC (2008) 404} {SEC (2008) 405} {SEC (2008) 406} COM/2008/0165 final.

[37] OJ 2014, L 349, pp 1–19.

[38] Case 102/81 *Nordsee v Reederei Mond*.

[39] Case C-126/97 *Eco Swiss China Time Ltd v Benetton International NV*.

[40] The Commission adopted seven decisions: *Nitrile butadiene rubber*, *International removal services*, *Sodium chlorate paper bleach producers*, *Aluminium fluoride*, *Paraffin wax*, *Bananas* and *Car Glass*.

[41] Annual Report on Competition Policy 2009, para 66.

[42] IP/16/2582.

The Commission's enforcement policy on abuse of dominant positions is equally characterised by the pursuit of high-profile cases. The *Microsoft* and *Intel* cases are prominent examples of this approach. The *Microsoft* case ended with a truce when Microsoft decided not to appeal the full court judgment of the CFI.[43] Yet both parties have been drawn into long and protracted discussions about the remedies. In the meantime, the effect of the decision could be seen from the features of the subsequent version of the Windows operating system which allowed the client to install its own choice of Internet browser. The General Court dismissed Intel's appeal on 12 June 2014. It upheld the Commission decision on all counts, thus confirming the £1.06 billion penalty.[44]

9.4.4 Sector Inquiries

Sector inquiries have become very popular with the Commission. They provide it with considerable insight, allowing it to take follow-up action. As such, they fill, to some extent, the gap that was created by the abolition of the notification procedure. So far there have been eight such inquiries: the retail banking sector, the energy sector, the pharmaceutical sector, E-commerce, the local loop, leased lines, roaming, media -3G. The results of the banking inquiry have helped the Commission face the avalanche of notifications of State aid measures in the financial sector since 2008. This was evident in the *Northern Rock* and the *German Landesbanken* cases. The energy sector inquiry has resulted in several decisions, of which three are commitment decisions: the *Distrigas* commitment to open up the Belgian gas market; the *E.ON* and *RWE* commitments on the opening of the German electricity and gas markets; and finally the *Gaz de France* commitment to open up the French gas market allowing competitors to import gas into France. One decision condemned the market sharing agreement between *E.ON* and *GDF* on the German and French gas markets.[45] Follow-up action has also been taken in the pharmaceutical sector, where the Commission adopted a decision imposing fines totalling €427.7 million on the French pharmaceutical company Servier and five producers of generic medicines. Commission Vice-President Almunia, said:

> Servier had a strategy to systematically buy out any competitive threats to make sure that they stayed out of the market. Such behaviour is clearly anti-competitive and abusive. Competitors cannot agree to share markets or market rents instead of competing, even when these agreements are in the form of patent settlements. Such practices directly harm patients, national health systems and taxpayers. Pharmaceutical companies should focus their efforts on innovating and competing rather than attempting to extract extra rents from patients.[46]

---

[43] Case T-201/04 *Microsoft v Commission*.
[44] Case T-286/09 *Intel v Commission*. Appeal C-413/14 P.
[45] See IP/09/1872 of 3 December 2009. See also the memo 09/536 of 3 December: frequently asked questions. See further the speeches by Commissioner Kroes on 3 December 2009 published on the DG Comp website http://ec.europa.eu/competition/index_en.html.
[46] IP 14/799 9 July 2014.

9.4.5 Commitment Decisions and Settlements

The use of commitment decisions was, formally, a new instrument created under Regulation 1/2003. It does, however, bear some resemblance to the way the Commission previously used its power to grant individual exemptions. Under the old regime, the Commission often negotiated a limitation of restrictions of competition during the process of granting an individual exemption and subsequently granted the exemption conditionally. The instrument of commitment decisions allows the Commission to achieve similar results without having to go all the way by adopting a full infringement decision. It is therefore attractive for the Commission. It is also attractive for the undertakings concerned in that they may avoid being hit by ever increasing fines and the risk of private damages litigation. It is, however, less attractive from the point of view of legal protection. The fact that the Commission can adopt the decision without having to prove that there was an actual infringement will necessarily have an effect on judicial protection. In the *GDF* case the Commission notes that *GDF might have*[47] infringed Article 102 TFEU. Moreover, the commitments imposed can, of course, have a very considerable financial and commercial effect. The Commission observes that it can impose a fine of up to 10 per cent of the company's annual turnover if the firm were to break its commitments.

Another interesting development in respect of public enforcement are the settlements that are increasingly common to terminate enforcement procedures. Parties involved in cartel enforcement may at some point of the investigation prefer to acknowledge their participation and thus be willing to settle. This may save them money and it will save the Commission time and effort. As was discussed in Chapter 6.4.2.2 there have been a significant number of settlements.[48]

9.4.6 Merger Control

The amendment of the Merger Regulation resulted in recasting the relevant thresholds. In the meantime, all Member States have enacted national merger control rules. There has also been an enormous proliferation of merger control regimes all over the world and we now have over 100 merger control systems. Thus, cooperation will become an even more important topic for the future. And we do see signs of such closer cooperation, for example the merger of Panasonic and Sanyo, where the Commission acted in close cooperation with the US FTC and the Japanese Fair Trade Commission in the context of the bilateral framework agreements.[49] Now cooperation with China is also enhanced on the legislation/personnel training aspect through the creation of the EU-China Competition dialogue. This may well lead in the future to a new bilateral agreement. The US Department of Justice has drawn up a list of current US antitrust investigations to help antitrust enforcement agencies of other jurisdictions reviewing

---

[47] Authors' italics.
[48] 17 as of the end of 2014.
[49] IP/09/1383.

such deals or behaviour. The ECN and ICN also provide a forum for discussing frictions that may arise between states in their enforcement policy.

9.4.7 Article 102 TFEU

In February 2009 the Commission published a Policy paper on Article 82 'Guidance on the Commission's Enforcement Priorities in Applying Article 82 EC Treaty to Abusive Exclusionary Conduct by Dominant Undertakings'.[50] As is indicated in the title, the paper is limited to exclusionary conduct, thus, it does not deal with exploitative abuses. The paper is also limited in the sense that it only sets out the Commission's enforcement policies. In the paper the Commission refers regularly to consumer interest, which reflects the substantive focus of EU competition law on consumer welfare. As the ECJ held in *T-Mobile and others*, however, consumer welfare is not the only parameter of the competitive process that EU competition law seeks to protect.[51]

9.4.8 Evaluation of Regulation 1/2003

The Commission has published a report on the functioning of Regulation 1/2003. In this report it stresses that the enactment of Regulation 1/2003 has effected a system change that allows it to target its enforcement priorities to areas where it can make a significant contribution to the enforcement of Articles 81 and 82 EC.[52] The Commission concludes that Regulation 1/2003 has significantly improved the enforcement of Articles 81 and 82 EC, allowing it to become more proactive and address the competiveness of key sectors of the economy. It notes that cooperation in the ECN has contributed towards a coherent application and that the network is an innovative model of governance for the implementation of competition law by the Commission and Member State authorities. It also notes that there are areas that merit further attention.

---

[50] Communication from the Commission, Brussels 9.2.2009 C(2009) 864 final.

[51] Case C-8/08 *T-Mobile and others* at para 38.

[52] As the Commission puts it: '12. The change from a system of notification and administrative authorisation to one of direct application has been remarkably smooth in practice. Overall, neither the case practice of the Commission and the national enforcers, nor the experience reported by the business and legal community, indicate major difficulties with the direct application of Article 81(3) EC which has been widely welcomed by stakeholders. The system change has supported a shift in priorities of the Commission, enabling it to focus its resources on areas where it can make a significant contribution to the enforcement of Articles 81 and 82 EC. This proactive approach is clearly illustrated by the launch of large scale inquiries in key sectors of the EU economy which directly impact consumers. The Commission has further implemented a more effects-based approach in all areas of antitrust case work and policy, outside the field of cartels. The more pro-active stance of the Commission is further illustrated by an increase in the number of enforcement decisions adopted, compared with earlier periods.'

9.5 Since 1 December 2009 We Have Articles 101 and 102 TFEU, Arbitration and Human Rights

9.5.1 Changes in the Lisbon Treaty

Although the Lisbon Treaty has brought fundamental changes in EU law, the provisions on competition policy have changed numbers but their substance remains the same. There are exceptions: one is that Article 3 TEU no longer makes a reference to 'a system of undistorted competition'. Instead, there is the Protocol No. 27 on the internal market and competition stating that: 'considering that the internal market as set out in Article 3 of the Treaty on European Union includes a system ensuring that competition is not distorted…'[53] Will this make any difference? One could think in particular about the case law on Articles 3(1)(g), 10 and 81 EC. In this context it is important to note that later case law no longer refers to Article 3(1)(g).[54] Furthermore, Article 10 EC is now found in Article 4(3) TEU. It seems therefore unlikely that the ECJ will no longer apply its case law. Moreover, since the ECJ's case law leaves Member States a considerable margin of discretion,[55] it seems unlikely that this case law will be watered down.

Another amendment is found in Article 105 TFEU where a new paragraph is added:

> The Commission may adopt regulations relating to the categories of agreements in respect of which the Council has adopted a regulation or a directive pursuant to Article 83(2)(b).

This seems to codify the long standing practice.

Finally, Article 3.1(b) TFEU lists competition as an area where the Union shall have exclusive competence:

> (b) the establishing of the competition rules necessary for the functioning of the internal market.

It may be questioned whether the fact that the competition rules are now explicitly designated as an exclusive competence will have an impact on Article 3 of Regulation 1/2003 which requires national competition authorities to apply Articles 101 and 102 TFEU when applying national competition law to agreements or abuses of dominant positions that have an effect on trade between Member States. Such fears, however, seem to be unwarranted given that, after all, these provisions have direct effect. Moreover, it is not uncommon that Member States or their emanations, implement EU law.

---

[53] See R Barents, 'Constitutional Horse Trading: Some Comments on the Protocol' and R Lane, 'EC Competition Law Post Lisbon: A matter of Protocol' in *Views of European Law from the Mountain Liber Amicorum Piet Jan Slot*, Wolters Kluwer 2009,123–132 and 167–179.

[54] See Case C-35/96, *Commission v Italy*.

[55] See N Reich, 'The "November Revolution" of the European Court of Justice: *Keck, Meng* and *Audi* Revisted' (1994) 31 *Common Market Law Review* 1, 459–492.

9.5.2 Arbitration[56]

Ever since the *Nordsee* judgment[57] the relationship between arbitration and EU competition law was uneasy. When the competition rules were raised in arbitral proceedings and their application by arbiters was unsatisfactory, only national courts could be relied upon to redress this. Moreover, national courts could only act if the legislation of the Member State allowed them to review arbitral awards. This was clearly demonstrated in the *Bennetton* case.[58] For a number of years the Commission has been involved in arbitral proceedings by writing submissions. There are also Commission State aid decisions that have taken into account that arbitral proceedings were going on. Similar developments may take place in the area of classical antitrust. Also, the Commission is more active in national proceedings as amicus curiae—this is likely a result of increasing damages litigation following on from Commission infringement decisions.

9.5.3 Human Rights

An area where we will certainly see discussions continuing is the area of protection of human rights in the context of competition law procedures, especially after the entry into force of the Lisbon Treaty.[59] The calls for a change of the system have become increasingly louder.[60] The central tenet of criticism is the fact the Commission is both the prosecutor and judge. At the time when Regulation 17 was enacted, the case law of the ECtHR on Article 6 was still in its infancy. In the EU, the only judicial protection provided for was laid down in Article 230 EC, which allows undertakings to whom decisions are addressed and those who are directly and individually concerned—ie, those with standing—to challenge Commission decisions.[61] In the *KME Germany and Chalkor* cases the Court ruled that the enforcement system of Regulation 1/2003 is in

---

[56] See Gordon Blanke and Phillip Landolt (eds), *EU and US Antitrust Arbitration* (Wolters Kluwer, 2011) 1–2211. This publication provides an comprehensive overview of the issues involved in arbitral proceedings including the application of EU competition law.

[57] Case C-102/81, *Nordsee Deutsche Hochseefischerei*. In this judgment the ECJ ruled that arbiters cannot refer questions under the preliminary procedure.

[58] Case C-126/97, *Eco-Swiss China Time Ltd v Bennetton*.

[59] Art 6(1) TEU recognises the rights, freedoms and principles set out in the Charter of Fundamental Rights. Art 6(2) provides that the Union shall accede to the ECHR although the ECJ Opinion from 2014 seems to have put plans for this on hold (Opinion 2/13, delivered on 18 December 2014 EU:C:2014:2454). For a discussion on the impact of these changes see M Dougan, 'The Treaty of Lisbon 2007: Winning minds not hearts', (2008) 45 *Common Market Law Review* 3, 661–672.

[60] See the leader in *The Economist* 20–26 February 2010 and, subsequently, the article on p 57.

[61] For discussion of the intricacies of this provision in general, see (eg) A Arnull, *The European Union and its Court of Justice* (Oxford, Oxford University Press, 1999) 31–48 and PP Craig and G de Búrca, *EU Law: Text, Cases, and Materials*, 5th edn (Oxford, Oxford University Press, 2011) ch 11. For its application in the competition law field, see (eg) R Whish & D. Bailey, *Competition Law*, 8th edn, (Oxford, Oxford University Press, 2015) 308–309 and C Kerse and N Khan, *EC Antitrust Procedure*, 5th edn (London, Sweet & Maxwell, 2005) ch 9.

conformity with the case law of the ECtHR.[62] The Court of Justice concluded that there was no infringement of the principle of effective judicial protection laid down in Article 47 of the Charter of Fundamental Rights.

As in many other areas of the law, the protection of fundamental rights has been gaining increased attention, and judgments of the ECJ and, after 1989, also of the CFI (now GC), have defined the scope of such rights in the area of competition law. In the *Kali & Salz* judgment of the ECJ,[63] the question was raised whether or not Article 2 of the EC Merger Control Regulation (ECMR) could also be applied to collective dominant positions. The applicants argued that such an interpretation could not be accepted as the Regulation did not provide for legal protection of the companies that would thus be involved but were not party to the approval procedure.

Another prominent case that should be noted under this heading is the *Roquette*[64] judgment, which was almost instantaneously incorporated into the text of Articles 20(8) and 21(3) of Regulation 1/2003.

The *TACA*[65] case and especially the position of, and appeals by, *DSR-Senator Lines*[66] illustrate the intricate relationship between EC procedural law and, in particular, the application of the general principles and fundamental rights as developed under Article 6 ECHR. The Commission adopted a decision against the Trans-Atlantic Conference Agreement imposing a fine on its members.[67] One of them, Senator Lines, was fined €13.75 million. As is standard practice, the Commission indicated that it would not take steps to recover the fine if Senator could provide a bank guarantee. Senator's dire financial situation made it impossible to get such a guarantee. Senator appealed against the Commission's Decision and filed for interim measures. Its main argument was that, because it could not provide a bank guarantee, it would not be able to have full judicial recourse. After a failed attempt to reach a settlement, the President of the CFI rejected the request for interim measures.[68] An appeal to the President of the ECJ also failed.[69] Faced with the prospect of steps by the Commission to recover the fine, Senator brought an application to the ECtHR against all the Member States of the EC.[70] It alleged that, in denying the suspensory effect of the appeal, the Commission and the CFI, as well as the ECJ, had deprived the applicant of its fundamental right to have recourse to a judicial instance under Article 6 ECHR.

The Strasbourg Court scheduled a hearing for 22 October 2003. It so happened that the CFI annulled the Commission's decision in the *TACA* case on 30 September.[71]

---

[62] C-272/09 P, C-386/10, C-389/10, *KME Germany and Chalkor v Commission*. The view of the Commission was expressed in: *Commission Staff Working paper accompanying the Report on the Functioning of regulation 1/2003*. SEC(2009) 574 final.

[63] Joined Cases C-68/94 and C-30/95 *France v Commission*, at paras 172–175.

[64] Case C-94/00 *Roquette Frères SA v Directeur général de la concurrence, de la consommation et de la répression des fraudes, and Commission of the European Communities* 1.

[65] Joined Cases T-191/98 and T-212-214/98 *Atlantic Container Line et al v Commission*.

[66] ibid.

[67] [1999] OJ L95/1 in the so-called *TACA* Decision (Commission Decision 1999/243/EC of 16 September 1998).

[68] Case T-191/98 R *DSR-Senator Lines GmbH v Commission*.

[69] Case C-364/99 P (R) *DSR-Senator Lines GmbH v Commission*.

[70] *Senator Lines GmbH v 15 States of the European Union*, Series A No. 256-A; (1993) 16 EHRR 297.

[71] Joined Cases T-191/98 and T-212/98 to 214/98, *Atlantic Container Line et al v Commission*.

The ECtHR postponed the hearing and removed the case from the register after the judgment of the CFI was handed down. The Commission refrained from taking steps to recover the fine during the procedure before the Strasbourg Court.

9.6 Conclusions

Since the entry into force of the EEC treaty in 1958, competition law has come of age. As can be seen from the above it has evolved into a mature system of law both in terms of substance as well as procedure. As a result, the impact of competition law on society has greatly increased, be it in terms of changing the behaviour of business, fines meted out to undertakings, claims for damages and last but not least providing jobs for legal practitioners. In his much acclaimed book *Antitrust and the Bounds of Power* Amato[72] has argued that competition law is addressing fundamental issues of a modern democracy. This is demonstrated most clearly when the behaviour of the giants of modern global industry such as Microsoft, Intel and Gazprom is challenged under Article 102 TFEU. Similarly, the merger control rules provide means to address the negative effects of mergers in highly concentrated industries. It is with these perspectives in mind that studying competition law will offer future generations of legal practitioners a challenging and interesting professional life.

---

[72] G Amato, *Antitrust and the Bounds of Power. The Dilemma of Liberal Democracy in the History of the Market* (Oxford, Hart Publishing, 1997). Amato uses the term 'antitrust policy' also referring to competition policy.

Index